State and Society in
Early Modern Scotland

JULIAN GOODARE

OXFORD

UNIVERSITY PRESS

OXFORD
UNIVERSITY PRESS

Great Clarendon Street, Oxford OX2 6DP

Oxford University Press is a department of the University of Oxford.
It furthers the University's objective of excellence in research, scholarship,
and education by publishing worldwide in

Oxford New York

Athens Auckland Bangkok Bogotá Buenos Aires Calcutta
Cape Town Chennai Dar es Salaam Delhi Florence Hong Kong Istanbul
Karachi Kuala Lumpur Madrid Melbourne Mexico City Mumbai
Nairobi Paris São Paulo Singapore Taipei Tokyo Toronto Warsaw

with associated companies in Berlin Ibadan

Oxford is a registered trade mark of Oxford University Press
in the UK and in certain other countries

Published in the United States
by Oxford University Press Inc., New York

British Library Cataloguing in Publication Data

Data available

Library of Congress Cataloging in Publication Data

Data applied for
ISBN 0-19-820762-X

1 3 5 7 9 10 8 6 4 2

Typeset in Baskerville
by Best-set Typesetter Ltd., Hong Kong
Printed in Great Britain
on acid-free paper by
Biddles Ltd,
Guildford and King's Lynn

To Jackie

ACKNOWLEDGEMENTS

In writing this book I have been helped by numerous scholars. Dr Michael Braddick, Professor Keith Brown, Professor J. H. Burns, Dr David Caldwell, Dr Jane Dawson, Professor Maurice Lee Jr., Dr Alan R. MacDonald, and Dr Athol Murray all kindly read and commented on draft chapters. Special thanks are due to Professor Michael Lynch, who read the whole book.

Over the years my thoughts have been shaped by discussions with many other friends and colleagues. These include Professor Geoffrey Barrow, Dr Steve Boardman, Professor Richard Bonney, Professor Archie Duncan, Dr Alexander Grant, Dr Maureen Meikle, Professor Conrad Russell, Mr David Sellar, Dr Fiona Watson, Dr Jenny Wormald, and Dr Louise Yeoman. The published works of these scholars have set a high standard for me to emulate. None of them may be held responsible for the views expressed here, and any errors are also my own responsibility.

Chapter 8 was drafted while I was a visiting fellow in the School of Advanced Study, University of London. The facilities of the School, and of the Institute of Historical Research, were much appreciated. An early version of Chapter 4 formed part of my 1989 University of Edinburgh Ph.D. thesis. Papers based on early versions of Chapters 2 and 3 were presented to the Association of Scottish Historical Studies and to the Department of History, University of Aberdeen. Part of Chapter 5 was drafted outside the north gate of Faslane nuclear submarine base.

Oxford University Press has been an exemplary publisher. Tony Morris provided support and encouragement over several years of writing, Anne Gelling offered invaluable help and advice at a crucial moment, and she, Ruth Parr, and Sarah Ridgard have seen the book efficiently through the press.

The tradition whereby a male academic author thanks his wife for providing him with domestic support services is not yet dead, but I am not going to prolong its life; Jackie had more important things to do. However, her own studies in the social sciences have led to some intellectual cross-fertilization for which this book is richer—and it is to her that I dedicate it.

J. G.

Edinburgh
October 1998

CONTENTS

CONVENTIONS AND ABBREVIATIONS

Money: All sums are in pounds (£s) Scots unless otherwise stated, sometimes rounded to the nearest £. A merk was 13s. 4d., two-thirds of a £ Scots. In 1560 the English £ (sterling) was equal to about £4. 10s. Scots at par, and the French crown to £1. 6s. 8d. Scots; by 1601 they were worth £12 Scots and £3. 6s. 8d. Scots respectively. The Scottish currency was pegged to the English in 1603, and between then and 1625 there were no major fluctuations in currency values.

Dates: These are given in old style (i.e. Julian calendar), but with the year beginning on 1 January.

Style: Contemporary documents are quoted in the original spelling, but the letters i/j and u/v are modernized; 3 (yogh) is given as y. Contractions are expanded, and modern capitalization and punctuation used. In the text, names of people and places use the standard modern form where one exists. Translations not otherwise attributed are my own.

The following abbreviations are used:

Aberdeen Letters	*Aberdeen Council Letters*, 6 vols., ed. L. B. Taylor (London, 1942–61)
ADCP	*Acts of the Lords of Council in Public Affairs, 1501–1554*, ed. R. K. Hannay (Edinburgh, 1932)
Add. MS	Additional MS (BL)
Adv. MS	Advocates' MS (NLS)
APS	*Acts of the Parliaments of Scotland*, 12 vols., ed. T. Thomson and C. Innes (Edinburgh, 1814–75)
Ayr Accounts	*Ayr Burgh Accounts, 1534–1624*, ed. G. S. Pryde (SHS, 1937)
Balfour, *Practicks*	Sir James Balfour of Pittendreich, *Practicks*, 2 vols., ed. P. G. B. McNeill (Stair Society, 1962–3)

BL	British Library, London
BUK	*Booke of the Universall Kirk: Acts and Proceedings of the General Assemblies of the Kirk of Scotland*, 3 vols., ed. T. Thomson (Bannatyne and Maitland Clubs, 1839–45)
Calderwood, *History*	David Calderwood, *History of the Kirk of Scotland*, 8 vols., ed. T. Thomson and D. Laing (Wodrow Society, 1843–9)
Craig, *De Unione*	Thomas Craig of Riccarton, *De Unione Britanniae Tractatus*, ed. C. S. Terry (SHS, 1909)
Craig, *Jus Feudale*	Thomas Craig of Riccarton, *Jus Feudale*, 2 vols., ed. J. A. Clyde (Edinburgh, 1934)
CSP Dom.	*Calendar of State Papers, Domestic Series*, 94 vols., ed. R. Lemon *et al.* (London, 1856–)
CSP Scot.	*Calendar of the State Papers Relating to Scotland and Mary Queen of Scots, 1547–1603*, 13 vols., ed. J. Bain *et al.* (Edinburgh, 1898–1969)
Eccles. Letters	*Original Letters Relating to the Ecclesiastical Affairs of Scotland*, 2 vols., ed. D. Laing (Bannatyne Club, 1851)
Edin. Recs.	*Extracts from the Records of the Burgh of Edinburgh*, 13 vols., ed. J. D. Marwick *et al.* (SBRS and Edinburgh, 1869–1967)
EHR	*English Historical Review*
ER	*Exchequer Rolls of Scotland*, 23 vols., ed. J. Stuart *et al.* (Edinburgh, 1878–)
Gordon, *Sutherland*	Sir Robert Gordon, *Genealogical History of the Earldom of Sutherland* (Edinburgh, 1813)
HMC	Historical Manuscripts Commission
HMC, *Mar & Kellie*	HMC, *Report on the Manuscripts of the Earl of Mar and Kellie*, 2 vols., ed. H. Paton (London, 1904–30)
HMC, *Salisbury*	HMC, *Calendar of the Manuscripts of the Marquis of Salisbury*, 24 vols., ed. S. R. Bird *et al.* (London, 1883–1976)

Hope, *Major Practicks*	Sir Thomas Hope, *Major Practicks*, 2 vols., ed. J. A. Clyde (Stair Society, 1937–8)
HP	*Highland Papers*, 4 vols., ed. J. R. N. Macphail (SHS, 1914–34)
IR	*Innes Review*
Jacobean Union	*The Jacobean Union: Six Tracts of 1604*, ed. B. R. Galloway and B. P. Levack (SHS, 1985)
James VI & I, *Political Writings*	King James VI & I, *Political Writings*, ed. J. P. Sommerville (Cambridge, 1994)
JR	*Juridical Review*
Knox, *History*	John Knox, *History of the Reformation in Scotland*, 2 vols., ed. W. C. Dickinson (Edinburgh, 1949)
Knox, *Works*	John Knox, *Works*, 6 vols., ed. D. Laing (Wodrow Society, 1846–64)
Lindsay, *Works*	Sir David Lindsay of the Mount, *Works*, 4 vols., ed. D. Hamer (STS, 1931–6)
LP James VI	*Letters and State Papers during the Reign of King James VI*, ed. J. Maidment (Abbotsford Club, 1838)
Melros Papers	*State Papers and Miscellaneous Correspondence of Thomas, Earl of Melros*, 2 vols., ed. J. Maidment (Abbotsford Club, 1837)
Melville, *Diary*	James Melville, *Autobiography and Diary, 1556–1610*, ed. R. Pitcairn (Wodrow Society, 1842)
Melville, *Memoirs*	Sir James Melville of Halhill, *Memoirs of His Own Life*, ed. T. Thomson (Bannatyne Club, 1827)
Moysie, *Memoirs*	David Moysie, *Memoirs of the Affairs of Scotland, 1577–1603*, ed. J. Dennistoun (Maitland Club, 1830)
NLS	National Library of Scotland, Edinburgh
NAS	National Archives of Scotland
P & P	*Past & Present*
Pitscottie, *Historie*	Robert Lindsay of Pitscottie, *Historie and Cronicles of Scotland*, 3 vols., ed. Æ. J. G. Mackay (STS, 1899–1911)

RCRB	*Records of the Convention of Royal Burghs of Scotland*, 7 vols., ed. J. D. Marwick and T. Hunter (Edinburgh, 1866–1918)
RMS	*Register of the Great Seal of Scotland (Registrum Magni Sigilli Regum Scotorum)*, 11 vols., ed. J. M. Thomson *et al.* (Edinburgh, 1912–)
RPC	*Register of the Privy Council of Scotland*, 37 vols., ed. J. H. Burton *et al.* (Edinburgh, 1877–)
RSCHS	*Records of the Scottish Church History Society*
RSS	*Register of the Privy Seal of Scotland (Registrum Secreti Sigilli Regum Scotorum)*, 8 vols., ed. M. Livingstone *et al.* (Edinburgh, 1908–)
SBRS	Scottish Burgh Records Society
SHR	*Scottish Historical Review*
SHS	Scottish History Society
Skene, *DVS*	John Skene, *De Verborum Significatione: The Exposition of the Termes and Difficill Wordes Conteined in the Foure Buikes of Regiam Majestatem and Uthers . . .* (Edinburgh, 1599)
Source Book	W. C. Dickinson *et al.* (eds.), *A Source Book of Scottish History*, 3 vols. (2nd edn., Edinburgh, 1958–61)
Spottiswoode, *History*	John Spottiswoode, *History of the Church of Scotland*, 3 vols., ed. M. Napier and M. Russell (Spottiswoode Society, 1847–51)
SRS	Scottish Record Society
STS	Scottish Text Society
TA	*Accounts of the (Lord High) Treasurer of Scotland*, 13 vols., ed. T. Dickson *et al.* (Edinburgh, 1877–)
Taymouth Book	*The Black Book of Taymouth, with Other Papers from the Breadalbane Charter Room*, ed. C. Innes (Edinburgh, 1855)
TGSI	*Transactions of the Gaelic Society of Inverness*
Warrender Papers	*The Warrender Papers*, 2 vols., ed. A. I. Cameron (SHS, 1931–2)

RMS and *RSS* are cited by document number without comment; all other citations are to page numbers unless otherwise stated. Parliamentary statutes in *APS* have a chapter number as well as a page number; references to *APS* lacking such a number are not to statutes. Titles of secondary works, and of primary sources not listed here, are given in full on their first citation in each chapter, and thereafter shortened.

Observation tells us that every state is an association, and that every association is formed with a view to some good purpose. I say 'good', because in all their actions men do in fact aim at what they think good. Clearly then, as all associations aim at some good, that association which is the most sovereign among them all and embraces all others will aim highest, i.e. at the most sovereign of all goods. This is the association which we call the state, the association which is 'political'.

*

There is another type of monarchy, such as kingships found among certain non-Greeks. All these have power approximating to that of tyrannies, but they are legally established and ancestral. For it is because non-Greeks are by natural character more slavish than Greeks (and the Asiatics than the Europeans) that they tolerate master-like rule without resentment. Therefore, while such kingships are for these reasons like tyrannies, their legality and ancestral status make them safe. And for the same reason the ruler has a royal, not a tyrant's bodyguard; for a king's bodyguard is composed of citizens carrying arms, a tyrant's of foreigners. And the king rules over willing subjects according to law, the tyrant over unwilling subjects.

Aristotle, *The Politics*, trans. T. A. Sinclair and T. J. Saunders (Penguin Classics edn., Harmondsworth, 1981), I: i, III: xiv.

① The newly heathen
military power removed.

he also presided over the
protestant church

Did not give all orders on
his own.

Introduction

> This I must say for Scotland, and I may trewly vaunt it; Here
> I sit and governe it with my pen, I write and it is done, and
> by a clearke of the councell I governe Scotland now, which
> others could not doe by the sword.[1]

> The sixteenth century forms the watershed in the political
> development of Europe and via Europe, of the entire world,
> for Europe is the birthplace of the modern state.[2]

This book is a study of a medium-sized European state as it underwent a far-reaching transition in the exercise of power. Out of the
parcellized, localized, fragmented authority-structures of the late
middle ages, a sovereign state arose. Political power now had a
single focus.

James VI, as his famous remark of 1607 shows, knew that something new and decisive had happened. What he mainly meant was
that the Scottish nobility had had their autonomous military power
removed; he had established warfare as a state monopoly. He could
also claim to have presided over the reduction of the new Protestant church to obedience. In fact these achievements were still
incomplete in 1607, though things were moving the way James
wanted. But his remark, though penetrating, needs to be qualified
in a more important way. Having a single focus of power did not
mean that the king gave all the orders himself; that was a convenient legal and ideological fiction. It meant that there was a
single dominant *structure* within which authority was exercised.
This book is about that structure.

According to Samuel Finer's recent synthesis, the establishment
of territorial sovereignty in a new and dynamic form was the crucial
governmental development of early modern European states. The
sovereign state of the sixteenth century arose from an earlier polity
with no ultimate sovereignty. There had been kingdoms in

---

[1] James VI & I, speech to parliament, 1607, in *Political Writings*, 173.
[2] S. E. Finer, *The History of Government from the Earliest Times*, 3 vols. (Oxford,
1997), iii. 1261.

medieval Europe, which can legitimately be described as 'states', but few if any of them had been fully integrated. Medieval kings had often been powerful, but power had been shared between kings and bishops, between kings and popes, and above all between kings and magnates. In this, medieval European 'states' had been unusual, for in other places and at other times, from the city-states familiar to Aristotle onwards, governments had generally been integrated enough to possess something more like sovereignty.[3] Once the diverse strands of medieval authority were gathered together, not only was the state more integrated, but the scope of its activities became a good deal broader.

The subsequent history of Europe would see periodic contests between alternative forms of political organization: on the one hand the sovereign state, on the other hand the universalizing claims of large empires. The empires failed, and Europe remained a single civilization divided into a plurality of aggressively competing states. This has often been regarded as part of the so-called 'European miracle'—the decidedly profane miracle whereby a backward corner of the late-medieval globe was enabled to lift itself to world dominance.[4] Clearly, the victory of the sovereign state over the universalizing empire mattered. That victory was not a simple affair, and the 'rise of the state' involved the *destruction* of many small states. Still, the smaller states played their part in the development of the European state system. The system relied, not just on a few large and influential states, but also on the tendency of *all* Europe's political classes to attach themselves, actually or potentially, to sovereign states rather than to empires.

The tendency of early modern Scottish elites to think and act as 'Scots' is thus a part, if only a small one, of the story of the modern state as a whole. One interesting aspect is that they did not all do so, or not all the time. The spiritual leader of the Scottish Reformation, John Knox, developed many of his ideas in a British context, and sometimes sent different messages to Scottish and British audiences. One of Scotland's most prominent intellectuals, John Napier of Merchiston, formulated a cosmic scheme in which neither Scotland nor any other national state could claim a special

[3] Ibid. i. 4–5, 93; iii. 1298.
[4] E. L. Jones, *The European Miracle* (Cambridge, 1981), chs. 6–7; I. Wallerstein, *The Modern World-System*, i. *Capitalist Agriculture and the Origins of the European World-Economy in the Sixteenth Century* (New York, 1974), 15–18.

role.[5] Napier's cosmopolitanism was perhaps *sui generis*, but the ambivalences of Knox's Scottish and British context would be experienced by many others in Scotland during the next century and even later. Smaller states had complex relationships with their larger neighbours, and these ambivalences add both light and shade to the picture of the 'rise of the state'. That is one reason to study, not just heavyweights like the French or Spanish states, but also their smaller and more numerous counterparts like the Scottish state. The picture of the 'rise of the state' is a mosaic with many pieces: the general themes of state formation are multifarious, and these themes arise in different ways within specific states of different types. This book can contribute only a few small pieces to this mosaic, but these pieces can and should be seen in context of the broader picture.

Scotland as a case-study can add light and shade to the European picture in several ways. One reason for this is that the early modern Scottish state was an indigenous development. The proudest boast of Scots in this period was that their country had never been conquered. They were thus able to develop their own governmental forms from native roots. It is a pity that the borrowings of administrators from other European models have not been researched in the way that those of masons and architects have been; but if the borrowings of the latter could be synthesized into a Scottish 'national style', so surely could those of the former.[6]

The country that had never conquered Scotland was, above all, England. Yet in our period, Scottish governments abandoned their traditional hostility to England and adopted a more friendly stance—varying from distrustful cooperation to enthusiastic support for Anglo-Scottish union. Just as architectural borrowings from England increased during our period, so probably did governmental ones. But this was not simply one-way traffic. Since seventeenth-century England had a vast contribution to make to the development of the early modern state, seventeenth-century Scotland deserves its own small but visible place in this picture too. Professor Finer pointed out the significant English 'invention' of

---

[5] A. H. Williamson, *Scottish National Consciousness in the Age of James VI* (Edinburgh, 1979), ch. 1; J. E. A. Dawson, 'The two John Knoxes: England, Scotland and the 1558 tracts', *Journal of Ecclesiastical History*, 42 (1991), 555–76.

[6] Cf. D. Howard, *Scottish Architecture: Reformation to Restoration, 1560–1660* (The Architectural History of Scotland, Edinburgh, 1995), 218–20.

'procedurally limited monarchy—to become known as "constitutional monarchy"'.[7] Well, maybe the English did not invent it entirely on their own. Constitutional monarchy was established in England through the collapse of Charles I's regime and the victory of parliament in the subsequent civil war. Whether or not one accepts in its entirety the claim that the Scots caused this chain of events,[8] it is clear that English parliamentarianism was paralleled, supported, and sometimes *preceded* by Scottish parliamentarianism.

'Scotland', although usually perceived as a unit, was unusually diverse for its size—both geographically and culturally. This had implications for the state. There was a fundamental Highland–Lowland divide, and the state was deeply marked by its inability to penetrate the Highlands except as a military invader. Other regions were geographically peripheral (the Borders, the Northern Isles) and thus had to be distinctively governed; even some Lowland regions were semi-detached from the state. Chapter 7 surveys some of the ways in which more precise state boundaries were delineated. Scotland also had a complex relationship with England, but remained a sovereign state even after the union of crowns in 1603. Chapter 8 returns to the 'problem' of the Highlands and Borders, and the distinctive means that were used to assert state authority.

As a study of state formation and state power, the book often deals in broad themes—though there is a good deal of detail in places. Some themes would have been detailed more fully had I not been able to build on other work. The clashing ideologies that pervaded political debate and hampered the unquestioned acceptance of authority have been elucidated by J. H. Burns, Roger Mason, and Arthur Williamson.[9] The reorientation of the nobility away from autonomous war-making, so essential to state sovereignty, has been explained by Keith Brown and Jenny Wormald.[10] The institutions and mechanics of government would have been

[7] Finer, *History of Government*, i. 93.

[8] The claim is made most eloquently by C. Russell, *The Causes of the English Civil War* (Oxford, 1990), 29, 217–18.

[9] J. H. Burns, *The True Law of Kingship: Concepts of Monarchy in Early-Modern Scotland* (Oxford, 1996); R. A. Mason (ed.), *Scots and Britons: Scottish Political Thought and the Union of 1603* (Cambridge, 1994); Williamson, *Scottish National Consciousness*.

[10] K. M. Brown, *Bloodfeud in Scotland, 1573–1625* (Edinburgh, 1986); J. Wormald, *Lords and Men in Scotland: Bonds of Manrent, 1442–1603* (Edinburgh, 1985).

more prominent in this book if I had not been dealing with them at more length elsewhere.[11]

Still, most of the book is based on primary sources. The basic source material for the Scottish state is the records it created—most notably the records of parliament and the privy council. Some official records are virtually unusable, such as the 400-odd manuscript volumes of decrees of the court of session, lacking any indexes or finding aids. There are, however, contemporary extracts giving what were regarded as the *significant* decrees of the court. Other state papers, both printed and manuscript, have been used extensively, as have private and public collections of correspondence. Then there are local records. Few rural records survive, but many urban ones. There is a good deal of such material in print, so it has made sense to concentrate on that. I have examined some unpublished burgh records, but the small number of occasions on which they appear in the footnotes suggests that continuing to pursue such material would have delayed the book's completion without changing it much.

The book's central focus is on the period 1560–1625—from the Reformation to the death of James VI and I. The Reformation of 1560 makes a natural starting-point; if the sovereign state was created at any one moment, it was when papal authority was abrogated. The terminal date of 1625, on the other hand, is *not* a major turning-point; it is a date that allows me to stand back from the major turning-point of the century, the covenanting revolution of 1638. Had I continued to 1638, the book would have tended to become a study of the collapse of a regime. That is certainly an important topic, but it is not the only one. I have distanced myself from the question of how the regime failed, because in many ways it succeeded. It lasted for at least two reigns, and could boast many practical achievements. Nor *need* it have failed in 1638. This book is to a large extent a story of success.

Our core period, 1560–1625, is also set in a broader context. Chapters 1 and 2 also deal in large measure with the previous century, back to about 1469; Chapter 10 focuses on the subsequent century, up to about 1725. Some important late-medieval themes—notably the exercise of lordship, and relations between crown and nobility—provide the roots from which sprang the absolutist state

---

[11] J. Goodare, *The Government of Scotland, 1560–1625* (forthcoming).

of Chapter 3. The early chapters thus bridge the late medieval and early modern periods. Similarly, Chapter 10 takes some of the themes of the period 1560–1625—those outlined in Chapter 9— and traces their continued evolution forwards. The result is not a complete account of the Scottish state throughout the period 1469–1725; it focuses on certain key themes. The book could be visualized diagrammatically as T-shaped, anchored in the middle with in-depth analysis of 1560–1625, but with narrower arms extending horizontally on either side.

One of the book's broad themes is the concept of the absolutist state, discussed most directly in Chapter 3. Now, such a sweeping term appears to make vast claims and to demand allegiance to a large body of theory. In fact, my aims are more modest than critics of the term might imagine. The term 'absolutist' is sometimes felt to have connotations of complete, all-embracing, total—connotations that I would disavow; while the term 'state' makes things worse by having its own claims to be all-embracing.[12] I use the term 'absolutist state', despite these disadvantages, because it has already been circulated by others; it seems better to continue to use it (with care) than to invent a new one.[13] But it needs defending, and defining.

Government has three basic functions: warfare, settlement of disputes, and allocation of resources. The absolutist state, as I use the term, is a distinctive form of authority that is often found being exercised over agrarian societies in early modern Europe. It develops gradually between the fifteenth and seventeenth centuries. Warfare is nationalized, so that legitimate political violence comes to be exercised solely by the state. The settlement of disputes, similarly, tends to be more centralized, and local courts find themselves implementing more central legislation, under supervision from the central executive. More of society's resources are extracted directly by central government, in the form of taxation,

---

[12] Today's physicists are sometimes criticized along similar lines for seeking what they have chosen to call a 'theory of everything'. They might be perceived as less immodest if they called it a 'theory unifying the four fundamental forces of electromagnetism, gravitation, and the strong and weak nuclear forces'. Cf. M. Riordan and D. Schramm, *The Shadows of Creation: Dark Matter and the Structure of the Universe* (Oxford, 1991), 46–7.

[13] Had it been possible to start from scratch, I would have preferred some such term as 'centralized feudal state'—though that would have brought its own problems, particularly over the definition of 'feudal'.

and are distributed through the royal court—for the absolutist state is almost always a monarchy. The leading nobility, as courtiers, play a crucial role in the process; they and their clients command the state's armies, staff the state's courts, and collect the pensions, fees, and other rewards for service that the state provides.

None of this is static; the 'absolutist state' is a process as well as a thing. It is not so much that it *is* centralized—an idea which any study showing decisions being made locally can claim to refute; rather that there is a trend towards *more* centralization—and towards increased taxes, bigger armies, a more lucrative gravy train. Perhaps if these forward-moving trends are halted (eighteenth-century France may come to mind here), the state is in danger of collapsing or being radically reshaped; this is speculation that only a wider comparative study could confirm. It would help to explain why we find the absolutist state fading away in the eighteenth and nineteenth centuries, but that is not the subject of this book.

As for what I do *not* mean by the 'absolutist state': I do not suggest that it had total control of its people's lives, or that it was arbitrary or tyrannical. It could never have total control; it could be tyrannical, but no more so than other polities. There was a rule of law. Monarchs claimed, and were generally believed, to be governing legitimately in the interests of the political nation—the propertied classes—who in turn had opportunities for active participation.

Two vital things that no government could be without—money and troops—are discussed in Chapters 4 and 5. As with other magnates, the crown's main traditional revenues came from land, but these revenues declined, and new sources of royal income began to emerge. Taxation, hitherto rare, became heavy and regular. Meanwhile, the decline of Lowland nobles' autonomous military authority also meant the decline of the crown's traditional unpaid 'common army', mustered and led by local lords. James VI could often hardly afford a small royal guard, but the government's military system was gradually updated until by the 1620s it resembled those of other states in all but size.

Money and troops were of course linked. One of the most thoughtful authorities on state formation, Charles Tilly, has compared the early modern European state to a protection racket, in which the people had resources extracted from them in order to guard against threats created by other states engaged in the same process.[14] Sheltered as it was from the most murderous excesses of European warfare, the Scottish state did not need to offer as much protection as some, and this limited its ability (and need) to raise such large taxes for war.

It did, however, need to regularize its relationship with the terrestrial mediators of divine authority. Chapter 6 examines the relationship between church and state . . . or are we really looking at the functioning of the church as an arm of government? The Reformation created powerful central and local institutions, both of which had an ambivalent relationship with the state. A royal supremacy was established—not, as in England, at the expense of the papacy, but at the expense of the presbyterian movement. The church, autonomous in the early years, became a department of state. Presbyterian dissidence was a problem, but there was always a good deal of church–state cooperation over aspects of social control.

 The changing nature of state power is the subject of Chapters 9 and 10, which together form something of a conclusion. How was state power differentiated from other, private forms of power? How and why did the scope of government expand during this period? And what were the tools that enabled it to do so? Here, the Scottish state makes a fascinating case-study of the European experience of state formation. Unlike many states, it developed an integrated state structure without being pressured to do so by warfare. Instead, the Scottish absolutist state—the political configuration of a landed nobility operating within a centralized administrative structure—developed because it was politically effective. On the other hand, there were limits to its effectiveness, resting as it did on a narrow social base of active support, and lacking wholehearted ideological consensus in its favour. In Chapter 10, much of this is reviewed in a longer-term framework extending into the early eighteenth century. The Scottish state in the sixteenth and early seventeenth centuries was a success story at the time—but it was finally absorbed by England in 1707, and some of the long-term reasons for its failure to maintain its independence are discussed.

[14] C. Tilly, 'War making and state making as organized crime', in P. B. Evans *et al.* (eds.), *Bringing the State Back In* (Cambridge, 1985). St Augustine and Sir Thomas More are among those who could be cited to similar effect.

The issue of Scottish 'independence' may offer a final perspective on the central theme of this book. At the time of writing, the Scots have recently voted for the establishment of a devolved parliament in Edinburgh. This has generally been welcomed as worthwhile in its own right. It has also been seen, more controversially, as a potential step towards full Scottish independence: an appealing prospect to some, an appalling one to perhaps a rather smaller number. To believe the more impassioned commentators, independence will solve—or create—all imaginable modern problems. But if independence comes, will either side be proved right? We will still be voting, paying taxes, and worrying about the environment or the health service. The locus of public authority will sometimes be relevant to this, but not necessarily. In an 'independent' Scottish state, many decisions will be taken in Edinburgh; but many decisions have been taken there for some time.[15] In an 'independent' Scottish state, we will still have to worry, as we do now, about decisions taken in London—and in Brussels, Frankfurt, Washington, and Tokyo. Can a state like Scotland, or even Britain, ever really be 'independent'?

These latest challenges for the Scottish national question come at a time when the traditional European polity of multiple competing states is being reshaped. Europe's refusal to become a single empire served it well in the early modern period, and in the eighteenth and nineteenth centuries the sovereign state gained a new lease of life from mobilizing the forces of nationalism. The concept of a 'nation-state' retains its popular appeal. But when states are played off against one another by transnational business and finance, the nation-state may have the trappings of 'independence' but can no longer be *sovereign* in the way that it began to be in the period of this book. Perhaps the era of the sovereign state is now coming to an end.

But even if today's sovereign state, or nation-state, is not what it used to be, state authority itself shows no sign of fading away. For good or ill, public regulation still pervades our lives: official brown envelopes still drop through our doors. Indeed, can we any longer imagine a world *without* those brown envelopes? The Scottish national question, today, is a matter of adjusting the balance of authority between Edinburgh and London; no doubt it will make

[15] L. Paterson, *The Autonomy of Modern Scotland* (Edinburgh, 1994).

a difference if we get the balance right. If, however, the state were to disappear altogether—and in today's interdependent world this could happen only on a global scale—we would notice a rather larger difference.

It is the unfolding of that difference—between not having state authority, and having it—that this book seeks in a small way to elucidate.

1

Sovereignty

Laws cannot be made by any one who has a superior, nor can any man call a parliament who hath not the right of soveraignty and majesty.[1]

In 1469, an act of parliament declared Scotland an empire, an act that has been compared with the famous 1533 Act of Appeals which did the same for England.[2] The English act terminated the authority of the pope, while the Scottish one abolished only the exiguous power of the Holy Roman Emperor (the power in question was the right to create notaries), but both acts were steps towards the creation of an integrated monarchy owing allegiance to no superior. The creation of notaries was one of the five chief marks of sovereignty claimed by medieval emperors as unique to them.[3] It is true that the Scottish act explicitly reserved the right of the pope to create notaries; other developments were whittling away papal control over the Scottish clergy, but papal power remained a reality until 1560, as we shall see. The inspiration behind the 1469 act was probably the recent assumption of personal authority by the young James III, and James also pursued the ideal of imperial kingship in other ways, adopting the closed or arched imperial crown on his last coinage. James IV (1488–1513) used the older open crown on his coins, while James V (1513–42) used both, but Mary's coins and all later ones were careful to depict

---

[1] Thomas Craig, *Scotland's Soveraignty Asserted*, trans. G. Ridpath (London, 1695), 422. This work was written in 1602.

[2] *APS* ii. 95, c. 6; W. Ferguson, 'Imperial crowns: A neglected facet of the background to the Treaty of Union of 1707', *SHR* 53 (1974), 22–44, at pp. 37–8.

[3] W. Ullmann, 'The development of the medieval idea of sovereignty', *EHR* 64 (1949), 1–33, at p. 3. The others were that the crime of *lèse-majesté* could be committed only against the emperor, that he was the only authority able to issue binding laws, the only authority able to legitimate bastards, and that appeals lay from kings to the emperor.

the imperial crown.[4] These early imperial developments symbolized Scotland's aspiration to take its place among the select grouping of European political units that were transforming themselves into sovereign states.

However, the medieval concept of sovereignty was not quite the same as the sovereignty that began to take shape in the sixteenth century. Perhaps we need to define what it is that we are looking for. Ours is the familiar quarry of early modern historians—familiar, if sometimes strangely elusive: the sovereign state. The 'state' is a protean term, used here to mean a political community or society with some form of publicly exercised power or authority. This loose definition is sufficient, because it acquires precision with the adjective 'sovereign'. There had been a state—a kingdom—in Scotland since the middle ages; when and how did it become a *sovereign* state? This chapter will argue that many essential attributes of sovereignty were acquired in the sixteenth century.

The starting-point for the concept of sovereignty is the nineteenth-century legal-positivist work of John Austin, who revolutionized jurisprudence by separating considerations of law from those of morality. He defined the sovereign as the individual or body of individuals within a given territory who gave authority to existing laws, made new ones, and rendered no obedience to any superior in the exercise of these functions:

1. The *bulk* of the given society are in the *habit* of obedience or submission to a *determinate* and *common* superior: let that superior be a certain individual person, or a certain body or aggregate of individual persons.
2. That certain individual, or that certain body of individuals, is *not* in a habit of obedience to a determinate human superior.[5]

Law was thus a command which people had a habit of obeying, rather than a moral obligation; morality, although a real force, was not an obligation to a defined superior. Law as command remains the basis for modern definitions of the state, such as that of Michael Mann (following Weber):

---

[4] J. D. Bateson and N. J. Mayhew, *Sylloge of Coins of the British Isles*, xxxv. *Scottish Coins in the Ashmolean Museum, Oxford, and the Hunterian Museum, Glasgow* (Oxford, 1987), pls. 47–51; P. Grierson, 'The origins of the English sovereign and the symbolism of the closed crown', *British Numismatic Journal*, 33 (1964), 118–34.

[5] J. Austin, *The Province of Jurisprudence Determined*, ed. W. E. Rumble (Cambridge, 1995), ch. 6; quotation at p. 166. Author's emphasis. Cf. W. E. Rumble, *The Thought of John Austin* (London, 1985), 88–108.

The state is a differentiated set of institutions and personnel embodying centrality, in the sense that political relations radiate outward to cover a territorially demarcated area, over which it claims a monopoly of binding and permanent rule-making, backed up by physical violence.[6]

Some writers have, however, disagreed with aspects of Austin. Hans Kelsen has interpreted laws as 'valid norms' to which sanctions are attached, while Herbert Hart has even suggested that laws should be seen 'primarily' as what people themselves think *ought* to be done (thereby reintroducing morality), and only 'secondarily' as what government orders them to do. This seems to me unhelpful when considering government, for government (I must insist with Austin) *makes* law. Kelsen, indeed, explaining how laws are made, is obliged to fall back on laws as commands.[7] However, these writers are more useful when considering the attitude of the people to the government, and how that affected the government's business. Austin said little about the legitimacy of laws, not because he thought that this was unimportant—on the contrary, he was well aware that morality was so vital that even the sovereign might have to defer to its dictates—but because legitimacy and morality belonged to a separate province from law.

Sovereignty in a recognizably Austinian sense was first identified by Jean Bodin in 1576.[8] Bodin's theory, although it had defects

---

[6] M. Mann, *The Sources of Social Power*, i. *A History of Power to AD 1760* (Cambridge, 1986), 37.

[7] H. Kelsen, *General Theory of Law and State*, trans. A. Wedberg (New York, 1961), 30–5, 186–8. The criticisms of Austin made here are that (i) legislators do not 'will' the law all the time, or after their death, and that (ii) customary laws are not 'commands'. But (i) the *current* authorities *do* 'will' the law of their predecessors and cause it to be enforced—a point originally made by Hobbes; (ii) the *enforcement* of customary law *is* done by the command of the ruler who validates it.

H. L. A. Hart, *The Concept of Law* (Oxford, 1961), ch. 4 and *passim*, makes the following criticisms: (i) the legislators' coercive orders apply also to themselves, so they are not fully 'above' the law; (ii) many laws confer *powers* on the subjects, rather than coercing them; (iii) there are difficulties in identifying the Austinian 'sovereign' in a democratic state (Austin wrote in the late 1820s). I would accept (i), as indeed Austin might have done; (ii) is unacceptable, as one person's legal power is another's legal coercion; while (iii), although important, is not relevant to our period.

[8] Jean Bodin, *The Six Bookes of a Commonweale*, ed. K. D. McRae (Cambridge, Mass., 1962); A. P. d'Entrèves, *The Notion of the State* (Oxford, 1967), 99–103. A thought-provoking survey of the changing concept of sovereignty at this time is provided by F. H. Hinsley, *Sovereignty* (2nd edn., Cambridge, 1986), ch. 3.

that need not concern us,[9] reflected the growing importance
of sovereign states at the time when he wrote. In the late middle
ages, Europe still possessed a rich diversity of models of political
organization: empires, kingdoms, lordships, federations of towns,
crusading orders, ecclesiastical principalities, city-states. Power was
diffused widely, and shared at many levels, from the most high and
dignified—the pope, the Holy Roman Emperor—to the local—the
bishop in his cathedral, the baron in his castle; power was also
differentiated into sacred and secular. The sovereignty claimed by
medieval emperors seemed to be a claim to be the strongest power,
but it was partly a claim to be the highest (as with the sole right to
create notaries, which was hardly a claim to strength). Gradually—
and the outlines of the process are familiar to all students of
fifteenth- and sixteenth-century Europe—power structures crystallized. Sovereign states, with defined territories, developed.
Other forms of power declined, or were subsumed into the state;
if bishop and baron survived, they did so because they were useful
to the king, exercising a delegated royal authority.[10] This chapter
aims to show how Scotland took many of the decisive steps towards
becoming a state of this kind.

The traditional concept of sovereignty—formal overlordship but
not direct power to command—was still being used in connection
with Scotland in 1559. In a scheme to resolve the Scottish-
international crisis of 1559–60, the English statesman Sir William
Cecil proposed 'to gyve to the French the interest of soveraynte with
some shews of honor', while reserving real power to the Scots.[11]

---

[9] He denied the possibility of sovereignty residing in a composite body such as
the crown in parliament, but critics soon sorted out this anomaly: J. H. Franklin, *Jean
Bodin and the Rise of Absolutist Theory* (Cambridge, 1973), 29–31. For a claim that
Bodin did *not* advocate a theory of sovereignty, see K. Pennington, *The Prince and the
Law, 1200–1600: Sovereignty and Rights in the Western Legal Tradition* (Berkeley and
Los Angeles, 1993), 276–82. The argument is that Bodin used medieval terminology, and denied that the king could break his own contracts, expropriate property,
or act as a judge. The second and third points might indeed seem a limitation on
the king, and the third has been much discussed (it will be taken up below); the first
and fourth, however, did not limit him (he appointed the judges).

[10] An incisive recent study is C. Tilly, *Coercion, Capital and European States, AD
990–1990* (Oxford, 1990), 2, 43–4. Professor Tilly uses the term 'national state',
which seems clumsy—he has to differentiate it carefully from 'nation-state'—but
the 'sovereign state' discussed in this chapter is the same thing. For the lack of
sovereignty among fifteenth-century European states generally, see B. Guenée,
States and Rulers in Later Medieval Europe, trans. J. Vale (Oxford, 1985), 6.

[11] Cecil to William Maitland of Lethington, 7 Apr. 1559, in H. James (ed.),
Facsimiles of National Manuscripts of Scotland, 3 vols. (Southampton, 1868–71), iii,

This was the kind of sovereignty that the Holy Roman Emperor possessed—a high, honourable, but somewhat empty dignity.

By the end of the century, the new concept of sovereignty had been fully accepted in Scotland. James VI would certainly not have been satisfied with Cecil's version of it. He agreed cordially with the concept of law as command: 'I will tell thee, man, what is obedience. The centurion, when he said to his servants, to this man, Goe, and he goeth, to that man, Come, and he cometh, that is obedience.' He also had, for his time, a clear conception of sovereignty: 'The king is above the law, as both the author and giver of strength thereto: yet a good king will not onely delight to rule his subjects by the lawe, but even will conforme himselfe in his own actions therunto'.[12] Similarly the great jurist Thomas Craig: 'There can be no majesty where there is not a soveraign command; neither does he retain the rights of soveraignty, who acknowledges another to be superiour to himself, or is obliged when call'd on, to answer at his court'. Craig approved Bodin's work, though he tried to assimilate it to his own ideas on feudal monarchy.[13]

When we think of the sovereign, we think at once of the king;[14] who else could it have been? After all, the king was the pre-eminent, permanent ruler. Nobody could call him to account, or limit his power, or remove him. As John Mair wrote in 1521: 'Unless under a solemn consideration of the matter by the three estates, and ripe judgement passed wherein no element of passion shall intrude, kings are not to be deposed'.[15] But of course, Mair's qualification was the vital element; the three estates—parliament— also participated in sovereignty. Not everyone accepted Mair's view of political authority, but all knew that legislation was made by parliaments summoned by the king. With the consolidation of the

no. 41. Cf. also the ingenious argument, advanced unsuccessfully in 1528, that parliament could not be held during Christian festivals, and that 'thair is na superior to the kingis grace to dispenss with him to hald his parliament in this feriate tyme, for he has na superior in the erd [i.e. earth] in temperalite': *APS* ii. 322. The reasoning was that if the king *had* had a superior, he could have obtained a dispensation; lacking a superior, he was powerless in the matter.

[12] Calderwood, *History*, vii. 263; James VI, *Trew Law*, in *Political Writings*, 75.

[13] Craig, *Scotland's Soveraignty Asserted*, 6; cf. ibid. 426, in which Bodin is cited in support. Cf. also J. W. Cairns *et al.*, 'Legal humanism and the history of Scots law: John Skene and Thomas Craig', in J. MacQueen (ed.), *Humanism in Renaissance Scotland* (Edinburgh, 1990), 62.

[14] Perhaps remembering that there might be a queen.

[15] John Major (Mair), *History of Greater Britain*, ed. A. Constable (SHS, 1892), 219.

sovereign state, the sovereign authority would come to be the crown in parliament. Without parliament, the crown could not make laws or raise taxes. Not all existing laws were parliamentary statutes, but if a sixteenth-century government wanted to change the law—and is it possible to govern actively without wanting this?—it required a statute.[16]

This meant that the Scottish government was a mixed monarchy rather than an absolute monarchy, or (in the well-known fifteenth-century distinction drawn by Sir John Fortescue) a *dominium politicum et regale* rather than *dominium regale*.[17] A tract of 1583–4 recognized this, comparing Scotland's polity to the Spartan '*mixta basilaristokrasia*' (mixed monarchy and aristocracy).[18] This was not a problem before the 1590s, as there was little or no conflict between crown and parliament. This harmony stands out more strongly when it is recalled that there had sometimes been such conflict before, in the fourteenth and fifteenth centuries, and would be again, more seriously, in the seventeenth. At the time when state sovereignty was being established, both crown and parliament were essential components of the centralized state, and they acted together to cement its power against other power centres.

The crown in parliament—or, between sittings of parliament, the executive and judicial institutions headed by the crown—did not do all the governing directly. Much had to be done by subordinate authorities. They acted in the name of the crown, and administered the law as laid down by the crown in parliament, the body to which they were ultimately answerable and by which they were ultimately supervised. There was no regular appeal to parliament from the court of session, but why should parliament have involved itself in these details?—the law that the court was implementing was the law as made in parliament.

---

[16] Balfour, *Practicks*, i. 1–4.

[17] As was recognized by Fortescue himself: J. H. Burns, *The True Law of Kingship: Concepts of Monarchy in Early-Modern Scotland* (Oxford, 1996), 12. The theory of a monarchy limited by the political community in parliament was elaborated fully in the works of John Mair: J. H. Burns, '*Politia regalis et optima*: The political ideas of John Mair', *History of Political Thought*, 2 (1981), 31–61, at pp. 36–42.

[18] 'The general state of the commonwealth of Scotland', in *CSP Scot.* xiii, II. 1115–20. The date of this tract was established by M. Lynch, 'The crown and the burghs, 1500–1625', in id. (ed.), *The Early Modern Town in Scotland* (London, 1987), 56–8.

At this point a suggestion of 'separation of powers' may arise. Like Austin, I find the concept unhelpful. It is usually held to mean that legislative, judicial, and executive authority are held by separate, if interdependent, governmental bodies. Such a concept may be useful for states that have based their own constitutional arrangements upon it, but it is not a jurisprudential universal and need not be imported into discussion of a government that does not force it on our attention.[19] In sixteenth-century Scotland, parliament (legislature), court of session (judiciary), and privy council (executive) all operated in the name of the crown, and cannot be said to have had fully separate spheres of action; certainly the two latter were not co-equal with the first. If there is a distinction to be drawn, it is that made by Kelsen between legislation (making law) on the one hand, and judicial and executive action (implementing it) on the other. Thus, court of session and privy council refrained from claiming the plenary legislative authority that belonged solely to crown in parliament.[20] Even this should not be allowed to obscure the unity of the government as the forum within which law was constituted. It was this unity that the crown symbolized: the name of the crown—which was not necessarily the personal command of the king—bound the structure together.

A further red herring should perhaps be dealt with at this point. In the pages that follow I shall consider government as an integrated whole, and shall treat with caution and scepticism many common assumptions that government was a matter of the personal will and inclinations of the monarch. But scepticism about monarchical authority can be taken too far. Even among scholars, there are found a few who repeat the modern folk-tale that in Scotland, 'sovereignty rested not with the King but with the people' or 'in the hands of the whole community'.[21] In fact, those

[19] Austin, *Province of Jurisprudence Determined*, 196–9. The most famous exponent of the concept, Montesquieu, regarded it as beneficial but not universal: *The Spirit of the Laws*, ed. A. M. Cohler *et al.* (Cambridge, 1989), 156–66.

[20] Kelsen, *General Theory of Law and State*, 255–7. The separation into legislative and executive powers, with the legislative as supreme, was recognized by John Locke, *Two Treatises of Government*, ed. P. Laslett (2nd edn., Cambridge, 1967), 382–7. Locke added a 'federative' power, dealing with foreign policy, usually held by the same person or persons as the executive power. The belief that the privy council possessed legislative powers is contested in J. Goodare, *The Government of Scotland, 1560–1625* (forthcoming), ch. 6.

[21] P. H. Scott, *Andrew Fletcher and the Treaty of Union* (Edinburgh, 1992), 24, 47; cf. G. W. Iredell, 'The Law, Custom and Practice of the Parliament of Scotland, with

sixteenth-century commentators who claimed that the king was answerable to the people did not do so in terms of sovereignty; George Buchanan was no follower of Bodin. The modern folk-tale about community sovereignty rests on an inadequate understanding of the concept of sovereignty, and fails altogether to explain why (or indeed how) Scotland should have differed from other states. In fact, sixteenth-century Scotland was a state like any other in western Europe, and its kings and parliaments exercised the authority that they did in much the same way. That does not mean that they held unlimited authority; but there was nothing unusual about either the theoretical or the practical constraints on their rule.

It may also be suggested, with more plausibility, that there were other, higher laws, to which statutes were obliged to conform. Certainly nobody in our period would have said that statute law was, or should be, supreme over *all* other laws; Hobbes was the first to say this, and even then few agreed with him. Until then, all agreed that divine law and natural law were paramount.[22] But this does not diminish the legal sovereignty of the state. The law of the supreme human authority was statute law, which was not constrained by these alleged higher laws. All the statutes ever made were said (and even believed) to be consonant with divine law and with natural law; no court would admit a plea to the contrary, though some people sometimes wished they would. The

Particular Reference to the Period 1660–1707', Ph.D. thesis (London, 1966), 12. In both cases, the only evidence cited is the Declaration of Arbroath of 1320 and the Claim of Right of 1689. In the Claim of Right, sovereignty rested with parliament; on this, see Ch. 10 below. The Declaration of Arbroath was a letter, not a binding constitutional enactment like the English Magna Carta, and it promised to depose, not a tyrant (as in early modern resistance theory), but a deserter. It was a commonplace that medieval monarchs could not alienate their kingdom; the Scottish barons of 1320 were only saying what any other barons would have said (although not necessarily with such eloquence) had they been in the same unusual situation. Cf. Sir George Mackenzie, *Jus Regium: or the Just and Solid Foundation of Monarchy in General, and More Especially of the Monarchy of Scotland* (Edinburgh, 1684), 66.

[22] Divine law was the law or will of God as received, understood, and expounded by religious authorities; natural law was either the customs that humankind shared with other animals, or (perhaps inconsistently) the dictates of human reason. Divine and natural law were sometimes equated (as when Christianity was regarded as an achievement of reason), sometimes separated. I take Hobbes in this context (though he is not essential to my argument) as having located the basic need for government in human nature, which is not quite the same as natural law. For learned contemporary comment, see Craig, *Jus Feudale*, 1.8.6.

existence—still more the superiority—of divine law and natural law was a moral claim rather than a legal fact. Sixteenth-century resistance theory, which drew liberally on divine and natural law, was influential not as law, but as ideology; it might legitimize revolution, but that is never a *legal* act, just as it is never the act of a government. An integrated government obeying no human superior is sovereign.

This still leaves one further type of law, or alleged law: fundamental law. People thought that there were laws—constitutional laws, in modern terms—that could not be transgressed; the *lex regia*, or law of succession to the crown, is a case in point. The trouble is that people were not consistent over this. King James propounded at least two different versions of fundamental law. He told his English parliament that the fundamental law of Scotland was solely the *lex regia*, for there was no English-style common law there. But when planning to restore bishops, he had written that this would restore the three estates which were the 'ancient and fundamentall policie of our kingdome'.[23] The corollary was that any *other* law was *not* fundamental—so that the king was at liberty to change it. Others were inclined to see a much wider scope for fundamental law. The Scottish parliament in 1604, suspicious of the proposed union, insisted on it 'nocht dirogating onywayes ony fundamentall lawes, ancient privileges, offices, richtis, digniteis and liberteis of this kingdome'.[24] The laws that constituted a parliament were here 'fundamentall', as important as the laws that constituted a king. Contemporaries thought that fundamental laws existed, but the statement that a law was fundamental was essentially no more than a claim that it was important and ought not to be altered by the government.[25]

[23] James VI & I, *Basilicon Doron*, and speech to the English parliament, 1607, in *Political Writings*, 25, 27, 172. To complicate matters further, James also thought that parliaments with these 'fundamentall' estates existed solely at the royal behest. Conceivably by 'policie' he meant something slightly different from law, and in his original MS he in fact wrote 'fundamentall lawis' before altering it to 'policie': James VI, *Basilicon Doron*, 2 vols., ed. J. Craigie (STS, 1944–50), i. 72. J. H. Burns suggests that this indicates 'uneasiness' with the concept of fundamental law: *True Law of Kingship*, 287–8.

[24] *APS* iv. 264, c. 1; cf. estates to James, Aug. 1607, *RPC* vii. 535. James's 1607 speech was an embarrassed attempt to put a more monarchical gloss on this for the English. Cf. B. P. Levack, *The Formation of the British State: England, Scotland and the Union, 1603–1707* (Oxford, 1987), 32–3.

[25] Cf. J. W. Gough, *Fundamental Law in English Constitutional History* (Oxford, 1955), chs. 2–5.

The apparent inconsistencies in such claims were not a problem
at the time; James contradicting himself hardly denoted constitutional conflict. In practice, the laws that constituted a king, and
the laws that constituted a parliament, were what the sovereign
government said they were; unless that government was divided
on real issues, there was no occasion to argue. In practice, parliament's constitution was changed from time to time.[26] In practice,
moreover, traditions of royal succession were neither precise,
consistent, nor unalterable. James's own stress on indefeasible
hereditary succession was a ploy to bolster his hopes of the English
crown, for it was on this ground that his claim was strongest; had
he stood next in line under Henry VIII's will, he might have discovered the virtues of the parliamentary statute that had legiti-
mated that will.[27] That was English law, but the greater regularity
of the Scottish succession was due merely to the genealogical accident that the Stewart dynasty had long produced clearly legitimate
direct heirs but few collateral branches. James might have reflected
that had he himself died without direct heirs, the Scots would suddenly have found themselves having to reinvent the *lex regia* on the
back of an envelope, with little in his writings on fundamental law
to guide them.

What about property rights—were these fundamental, and if so
did they transcend the authority of the state? Medieval jurists had
discussed inconclusively whether sovereigns such as the emperor
had the right to take their subjects' property at will; as European
monarchs' tax demands began to bite, an answer to this question
was now required.[28] In our period, it was commonly thought that
while kings had the right to sovereignty, subjects had the parallel
right to property; to complicate matters, the same Latin word,
dominium, could be used to mean both. Bodin himself saw the subjects as having fundamental rights not to be taxed, a view that
caused him many difficulties.[29] In 1597, Sir John Skene wrote
(quoting medieval jurists) that the king 'is called our liege king,

---

[26] For changes in the number of estates, accompanied by claim and counter-
claim that various estates were fundamental, see J. Goodare, 'The estates in the
Scottish parliament, 1286–1707', *Parliamentary History*, 15 (1996), 11–32.

[27] Cf. G. R. Elton (ed.), *The Tudor Constitution* (2nd edn., Cambridge, 1982), 3.

[28] Pennington, *The Prince and the Law*, ch. 1; S. E. Finer, *The History of Government
from the Earliest Times*, 3 vols. (Oxford, 1997), iii. 1298–9.

[29] M. Wolfe, 'Jean Bodin on taxes: The sovereignty-taxes paradox', *Political Science
Quarterly*, 83 (1968), 268–84.

because he suld maintene and defend us. . . . *Just as the emperor is said to be lord of the world, in the same way the king is lord of his kingdom.* . . . quhilk suld be understand, concerning the defense and maintenance, and not anent the propertie', for 'kings are not lords of private possessions'.[30] This established that a line ought to be drawn between sovereignty and property, but evaded saying where to draw it. When it came to taxation, people tended to frame the question along traditional lines—'under what circumstances does the king have the right to take his subjects' property?'—but it gradually became clear that this was the wrong question. The unspoken convention grew up in the 1580s and 1590s that parliament—*not* the king—had the right to impose taxation under *any* circumstances.[31] Here again, parliament was sovereign.

Another possibility was that the law governing succession to landed property—feudal law—might be supranational and thus beyond the government's reach. The leading authority on this, Craig, contrasted the European 'feudal law' with the 'municipal law' of a nation. However, the feudal law in any given country had been imposed, as he saw it, by the crown or with the assent of the crown; thus, in Scotland, various components of feudal law had been adopted by early kings such as Kenneth II (971–95) and Malcolm II (1005–34). Craig tended to speak of the laws' 'adoption by the Scottish people' rather than simply making the king a legislator, but his feudal law was an adjunct to royal authority, not an alternative to it.[32] James VI also thought that the Scottish laws on land tenure, which were feudal through and through, rested on royal authority: 'James the first, bred here in England, brought the [feudal] lawes thither in a written hand'.[33] He declared his intention to respect property, but only in a menacing passage in which his reasons for doing so were not entirely explicit. Scottish kings existed before the law, he wrote, 'and by them was the land

---

[30] Skene, *DVS*, s.v. ligeantia. Emphasis added to translation from Latin. For the similar if more sophisticated view of John Mair, see Burns, *True Law of Kingship*, 67.

[31] J. Goodare, 'Parliamentary taxation in Scotland, 1560–1603', *SHR* 68 (1989), 23–52, at p. 41.

[32] Craig, *Scotland's Soveraignty Asserted*, 2; id., *Jus Feudale*, 1.8.1–3; J. G. A. Pocock, *The Ancient Constitution and the Feudal Law* (2nd edn., Cambridge, 1987), ch. 4.

[33] James VI & I, speech to parliament, 1607, in *Political Writings*, 173–4. Craig saw the practice of giving of sasine as having been introduced about 1430, and this may be what James had in mind: Craig, *Jus Feudale*, II.7.2.

distributed (which at first was whole theirs)'. What the king could give, could he under certain circumstances take back?

The king might have a better colour for his pleasure, without further reason, to take the land from his lieges, as over-lord of the whole, and doe with it as pleaseth him, since all that they hold is of him, then, as foolish writers say, the people might unmake the king, and put an other in his roome: But either of them as unlawful, and against the ordinance of God, ought to be alike odious to be thought, much lesse put in practise.[34]

In 1626, the earl of Mar protested to Charles I that his revocation scheme would undermine the security of property: 'no subjectt could be seur of any inheritans . . . nether (give itt should ons be maed aine actt of parliament) could his majestie or any of his successor kings mak thaem any securitie in tym cuming'.[35] Here, Mar was dimly realizing one implication of sovereignty: no sovereign can bind its successor. He clearly thought that property rights ought to be fundamental law—above the king, or rather, above parliament, since it was parliamentary ratification of the revocation that was crucial to him. We, however, can see that Mar was wrong; there was no such fundamental law restraining governments.

Shortly after this, a Scot for the first time articulated a more extreme theory: not only is the king above the law, but he can dispose of his subjects' property at will. This was Lord Napier, in his Bodinian essay 'Of laws', written probably in the 1630s. Under the laws of God and nature, all things had originally been held in common; so property law could be placed no higher than the civil law of particular states. Napier insisted that the sovereign was above this civil law: 'Civil lawes ar reules for the subjects to live by; but the Soverane is exempt from them, becaus they ar his own commands; *nemo potest sibi imperare* [nobody can command himself].' Napier seems to have been atypical; his fellow-royalists would find his arguments hard to stomach in the 1640s.[36]

---

[34] James VI, *Trew Law*, in *Political Writings*, 73–4. Related positions were taken by two expatriate Scots with high views of monarchy. Adam Blackwood in 1581 held that the king might take property without consent in emergencies, while Alexander Irvine in 1627 held that while he could do so at any time, he ought not to. J. P. Sommerville, 'English and European political ideas in the early seventeenth century: Revisionism and the case of absolutism', *Journal of British Studies*, 35 (1996), 168–94, at pp. 177–9.

[35] HMC, *Mar & Kellie*, i. 139.

[36] Lord Napier, 'Of laws', in *Memorials of Montrose and his Times*, 2 vols., ed. M. Napier (Maitland Club, 1848–50), i. 76–8; cf. D. Stevenson, 'The "Letter on

We have traced some of the lineaments of sovereignty; perhaps we should investigate where it came from. In Scotland, it arose gradually in the sixteenth century, particularly after 1560. Sovereignty is not a simple, unchanging, or (as we shall see) absolute concept, and in this early period it did not look quite as it would do in the nineteenth or even eighteenth centuries. There were other autonomous authorities, both above and below the level of the kingdom, whose powers had to be curtailed or incorporated; this process took some time, and even when it was more or less complete (as it was by 1625) the sovereign state was not a unitary one. The composite nature of the Scottish-British state after 1603 perplexed and agitated contemporaries, and continues to pose conceptual difficulties for the historian, although it is by no means the only issue with which we shall have to grapple. But let us begin at the beginning. Fifteenth-century Scotland was not sovereign, because—sad to say—the people of Scotland were not in the *habit* of obeying the king. They did obey him sometimes—quite often, in fact; but they also obeyed several other people, without asking the king's permission. We therefore have to look at who these people were, and how the shared and parcellized authority of the later middle ages became the more concentrated authority of the seventeenth century.

Usually, the authority-figure whom people obeyed was their immediate feudal lord. This may seem a large claim, but it could be falsified only by showing that when people had a choice (as they often did) between obeying their lord and obeying the king, they chose to obey the king. Of course they did not. This point could be demonstrated at length, but one example may suffice: James III's protracted struggle with the Home family over the priory of Coldingham, which came to a head in the mid-1480s. Alexander Home, grandson and heir of the elderly first Lord Home, was able to chart his own political course—loyal to the king in the crisis of 1482–3, dissident in that of 1487–8—with the full support of his numerous family. The Homes' aim was to get John Home (Alexander's uncle) confirmed in possession of the priory, regardless of the king's plans to suppress it and annex its revenues to the chapel royal. John Home appealed from the king to the pope, visiting

sovereign power" and the influence of Jean Bodin on political thought in Scotland', *SHR* 61 (1982), 25–43, which discusses the reception of a later and better-known work of Napier's.

Rome in 1484–5, but ultimately showed himself prepared to defy both king and pope. Thanks to the political divisions which led to James III's downfall in 1488, the Homes were to succeed in their defiance; what is significant here is not so much that they succeeded as that defiance of the king—ultimately, armed defiance—by a local noble family was a possible and in some senses routine eventuality in fifteenth-century politics. There is no suggestion that the loyalties of other Homes should have been to the king rather than to the head of the family.[37] The normal position of a noble's following is well summed up by Jenny Wormald:

And in the localities, who better—indeed, who other—to maintain royal authority than the nobles with their pre-eminent position based on their widespread alliances with their kindreds, the lairds and their tenants and servants, alliances based on protection by the magnates in return for the service and loyalty of their dependants.[38]

Thus the crown did not possess a monopoly of political violence—something that all modern states regard as essential. Feudal lords had their own armies, made up of their vassals and leading kinsmen and tenants. The crown had no separate army of its own: the medieval Scottish army was largely composed of the followers of nobles. Feudal lords and their vassals were all expected to be loyal to the crown, of course, and they often were. We are reminded of this by Dr Wormald, who stresses the frequency of cooperation between crown and nobles in the fifteenth century. But it was still cooperation, with a strong voluntary element, rather than compulsion by the crown. If for any reason a lord fought against the crown, his vassals would be expected to do so too.[39]

A detailed discussion of the position of the nobility must, however, wait until the next chapter, which will provide the opportunity to see how government functioned within the traditional

[37] N. Macdougall, 'The struggle for the priory of Coldingham, 1472–1488', *IR* 23 (1972), 102–14.

[38] J. Wormald, 'Taming the magnates?', in K. J. Stringer (ed.), *Essays on the Nobility of Medieval Scotland* (Edinburgh, 1985), 278.

[39] Whether they would do so in practice might depend on immediate political realities. Many of the fourth earl of Huntly's followers deserted him in his 1562 rebellion, feeling that it was a 'lost cause': A. White, 'Queen Mary's northern province', in M. Lynch (ed.), *Mary Stewart: Queen in Three Kingdoms* (Oxford, 1988), 61–2. The same kind of desertion was experienced by the outnumbered *royal* army at Carberry Hill in 1567.

Scottish social structure. In the meantime, the theme of sovereignty can be pursued by examining supranational authority.

People also sometimes obeyed the pope, again without asking the king. Not always, of course. Analysis of papal powers in Scotland is difficult, because the historiography of the papacy's relations with Scotland (and indeed the whole of northern Europe) in the century before 1560 tends to stress the seemingly inevitable erosion of Rome's influence.[40] But Rome was not dead yet; a declining power may still be formidable. The power of the late-medieval papacy was based on its position at the apex of a vast pyramid of church benefices with uncounted wealth and extensive privileges; on its custody of canon law, regulating not only those benefices but also wide areas of human behaviour; and on people's acceptance of the pope's claim to wield spiritual sanctions based on the possession of the keys of heaven. It was a potent combination.[41]

Some of the papal powers belonged only to the recent past; the idea that something immemorial was passing away with the papacy should be resisted. During the fourteenth century, the period of the Avignon papacy, there was a dramatic expansion of papal provisions to benefices (grants of vacant benefices, or grants of the right to succeed to a benefice). Provisions were not particularly unpopular in Scotland (much of the hostility they attracted in England was due to pro-French popes), and the bureaucratic way in which they were administered made the system fairly reliable. This system was used by churchmen at every level: junior priests hoping for benefices, and bishops, cardinals, and senior clergymen seeking to top up their own income or to reward valued servants. It was 'very much based on law rather than on papal whim'—a law recognized by all, from Easter Ross to Avignon, and by the royal court as much as the papal curia.[42]

Along with powers of appointment to benefices went powers to

---

[40] For a general introd. to this subject, see W. J. Anderson, 'Rome and Scotland, 1513–1625', in D. McRoberts (ed.), *Essays on the Scottish Reformation* (Glasgow, 1962).
[41] W. Ullmann, *Principles of Government and Politics in the Middle Ages* (4th edn., London, 1978), 32–86.
[42] A. D. M. Barrell, *The Papacy, Scotland and Northern England, 1342–1378* (Cambridge, 1995), ch. 2; quotation at p. 123. Papal influence in the appointment of abbots increased between the 13th and the 15th cents.: M. Dilworth, *Scottish Monasteries in the Late Middle Ages* (Edinburgh, 1995), 13–15.

tax those benefices. There were several papal taxes, of which the most important was annates—a levy on the first year's income of a benefice filled by papal provision. Again in the fourteenth century the incidence of this tax was expanded by the Avignon papacy. It was hard to collect, but the tribulations of the papal collectors seem to have been no worse than what one would expect from any other late-medieval tax, and certainly should not be used to infer any inherent papal weakness.[43] The papacy also supervised benefice-holders' use of their property; right up to the Reformation, permanent alienation of such property through feuing could only be achieved by obtaining permission (and paying the requisite fee) in Rome.[44]

The papacy was thus involved in Scottish life at every level. A dispute between the bailies and friars of Ayr in 1386 was settled, not by the crown, but by a papal legate.[45] Thousands of cases to do with benefices or teinds were decided by the pope, as the *Calendars of Scottish Supplications to Rome* make clear; real power is power exercised in a routine way. The pope was asked, in 1433, to confirm a royal grant of a market and trading rights to the ecclesiastical burgh of Brechin.[46] He could involve himself in nobles' feuds, as when he ordered the bishop of Lismore to use the threat of excommunication to force Walter Stewart, Lord Lorne, and his followers, to underlie the law for attacking the castle of the earl of Argyll.[47] Papal influence in diplomacy and war was illustrated in 1455, when a Scottish army marching to besiege Berwick was met by two 'papal nuncios' who persuaded the king to abandon the attack—although they later turned out to have been English agents in disguise.[48]

The ultimate governing bodies of Scottish monasteries were supranational institutions such as the Cistercian general chapter. Many monastic orders enjoyed a good deal of freedom from the influence of bishop or papacy, and the influence of the crown was

---

[43] A. D. M. Barrell, 'William de Grenlaw, papal collector in Scotland, and his account', *IR* 42 (1991), 3–18; id., *The Papacy, Scotland and Northern England*, 33–55.

[44] R. K. Hannay, 'On the church lands at the Reformation', *SHR* 16 (1919), 52–72, at pp. 58–9.

[45] E. L. Ewan, *Townlife in Fourteenth-Century Scotland* (Edinburgh, 1990), 47.

[46] *Calendar of Scottish Supplications to Rome, 1433–1447*, ed. A. I. Dunlop and D. MacLauchlan (Glasgow, 1983), no. 87.

[47] S. I. Boardman, 'Politics and the Feud in Late Medieval Scotland', Ph.D. thesis (St Andrews, 1990), 35.

[48] C. McGladdery, *James II* (Edinburgh, 1990), 97.

even more indirect. The orders' governing bodies continued to exercise a periodic supervision over the Scottish monasteries, occasionally in defiance of the crown's wishes but seldom with crown involvement, until the 1530s at least, although the comprehensive interference of James V in appointments to senior church posts disrupted monastic governance. The Knights Hospitallers had to defer not just to a grand master in Rhodes, but also to a prior in England—and generally did so.[49]

This reminds us that the medieval church was not an effective monarchy, however great the pope's power. It was too decentralized for that. Authority could spread bewilderingly in all directions. The abbey of Iona in the thirteenth century gained independence from all ecclesiastical superiors, becoming subject to the pope alone—and in the process it had to contend with claims to control from the abbey of Dunfermline, the bishop of the Isles (based on the Isle of Man), the abbey of Derry in Ireland, and the archbishop of Trondheim in Norway.[50] The pre-Reformation Scottish universities were always subject to episcopal authority, probably because they were founded by bishops, but that was not a universal pattern—the university of Paris acknowledged no superior at all in the fourteenth century, and in the fifteenth century it recognized the authority of the crown.[51] Not only was there no unitary sovereign state: there was no unitary church state either.

The concept of parliamentary sovereignty over all estates had not been fully accepted by the church, or imposed by the state, at the outset of our period. In 1543, parliament agreed to the circulation of the bible in the vernacular, but the bishops objected to the act's statement 'that the thre estatis concludit the samin'; they, 'being present as ane of the thre estatis of the said parliament, dissentit thairto simpliciter', and declared that they would not recognize the act until a provincial council of the church could discuss it.[52] In 1546, 'my lord governour, in face of parliament, desyrit the lordis spirituale to vote' in a case in which a papal decree was alleged to infringe the royal rights. They evaded doing so, however,

[49] M. Dilworth, 'Franco-Scottish efforts at monastic reform', *RSCHS* 25 (1993–5), 204–21; A. Macquarrie, 'A problem of conflicting loyalties? The Knights Hospitallers in Scotland in the later middle ages', *RSCHS* 21 (1981–3), 223–32.

[50] A. Macquarrie, 'Kings, lords and abbots: Power and patronage at the medieval monastery of Iona', *TGSI* 54 (1984–6), 355–75, at pp. 357–9.

[51] I am grateful to Prof. J. H. Burns for making this point to me.

[52] *APS* ii. 415, c. 12.

and the regent was reduced to protesting 'that na wyte suld be imputt to him thairthrow'.[53] Claims that an act of the estates was illegitimate because one of the estates had not consented to it would later be made by the burghs;[54] but the burghs failed to sustain their claim, while the pre-Reformation church seems to have had a good deal of success.

The canon law, and the church courts that administered it, were essentially supranational, even if there was little central control guiding it. The Scottish church passed few statutes, fewer than in England; even once it started legislating more actively, between 1549 and 1559, it was often content to copy the statutes of the Council of Trent.[55] We are told that William Hay, who lectured on the law of marriage in Aberdeen early in the sixteenth century, 'makes scant reference to things Scottish'.[56] Church courts heard not only narrowly religious and matrimonial cases but all actions concerning teinds, testaments, slander, oaths (thus bringing many contracts under ecclesiastical jurisdiction, as a breach of contract might involve breach of an oath), and any action with a clergyman as defender.[57] The prior and canons of Pittenweem committed homicide in 1531, but were able, despite royal protests, to obtain absolution from an ecclesiastical court.[58] These courts were answerable to no secular authority at any level, and appeal lay ultimately to Rome. Most of the cases going all the way to Rome related to the possession of benefices. The church courts fitted harmoniously into the legal system, with regular adjustment of boundaries but no systematic rivalry between 'church' and 'state'—at least not in the 1540s, from which our fullest evidence comes.[59] There seems to have been little or no desire to establish unitary sovereignty within the legal system.

Of course, the king was an influential figure in the politics of the late medieval church. For the time being, his influence was

---

[53] *APS* ii. 479. 'Wyte' = blame.   [54] *RCRB* i. 210; cf. ii. 190.

[55] S. Ollivant, *The Court of the Official in Pre-Reformation Scotland* (Stair Society, 1982), 129–30.

[56] William Hay, *Lectures on Marriage*, ed. J. C. Barry (Stair Society, 1967), p. xxxi.

[57] Teinds, however, were increasingly set in tack (i.e. leased) in this period, and tacks of teinds came under the secular courts, as did actions for spulyie (i.e. spoliation) of teinds: Hope, *Major Practicks*, i. 224–6.

[58] *St Andrews Formulare, 1514–1546*, 2 vols., ed. G. Donaldson (Stair Society, 1942–4), ii, p. xv and no. 341.

[59] Ollivant, *Court of the Official*, 133–8; cf. I. B. Cowan, *The Scottish Reformation* (London, 1982), 20–1.

mainly indirect, although it is easy enough to discern the outlines of a future royal supremacy; indeed it has been argued that the papacy was already, in the mid-fifteenth century, operating in effect by royal permission as 'the greatest of the jurisdictional franchises in the country'.[60] Kings were certainly well versed in the art of making the pope an offer he could not refuse, and limitations on papal power were sufficiently evident for it to be clear that there was no question of the *pope* being sovereign. But in the fifteenth century, a royal supremacy was at best latent; its realization would have to wait until after the Reformation. In the meantime, there was nothing special about (for instance) resistance by the king to an obnoxious papal provisor, for the provisor could equally well be resisted in the locality. Whether the resistance would succeed depended on the balance of political forces in the case. For the crown, this was partnership; it was not sovereignty.[61]

Eventually, this did change, and the authority of the pope was abrogated. To some extent this was the result of a sudden catastrophe for the papacy—the legislation of the Reformation Parliament of 1560. But could we also see the establishment of ecclesiastical sovereignty as a gradual process? Half of Europe never repudiated the pope; Catholic states were able to establish sovereignty by circumscribing but not abrogating papal powers. The papacy was made to operate by *permission* of the state, so that the relative authority of the two was reversed; the pope remained a partner in government, but a junior one. Contrary to what is sometimes thought, it was not a matter of confining the pope to spiritual matters; these were and remained an essential field for government.[62] The ultimate reason for the states' success was that, since the Reformation, rulers had a choice of religion.[63]

---

[60] D. E. R. Watt, 'The papacy and Scotland in the fifteenth century', in B. Dobson (ed.), *The Church, Politics and Patronage in the Fifteenth Century* (Gloucester, 1984), 119.

[61] Cf. J. A. F. Thomson, *Popes and Princes, 1417–1517* (London, 1980), 214.

[62] R. J. Knecht, 'The Concordat of 1516: A reassessment', in H. J. Cohn (ed.), *Government in Reformation Europe, 1520–1560* (London, 1971); P. Prodi, *The Papal Prince: One Body and Two Souls: The Papal Monarchy in Early Modern Europe*, trans. S. Haskins (Cambridge, 1987), ch. 8.

[63] If the Great Schism had continued, it might have had the same effect. Diplomatic questions about the Schism were decided in Scotland by parliament, not by the provincial council of the church: D. E. R. Watt, 'The provincial council of the Scottish church, 1215–1472', in A. Grant and K. J. Stringer (eds.), *Medieval Scotland: Crown, Lordship and Community* (Edinburgh, 1993), 154.

In Scotland, regular state assertiveness towards the papacy seems to date from 1471, two years after the 'imperial' statute with which we began.[64] In that year, a hard-hitting statute was passed against the purchase of any benefice in Rome when this had not been the custom for that benefice—there was 'gret damnage and skaith dayli done to al the realme be clerkis religious and secularis quhilkis purchessis abbasyis and utheris benefice[s] at the court of Rome'. The act also restricted papal taxations to former levels, and curbed some appropriations of parish benefices.[65] Next year, however, Patrick Graham, bishop of St Andrews, persuaded Pope Sixtus IV to promote him to archbishop, in an episode which is still obscure—was it with, or without, the king's permission? Traditionally the creation of the archbishopric was seen as a papal initiative; more recently it has been argued that the king initially supported it, but that Graham was also appointed as papal collector and legate *a latere* by the pope who wanted him to reform the Scottish monasteries as a quid pro quo. Either way, the episode does not demonstrate untrammelled royal power; crown and papacy had to reach what seems to have been a more or less equal compromise. It did have the result of incorporating within the Scottish province the bishoprics of Galloway and Orkney (hitherto technically subject to the archbishoprics of York and Trondheim respectively), thus making the Scottish church and kingdom conterminous.[66]

James III was still far from all-powerful *vis-à-vis* the pope in the 1480s; he had to accept the papal nominee to the bishopric of Dunkeld, George Browne, despite the latter's links with the dissident earl of Angus and the claims of a royal candidate, Alexander Inglis. James also reached an unfavourable compromise with the pope over the bishopric of Glasgow.[67] A reforming bishop like

---

[64] Instances of earlier conflict are noted by Watt, 'The papacy and Scotland', 118–22, who stresses, however, that cooperation was more common. The reign of James I saw a number of acts passed against purchase of benefices at Rome without royal permission, which came to be defined as 'barratry'; these and later acts on the subject are conveniently collected in *Source-Book*, ii. 83–93.

[65] *APS* ii. 99, c. 4. The act was repeated in 1488: *APS* ii. 209, c. 13.

[66] L. J. Macfarlane, 'The primacy of the Scottish church, 1472–1521', *IR* 20 (1969), 111–29, which is probably too pessimistic about the pope's undoubtedly diminishing authority over this period; N. Macdougall, *James III* (Edinburgh, 1982), 104–8; Watt, 'The papacy and Scotland', 123–6.

[67] Macdougall, *James III*, 222–5; L. J. Macfarlane, *William Elphinstone and the Kingdom of Scotland* (Aberdeen, 1985), 180.

William Elphinstone of Aberdeen might well face problems from both royal and papal interference.[68] Parliament in 1493 attempted to reconcile Scotland's two feuding archbishops, begging them to drop their appeals to Rome; the wording—'that the kingis hienes gar wryte his lettrez to baith the said prelatis exhorting them and praying thame to leif thair contentiounis, litis, and pleyis'—is redolent of a polity in which the government could not command. The act proved a dead letter.[69]

The crown scored its most notable victory against the papacy in the Indult of 1487, which seems to have been the crown's retaliation for the Browne affair.[70] By it, the pope was made to agree to wait for eight months before making provisions to major benefices, and to provide the crown's candidate if one was nominated. It was agreements of this kind in the post-conciliar period that did most to undermine papal power. The Indult was not perpetual, however, and was confirmed by the popes of the early sixteenth century only after complex struggles in which they sometimes regained ground. It seems, for instance, that Andrew Forman, bishop of Moray, was the pope's choice (though not his first choice) for the archbishopric of St Andrews in 1514.[71] A statute of 1526, asserting that 'quhen prelacyis sic as bischeprykis or abbacys hapnis to vaik, the nominacioun therof pertenis to our soverane lord, and the provisioun of the samyn to our haly fader the paip', seems to have restored the position of 1487 and perhaps went further.[72] In 1534, a papal bull granted the king the right to nominate to the major benefices, and to receive a year's rents from them.[73] By this time, the crown seems to have been in full and effective control of these benefices—at least if the political nation was prepared to support

[68] Macfarlane, *William Elphinstone*, 217–23; cf. G. Donaldson, *The Scottish Reformation* (Cambridge, 1960), 20.

[69] *APS* ii. 232–3, c. 7; L. J. Macfarlane, 'The elevation of the diocese of Glasgow into an archbishopric in 1492', *IR* 43 (1992), 99–118, at pp. 111–12.

[70] Watt, 'The papacy and Scotland', 127–8.

[71] Leo X to Queen Margaret and council, 8 Dec. 1514, and duke of Albany to Leo, [Feb. 1517,] *Letters of James V*, ed. R. K. Hannay and D. Hay (Edinburgh, 1954), 15–17, 41; J. Dowden, *The Bishops of Scotland* (Glasgow, 1912), 38–9. Cf. Cowan, *Scottish Reformation*, 29–30; Dilworth, *Scottish Monasteries*, 18; Prodi, *Papal Prince*, 159–61.

[72] *APS* ii. 309–10, c. 1.

[73] Robert Keith, *History of the Affairs of Church and State in Scotland, from the Beginning of the Reformation to the Year 1568*, 3 vols., ed. J. P. Lawson and C. J. Lyon (Spottiswoode Society, 1844–50), i. 461–4.

it; division, however (as in the 1550s), might still be exploited by the papacy to give itself a little room for manoeuvre.[74] Despite the spread of noble and royal lay commendators, one-third of monasteries still had regular abbots in 1560—apparently largely because of papal resistance.[75]

From the early sixteenth century we have signs of an ideologically motivated desire to curb papal power. The courtier and poet Sir David Lindsay of the Mount made a blistering attack on the 'papall monarchie', seen as

> the potent pope of Rome,
> Impyrand ovir all Christindome,
> To quhome no prince may be compare,
> As canon lawis can declare.[76]

We should probably regard this, not as evidence of how 'potent' the papacy really was, but as suggesting that opinion would endorse further royal inroads into its power.

With the sanction of parliament, the crown was able to tax the three estates, including the clergy, because the clergy were members of parliament. In fact such taxes were hardly ever demanded. From 1531, however, the crown began frequent taxation of the church alone, taxation that soon became heavy. To achieve this it needed, and gained, the consent of the pope. Although the papacy was too weak to refuse the crown's demands altogether, it did at least manage to evade the imposition of the *regular* tax that James V demanded.[77]

One way of increasing state control over the Scottish church would have been to get a suitable churchman made papal legate *a latere*, able to exercise many papal powers locally, including granting dispensations and hearing appeals from church courts. James

---

[74] In 1547, a wartime emergency ordinance provided that if any benefice-holder died in the coming campaign, his nearest heir 'maist abill thairfor' should simply have the benefice without further ado (*APS* ii. 599–600); but such measures may not be a good guide to normal practice or powers. For papal influence on a weak regime in the early 1550s, see R. K. Hannay, 'Some papal bulls among the Hamilton papers', *SHR* 22 (1925), 25–41.

[75] Dilworth, *Scottish Monasteries*, 23.

[76] Lindsay, 'The monarch', in *Works*, i. 325–6. For more on Lindsay's religion, see C. Edington, *Court and Culture in Renaissance Scotland: Sir David Lindsay of the Mount* (Amherst, Mass., 1994), part 3.

[77] W. S. Reid, 'Clerical taxation: The Scottish alternative to dissolution of the monasteries', *Catholic Historical Review*, 35 (1948), 129–53.

V regularly asked the pope for legatine powers for the archbishop of St Andrews, but without success. Only in 1544 did David Beaton achieve the coveted office, and unfortunately there is at present too little evidence to assess how he exercised his powers before his death in 1546. He seems to have gained the office partly through persuading Marco Grimani, the visiting papal legate *a latere* in Scotland in 1543–4, of his suitability and the need for the appointment.[78] It may be here that power devolved was power retained as far as the pope was concerned; at any rate, Beaton was not replaced.

None of this nullified the pope's authority entirely. Even in 1559, a provincial council of the church, while legislating against the collation of priests' sons to their fathers' churches, 'deemed it expedient earnestly to implore the queen to write supplicatory letters to our holy lord the pope, beseeching his holiness never more to grant any dispensations from the aforesaid statute'.[79] But the next year, the legislation of the Reformation Parliament put an end to centuries of papal influence. The regular flow of routine business for decisions in Rome ceased abruptly—a fact of momentous consequence for Scottish government.

If the power of the pope was real enough in early sixteenth-century Scotland, what about that of the emperor, with whom this chapter began? Here, it is not so much a matter of real power—though the emperor was still creating some notaries even after James III's Scottish-imperial statute of 1469 had supposedly banned this.[80] Rather, it was the *idea* of the empire as possessing a form of authority higher than that of a mere kingdom which may have inhibited legislators. So long as the emperor was seen as having a higher dignity than kings, it was hard to escape the corollary that mere kings—even those outside the boundaries of the Holy Roman Empire itself—lacked full plenary powers.

In the fifteenth century, there was still life in the concept of *universal* empire—the idea of the Holy Roman Emperor as having a

[78] Donaldson, *Scottish Reformation*, 43; M. H. B. Sanderson, *Cardinal of Scotland: David Beaton, c.1494–1546* (Edinburgh, 1986), 114–19.

[79] *Statutes of the Scottish Church, 1225–1559*, ed. D. Patrick (SHS, 1907), 165.

[80] J. Durkan, 'The early Scottish notary', in I. B. Cowan and D. Shaw (eds.), *The Renaissance and Reformation in Scotland* (Edinburgh, 1983), 31. For the prosecution of an imperial notary in 1478, see *APS* ii. 115–16. James III's imperial policy is discussed by R. Nicholson, *Scotland: The Later Middle Ages* (Edinburgh, 1974), 483–4, and Macdougall, *James III*, 98. The English had abolished imperial notaries in 1320.

jurisdiction superior to those of mere kings.[81] Universal empire was not, and had never been, a reality; its importance lay in its attraction as an ideal—an importance that grew in the early sixteenth century, and did not so much decline thereafter as become transferred to national monarchies.[82] But the transfer was a gradual process, and some residue of the old respect for the empire remained. This was shown in a visual representation of the state of Christendom in about 1520, on the painted ceiling of St Machar's Cathedral, Aberdeen. Along with the king and the Scottish earls and bishops, there were represented the arms of the pope, the emperor, and the kings and prominent dukes of Europe. The key positions assigned to the pope and emperor reflected their combined role as ecclesiastical and secular leaders of Christendom.[83]

Meanwhile, Scottish monarchs were late to adopt the title 'his majesty', traditionally reserved for the emperor; Mary was the first to do so regularly, and parliamentary statutes referred to 'the quenis majestie' after 1563.[84] Skene cited numerous imperial laws in his *De Verborum Significatione* (1597), such as the law of Charlemagne that churches should have manses.[85] He gave every appearance of believing that these laws were in some sense valid for Scotland. A memorandum written about 1603 said that Scotland's main law was its parliamentary legislation, but 'that faylinge they have recourse and doe decide accordinge to the ymperiall civill lawe'.[86] This civil law may have been 'ymperiall' only in the ancient Roman sense, and its conceptual links with the contemporary emperor, Rudolf II, were probably slight; statute law, moreover, was given precedence. But in 1604, the imperial ideal was still alive in a form that Rudolf would have welcomed. Commenting on the contention by the English House of Commons that the adoption

---

[81] J. H. Burns, *Lordship, Kingship and Empire: The Idea of Monarchy, 1400–1525* (Oxford, 1992), ch. 5.

[82] F. A. Yates, *Astraea: The Imperial Theme in the Sixteenth Century* (Peregrine edn., Harmondsworth, 1977), ch. 1.

[83] D. McRoberts, *The Heraldic Ceiling of St Machar's Cathedral, Aberdeen* (Friends of St Machar's Cathedral, Aberdeen, 1976).

[84] The title had been adopted by Henry VIII in 1534–5: S. J. Gunn, *Early Tudor Government, 1485–1558* (London, 1995), 164. Scotland's decision not to follow suit at this time is underlined by a parliamentary minute of 1543 discussing 'the kingis maistie of Ingland' and 'the quenis grace our soverane lady': *APS* ii. 426.

[85] Skene, *DVS*, s.v. mansus.

[86] 'Relation of the manner of judicatores of Scotland', ed. J. D. Mackie and W. C. Dickinson, *SHR* 19 (1922), 254–72, at p. 268.

of the name 'Britain' would imply the founding of a new kingdom, Craig wrote that 'the power of creating new kingdoms belongs solely to the emperor and the pope'.[87]

Imperial kingship, however, was gradually but inexorably corroding these archaic concepts. When Sir David Lindsay envisaged the young James V, in about 1529, 'havand power imperyall', this probably meant no more than that he should rule in person, though Lindsay's role as herald would certainly have made him sensitive to such terminology.[88] But the fashion for elaborately staged royal 'triumphs' was consciously imperial; one of the earliest in Britain was staged by Mary queen of Scots in 1566.[89] One of Mary's judges, David Chalmers of Ormond, informed her in that year that

> your majestie and your most noble progenitouris, as alsua all wther princis not recognoscand ony superiouris, hes alss grete powar and auchtoritie within your awin realmess to statut, mak lawes and ordinances for the politie and governament of your commoun welthis and contrayis as ewer had ony empreour within thair empyre.[90]

Chalmers projected the imperial authority back to all the queen's 'progenitouris'; the concept of imperial kingship possessed traditional elements predating Bodin. A significant novelty in Bodin's concept of sovereignty was his dethroning of the Holy Roman Emperor, who, he declared (upsetting the Germans), was no sovereign. This overturned the common medieval idea that the emperor was the *only* prince able to legislate (*legibus solutus*, free of the laws). By 1581, Adam Blackwood could write that the emperor was *below* a king in status, because he lacked the plenary power of an absolute monarch like the king of Scots.[91]

By the late sixteenth century, Protestants were developing a

---

[87] Craig, *De Unione*, 402. He did also remark (apropos Edward I and the Scots) that the pope had never been 'judg in Scots affairs': id., *Scotland's Soveraignty Asserted*, 396.

[88] Lindsay, 'The complaint of Sir David Lindsay', in *Works*, i. 43; Edington, *Lindsay*, 110–11.

[89] Yates, *Astraea*, 112; M. Lynch, 'Queen Mary's triumph: The baptismal celebrations at Stirling in December 1566', *SHR* 69 (1990), 1–21, where it is noted (p. 6) that the prince's name of 'Charles James' evoked not just Charles IX of France but also Charlemagne.

[90] BL, David Chalmers, 'Dictionary of Scots law' (1566), Add. MS 27 472, fo. 1[r–v].

[91] J. H. Burns, 'George Buchanan and the anti-monarchomachs', in R. A. Mason (ed.), *Scots and Britons: Scottish Political Thought and the Union of 1603* (Cambridge, 1994), 149.

concept of the monarch as 'Christian Emperor' on the model of Constantine. This led to intricate intellectual debate—the Scottish Reformation was cautious about imperial thinking, associated as it was with the Elizabethan royal supremacy over the church. The anti-imperial, anti-papal arguments of John Napier of Merchiston have attracted particular attention. But the debate focused attention either on the authority of James VI or on the autonomy of the church, and precluded any idea that Rudolf II might have special powers.[92] James himself was certainly keen on imperial kingship (as indeed he was on the royal supremacy). In 1603 he was thinking of calling himself 'Emperor of Great Britain'.[93] This image soon faded, but the union of crowns raised the status of the monarchy so much that its imperial powers within its territories could no longer even be questioned.

In the century and a half after the symbolically imperial date of 1469 with which this chapter began, patterns of political power had been in flux, and some recognizably new structures had emerged. Late-medieval Scots (to adapt a slogan familiar to their modern compatriots) possessed independence in Christendom. In the area known as Scotland there were a number of more or less self-contained power centres, floating loosely in a viscous plasma of interconnected power relations. The crown formed an important solid nucleus, but so did each territorial magnate; power in the localities flowed mainly from the magnates, who were thus at the centre of their own political world. Moreover, the plasma extended well beyond the borders of Scotland (which were themselves permeable and indefinite), so that power could be exercised even from Rome. Gradually, the state's external borders calcified, while local power structures tended to dissolve, losing their individual identity and instead beginning to form part of a more integrated, centralized structure.

The rise of territorial sovereignty, and the concomitant decline of autonomous local power centres, had profound implications for the nature of the state. This chapter has looked mainly at the state's

---

[92] W. M. Lamont, *Godly Rule: Politics and Religion, 1603–1660* (London, 1969), 34; A. H. Williamson, *Scottish National Consciousness in the Age of James VI* (Edinburgh, 1979), ch. 1; R. A. Mason, 'The Reformation and Anglo-British imperialism', in id. (ed.), *Scots and Britons*, 181–3.

[93] B. Galloway, *The Union of England and Scotland, 1603–1608* (Edinburgh, 1986), 21.

triumph over external rivals, although internal rivals have also been mentioned. But these internal rivals—particularly the magnates of Scotland, with their vast feudal followings—included some of the most powerful men in the country. Did the state really 'triumph' over them? Were they, indeed, 'rivals' to it? In a sense, it did, and they were; but in a more fundamental sense, the magnates were incorporated—recruited, even—rather than overcome. The state that emerged bore the marks of its origin, being forged in a complex struggle both *against* the magnates and *with* the magnates against other forces. To the details of that struggle we now turn.

2

The Roots of Authority

Trait ilk trew barroun as he war thy brother,
Quhilk mon, at neid, the[e] and thy realme defende:
Quhen, suddantlie, one doith oppresse one uther,
Lat justice, myxit with mercy, thame amende.
Have thou thare hartis, thou hes yneuch to spend:
And, be the contrar, thou arte bot kyng of bone,
Frome tyme thyne hereis hartis bene from the[e] gone.[1]

The previous chapter discussed the erosion of supranational ties, showing that the sovereign state became the highest forum for government. But it also noted that an even more serious constraint on state power was the authority, exercised independently of the state, of local lords and local institutions. This constraint was not necessarily a problem: as Sir David Lindsay's advice to James V shows, it was accepted that a king had to cooperate with his magnates and to win their trust. This consensual and decentralized structure of power was, however, beginning to be eroded. The purpose of this chapter is to examine the traditional power structure of the fifteenth and sixteenth centuries, paying particular attention to the points which were undermined by the emergence of the absolutist state; the next chapter will look in more detail at that state.

Medieval power was exercised through lordship. At its most fundamental level, this was the coercive power wielded by landlords over peasant tenants. But there were also lords of lords. Here, it was not just a matter of coercion, but also of clientage and mutual aid. Followers served their lord, in his courts or in his army, and were rewarded for it. Their service might consist of bringing their own followers, so there was a chain of dependence. At the top of the chain was the king, who was served by his followers, in his

---

[1] Lindsay, 'The testament of the papyngo', in *Works*, i. 66. 'Hereis'=nobles.

courts or in his army, in much the same way. As well as these chains of delegation and dependence from one individual to another, there were also collective institutions, at local, national, and supra-national levels.[2] Ties binding lords or institutions to the crown existed, but they were not necessarily any stronger than other, unrelated ties.

Absolutism was no root-and-branch replacement for this polity, but it did change some things drastically. By strengthening central authority and integrating local and regional lordships into a national system, it transformed the business of government near the top of the political ladder. Ordinary people were affected least, the crown and nobility most. The central institutions of government, those most amenable to direct state control, were augmented in power and extended their influence into formerly autonomous provincial lordships. The crown's role was enhanced as it found itself at the centre of the state's executive machinery; much of the role of parliament in high politics was taken over by the royal court, but the state's increased need for legislation and taxation meant that parliament survived, reconfigured, to provide these. Leading nobles had their old role as supreme local magnates removed, and had to learn a new role at court: in doing so, they claimed their share of royal authority by helping to make central policy, while also acting as royal officers in helping to implement the policy.[3] But other lords—prelates and lesser lay landlords—also felt the heavy hand of royal and central authority, as did other local institutions and power centres.

The heavy hand was nevertheless quite legal, and indeed arose largely with the approval of the elite. This point needs to be stressed, since criticism of the term 'absolutism' often takes the form of a challenge (in the words of an English historian) to what is taken to be 'the assumption that, for the early Stuarts, divine right meant absolutism, which in turn meant arbitrary rule by the Crown'.[4] I hope such challenges will not be necessary against me,

---

[2] For the place of communities in the chains of dependence characteristic of feudalism, see S. Reynolds, *Kingdoms and Communities in Western Europe, 900–1300* (Oxford, 1984).

[3] J. Goodare, 'The nobility and the absolutist state in Scotland, 1584–1638', *History*, 78 (1993), 161–82.

[4] P. Christianson, 'Royal and parliamentary voices on the ancient constitution, c.1604–1621', in L. L. Peck (ed.), *The Mental World of the Jacobean Court* (Cambridge, 1991), 72. For an equally representative comment, see C. S. R. Russell,

because I do not share this assumption. Divine right, yes: nobody would deny its importance in the ideology of the period. Arbitrary rule, no: there was always a rule of law. As for the term 'absolutism' itself (or rather, the absolutist *state*, for absolutism was a process within a state, and the importance of state formation is sometimes overlooked): I use it as a long-established word for certain of the monarchies of early modern Europe, in the way that Perry Anderson did when he offered an interpretation of the period using the familiar term.[5] In these pages, an absolutist regime is simply a feudal regime onto which a strong, centralized monarchy has been grafted.

Nobles retained their role as landlords, and this helped them to continue in power, sometimes estranged from the state, more often in alliance with it. This represented a differentiation of functions within the state, since the absolutist monarchs of the late sixteenth and early seventeenth century—in Scotland, England, and France, to look no further—were all parting with their demesnes. There had been an earlier phase when royal power did lead to the accumulation of land: the all-time high points of royal landholding were 1517 in France, 1540 in England, and 1542 in Scotland.[6] But in our period, the absolutist state was raising revenue through a different means, one that would forge a relationship with all its subjects equally: taxation.

Taxation was not entirely new, of course. Indeed, the phase of royal landholding may have been preceded by an earlier phase of taxation, for David II in the mid-fourteenth century taxed more than his successors. Much of the taxation was customs duties which

'Monarchies, wars and estates in England, France and Spain, c.1580–c.1640', *Legislative Studies Quarterly*, 7 (1982), 205–20, at p. 214.

[5] P. Anderson, *Lineages of the Absolutist State* (London, 1974). Cf. Goodare, 'The nobility and the absolutist state', where I offered the view that his argument was applicable to Scotland. I have my differences with Professor Anderson, but he did at least set out a coherent and thought-provoking framework. For a recent analysis along similar lines, see A. Mączak, 'The nobility–state relationship', in W. Reinhard (ed.), *Power Elites and State Building* (Oxford, 1996), 198.

[6] D. Parker, *The Making of French Absolutism* (London, 1983), 3–4; R. Bonney, *The King's Debts: Finance and Politics in France, 1589–1661* (Oxford, 1981), 33; P. McNeill and R. Nicholson (eds.), *An Historical Atlas of Scotland, c.400–c.1600* (Conference of Scottish Medievalists, 1975), 72–3, 185. The Scottish pattern is complicated because the lands were alienated by feuing rather than by outright sale, a topic as yet scarcely researched. The English picture, in which the dissolution of the monasteries was completed in 1540, is clearest.

fell on the burghs. Similarly in England, there was more taxation in the early fifteenth century, after which the crown lands became more significant; though the picture is complicated by the fact that the reign of Henry VIII, which saw crown lands at their greatest extent, also saw the greatest political success in tapping the wealth of subjects through direct taxation.[7] In Scotland, the pattern is clearer: just as fourteenth-century taxation of burgesses had led to the incorporation of the burghs as full members of the political community, so the establishment of regular direct taxation from the 1580s onwards would lead to the further extension of that community to include lairds as well.[8]

To explain the roots of all this, it is necessary to return to the nobility. The rise of the authority of the crown and central administration, characteristic of absolutism, took place in our period, with some particularly important developments between about 1584 and 1598, but the roots of the change can be traced back at least to the mid-fifteenth century. The fifteenth and early sixteenth centuries in Scotland are usually discussed in terms of the relationship between crown and nobility—either a relationship of regular conflict, as in most older works, or a relationship with relatively *little* conflict, according to a more recent school of thought.[9]

Certainly no *structure* of conflict, or even tension, between crown and nobility, could have had more than a tenuous and intermittent existence in the fifteenth and early sixteenth centuries, for the reasons usually cited but also because crown and nobility, although often discussed as if they were different species (indeed, the following chapter will adopt such an approach), were not always so different. Fifteenth-century Stewart monarchs were nobles themselves. Lindsay commented of James IV that 'ane greater nobyll rang nocht into the eird'. Kings exercised power through lordship. Their buildings (until the reign of James IV or perhaps James III)

---

[7] B. P. Wolffe, *The Crown Lands, 1461–1536* (London, 1970); R. Schofield, 'Taxation and the political limits of the Tudor state', in C. Cross *et al.* (eds.), *Law and Government Under the Tudors* (Cambridge, 1988).

[8] Cf. J. Goodare, 'The estates in the Scottish parliament, 1286–1707', *Parliamentary History*, 15 (1996), 11–32, where the estates in parliament (including lairds after 1587) are discussed in terms of their place in the political community.

[9] M. Brown, 'The taming of Scotland? Kings and magnates in late medieval Scotland: A review of recent work', *IR* 45 (1994), 120–46.

were similar to those of the nobility, with little unique about royal palaces.[10] One of the factors that helped to lift the fifteenth-century crown above the nobility was the practice of James I and James II of retaining the lands confiscated from forfeited nobles. As a result, the successors of the fallen Albany Stewarts and Black Douglases could not accumulate vast territorial lordships in the same way.[11] But that process also made the *crown* into a vast territorial lord—more so than in the fourteenth century, when Scottish kings had often relied more on taxation. The strength of James I and II, although always great, ultimately derived less from any special constitutional status than from having more lands, and thus more rents and followers, than any other noble.

If we look at what fifteenth-century kings actually did, much of it turns out to be the same as what other fifteenth-century lords did: protecting their followers (that is, their subjects), allocating patronage among their followers, and settling their followers' disputes for them.[12] Parliament declared in 1455, annexing certain lordships to the crown, that 'the poverte of the crowne is oftymis the caus of the poverte of the realme, and mony uther inconvenientis the quhilkis war lang to expreyme'.[13] This was an effort to *restrict* certain kinds of patronage—the permanent alienation of crown lands; it is usually explained as an effort to avoid future taxation, but it was also an effort to endow the crown with a revenue that could be distributed positively among a wider circle of royal servants. Apart from outright alienation, the crown lands could also be used for patronage in other ways, such as leasing them out to powerful families: this happened with the earldom of Mar from at least 1473.[14]

---

[10] Lindsay, 'The testament of the papyngo', in *Works*, i. 70. 'Rang' = reigned; 'eird' = earth. Medieval English kings and lords both exercised 'lordship' (*dominium*): F. Pollock and F. W. Maitland, *The History of English Law*, 2 vols. (2nd edn., Cambridge, 1898), i. 511–26. On buildings, see G. Stell, 'Kings, nobles and buildings of the later middle ages: Scotland', in G. G. Simpson (ed.), *Scotland and Scandinavia, 800–1800* (Edinburgh, 1990), 65, where the early building work at Linlithgow under James I is noted as an exception to the rule.

[11] A. Grant, *Independence and Nationhood: Scotland, 1306–1469* (London, 1984), 196.

[12] The first and third of these duties are cited by R. Mason, 'Kingship, tyranny and the right to resist in fifteenth-century Scotland', *SHR* 66 (1987), 125–51, at p. 127.

[13] *APS* ii. 42, c. 1.

[14] C. A. Madden, 'Patronage or profit: Royal exploitation of the earldom of Mar', *Aberdeen University Review*, 46 (1975–6), 393–8.

As for the settlement of disputes, it was the failure to provide justice that was the single most serious complaint of parliament against Robert II and Robert III.[15] People did not always separate out provision of 'justice' and allocation of patronage, since the latter had to be done 'justly': there is mention of 'that part of justice quhilk consistis in distribution of panis and rewardis'.[16] Patronage and the settlement of disputes are the two main topics discussed by Trevor Chalmers in his influential study of the royal council in the late fifteenth century. The council developed a more professional secretariat in order to keep track of grants of royal patronage, and also came to be, at least in outline, a bench of judges. In the process they allowed the king to take a more considered approach to the dispensing of patronage, and allowed his council to take a step towards the replacement of the judicial committees of parliament that had dispensed central civil justice hitherto.[17] But the 'daily council' described by Dr Chalmers had the same range of basic tasks as the government of James II, and probably that of James I too.[18] Much of high politics consisted of the resolution of disputes among the nobility over access to landed resources: a successful king, like a successful magnate, was one who could keep these disputes among his followers under control.

Protecting their followers was another matter. Defence of the realm was a more distinctive function; it was this that might enable kings to differentiate themselves from lords most effectively. Thinkers recognized the importance of defence, so much so that Sir David Lindsay's stress instead on the provision of justice has been seen as unusual.[19] In practice, king and lords had to cooperate over national defence, as when (in 1481) 'oure soverane lord has ordanit to ger purway and stuff his castellis . . . and als[o] his hienes commandis and chargis al the lordis of the realme, baith spirituall and temporale, that has castellis near the bordouris or

[15] S. I. Boardman, *The Early Stewart Kings: Robert II and Robert III, 1371–1406* (East Linton, 1996), 131, 211; R. Nicholson, *Scotland: The Later Middle Ages* (Edinburgh, 1974), ch. 8.

[16] NAS, 'Buchanans opinioun anent the ordering of the north, 1569', in GD149/265, pt. 2, fo. 18ʳ.

[17] T. M. Chalmers, 'The King's Council, Patronage, and the Governance of Scotland, 1460–1513', Ph.D. thesis (Aberdeen, 1982).

[18] A. R. Borthwick, 'The King, Council and Councillors in Scotland, c.1430–1460', Ph.D. thesis (Edinburgh, 1989), 4.

[19] C. Edington, *Court and Culture in Renaissance Scotland: Sir David Lindsay of the Mount* (Amherst, Mass., 1994), 82–4.

on the sey coist . . . that ilk lord stuff his aun hous and strenth'. In Carnwath, the wealthier tenants at least had to be 'redy to the kingis weiris for the debaitting of the rewme and for the debaitting of my lord thair selffis and the baronie'.[20] Royal and aristocratic war-making were similar in character. James IV did something new when he developed a fleet, but it did not last.[21]

The royal court was by no means as distinctive then as it was to become in the late sixteenth century. It has been doubted whether a court literature existed in fifteenth-century Scotland, except during the reign of James IV.[22] It may be that early stirrings of such literature will be identified also in the reign of James III, but hardly before then. We thus see a pattern in which new cultural developments, architectural and literary, arise at the courts of James III and especially James IV. This fits well with the argument on sovereignty advanced in the previous chapter, and—more importantly—with the development of the absolutist state, to be examined in Chapter 3.

But courtly literature also illustrates the difficulties of differentiating late-medieval kings and nobles from one another. Much of the literary advice to princes—a combination of classical and Christian advice to live chastely, administer justice, defend the weak, listen to good counsel, and avoid flattery—was also advice to lords and knights. Kings in this respect were no different from other virtuous lords, except that they acted in that somewhat larger sphere, the nation. When ideal Scottish kings were expected to be patriotic, and the chivalric code enjoined patriotism on knights too, this in some ways brought kings and knights closer—but it might also, in the right circumstances, integrate the knights into a national structure.[23] Still, loyalty to the monarch had in practice to take its

---

[20] *APS* ii. 133, c. 6; *Court Book of the Barony of Carnwath, 1523–1542*, ed. W. C. Dickinson (SHS, 1937), 164–5. 'Debaitting of the rewme' = defending of the realm.

[21] N. Macdougall, ' "The greattest scheip that ewer saillit in Ingland or France": James IV's "Great Michael" ', in id. (ed.), *Scotland and War, AD 79–1918* (Edinburgh, 1991). For more on military matters, see Ch. 5 below.

[22] S. Mapstone, 'Was there a court literature in fifteenth-century Scotland?', *Studies in Scottish Literature*, 26 (1991), 410–22. Cf. the dearth of English writing in this period praising kings or giving theoretical backing to kingship: J. R. Lander, *The Limitations of English Monarchy in the Later Middle Ages* (Toronto, 1989), 4.

[23] R. A. Mason, 'Kingship and Commonweal: Political Thought and Ideology in Reformation Scotland', Ph.D. thesis (Edinburgh, 1983), 32–8; cf. R. Mason, 'Chivalry and citizenship: Aspects of national identity in Renaissance Scotland', in id. and N. Macdougall (eds.), *People and Power in Scotland* (Edinburgh, 1992), 58.

place among many other loyalties. Even members of the royal household might have their primary loyalties to other magnate houses. When James I fell into conflict with certain magnates, there were members of his own household who took the magnates' side and helped to murder him.[24] This was, of course, a crime, but there is no suggestion that the priority of loyalty behind it was itself unusual.

Another national institution, parliament, was an important component of fifteenth-century government, but not at all for the same reasons as in our own period. Legislation was sometimes important, but not often before 1584. Some apparently general legislation was intended to solve particular local problems, and was not necessarily intended to be applied nationally or permanently.[25] Another parliamentary function, direct taxation, was abandoned after a brief attempt by James I, and taxes were few and small thereafter until the 1580s.[26] Yet parliaments met with remarkable frequency, typically annually. They did so for two related reasons: to provide justice, and to oversee government generally. As mentioned earlier, the central courts came under James IV to be connected more closely with the royal council: this, however, reversed an earlier trend, in the reign of James II, for parliament to exercise *increasing* influence over justice.[27]

The crown, meanwhile, did not control parliament. Its membership was not determined by the crown, and even in the election of lords of the articles (the parliamentary steering committee), the crown's influence was small in the fifteenth century and most of the sixteenth.[28] Parliamentary supervision of the government's political direction was seen most clearly during political crises: these invariably led to frequent meetings of parliament. The fifteenth-century record is perhaps held by the sixteen months between March 1482 and July 1483, when four parliaments met;

For the general similarity between books on chivalric conduct and books on government (the 'mirrors of princes'), see M. Keen, *Chivalry* (New Haven, 1984), 16.

[24] M. Brown, *James I* (Edinburgh, 1994), 206.

[25] Several examples are given in M. Lynch, 'Towns and townspeople in fifteenth-century Scotland', in J. A. F. Thomson (ed.), *Towns and Townspeople in the Fifteenth Century* (Gloucester, 1988), 174.

[26] Grant, *Independence and Nationhood*, 188; J. Goodare, 'Parliamentary taxation in Scotland, 1560–1603', *SHR* 68 (1989), 23–52, at pp. 45–6.

[27] Borthwick, 'King, Council, and Councillors', 277–8.

[28] I. E. O'Brien, 'The Scottish Parliament in the 15th and 16th Centuries', Ph.D. thesis (Glasgow, 1980), ch. 3.

but biannual parliaments were common enough. There were nine parliaments in the first six years of the reign of James IV, for instance.[29] These parliaments were hammering out real decisions, not ratifying prearranged programmes. Similarly the period 1567–73, one of instability and civil war, saw ten parliaments and nine conventions of estates, not to mention three parliaments held by the rebel party, although the tradition of annual parliaments had ended well before.[30]

That the king, meeting with his magnates assembled in parliament, was still *primus inter pares* in the fifteenth century is illustrated by the freedom with which the magnates in parliament treated him. Sir Robert Graham, chosen as speaker of the estates in 1436, tried to arrest the king in their name; they failed to back him, but Graham's action was in a mode that they would have understood.[31] In 1450, it was enacted 'that gif ony man as God forbede committis or dois treson agaynis the kingis persone . . . *without the consent of the thre estatis*, [they] sal be punyst as tratouris'.[32] The estates could thus sanction treason. In 1473, parliament's 'avisment' to James III was perhaps loyal but certainly blunt. His plan to lead an army to the Continent was attacked—'the lordis can nocht in na wiss gif thar consale to his passage'—and if he insisted on going, he was urged 'in the meyntyme to tak part of labour apoun his persone and travel throw his realme and put sic justice and polycy in his awne realme that the brute and the fame of him myght pas in utheris contreis'.[33] It is inconceivable that such frankness could have been used a century later, when governmental decisions were no longer being hammered out in the parliament house itself. Decisions were made at court, and only then submitted to parliament, which usually ratified them. That does not mean that parliament was insignificant: after all, governmental decisions today are made in the cabinet, and parliament usually ratifies them. The governments of early modern times did not depend for their

[29] N. Macdougall, *James IV* (Edinburgh, 1989), 171–2.
[30] J. Goodare, 'Parliament and Society in Scotland, 1560–1603', Ph.D. thesis (Edinburgh, 1989), app. A, nos. 10–32; cf. id., 'The Scottish parliamentary records, 1560–1603', *Historical Research*, lxxii (1999, forthcoming).
[31] Brown, *James I*, 175–7.
[32] *APS* ii. 36, c. 12. Emphasis added. Cf. the numerous late-medieval states in which noble rebellion was legitimate, sometimes requiring the estates' sanction: M. Bush, *Noble Privilege* (New York, 1983), 105.
[33] *APS* ii. 103–4.

existence on a parliamentary majority, but such a majority was sometimes—in 1621, for example—both important for the government, and difficult to obtain.[34]

Institutions of local government, too, were pervaded by channels of control based on lordship. Even for government in the name of the crown, control often rested in the hands of a lord and his affinity. Magnates took care to insert members of their affinity into royal offices in their locality, thus making sure that the system of royal administration worked primarily for *them*. Thus, as part of a settlement between Malcolm Drummond of Concraig and Sir David Murray of Tullibardine in 1441, it was 'accordit' that the offices of steward, coroner, and forester of Strathearn, held by Drummond, 'salbe governit be the avise and ordinance of the said Schir Davy'; the 'profits' of the offices were to be divided between the two. The crown, which held the earldom of Strathearn on which these offices depended, was not consulted. Eventually the Murrays displaced the Drummonds, and this was ratified by the crown, accepting the inevitable, in 1473.[35] To take another example, Sir Alexander Guthrie of that Ilk, a client and councillor of the earl of Crawford, was king's bailie of the thanage of Kincardine between 1474 and 1480, and depute to the earl as sheriff of Forfar until at least 1483. He was accused of packing a jury of inquest in 1479, leading to his loss of the bailiary, but his successor and adversary, Thomas Fotheringham of Powrie, was unable to distrain for Guthrie's arrears in office because he was protected by Crawford as sheriff. Guthrie did not pay the arrears until 1501.[36] Keith Brown, in his seminal study of the bloodfeud, gives a number of examples of local jurisdictions which were fought over by rival families in the late sixteenth century: there seems to have been a higher level of intervention by the crown in these disputes, but there were still times when the crown could do no more than ratify the outcome of a local power struggle.[37]

As well as acquisition of offices, there was also the possibility of magnates influencing the royal courts in order to produce

---

[34] J. Goodare, 'The Scottish parliament of 1621', *Historical Journal*, 38 (1995), 29–51.

[35] S. I. Boardman, 'Politics and the Feud in Late Medieval Scotland', Ph.D. thesis (St Andrews, 1990), 162–5.

[36] C. A. Kelham, 'Bases of Magnatial Power in Later Fifteenth-Century Scotland', Ph.D. thesis (Edinburgh, 1986), 86–7.

[37] K. M. Brown, *Bloodfeud in Scotland, 1573–1625* (Edinburgh, 1986), 72–6.

judgements more in keeping with the kin-group's idea of justice. If this was less important than in England, it was only because the Scots nobles already had *direct* control over much royal justice, in the form of heritable jurisdictions: both sheriffships (the normal royal courts in the localities) and regalities (grants of jurisdiction covering one's own lands). Being heritable may not have made these courts more impartial, but they *were* less open to manipulation. Spheres of influence were clear-cut. Here, the crown did not control the machinery of justice, either directly or indirectly.[38]

Legislation was less important in the fifteenth century than it was to become later; but at least it was all done by the authority of the king, thus differentiating him from the nobility. Or was it? In 1448, 'Erl Williame of Douglas assemblit the haill lordis, frehaldaris, eldest bordouraris that best knawledge had at the college of Lynclowden': they compiled a set of Border laws from those made by previous earls of Douglas. 'Item, the said Williame and lordis and eldest bordouraris maid certane punctis to be tresoun in tyme of weirfar to be usit, the quhilkis war na tresoun befoir his tyme bot to be tresoun in his tyme and eftir'.[39] The 'tresoun' referred to was 'march-treason'—cowardice or disloyalty, rather than an attack on the king; but this is still a clear (though rare) example of legislation by an earl. It might not have been acceptable to do such a thing in the heartland of the state: John, Lord of the Isles and earl of Ross, in 1461 granted a licence to build a fortified tower, but elsewhere this power was reserved to the crown.[40]

Another mark of a sovereign state was taxation. Again, this was usually done by the crown, but not always. The royal burghs

---

[38] A. Grant, 'Crown and nobility in late medieval Britain', in R. A. Mason (ed.), *Scotland and England, 1286–1815* (Edinburgh, 1987), 45–9; J. Wormald, *Lords and Men in Scotland: Bonds of Manrent, 1442–1603* (Edinburgh, 1985), 131–6. Leading examples of regalities which 'could exist side-by-side in peace' were those of Alexander Stewart, lord of Badenoch, and John Dunbar, earl of Moray. Stewart fell out not with the earl but with the *bishop* of Moray. A. Grant, 'The Wolf of Badenoch', in W. D. H. Sellar (ed.), *Moray: Province and People* (Scottish Society for Northern Studies, 1993), 157.

[39] 'The March Laws', ed. T. I. Rae, *Stair Society Miscellany*, i (1971), 40.

[40] *Acts of the Lords of the Isles, 1336–1493*, ed. J. Munro and R. W. Munro (SHS, 1986), no. 70. However, the crown probably did not *use* the power regularly. The first systematic attempt to regulate the building of 'ony strenth or fortalice' relates only to the Borders and dates only from 1528: Balfour, *Practicks*, ii. 595. For more on licences to crenellate, see G. Stell, 'Late medieval defences in Scotland', in D. H. Caldwell (ed.), *Scottish Weapons and Fortifications, 1100–1800* (Edinburgh, 1981), 30–1.

could tax themselves, either individually or collectively. Taxation by nobles, however, seems to have been rare. The earl of Argyll had his own taxes in the mid-sixteenth century; so had the earl of Orkney in the 1590s. But by then, this was something that got him into trouble.[41] The very things that were becoming more important to government were things that only central government could do.

Magnates, of course, always thought of themselves as governors, and rightly so. Not only did they rule their own followers and territories, but they had a special place in the state through their privileged access to the king and right to give him counsel. This was partly exercised through parliament, which has already been discussed, but the right to offer counsel extended more widely than the right to attend parliament—and, at court, or in the army (as in the arrest of James III at Lauder Bridge in July 1482), this was most definitely a *right*.[42] Behind this was the belief in a collective of magnates, with extensive and innate rights not depending on the crown. This collectivism was reinforced by the frequent royal minorities in Scotland—a topic that will recur.[43]

Noble privilege even created its own myths. The most striking European example is the alleged oath of the Aragonese nobility, which began to circulate in the later sixteenth century: 'We, who are worth as much as you, have you as our king and lord, provided that you preserve our privileges and liberties: and if not, not.'[44] Scotland had a native myth with the same message, the story of the 'Sewed Charter' of the earl of Morton. James III, it was said, had objected to 'the largeness and absoluteness of it', and had torn it in half, but 'was forced by the nobility to sit down and sew it up

---

[41] J. Dawson, 'The fifth earl of Argyle, Gaelic lordship and political power in sixteenth-century Scotland', *SHR* 67 (1988), 1–27, at p. 25; P. D. Anderson, *Black Patie: The Life and Times of Patrick Stewart, Earl of Orkney, Lord of Shetland* (Edinburgh, 1992), 63, 65, 67. At the even later date of 1620, the vassals of the earldom of Sutherland gave a 'generall contribution (everie one according to his estate and habilitie)'. Gordon, *Sutherland*, 382. Whether this was compulsory taxation is unclear. Cf. Sir Alexander Gordon of Navidale to Sir Robert Gordon, 22 Nov. 1616, W. Fraser, *The Sutherland Book*, 3 vols. (Edinburgh, 1892), ii. 128–9.

[42] On the crisis of Lauder Bridge, see N. Macdougall, *James III* (Edinburgh, 1982), ch. 8, and id., ' "It is I, the earle of Mar": In search of Thomas Cochrane', in Mason and Macdougall (eds.), *People and Power in Scotland*.

[43] See Ch. 3 below.

[44] R. E. Giesey, *If Not, Not: The Oath of the Aragonese and the Legendary Laws of Sobrarbe* (Princeton, 1968). The oath circulated in different versions.

again with his own hand'.[45] Whether this had really happened is
not the point: people in the sixteenth century thought that it had.
But although such stories were still told, they were beginning to
represent an ideal past rather than contemporary reality, by the
1590s at least. The fifth earl of Bothwell campaigned against that
'puddock-stool of the night', Chancellor Maitland: he appealed to
his fellow-nobles, claiming to be following the 'lovable custome of
our progenitouris at Lauder' from the precedent of the nobles who
had lynched the low-born councillors of James III. He attracted a
good deal of passive sympathy, but was ultimately unable to maintain his position.[46]

The Reformation brought some new support for nobles' autonomous privileges: the Protestant church needed 'godly magistrates'
to help implement its programme.[47] Such men enforced godliness
upon their families and localities, promoting doctrine and backing
up church discipline; occasionally, as the leading presbyterian minister James Melville said, they 'corrected and brought in ordour'
tyrannical kings, thus demonstrating the independent roots of
their authority.[48] This stress on the nobility as bridles on tyranny,
although with a slightly different emphasis, draws on the same
ideas as the stories of noble autonomy: it was a central concern of
George Buchanan, and reached the presbyterians through his
work.[49] Godly magistrates could actually be found in the first generation after 1560, but as the church became committed to presbyterianism and insisted more and more on high standards of
personal conduct and political activism for its supporters, and as
alternatives came to be offered by James VI, the nobles came to
show less interest in a godly programme; there were few nobles
committed to presbyterianism by the 1590s.

The early 'godly magistrates' were backed by England. From the

---

[45] *CSP Scot.* xiii, ii. 1116.

[46] Calderwood, *History*, v. 156 ('puddock-stool'=toadstool); *Warrender Papers*, ii.
154–64, 264; R. G. Macpherson, 'Francis Stewart, fifth Earl Bothwell, c.1562–1612:
Lordship and Politics in Jacobean Scotland', Ph.D. thesis (Edinburgh, 1998). Both-
well's chief adviser, and very likely the author of his propaganda, was Mr John
Colville, who has also been proposed as the author of the report containing the
'Sewed Charter' story; further investigation of his role might be worthwhile.

[47] K. M. Brown, 'In search of the godly magistrate in Reformation Scotland',
Journal of Ecclesiastical History, 40 (1989), 553–81.

[48] Melville, *Diary*, 192. See also Ch. 3 below.

[49] R. A. Mason, 'George Buchanan, James VI and the presbyterians', in id. (ed.),
Scots and Britons: Scottish Political Thought and the Union of 1603 (Cambridge, 1994).

1560s to the early 1580s, the Protestant, Anglophile faction received subsidies and other assistance in attempting to coerce the government into supporting its line. It was while hoping for English assistance that the earl of Moray and other noble 'Chase-about' rebels in 1565 issued the following manifesto against Queen Mary:

Concerning the policie and commoun wealth, we that are of the cheefe of the nobilitie and counsellers of this realme, to whom of duetie it apperteaneth to have a speciall care of the publict effaires of the same, and of the preservatioun of the estate therof, als weill by reason of our birth and blood, as also by defence of the countrie, (in whose hands hath stand the defence therof by our blood shedding,) having advisedlie considered the great misorder and danger ensuing to the estat forsaid by diverse enormities and misorders, can doe no lesse, than by all meanes possible sue the same to be repaired and redressed.[50]

This linked the English 'amity' with the traditional view of the magnates as having the right to advise the monarch. Once the English adopted James VI himself as their channel for supervision of Scottish affairs, however, with the treaty of 1586, they started to concern themselves with his authority.[51] In 1588, Sir Francis Walsingham regretted that the king of Scots seemed not to have the power to restrain his magnates: 'The use of a Starre Chambar myght worke a great redresse therin. Yt is almost impossyble for any prynce to be in suretye in a realme or kyngdome where the regall awthorytye is not merely deryved from the King.'[52] The English were still prepared to assist Bothwell against the king in the early 1590s, but this was unusual, and was outweighed (from this point of view) by their efforts to support James in bringing the dissident Catholic earls of the north to heel. English influence first helped to perpetutate autonomous noble authority, and then undermined it.

The Catholic earls of the 1590s were the last ever to mount a regional challenge to the crown. It is interesting that, within the increasingly complex framework of legal authority, they showed

[50] Calderwood, *History*, ii. 572.
[51] K. M. Brown, 'The price of friendship: The "well affected" and English economic clientage in Scotland before 1603', in Mason (ed.), *Scotland and England*; J. Goodare, 'James VI's English subsidy', in id. and M. Lynch (eds.), *The Reign of James VI* (East Linton, 1999, forthcoming).
[52] Walsingham to Thomas Fowler, 22 Dec. 1588, *CSP Scot.* ix. 651.

signs of vindicating magnate autonomy by appealing not to ancient tradition but to laws other than those of the state. They wrote to the magistrates of Aberdeen in 1594 that the latter's recent arrest of their supporters was 'agains the lawis of nationis'. However, the letter continued not with legal arguments, but with the threat to 'persew yow . . . with fyre and sworde' if the town did not submit.[53] Ultimately this use of 'law' would prove a dead end, and the law would work solely to integrate the state. But we are running ahead of the story.

In the fifteenth and early sixteenth centuries, nobles and other lords, as well as governing in their own localities, often appeared in recognizably national 'Scottish' history: on what terms? How did their relationship with the crown function? And what of the frequent periods when no adult monarch was present? The traditional view was that the nobles particularly enjoyed royal minorities, where they could grab more lands and revenues and feud happily with one another, without being challenged or restrained by the crown. Jenny Wormald and others have made trenchant criticisms of this view, and it does seem to reflect historians' distaste for what they saw as uncivilized baronial anarchy rather than detailed assessment of nobles' gains and losses during royal minorities. It would be useful to have a more detailed picture of this than is currently available, particularly for the period 1513–1560, but the overall picture is beyond dispute: during royal majorities the crown gained in resources at the nobles' expense, both through forfeitures and through royal revocations.[54] Dr Wormald observes that 'the repeated minorities which beset the Stewart dynasty had militated against the move towards absolutist rule, with its ideological underpinning, already detectable in the French and Spanish kingdoms by the fifteenth century'.[55]

This is not the end of the issue, however. Dr Wormald also points out that the noble ethic was one of service and loyalty to the

[53] Huntly and others to the magistrates of Aberdeen, 19 July 1594, W. Fraser, *The Douglas Book*, 4 vols. (Edinburgh, 1875), iv. 374–5. In regarding this as the last regional rebellion, the Highlands are omitted because they operated a different political system. On them, see Ch. 8 below.

[54] The point about forfeitures runs through all work on the subject; for revocations see Wormald, *Lords and Men*, 158–9, and ead., 'The house of Stewart and its realm', in ead. (ed.), *Scotland Revisited* (London, 1991), 19–20.

[55] Ead., 'James VI and I, *Basilikon Doron* and *The Trew Law of Free Monarchies*: The Scottish context and the English translation', in Peck (ed.), *The Mental World of the Jacobean Court*, 42.

crown.[56] Nobles did not *want* baronial anarchy; they wanted a good relationship with a sympathetic adult monarch. It is worth relating this ethic to nobles' material prospects. Royal service was a lottery in which the risks of losing outweighed the opportunities of winning; but many people enjoy lotteries, and take part even though they are likely to lose. History pays more attention to successes like the Hamiltons, so often on the right side before the 1570s,[57] than to such politically active and thoroughly loyal nobles as the third earl of Lennox, killed by the Douglases in 1527; the first Lord Methven, who returned to obscurity after the dissolution of his marriage to the queen dowager in 1537; the fourth Lord Innermeath, who became an extraordinary lord of session in 1544 and later attended the Reformation Parliament, but never made a mark on events; or the fifth Lord Home, who died under forfeiture for not choosing quite the right moments to change sides in the struggles of 1567–73.[58] The failures may well have been in the majority, but they did not give up. While the noble class as a whole was likely to lose by the activities of an assertive king like James V, *some* nobles would benefit, and many could aspire to do so. They not only served, but were (or hoped to be) rewarded for service. The 'service' was often self-serving, for it involved coming out on top in political struggle; still, that is how the great noble families of the sixteenth century—Hamiltons, Campbells, Angus Douglases, Gordons—had got where they were.

But having got there—to a position with lands, clients, hereditary offices, patronage—they had to maintain their position against their rivals. This they did by all available means. A stance of loyalty to the crown was an attractive option when you were under threat; it meant that you might get the royal courts on your side. But by the same token, loyalty would do you no good if your local enemy was better connected at court than you. It would then be your enemy who mobilized the machinery of royal 'justice' against you. Protestations of loyalty and service would be useless; what you needed was a couple of hundred well-armed followers,

[56] J. Wormald, 'Taming the magnates?', in K. J. Stringer (ed.), *Essays on the Nobility of Medieval Scotland* (Edinburgh, 1985), 278–9.

[57] E. Finnie, 'The house of Hamilton: Patronage, politics and the church in the Reformation period', *IR* 36 (1985), 3–28.

[58] J. B. Paul (ed.), *The Scots Peerage*, 9 vols. (Edinburgh, 1904–14), under the relevant title.

prepared if necessary to defy the messengers of the crown. Of the nobles who read the books on loyalty and service cited by Dr Wormald, how many did *not* deforce a royal herald at some point?[59]

Service to the crown, therefore, was not an obligation for nobles; it was an option, often freely chosen for self-interested reasons, and sometimes freely rejected for the same reasons. Nobles wanted to serve—but on their own terms. Despite the ethic of service, the patriotism, and the conservatism, nobody could ever say (before the early seventeenth century) that the most recent noble revolt would be the last. These revolts were all considered by their leaders to be justified; and the justifications for them must surely be considered as integral to the nobles' ethic. In 1452, after the murder of the eighth earl of Douglas by James II,

> thar was put on the nicht on the parliament hous dure ane letter under Sir James of Douglas sele [i.e. that of the ninth earl] and the sele of the erll of Ormond and Sir James Hamilton's declynand fra the king, sayand that thai held nocht of him nor wald nocht hald with him, with mony uther sclanderous wordis, calland tham traitors that war his secret counsall.[60]

This is the only example known to me of the formal *diffidatio*, or renunciation of feudal allegiance ('defiance'); but that there is even one case of it proves that it was known about and could be done.[61] Nobles' individual allegiance to the crown was, in the last resort, conditional and contractual. Even the rhetoric of service itself has been considered to be window-dressing for the defence of a noble's 'rightful heritage'.[62] However, to the extent that noble self-interest *had* to be dressed up as 'service', nobles lacked the rhetorical tools to challenge the way in which the crown was lifting itself above them. It would be hard to say whether this ideological

---

[59] A sixth of the English peerage were imprisoned for such offences between 1448 and 1455: J. R. Lander, *Crown and Nobility, 1450–1509* (London, 1976), 20.

[60] The Auchinleck chronicle, quoted in C. McGladdery, *James II* (Edinburgh, 1990), 166; cf. 78–80.

[61] That it *was* a formal *diffidatio* seems clear from the wording of the source, and this is supported by Nicholson, *Scotland: The Later Middle Ages*, 360; doubts are expressed by Mason, 'Kingship, tyranny and the right to resist', 143, but no reasons are given. The procedure for renunciation of an overlord was laid down in Robert III's reign: John Skene (ed.), *Regiam Majestatem* (Edinburgh, 1609), pt. II, pp. 55–6 (Rob. III c. 18). It was probably not intended for use against the king, but the king *was* undeniably an overlord.

[62] Boardman, 'Politics and the Feud', 431–2.

failure was a cause, or merely an effect, of noble conservatism. The failure was probably rendered more complete by the fall of the Black Douglases in 1455; their example was not a happy one. The Hamiltons were lucky not to be dragged down too, and when they and other nobles thought of the *diffidatio*, they may have done so with a shudder. Although the events of 1455 did not themselves alter the nature of lordship, the removal of the other noble family able to consider the crown as little more than an equal (the previous one having been the Albany Stewarts, destroyed in 1425) marked a stage in the process by which nobles' allegiance came to be obligatory. It was a portent.[63]

So far the late-medieval polity has been considered exclusively in terms of crown and nobility; but there were other kinds of lords. In particular, lordship was exercised by the church. It was an enormous feudal landholder, with castles, baronies, and regalities just like the lay magnates. A clerical magnate had his own following, which he built up much as laymen did—for example, by granting tacks (leases) of his lands to dependants, who might be his kinsmen. David Beaton did this as abbot of Arbroath. Beaton was also able to use ecclesiastical patronage, granting benefices to his followers on a larger scale than secular lords could do.[64] A fifteenth-century bishop like William Turnbull could buy a royal ward for his nephew to marry, just as a lay lord might have done.[65] Because ecclesiastical lordships were not hereditary, they were available for the crown to reward its professional supporters by making them bishops, while nobles rewarded their own followers with lesser benefices. It would almost always be a younger son, or an illegitimate one, who entered the church, while secular landlords themselves remained at arm's length.[66] A fifteenth-century magnate would probably have a parson or two on his staff, for

---

[63] It was also an episode in a related trend, not discussed in detail here: the conversion of the higher Scottish nobility from a small group of earls (and other provincial lords) ruling compact provinces to a larger number of nobles whose territories were scattered and whose status derived more from their title. The Black Douglases themselves were transitional, in that their lands were scattered but extremely extensive. See A. Grant, 'Earls and earldoms in late medieval Scotland, c.1310–1460', in J. Bossy and P. Jupp (eds.), *Essays Presented to Michael Roberts* (Belfast, 1976); A. Grant, 'The development of the Scottish peerage', *SHR* 57 (1978), 1–27.

[64] M. H. B. Sanderson, *Cardinal of Scotland: David Beaton, c.1494–1546* (Edinburgh, 1986), 24–5.

[65] J. Durkan, *William Turnbull, Bishop of Glasgow* (Glasgow, 1951), 31.

[66] Borthwick, 'King, Council and Councillors', 38, citing an exception, William Lauder, bishop of Glasgow.

instance as secretary or chamberlain.[67] This is why it was important for the crown to win out in its struggle with the pope: it wanted to have its own servants, not the pope's, in positions of power in the church. The crown under James III and James IV was making increasing use of clerics as administrators.[68]

The clergy were involved in the pattern of noble alliances and feuds, but only to a lesser degree. This is an impressionistic view, based partly on their relative absence from the standard accounts of Professor Brown (who does not deal, however, with the period before the Reformation) and Dr Wormald, and partly on the fact that alliances and feuds feature less prominently in studies of clerics. Numerous bishops, and some abbots, received bonds of manrent and gave bonds of maintenance; the last surviving example dates from 1553.[69] It was said in 1543 that Cardinal Beaton 'giveth great fees', while bishops built fortifications similar to those of the nobility.[70] But there seems to be less evidence of such behaviour than for nobles.

One may well wonder how clerical lords defended their lands, if secular lords had to have followers prepared to resort to violence. However, disputes have to be about something. Possibly the clergy's title to their property was more clear-cut: at least they were not involved in inheritance disputes, while before the Reformation a higher proportion of clerical income came from teinds, to which fewer laymen had title. Very likely, also, the non-heritable nature of benefices made it more difficult to recruit and maintain a following—although this would not explain why churchmen were not attacked by the laity. The most likely reason is that they were defended by lay relatives, into whose followings they were integrated. Church lands were pervaded by lay officials, particularly bailies, who were nobles and lairds exercising the regular judicial and occasional military functions of the estates.[71] Prelates like James Kennedy, bishop of St Andrews, were not only well connected but also wielded ecclesiastical sanctions. After a 'richt gret herschipe' made by the earl of Crawford in Kennedy's lands in

---

[67] Kelham, 'Bases of Magnatial Power', 47.

[68] Chalmers, 'King's Council', 335. For more on crown and papacy, see Ch. 1 above.

[69] Wormald, *Lords and Men*, 365–70.

[70] Ibid. 92; Stell, 'Kings, nobles and buildings', 65.

[71] P. J. Murray, 'The lay administrators of church lands in the fifteenth and sixteenth centuries', *SHR* 74 (1995), 26–44.

1445, Crawford was 'cursit solempnitlie with myter and staf, buke and candill' by the bishop: when the earl died, nobody dared bury him until Kennedy lifted the interdict.[72]

Late-medieval Scottish society also contained many lesser land-lords. They were typically the kinsmen of nobles, who would muster their followers to fight in these nobles' quarrels. In return, they received their lords' protection: it was their lords' duty to support them in their own quarrels, to control their political allegiance, and to settle their disputes. The crown could not do this without the lords' permission, nor did it wish to do so. The bond of manrent given to the lord did typically include the qualification 'my allegeance to our soverane lady the quenis grace allanerlie exceptit', as in this bond of James Kennedy of Blairquhan to the earl of Arran in 1545;[73] but this example shows what a meaningless qualification this was, for the 2-year-old queen was hardly likely to have intervened in Kennedy's relationship with Arran, even if Arran had not been regent of Scotland at the time.

Dr Wormald argues persuasively that in the later fifteenth century there was no separate Scottish class of gentry, unlike in England. The strength of the Scottish lairds made them less dependent on the nobles. The new nobility who emerged to replace the sprawling power of the Albany Stewarts and Black Douglases—the families of Campbell, Gordon, Hamilton, and others, still in place in the late sixteenth century—actively sought the allegiance of lairds, offering protection and the ability to settle disputes in return for support. As a result the lairds were not forced to give up their own status as lords, as happened in England.[74]

---

[72] N. Macdougall, 'Bishop James Kennedy of St Andrews: A reassessment of his political career', in id. (ed.), *Church, Politics and Society: Scotland, 1408–1929* (Edinburgh, 1983), 2.

[73] Wormald, *Lords and Men*, 53.

[74] Ead., 'Lords and lairds in fifteenth-century Scotland: Nobles and gentry?', in M. Jones (ed.), *Gentry and Lesser Nobility in Late Medieval Europe* (Gloucester, 1986), 192. Some historians, pointing out that lairds were lords (often formally *domini* with baron courts), refer to the peerage and lairds together as 'the nobility'. I do not follow this usage, preferring to stress that conferment of a peerage, membership of parliament, and access to the king, not to mention generally greater wealth, marked the peers off from other landlords; but the point is to a large extent a terminological one, and nobles and lairds had a good deal in common, especially in their dealings with those below them. A division between *leading* nobles, with wealth and an established court position, and other landlords (with or without peerages), probably became more important during the late sixteenth century. M. M. Meikle, 'The invisible divide: Lords and lairds in Jacobean Scotland', *SHR* 71 (1992),

But although lairds were lords, they have to be considered as followers of magnates: at least, this is the way in which they have
usually been studied.[75] About half of the members of the affinities
of those late fifteenth-century magnates studied by Charles Kelham
were kinsmen of some kind, although he was not convinced that
kinship alone formed the rationale for their relationship; most of
the rest were linked to the lord by feudal land tenure (a declining
element) or by bonds of manrent (a growing one), and again it is
not clear exactly which element was decisive. Some followers
received material rewards—lands or cash from the lord; but more
often service was given for the intangible benefit of maintenance
and protection.[76] When bonds of manrent by followers are linked
to superiors' grants to them of lands in liferent, this is recognizable as the classic feudal contract—grants of land in return for
service—in its purest form.[77] This retained some residual political
legitimacy to the end of the sixteenth century: James VI's indict-
ment of the 'iniquitie' of his nobles included the complaint that
they 'thrall by oppression, the meaner sort that dwelleth neere
them, to their service and following, *although they holde nothing of
them*'.[78]

Lesser lords could behave just like greater ones, with their own
local followings. Alexander Ross of Balnagown does not appear on
the national stage, but in Easter Ross he was regarded as a leader
of the 'name and arms of Ross'. He had a fully developed client
network; in 1565 he sought financial contributions from twenty-
three Rosses (twenty complied) and twenty-five others (six complied). He pursued a vigorous expansionist policy, gaining many
lands from the church, and one victim complained that he 'usurps
his hienes authoritie in taking of fre personis . . . and detening of
thame in ward in irnis'.[79] This point—the autonomous exercise of

70–87, points out the existence of a group of wealthy lairds who equalled nobles
in many things. They were, however, exceptions, and in due course they received
peerages.

[75] This is so in England too, although it has been argued that 'in terms of their
formal membership bastard feudal affinities only scraped the surface of political
society': G. Harriss, 'Political society and the growth of government in late medieval
England', *P & P* 138 (Feb. 1993), 28–57, at p. 55.

[76] Kelham, 'Bases of Magnatial Power', 351–60.

[77] Boardman, 'Politics and the Feud', 8.

[78] James VI, *Basilicon Doron*, in *Political Writings*, 28. Emphasis added.

[79] *The Calendar of Fearn: Text and Additions, 1471–1667*, ed. R. J. Adam (SHS,
1991), 155–61, 243–4.

authority—is echoed in the ballad of another local hero, Johnny Armstrong:

> When Johny came before the king,
> With all his men sae brave to see,
> The king he movit his bonnet to him;
> He weind he was a king as well as he.[80]

So there were four integrated types of feudal landholding: crown, church, nobles, and lesser landlords. The term 'landownership' is best avoided, because the concept of absolute ownership of land was alien to the feudal system. Instead of a single owner, there were several people with rights in the land. To Roman lawyers, *dominium* had been a matter of absolute possession. But feudal lordship, which was not absolute, observed a distinction between *dominium utile* (the use-right of the vassal) and *dominium directum* (the ultimate rights of the overlord).[81] The two most important people in this system were the feudal superior and the feudal vassal. Typically the feudal superior might be a noble (or sometimes a larger laird), and the vassal might be his kinsman or dependant. In a detailed study of lairds in the eastern Borders, Maureen Meikle found eighty-seven lairds holding their principal lands in chief from the crown, ninety-seven holding from another laird, thirty-three from Lord Home, and eight from other nobles.[82] Magnates may have been more prominent as superiors elsewhere; this was a region without a dominant magnate. The vassal collected the rent from the peasants and used it to provide fighting men which would maintain his possession of the land, in cooperation with the superior. But both feudal superior and vassal had certain rights: for instance, when a vassal died, if his heir was a minor the superior

---

[80] F. J. Child, *English and Scottish Popular Ballads*, ed. H. C. Sargent and G. L. Kittredge (London, 1904), no. 169. 'Weind'=believed. Armstrong was laird of Gilnockie in the Debatable Land, and was then attempting to establish himself and his family there. His execution in 1530 represented a bid to establish royal control in that area of the Borders: W. M. Mackenzie, 'The Debateable Land', *SHR* 30 (1951), 109–25, at p. 120.

[81] J. H. Burns, *Lordship, Kingship and Empire: The Idea of Monarchy, 1400–1525* (Oxford, 1992), 18.

[82] M. M. Meikle, 'Lairds and Gentlemen: A Study of the Landed Families of the Eastern Anglo-Scottish Borders, c.1540–1603', Ph.D. thesis (Edinburgh, 1989), 42. There were twenty-three further lairds holding in feu from the crown, and forty-nine in feu from the church: these were relatively autonomous in feudal terms, with few obligations to their superiors, though they may have had links to lords not based on tenure of land.

had the right to his wardship. This could be lucrative: it involved the right to administer the estate until the heir came of age. The feudal superior of all superiors was the crown, which also had a share in the holding of the land. The crown had an advantage over other lords here, both because it was always lord and never vassal, and because it had a prior claim to wardship if a vassal held both from the crown and from other lords.[83] However, the crown could not in practice move in and take over the estate: it had to proceed by negotiation with the kin.[84]

This picture is complicated by the fact that some feudal relationships were purely formal, giving the vassal a legal title to his land but no real ties of obligation to the superior. Meanwhile, other ties were created in which lords gave bonds of maintenance to followers who might well not hold of them in feudal terms, receiving bonds of manrent in return. Such bonds became common from the mid-fifteenth century, dying away in the early seventeenth. In this exchange of obligations, although land tenure played little part, the function—to create a chain of personal dependence, and a military following—was the same. Land was also, of course, the ultimate reason for the bonds. As with the pure feudal relationship, they gave both lords and followers the means to fend off challenges to their possession of land. A lord with a personal following linked to him by bonds did not expect to have to go to the royal courts to settle his disputes: 'once the courts were involved, the bond was already dead'.[85]

Not that Scottish lords were uninterested in courts. The characteristic form of late-medieval lordship was the baron court, a private jurisdiction of feudal landlords over peasant tenants. All four types of lords had baron courts. The classic form of feudalism had had the peasants as actual serfs of their lords, and although serfdom had died out in Scotland in the fourteenth century, baron courts still gave the lords similar (though not so strong) powers of direct coercion over their tenants; the landlord–tenant relationship was not primarily a contractual one.[86]

[83] Balfour, *Practicks*, i. 250–1.
[84] R. Nicholson, 'Feudal developments in late medieval Scotland', *JR* NS 18 (1973), 1–21; C. Madden, 'Royal treatment of feudal casualties in late medieval Scotland', *SHR* 55 (1976), 172–94.
[85] Wormald, *Lords and Men*, 11–12, 131, and *passim*.
[86] This was also the case in England. 'In the fifteenth century, broadly speaking, the mark of gentility seems to have been lordship over men, therefore possession

When in 1527 'all the tennandis in Quodquen and Kerswell', thirty-three named peasants, were condemned by Lord Somerville for having 'baith harrowit, telit and sawin the saidis landis vithout lecens of the said lord', we see where the power lay in feudal society.[87]

James VI said that parliament itself was 'the head court of the king and his vassals'.[88] There was traditionally little functional difference, except in scale, between parliament and a baron court, just as the difference between the lordship of James V and that of Johnny Armstrong was one of scale. The people in parliament had the right to be there because they were the king's feudal vassals assembled in his court. These people had their own feudal vassals and their own courts, and so on down the chain. Absolutism tried to reinforce and exploit this chain of rights in land, strengthening the links at the top of the chain and thus increasing the crown's power:

The king is *dominus omnium bonorum*, and *dominus directus totius dominii*, the whole subjects being but his vassals, and from him holding al their lands as their over-lord, who according to good services done unto him, changeth their holdings from tack to few, from ward to blanch, erecteth new baronies, and uniteth olde, without advise or authoritie of either parliament or any other subalterin judiciall seate.[89]

James's refusal to see the English feudal tenures abolished during the negotiations for the 'Great Contract' in 1610 played a part in the collapse of the scheme, because MPs realized that as a result, the proposed removal of the fiscal burdens on them could never be made secure.[90] It was a characteristic episode.

After this extended tour of the late-medieval polity from which it sprang, an approach can be made to the exercise of power in the absolutist state itself. The best way to begin is with a brief outline of some of the social and governmental developments in the sixteenth and seventeenth centuries which collectively amount to the

---

of at least a substantial segment of a manor, with seigneurial rights.' C. Carpenter, 'The fifteenth-century English gentry and their estates', in Jones (ed.), *Gentry and Lesser Nobility*, 38.

[87] *Court Book of Carnwath*, 85–8.

[88] James VI, *Trew Law*, in *Political Writings*, 74.

[89] Ibid. 73. 'Lord of the goods of all . . . overlord of the whole land'.

[90] A. G. R. Smith, 'Crown, parliament and finance: The Great Contract of 1610', in P. Clark *et al.* (eds.), *The English Commonwealth, 1547–1640* (Leicester, 1979).

rise of absolutism. Even its fall may be glanced at, though extended treatment of that would be beyond the scope of this book.

We begin, in around 1500, with a still-vigorous decentralized polity, resting on the four landed pillars of crown, church, nobility, and lesser lords. But change was afoot. In the course of the sixteenth century, the landholdings of both crown and church were gradually dissolved through feuing. This created a new class of heritable proprietors, liable to pay an annual feu duty but otherwise independent of the feudal superior. Feu duties, fixed in perpetuity, were going to be eroded by inflation. This system allowed the conveyancing formalities of the feudal system to continue into the twentieth century, long after the reality of shared feudal rights in land had evaporated. Margaret Sanderson has shown that most feuing of church lands took place between the 1540s and 1580s.[91] Little is known as yet of the feuing of crown lands, but it certainly took place during the sixteenth century. Henceforth, church and crown would derive *all* their authority from sources other than lordship over peasants and followers.

By 1600, the crown was exerting pressure on the nobles to renounce the autonomous exercise of force, and campaigning to bring the church under its control. Both campaigns looked set to succeed.[92] This enhanced the impact of the royal court in the localities: the hospitality accounts of the burgh of Ayr tell of the increasing need to stand well not only with local lords like the earl of Cassillis, but also with courtiers like Lord Balfour of Burleigh and court-connected entrepreneurs like Bernard Lindsay.[93] Direct taxation was expanding to become a regular source of revenue, and customs duties were being increased and extended in scope: already much of the crown's income came from sources radically different from those on which James IV had relied. The nobles were being groomed for a role as assistants to a personal monarchy—although they were unable to sustain this role without royal subsidies, which limited their usefulness. Meanwhile, although aspects of feudal lordship over land still had a bright future, the growth of a land market and the increasing independence of lesser

---

[91] M. H. B. Sanderson, *Scottish Rural Society in the Sixteenth Century* (Edinburgh, 1982), 65.

[92] See Brown, *Bloodfeud*, and, on the church, Ch. 6 below.

[93] *Ayr Accounts*, 244. These examples, taken at random, are from the year 1609–10.

landed proprietors from their traditional superiors curtailed the ability of crown and nobles to enforce their authority. Control of land, through a process as yet little researched, came to depend less on lordship and more on money. The new proprietor was often a feuar, who although he had absolute rights to control, inherit, and sell his land, was quite far down the scale in traditional terms.

If we now jump forward again to 1700, there had been vast changes. Consider the fate of the four landed pillars.[94]

The crown was subsumed in a more impersonal and bureaucratic governmental structure that had barely existed two centuries before—a structure presided over by parliament. Neither James IV nor James VI would have tolerated treasury commissions or parliamentary committees of public accounts wielding regular authority over public money: William and Mary in the 1690s had to accept parliamentary power. A survey of the Scottish administration after 1689 scarcely finds it necessary to mention the crown, though there is much on the treasury and the privy council.[95]

Secondly, the church also disappeared as a landholder, again thanks to feuing. It now derived its social authority from professional expertise rather than (as in medieval times) the size of its economic resources; bishops were no longer magnates. Religion was less central to political ideology, so official toleration of religious pluralism was now possible.

Those secular magnates, the nobles, thirdly, did much better: they continued to be landlords (in fact absolute landowners of a new kind), but lost their local autonomy in return for a share of influence on the government at a national level. Arguably this was quite a good bargain, since national government had a wider scope for its activities than ever before; but it was still a traumatic experience for some nobles.[96]

Finally, the lairds were participating directly in government, and were also absolute landowners, though on a smaller scale.

[94] Cf. a summary of English landholding, showing that in 1436 and 1688 the proportion of land held by the peers and richest gentry was about the same (15–20%), but that that held by lesser gentry rose from 25% to 45–50%, mainly at the expense of the crown and the church: F. Heal and C. Holmes, *The Gentry in England and Wales, 1500–1700* (London, 1994), 12.

[95] A. L. Murray, 'Administration and law', in T. I. Rae (ed.), *The Union of 1707: Its Impact on Scotland* (Glasgow, 1974), 30–4.

[96] K. M. Brown, 'Aristocratic finances and the origins of the Scottish revolution', *EHR* 104 (1989), 46–87; Goodare, 'The nobility and the absolutist state'.

Government office was more important than before: already in 1629, Sir James Pringle of Galashiels was considered 'a great man in his country' because 'he himself is sheriff of Ettrick and hath been these three years together, he is also a commissioner in the same sheriffdom . . . he is also a convener of justice[s], a justice of the peace'.[97] Sir John Stewart of Traquair wrote of his suits in the royal court in 1624:

I hawe desyrid not only to be made a barron but alsoe a commissionar for the borders, quhilk is a thing can afford me small or no commoditie; yit it is sume kynd of credit, and vithall giwis me a occasione to keip thos my nechbours from the oppressione and intrusione of uthers, quho, throuch the iniquitie of this tym, preasis to incroch on me more nor is reasonable.[98]

This scramble for government office in the localities, which began in our period, was very much a feature of the seventeenth and also of the eighteenth century.[99] Lairds were closer to central government in another way: feuars, those who had benefited from the dispersal of church and crown estates, were admitted to parliament in 1661. The lairds' relationship with the large landowners, though still deferential, was quite different from that of the lesser lords of the early sixteenth century, who had often been close kinsmen of the local noble whom they regarded as their chief. We have moved from lordship to patronage.[100]

These new landowners were integrated into a centralized administrative system. It is undoubtedly true to observe, as Professor Brown does, that 'in 1700 Scottish political life was every bit as hierarchical and exclusive as it had been in 1600': but it by no means follows from this that 'it is doubtful if there was any significant change in the underlying structure of political power, or its social distribution, throughout the entire early modern period'.[101] The titled nobility still *had* most of the power (though by 1700 the value of a title to a politician, though still considerable, was

[97] 'Account of a journey into Scotland', 1629, in HMC, *Report on the Manuscripts of the Earl of Lonsdale*, ed. J. J. Cartwright (London, 1893), 77.

[98] Stewart to Lord Carnegie, 30 Mar. 1624, W. Fraser, *History of the Carnegies, Earls of Southesk, and of their Kindred*, 2 vols. (Edinburgh, 1867), i. 88.

[99] R. M. Sunter, *Patronage and Politics in Scotland, 1707–1832* (Edinburgh, 1986).

[100] Cf. R. Mitchison, *Lordship to Patronage: Scotland, 1603–1745* (London, 1983).

[101] K. M. Brown, *Kingdom or Province? Scotland and the Regal Union, 1603–1715* (London, 1992), 34.

probably declining), but this is of limited interest for the present purpose. Power in 1700 was *exercised* quite differently from in 1500 and 1600: the 'structure of political power' was based on the institutions of an integrated sovereign state, which in 1600 had been under construction.

This emphasis on the structures of power is different from the question historians more often ask, about the *amount* of power that kings (or nobles) had. Maurice Lee, for example, describes James VI as 'more powerful than any king since Robert Bruce'.[102] How criteria could be established which could allow this assertion to be tested is not at all clear. Is the ability to deal with political dissidence the crucial criterion? Certainly a political historian like Professor Lee is likely to put a premium on political stability. But although much can be learned from an 'Off with his head!' approach to political history, it cannot answer *all* the relevant questions. In discussion of Robert I, or of the fifteenth-century kings whose 'terrifying power' Dr Wormald rightly stresses,[103] we also need to know what the scope of their activities was: not just whether they had power, but what they did with it, and how.

These questions will recur; in the meantime, a small example may be offered. What did late-medieval kings do in the field of poor relief? There were some statutes on the subject between 1425 and 1575, but evidence that they were enforced is entirely lacking.[104] Only in the latter year was an act passed that led identifiably to action—slowly at first, it is true, and not always as planned, but it was a development that created new state machinery and led to new forms of contact between government and people.[105] As with poor relief, so with witch-hunting, supervision of land transactions, or even simply the collection of a wider range of taxes: the government presided over by James VI began to behave in a different way, and the exercise of state authority was differentiated decisively from the exercise of private, baronial authority.

---

[102] M. Lee, 'Scotland and the general crisis of the seventeenth century', *SHR* 63 (1984), 136–54, at p. 142. Cf. id., *John Maitland of Thirlestane and the Foundation of the Stewart Despotism in Scotland* (Princeton, 1959), 79: 'unquestionably the most successful king of Scotland since Robert Bruce'.

[103] Wormald, 'The house of Stewart and its realm', 14.

[104] *APS* ii. 8, c. 21 (1425); 347–8, c. 29 (1535); 486–7, c. 16 (1552).

[105] R. Mitchison, 'The making of the old Scottish poor law', *P & P* 68 (May 1974), 58–93; Goodare, 'Parliament and Society', ch. 8.

3

The Absolutist State

> Of this hes sprung the absolut powar, wharbe, as a monster
> never hard of in anie just government, the haill priviledges of
> the thrie esteates of the realme is weakned and almost takin
> away; be the quhilk esteates, . . . kings, passing thair bounds
> to the wrak and oppression of the comoun-weill, war cor-
> rected and brought in ordour. In lyk maner, the privilages of
> towns and universities, yea of the holie kirke it selff, estab-
> lished be sa manie guid rewlars and parliaments, according
> to the word of God, ar owerthrawin.[1]

James Melville was writing of the climactic year 1584, when the government of Captain James Stewart, earl of Arran, was wielding
coercive statutes to oppress the presbyterian ministers, and interfering wholesale in local autonomy. Melville perceived correctly
that the balance between the central state and other institutions
of government was being shifted in a fundamental way. The self-
government of corporate bodies such as the three individual
estates was being undermined—particularly, in his mind, the estate
of the church, but also the burghs, several of which had centrally
nominated provosts imposed on them. The nobility, too, the other
estate, though not named by Melville, were clearly in his mind as
the estate who had 'corrected and brought in ordour' previous
kings. Lesser institutions like the universities were also having to
bow before the new 'monster'.

But it was not just a question of oppression and loss of traditional
privileges; the 'monster' was attractive to some. The rise of a new
form of power offered opportunities to those who found that they
could harness it. It deprived some groups and institutions of their
autonomy, but often offered them a new role in place of the old.

---

[1] Melville, *Diary*, 192. For the background to Melville's remarks, see
A. H. Williamson, 'A patriot nobility? Calvinism, kin-ties and civic humanism', *SHR*
72 (1993), 1–21, at pp. 1–4.

In its supporters' view, the absolutist state could defend national integrity, maintain political stability, prevent civil war (particularly that sixteenth-century horror, religious war), suppress violent feuds in order to offer impartial justice to all, and extend state authority and true religion into outlying regions, while providing employment for administrators and handouts for courtiers. There are no prizes for guessing that administrators and courtiers were prominent and vocal among the supporters of the system;[2] but the system worked, and its dynamism was seen positively as often as negatively.

Absolutism arose through central institutions and structures of power that would extend the scope of government and transform the nature of the state. What we need to grasp here are the underlying processes at work.[3] The previous chapter argued that crown and nobility had some quite similar functions in the fifteenth and early sixteenth centuries; it is perhaps worthwhile becoming more conventional and looking at some of the things that differentiated them. For central authority to establish itself, it was essential that noble autonomy—the option of rebellion—should become at first less attractive and ultimately barely possible. Such developments could not happen overnight, and the absolutism that emerged in our period had a prehistory of at least a century.[4]

It is here that we come up against the problem of royal majorities. This is not how most historians have put it, but the conventional wisdom—that the problem was one of frequent royal *minorities*—is not the most helpful, at least for the present purpose. It is easy enough to establish that majorities were not the norm: in the two centuries before 1584, there was an adult monarch present and ruling for less than half the time.[5] But even those historians

---

[2] Most Continental absolutist thinkers were royal servants or aspirants to royal service: W. Weber, ' "What a good ruler should not do": Theoretical limits of royal power in European theories of absolutism, 1500–1700', *Sixteenth Century Journal*, 26 (1995), 897–915, at pp. 898–9.

[3] There is more detail on the institutions in J. Goodare, *The Government of Scotland, 1560–1625* (forthcoming), chs. 3–7.

[4] In my use of the terms 'absolutism' and 'absolutist state', the former is shorthand for the latter or indicates a process leading to the latter. I draw a distinction between these terms and the narrower term 'absolute monarchy', which denotes a polity in which the monarch was not constitutionally answerable to the political nation. An absolutist state could well contain an absolute monarchy, but it also embodied a wider social and political system.

[5] Robert II (1371–90) ruled personally 1371–84; Robert III (1390–1406) not at all; James I (1406–37) ruled 1424–37; James II (1437–60) ruled 1449–60; James III (1460–88) ruled 1469–88; James IV (1488–1513) ruled c.1494–1513; James V

who have done most to rehabilitate the image of the late-medieval nobility have stopped short before treating a noble-run Scotland as normal; they have paid more attention to the majorities, perhaps because the approach has been defined as 'crown and nobility', or perhaps because change is more interesting than stasis, so that minorities and royal absences tend to appear as interludes or are even omitted altogether.[6] This may allow part of the case for the nobles to go by default. Could it be that they were perfectly capable of running the show on their own, without a king to supervise them? Naturally the presence of a king was assumed as an *ideal*— but people sometimes wait long for their ideals to be fulfilled, and in the meantime they have to get on with their lives. Also, alas, the ideals do not always come up to expectations.

Now, it is true that there were recurrent breakdowns of the political system during minorities, such as the bitter division and civil war of 1567–73 (exacerbated by religious conflict and foreign intervention), or the Angus Douglases' attempt to monopolize power in 1526–8. But were these inherently worse than what happened in the majorities—the chronic and destructive instability of the 1480s under James III, or the alienation of the nobility by James V that led to the fiasco of Solway Moss in 1542? The nobles certainly managed some things quite well. Could we have a better example of stable, consensual decision-making than the displacement of the duke of Châtelherault by Mary of Guise as regent in 1554? This took place with a notable lack of political turbulence, despite (or because of?) the unpopularity of the duke and latent distrust of the French-backed queen mother. The agreement between the two was made peacefully, and discussed and ratified (with some amendments) by parliament.[7]

This was all the easier because government was recognized as the nobles' business as well as the crown's. In the localities, much

---

(1513–42) ruled 1528–42; Mary (1542–67) ruled 1561–7; James VI (1567–1625) ruled from c.1585.

[6] S. I. Boardman, *The Early Stewart Kings: Robert II and Robert III, 1371–1406* (East Linton, 1996); M. Brown, *James I* (Edinburgh, 1994); C. McGladdery, *James II* (Edinburgh, 1990); N. Macdougall, *James III* (Edinburgh, 1982); id., *James IV* (Edinburgh, 1989).

[7] *APS* ii. 600–4; G. Donaldson, *Scotland: James V–James VII* (Edinburgh, 1965), 83–4. This kind of episode also forms an antidote to the suggestion, occasionally canvassed, that the entire period 1542–85 represented some kind of 'mid-Stewart crisis'.

of the formal government machinery—the sheriffships and regalities—was in their hands anyway; to make the institutions work, the magnates' local followings were also indispensable. Alexander Stewart, earl of Mar, ruled north of the Mounth with notable success until his death in 1435: his position as royal lieutenant helped, but his own following was more important. James I, even as the earl's heir, could not replace him, and the region fell into disorder.[8]

By contrast, an adult king could easily be a nuisance. Probably James IV was the only Stewart monarch to come up to the nobles' ideal.[9] Kings could stir up trouble in the localities, as when James V risked destabilizing the Hamilton family connection by first promoting and then arbitrarily destroying Sir James Hamilton of Finnart. In the minority of Queen Mary the Hamiltons recovered, and won a trial of strength with their local rivals, the Lennox Stewarts, in a way that should have been conclusive; but in 1564–5 the queen, largely by royal fiat, restored the earl of Lennox, causing quite unnecessary turmoil from a noble's point of view, in order to marry his son.[10] Solway Moss would never have happened under a regent, whose powers were more limited: Albany in 1522–3, and Mary of Guise in 1557, could not make the nobles cross the Border.[11]

But the restless and interfering character of royal majorities proved eventually to be a one-way ticket to absolutism. Monarchs were fashion-conscious, copying from one another and seeking the latest trends in styles of dress, chivalric entertainment, or designs of palace; their advisers did the same in forms of government. The new college of justice in 1532 was modelled on Italian bodies like that at Pavia, where the royal secretary, Thomas Erskine, had studied.[12] This is just one of many political and administrative developments which, once done, could not be undone. It has been argued by H. G. Koenigsberger that the crown had an inbuilt

[8] Brown, *James I*, 156–60.
[9] N. Macdougall, 'The kingship of James IV of Scotland: "The glory of all princely governing"?', in J. Wormald (ed.), *Scotland Revisited* (London, 1991), 35.
[10] C. McKean, 'Hamilton of Finnart', *History Today*, 43/1 (Jan. 1993), 42–7; J. Goodare, 'Queen Mary's Catholic interlude', in M. Lynch (ed.), *Mary Stewart: Queen in Three Kingdoms* (Oxford, 1988), 157–9.
[11] Donaldson, *James V–James VII*, 37, 88.
[12] P. Stein, 'The college of judges at Pavia', *JR* 64 (1952), 204–13.

advantage over a magnate-dominated parliament, and was likely in the long run to take over some of its functions.[13]

It is a commonplace observation that absolutist monarchies often developed in the aftermath of civil war, in which the shortcomings of traditional baronial power were vividly demonstrated. Scotland may partially fit this model—the seriousness of the divisions created in the turbulent period 1567–73 should not be underestimated; but on the whole the development of Scottish absolutism should be seen in a longer perspective stretching back to the fifteenth century. This is why the beginning of 'new monarchy'—a term widely used for a monarchy raised decisively above the nobility—has been identified with the advent on the scene of various different Scottish monarchs: James I (in his 1428–31 spending spree),[14] James IV,[15] James VI,[16] and the latter's successful 'pen government' following the union of crowns.[17] The oscillation between magnate-dominated and royal-dominated polities allowed adult monarchs to exploit the momentum created by their arrival on the political scene. They usually had no debts to pay or obligations to fulfil; it was natural that they should wish, however unconsciously in some cases, to do things in a new way, and to collect around themselves like-minded advisers and administrators with few ties to the past.

So if certain kings (and a queen) had not insisted on growing up and throwing their weight about—or, to put it more fully and accurately, if certain men had not insisted on associating themselves with an adult monarch whose word was unquestionable, and exploiting that connection to enhance their authority—'new monarchy' might never have developed; but the traditional Scottish polity might have continued quite happily. A kingdom in which the monarch never grows up is a Never-Never Land indeed, but its political trajectory—probably resembling that of the

[13] H. G. Koenigsberger, 'Monarchies and parliaments in early modern Europe: *Dominium regale* or *dominium politicum et regale*', *Theory and Society*, 5 (1978), 191–217, at p. 195.

[14] Brown, *James I*, 139, 207.

[15] R. Nicholson, *Scotland: The Later Middle Ages* (Edinburgh, 1974), 539–41.

[16] Donaldson, *James V–James VII*, 155; M. Lynch, 'The crown and the burghs, 1500–1625', in id. (ed.), *The Early Modern Town in Scotland* (London, 1987), 68.

[17] A. G. R. Smith (ed.), *The Reign of James VI and I* (London, 1973), 1. Similarities between 'new monarchies' and 'absolutist' states are noted by S. J. Gunn, *Early Tudor Government, 1485–1558* (London, 1995), 208.

elective monarchy of Poland as it became virtually a nobles' republic—is not hard to imagine.

In the end, of course, not just the kings but the Scottish state itself grew up. Chapter 1 of this book began with the symbolic date 1469, and the first declaration of Scotland's imperial crown: it was also the year of the coming of age of James III. From that date onwards, if not before, the innovative character of royal majorities becomes manifest.[18] James's biographer characterizes the early years of his personal rule as marked by 'aggression and illegality' in his 'determination to be an effective sovereign'.[19] He accumulated treasure, as did other 'new monarchs' in Europe such as Francis I and Henry VII, and developed a more exalted Renaissance image of the monarchy. He distanced himself from the nobility, and encouraged the ideology of imperial kingship. He was the first Scottish king to acquire and manufacture the new bronze field guns of the period. He made no attempt to make them a royal monopoly, however, and indeed there were statutes ordering the nobility to acquire 'cartis of weir'; it was the cost of artillery that made it so much a royal attribute.[20] Kings had always operated on a larger scale than individual magnates: now a quantitative difference was becoming a qualitative one.

The main long-term achievement of James IV was the forfeiture of the lordship of the Isles, an autonomous power centre which had had the potential to resist territorial integration into the Scottish state—a negative, but important, achievement.[21] He broke with the practice of his predecessors by holding far fewer parliaments; the tradition of annual parliaments was never restored. He was able to do this because of his elaborate and successful court, which fulfilled many of parliament's political functions and kept him in touch with the political nation in a way that *he* controlled; also because he travelled extensively (a medieval tradition rather than a new development) to build personal links with the localities. He did not need parliaments for taxation either, since he opened up new and

---

[18] The majority of James I also has claims to be considered innovatory.

[19] Macdougall, *James III*, 88.

[20] D. H. Caldwell, 'Royal patronage of arms and armour making in fifteenth and sixteenth-century Scotland', in id. (ed.), *Scottish Weapons and Fortifications, 1100–1800* (Edinburgh, 1981), 74–5.

[21] The forfeiture, in 1493, was before James assumed full control of the government; but he himself as king intervened periodically in the Highlands thereafter. Macdougall, *James IV*, 100–2, 175–91. For more on the Highlands, see Ch. 8 below.

lucrative sources of revenue in fiscal feudalism and increased rents on crown lands. He spent the money on prestige products like warships, at a time when a standing navy was still a rare thing for a European king to have.[22] His fiscal edifice proved ephemeral, and the developing absolutist state was to be financed through other means, but at the time it was a solid achievement.

If less can be said about the majority of James V, it may be because his reign has been less studied. He extended Scotland's political and cultural links with France, at a time when Francis I of France was the leading example of 'new monarchy' in Europe. He built impressive palaces in French style (something begun by his predecessors). He developed new forms of taxation—largely milking the church (again, James IV had begun this). Although he raised some large sums, the procedure was rather hit-and-miss, but such clerical taxation continued until 1560.[23] James's most lasting governmental achievement was linked with this: the creation of the college of justice as a permanent civil court. It may have been an excuse for the king to lay hands on church revenues, but it also possessed the jurisdictional potential to settle the nobles' disputes without feuding. Probably nobody intended it this way, but in due course this is how it came to be used.

Mary, in her briefer personal reign, did more. She enhanced the monarchy's prestige by playing a larger part on the European stage than any predecessor, exploiting her position in the English succession and pursuing active relations with England, France, and Spain. At home, she took advantage of the opportunities offered by the upheaval of the Reformation, systematizing and extending taxation of church lands by collecting 'thirds' of benefices. In 1564 the state took over the courts of the old church, which were relaunched as the commissary courts. The first complete edition of acts of parliament was published in 1566—a crucial event which encouraged the use of statute law.

How much of all this can be attributed to personal monarchical initiative is doubtful, but a polity focused on the monarch allowed

---

[22] L. O. Fradenburg, *City, Marriage, Tournament: Arts of Rule in Late Medieval Scotland* (Madison, 1991); Macdougall, *James IV*, chs. 7 (parliament), 6 (finance), 9 (navy).
[23] R. Fawcett, *Scottish Architecture from the Accession of the Stewarts to the Reformation, 1371–1560* (The Architectural History of Scotland, Edinburgh, 1994), 320–30; W. S. Reid, 'Clerical taxation: The Scottish alternative to the dissolution of the monasteries, 1530–1560', *Catholic Historical Review*, 35 (1948), 129–53.

it to happen. By contrast, a few governmental developments may
have been easier in minorities. In the minority of James V, in the
1520s, parliamentary statutes began to use the term 'commonweal
of the realm', or sometimes simply 'the commonweal', as an
accepted term for the national interest: eventually the term came
to acquire overtones of 'the state'.[24] To Mary's minority, in 1545,
belongs the creation of the privy council. The importance of the
parallel body in England has long been known, so perhaps more
attention should be paid in Scottish history to the creation of a
small, efficient working council with a stable, defined membership.[25] The 'council' under James V had been an *ad hoc* affair, like
other aspects of his government, because of his arbitrary nature,
but at least he was personally responsible for the orders he issued;
during the regency of the earl of Arran, the privy council emerged
to take formal collective responsibility for decisions.[26] It was during
Mary's absence in France that the Reformation came, in
1559–60—an event that owed much to the concept of the 'commonweal'.[27] Further research on royal minorities might identify
more governmental developments, refining or even diminishing
the distinction drawn here between majorities and minorities.

With the adult reign of James VI, government started to change
more rapidly and more fundamentally. In the early 1580s, the issue
of 'the absolut power', in the sense of royal supremacy over the
church, first came to the fore.[28] The legislation of two parliaments
in particular—those of 1584 and 1587—can be seen as an absolutist manifesto.

In 1584, the Black Acts were passed, asserting crown authority
over the church, banning presbyteries, and confirming the authority of parliament; seditious speeches against the king or his council

[24] R. A. Mason, 'Kingship and Commonweal: Political Thought and Ideology in
Reformation Scotland', Ph.D. thesis (Edinburgh, 1983), 69–70.

[25] See e.g. J. Guy, 'The privy council: Revolution or evolution?', in C. Coleman
and D. Starkey (eds.), *Revolution Reassessed: Revisions in the History of Tudor Government and Administration* (Oxford, 1986).

[26] For James V's council, see A. L. Murray, 'Exchequer, council and session,
1513–1542', in J. H. Williams (ed.), *Stewart Style, 1513–1542* (East Linton, 1996).
There had been an administrative council in James V's own minority, with some
similarities to the privy council of the 1540s. I am grateful to Dr Murray for a discussion of these matters.

[27] R. A. Mason, 'Covenant and commonweal: The language of politics in Reformation Scotland', in N. Macdougall (ed.), *Church, Politics and Society: Scotland,
1408–1929* (Edinburgh, 1983).

[28] *BUK* ii. 604 (Oct. 1582).

were banned; feuding by parties to lawsuits was to be more severly punished. A scheme was launched for a professional royal guard, to be financed from the revenues of the monasteries (which were largely in the hands of nobles).[29] In 1585 there was an act against private alliances of nobles.[30] Until the 1580s one of the important considerations in parliament had been that the lords of the articles (the parliamentary steering committee) should have a balance of geographical representation from different parts of the country; now this began to fade. Parliament was apparently ceasing to represent traditional locally based political communities, and its important members were becoming more linked to the central state directly.[31]

Then in 1587 came an avalanche of statutes: only a few can be mentioned here. An act of revocation claimed back crown lands that had been granted out to the nobles and others. An act of annexation transferred the remaining feudal superiorities of church land to the crown. Procedure was tightened up in parliament, privy council, and exchequer—the latter a new organ of active government. Various reforms were made to the administration of crown lands, designed to increase revenue. An act set out a programme for increasing crown authority in the Highlands and Borders. Local commissioners, the precursors of justices of the peace, were to be appointed: the scheme was never fully implemented, but the point is that they were trying. Inevitably, in this experimental period, some of the experiments failed. Finally, the nobles' position in parliament was undermined by the admission of representatives of the lairds as an independent estate.[32] All these measures affected the structure of government; but the 1587 parliament, which passed more acts than ever before (136 in all), also took new initiatives in government *policy*. One example among many is the legalization of interest payments up to a rate of 10 per cent.[33]

This governmental programme was probably not a deliberate attack on the nobility as such, though there are times when James's

---

[29] *APS* iii. 292–300, cc. 1–5, 8, 13–14.
[30] *APS* iii. 376–7, c. 6. This was a re-enactment of an act of 1555, but it now formed part of a wider programme.
[31] I. E. O'Brien, 'The Scottish Parliament in the 15th and 16th Centuries', Ph.D. thesis (Glasgow, 1980), 104–20.
[32] *APS* iii. 431–510, cc. 8, 13–14, 16–19, 49–59, 120.
[33] *APS* iii. 541, c. 35.

chancellor, John Maitland of Thirlestane, seems to have come close to it—notably in 1590, when he

devysed . . . many refourmations to be maid, and new fourmes and fassions to be set fordwart at his majesteis hamecommyng [from Denmark]; as to have na prevy consaill bot the chekker, and the nobilite to be debarrit therfra; . . . and caused pen ane proclamation . . . that nane of the nobilite suld com to court on [sc. unless?] being sent for, and then to bring with them sex persones and na mar.[34]

Whatever Maitland's motives, confrontational actions like this led to a troubled decade.[35] In 1590, there was an attempt to revoke the nobles' automatic right of access to the king, which infuriated many of them, and which certainly was a direct attack on an aspect of noble privilege. The royal guard also worried many nobles, although the king often lacked the money to keep it together. The revitalization of the exchequer in 1590 removed much policy-making from nobles' influence. Many nobles were privy council-lors, but few were lords of exchequer; either they really were 'debarrit therfra' or else they were insufficiently numerate. In 1594 the treasurer depute reportedly lamented that 'the nobilitie had left the king'.[36]

These were also the years of increasing pressure on nobles to bring their disputes to the royal courts instead of feuding. The 'act anent feuding' of 1598 was one of the most significant statutes of the century. By it, the nobility recognized at last that feuds had to be submitted to royal justice: private revenge was no longer legit-imate. The tradition of making of bonds of manrent suddenly died away; very few bonds were made after about 1600, and the number of feuds declined steadily until they were almost extinguished by

[34] Melville, *Memoirs*, 373.
[35] The classic analysis of this period, and of Maitland's role in it, is M. Lee, *John Maitland of Thirlestane and the Foundation of the Stewart Despotism in Scotland* (Princeton, 1959). For a recent restatement of Professor Lee's seminal views, see his *Great Britain's Solomon: James VI and I in his Three Kingdoms* (Urbana, Ill., 1990), 67–77. I would be more cautious about attributing so much to a coherent and con-sistent master-plan of Maitland's, when this plan is largely an *ex post facto* recon-struction and when so much of what James and Maitland did was in response to the immediate political events of a turbulent period. But my reservations on this should not be allowed to obscure the more important fact that Professor Lee's stress on the late 1580s and 1590s, as a critical period of realignments in the state, is similar to my own. I have also commented on this in J. Goodare, 'The nobility and the abso-lutist state in Scotland, 1584–1638', *History*, 78 (1993), 161–82, at pp. 166–70.
[36] Calderwood, *History*, v. 298.

1625. This was achieved to a large extent by persuasion rather than coercion, but the effect was the same: once a lord had discontinued his feuds, it was understood that he would not start new ones. Soon the machinery that had allowed him to do so—his network of armed local lordship—would atrophy. This was not the sort of development that hits the headlines at the time, but it was a momentous shift in the social and political structure of the Scottish Lowlands. The exercise of autonomous noble power petered out, and government would never be the same again.[37]

Meanwhile, the permanent exchequer was abolished in 1598, by the same convention of estates that passed the 'act anent feuding'; the hostility that the exchequer had attracted from courtiers makes it hard not to see this as a quid pro quo. The friction of the 1590s died away, to be replaced by a long period of harmony between crown and nobility, in which the latter regularly received generous subsidies. There were difficulties at first, because the 1590s were also years of fiscal crisis for the crown; but subsidies to the nobility became affordable after 1603, when the cost of the royal court was removed from the Scottish treasury. Eventually, the nobility learned that service to the crown was their only option for advancement; and it had to be done on the crown's terms.

Maitland's own father, Sir Richard Maitland of Lethington, in his diatribe 'Aganis the theivis of Liddisdaill', had seen their evil deeds as part of a magnate-dominated system:

> To se sa grit stouthe quha wald trowit
> onles sum grit man it allowit.[38]

But Liddesdale was a remote Border region. It was, indeed, in the Highlands and Borders that the traditional polity survived longest. Robert Pont wrote in 1604 of 'the fierce and insolent governours and pettie princes possessing large territories in the places most remote and abandoned of justice . . . seldome justice can be had against them . . . unless', he added, 'the king resume the cause and

---

[37] The 'act anent removeing and extinguischeing of deidlie feidis' is at *APS* iv. 158–9; 233–5, c. 31 (ratification in 1600). Cf. K. M. Brown, *Bloodfeud in Scotland, 1573–1625* (Edinburgh, 1986), chs. 7–9; J. Wormald, *Lords and Men in Scotland: Bonds of Manrent, 1442–1603* (Edinburgh, 1985), ch. 9; M. B. Wasser, 'Violence and the Central Criminal Courts in Scotland, 1603–1638', Ph.D. diss. (Columbia, 1995).

[38] *The Maitland Folio Manuscript*, 2 vols., ed. W. A. Craigie (STS, 1919–27), i. 302. 'Stouthe' = theft, robbery.

punish the outrage'.[39] Although the state's outlying regions were far from fully integrated—something that would continue well beyond our period—the level of state aggression against them was now higher than before. What Pont's comment omitted, however, was more significant still. In the core of the kingdom, state authority was well established, and there were no more 'pettie princes'. And even Border lords could be made to submit themselves to royal justice. The king was informed in 1605 that 'the greatest pleyars now . . . ar Jhonstons and Maxuellis, ane werye great and guid noveltie'.[40] These families, who had fought a pitched battle at Dryfe Sands near Lockerbie in 1593, were now fighting out their battles in the law courts.

Before the authority of the state was fully accepted by the nobles, there were some critical comments on life as a royal dependant at court. There already existed a literary tradition commenting on the insecurity of high office and the instability of the court—this is Sir David Lindsay on the subject:

> The vaine ascens of court quho wyll consydder,
> Quho sittith moist hie sal fynd the sait most slidder.[41]

There was no suggestion here that things had changed, no looking back to a lost golden age, although elsewhere in his works Lindsay was well willing to do this; on the contrary, he regarded such instability as normal. However, many French nobles at court in the sixteenth century began to complain that they preferred what they saw as the older noble existence—more rural, more self-sufficient, more military, less cultured, and with less of the intense competition for office and favour that took place at court. Only when they got used to it, in the late sixteenth and early seventeenth century, did the literature of complaint about the court die away.[42] The comparable literature in Scotland has been less studied for this purpose, but it would surely include Sir Richard Maitland's 'Na

---

[39] Pont, 'Of the union of Britayne', *Jacobean Union*, 22.

[40] Lord Fyvie to James, 3 Mar. 1605, *LP James VI*, 68. For more on the Borders and Highlands, see Ch. 8 below.

[41] Lindsay, 'The testament of the papingo', in *Works*, i. 66. For Lindsay's own experience of this instability, see C. Edington, *Court and Culture in Renaissance Scotland: Sir David Lindsay of the Mount* (Amherst, Mass., 1994), 21–2, 59–62.

[42] E. Schalk, 'The court as "civilizer" of the nobility: Noble attitudes and the court of France in the late sixteenth and early seventeenth centuries', in R. G. Asch and A. M. Birke (eds.), *Princes, Patronage and the Nobility: The Court at the Beginning of the Modern Age, c.1450–1650* (Oxford, 1991).

Kyndnes at Court without Siller', in which the 'kyndnes' referred to the bonds of kinship.[43] There could also be a frustration with the intensity of factional politics. Sir James Melville, embroiled in the manoeuvrings and rivalries over a plan to send an embassy to Denmark in 1588, exclaimed: 'Wald not this kynd of court handling skar any man to be a medler in sic weichty matters?'[44] This topic too could be pursued further, and any conclusions here can be only tentative, but seventeenth-century courtiers like Lord Napier, whom we shall meet shortly, seem to give no such impression of alienation. However much they may have disliked the intrigues, they accepted them as part of their world.

Now that the nobles were the crown's loyal servants, it was natural that the crown should think of creating more of them. But was it safe? In the late 1590s, Melville counselled the king against it:

Bot wher it apperis ye ar advysed, be creating ma noblemen, to increase your forces, wherby it rather makis them the starker; wheras dyvers uther princes pressit to mak them lawer and fewer, be raison of the auld emulation that hes lested betwen the kingis of Scotland and ther nobilite.[45]

The king, rightly, disregarded this advice. He needed servants, and after about 1598 he found that he could trust his nobles. From 1599 onwards, many more peerages were granted.[46] The fact that these men were his foremost servants has sometimes been obscured by arguments (by their nature inconclusive) about what *other* groups James used—whether the administration contained 'new men', or a *noblesse de robe*. Of course it was useful to have lairds and professional men serving the state, but when the state needed a marriage between local landed power and obedience to central authority, what it needed was not 'new men' but a reconstructed nobility. Their reconstruction would have to maintain continuity with many of the trappings of the old nobility, since nobility was traditional by definition; but James was not wrong in seeking noble servants. They were still disaffected when Melville wrote, but they soon ceased to be. In 1621, in an important parliamentary vote,

---

[43] *Maitland Folio Manuscript*, i. 335–6.   [44] Melville, *Memoirs*, 367.
[45] Ibid. 384. This memorandum is slightly garbled, and it may be a draft: we have only Melville's word for it that it was presented to the king. In its present form it dates from 1597 or later.
[46] Approximate figures for ennoblements and promotions in the peerage: 1560–9, 4; 1570–9, 2; 1580–9, 7; 1590–9, 7; 1600–9, 36; 1610–19, 14; 1620–9, 26.

the loyalty of the nobles whom James had created was conspicuous and influential.[47] New noble creations could also help to legitimize the nobility, by showing that it was no closed caste and encouraging the aspirations of lower groups.[48] This was probably less successful in Scotland, since there was certainly widespread disaffection among these groups in 1621; but it may have had some influence.

The new understanding between crown and nobility had much to do with refurbished ideals of service. What sort of service was now needed? It might seem that the crown, having established its authority, no longer needed the nobles so much. This impression might be borne out by a consideration of what the nobles actually did in return for their pensions, fees, grants of land and office: at first sight, it may not seem to be a lot. What did the second duke of Lennox do for James VI in all his long years at court, during which he held offices including that of chamberlain of the household? He had his own table at the highest level of the court—the only nobleman in this privileged position.[49] He performed periodic administrative duties, usually by proxy, and associated his name with numerous projects, but he was never an officer of state;[50] basically

---

[47] They voted 13 : 2 for the court, providing two-fifths of its majority: J. Goodare, 'The Scottish parliament of 1621', *Historical Journal*, 38 (1995), 29–51, at pp. 39, 48–9.

[48] M. Bush, *Noble Privilege* (New York, 1983), 142–3.

[49] A. Gibson and T. C. Smout, 'Food and hierarchy in Scotland, 1550–1650', in L. Leneman (ed.), *Perspectives in Scottish Social History* (Aberdeen, 1988), fig. 1, p. 38.

[50] He was a privy councillor for much of the 1590s; a commissioner to punish certain crimes in 1588 (*RPC* iv. 300–2); admiral from 1591 onwards (B. Seton, 'The vice admiral, and the quest of the "golden pennie"', *SHR* 20 (1923), 122–8, at p. 123); lieutenant of the north in 1594, after other nobles refused the task (*Warrender Papers*, ii. 269–70; *APS* iv. 99); a commissioner for the treasurership in 1597 (*CSP Scot.* xiii, I. 144–5); head of a costly but trivial embassy to France in 1601 (Spottiswoode, *History*, iii. 100–1); a collector of taxation in 1601, despite having defaulted on his own taxes in 1597 (*RPC* vi. 359; NAS, taxation accounts, 1597, E65/4, fos. 17ᵛ–23ʳ); royal commissioner to parliament in 1607 (*APS* iv. 365); a commissioner for the Isles in 1601 (*RPC* vi. 255–6); for war in 1602 (*RPC* vi. 330–1); a commissioner to punish certain crimes in 1609 (*RPC* viii. 263–4); and a commissioner on wool exports in 1623 (*Melros Papers*, ii. 500–2). Only as chamberlain (an honorific post), ambassador, lieutenant of the north, and royal commissioner to parliament does he seem to have acted personally: in a career of almost forty years at court, this hardly amounts to wearisome toil. Other wealthy nobles, such as the fifth Earl Marischal (founder of Marischal College, Aberdeen), appear more rarely in government records, but Marischal was no courtier and seems not to have wanted to be at the centre of affairs. The point is that Lennox did.

he was a dignified courtier whose main duty was to eat several square meals daily in the king's presence.[51]

Lennox's ventripotency, of course, had a symbolic function. He enhanced the status of the king: if you are served by a duke, you are greater than a duke. The king needed high-status people around him in order to demonstrate his own status. This may not have been the only way in which the king's status could be established, but it was an important one. If the court tended to become a soup kitchen for the nobility, this merely illustrates the *mutual* dependence of nobles and crown.

From the first noble in the soup kitchen, perhaps we could pursue the question by moving to the other end of the queue, where we find John Stewart, Lord Kinclaven, ennobled in 1607. This younger brother of the ill-fated second earl of Orkney survived the latter's fall to eke out an existence on the fringes of the court, surviving for years on his royal pension despite performing no identifiable services in return. He was even created earl of Carrick in 1628. Like his elder brother (and like Lennox), he was a cousin of the king, and numerous other Stewarts were honoured at James's court. But if the king was helping Kinclaven only as his relative, then he might also have helped a third brother, Robert, who rose no higher than the keepership of the royal park of Bewdley, and was dismissed even from that post in 1606.[52] It was simply thought useful to have nobles.

The nobility's tenure of many royal offices was also symbolic. The constable's court, held hereditarily by the earls of Errol, was no ancient relic: this supposedly traditional institution was freshly reinvented. Errol claimed in 1631 the 'previledges . . . due unto

---

[51] His obituary by Sir Robert Gordon praises him highly but makes it clear that he had obtained his popularity at court by his personal charm; no substantive achievements are mentioned, although Gordon was elsewhere most willing to record such achievements (including his own). Gordon, *Sutherland*, 385.

Lennox's evident courtliness did not interfere with his determination to maintain his hereditary privileges, mostly very recently conferred: 'It is not his majesties intention that I sould laike any of the olde privileges that ar so kindlei to me, as the bailierei and the ellection of the magistrats [of Glasgow] and the commandement theire, as I have had before. Therfor lett no man think that I will any vaise go from that.' Lennox to Sir William Livingstone of Kilsyth, 1 Apr. [1605?], HMC, *Reports on Manuscripts in Various Collections*, v (London, 1909), 111.

[52] P. D. Anderson, *Black Patie: The Life and Times of Patrick Stewart, Earl of Orkney, Lord of Shetland* (Edinburgh, 1992), 48–53, 142–4, 195. For Kinclaven's dependence on his pension see HMC, *Mar & Kellie*, i. 113. The privy council objected to the pension in 1621: *Melros Papers*, ii. 441–2.

him in the right of his office, and whereof as he alleadges his pre-
decessouris hes bene prejudged, and the same broght in discon-
tinuance, be reassoun of the manye ecclypses whiche that noble
house fra tyme to tyme hes suffered'. A commission investigated
the court, which had not actually existed in the sixteenth century,
and decided that the constable ought to have criminal jurisdiction
within a four-mile zone around the king. This was not much use
with an absentee king, so they added zones around parliament and
privy council also.[53] In practice, the constable was merely a nuisance, a source of jurisdictional disputes with the regular authorities such as the burgh court of Edinburgh. The burghs, 'resenting
the prejudice they ar licklie to sustein through the incroatching of
the grit constable upone thair liberties', lobbied against him in
vain.[54] The trappings of high authority had to be kept in the hands
of the nobility.

But surely the explanation for the crown's generosity to the
nobles goes deeper than these baubles? It does indeed. In studies
of state formation, not excluding the present one, much stress is
laid on the creation of centralized institutions, and it can easily be
imagined that these institutions were *replacing* the nobles. Not so.
They were, it is true, removing one sphere of action from them,
but only to give them another. The characteristic pattern of authority within the early modern state was one of patronage and clientage. As well as the allocation of material rewards—the late
medieval form of patronage, discussed in the previous chapter—
James VI was able to offer an increasing number of royal offices.
Some were financially profitable, but many were important
because of the power they wielded. James could not choose all his
officers personally: he had to have recourse to patronage-brokers
to advise him. And who better to perform this task than the nobles
who surrounded the king at court?

A courtier thus had a real function in government: he stood at
the head of a network of clients, and it was these clients who staffed
the lower levels of the administration and outer circles of the royal
court. Thus, William Beik shows that Richelieu's effectiveness in

[53] 'The Erroll papers', *Spalding Club Miscellany*, ii, ed. J. Stuart (1842), 217–27.
Cf. an earlier, unsuccessful request for the establishment of such a court: NLS, Errol
to James, 13 July 1606, Denmylne MSS, Adv. MS 33.1.1, vol. i, no. 71. For alternative arrangements made as recently as 1600, see *APS* iv. 239–40, c. 39.

[54] *Edin. Recs.* vii. 97–8; cf. Sir George Mackenzie of Rosehaugh, *The Laws and Customes of Scotland in Matters Criminal* (Edinburgh, 1678), 367–71.

France was due, not to institutions, but to a network of clients.[55] The point is, though, that they were clients *in* the institutions. Clients who did *not* have posts in the royal administration were not useful. This is what differentiated the system from its predecessor, in which a client had more often needed a band of armed followers. Kinship could still operate in this new context. During 1587–92, the period of Maitland's ascendancy, nine new members were appointed to the court of session: four were his relatives.[56]

Clientage was so all-pervasive that many examples could be given. The constable's court has already been discussed, but that was a largely ceremonial institution; the admiral's court, however, was a fully functional part of the administration. The duke of Lennox, as hereditary admiral, appointed the admiral depute or deputes, who in turn appointed and supervised the officers who did most of the actual work. The efficiency of the system depended on this chain of patronage; if a courtier wished to show his effectiveness and dedication in the royal service, he had to have able clients whom he could recommend for office. Once appointed, the clients not only had to demonstrate *their* effectiveness and dedication in the royal service, but had also to remember to whom they owed their posts.

Effectiveness was in fact none too evident in the admiral's court in 1607, although there was dedication of a kind. The skipper William Ashmore complained to the privy council that the admiral's officers in Leith, John Robertson and William Boustoun, had impounded the anchor of his ship: he had found caution to underly the law but had then been warded. Robertson and Boustoun were found to have exceeded their authority and were 'layed in the stokis'. Their superior, the admiral depute, Jerome Lindsay, was exonerated, but in 1608 Lennox had a new admiral depute— Henry Stewart of Craigiehall, who had been connected with him in 1598.[57] No sooner had this happened than two Dutch skippers brought another complaint: they had been loading coal when John

---

[55] W. Beik, *Absolutism and Society in Seventeenth-Century France: State Power and Provincial Aristocracy in Languedoc* (Cambridge, 1985), 15.

[56] Lee, *Maitland*, 153–4.

[57] *RPC* vii. 356. Lindsay was a tacksman of the customs, and son of David Lindsay, the veteran minister of Leith: *RPC* v. 141; vi. 107, 356. Stewart was a minor laird, sheriff depute of Edinburgh: *RPC* v. 435, 746. His chief claim to fame was as chancellor of the assize that had convicted a number of dissident ministers of treason in a state trial of 1606: Calderwood, *History*, vi. 391.

Wilson and Thomas Cownes, the new admiral's officers, had boarded them with a warrant and had demanded £40 or £50 to let them proceed. The privy council decreed that this was sheer extortion, and punished the officers. Next month there was an order to arrest Stewart himself for debt.[58] A statute of 1609, granting additional authority to the admiral, had to admit the 'insufficiencie, corruptioun and defectis whilkis were in the deputtis and memberis of these courtis', which had been 'weill amendit by the planting of hable, worthie and sufficient men in their places'.[59] In fact the complement of such men must still have been incomplete, since in 1610 Lennox granted a new commission to Sir John Wemyss of that Ilk as admiral of the Forth.[60] All this demonstrates the operation of patronage in practice, and the connections between life at the royal court and the minutiae of royal administration.

Nobles might always be expected to resolve the disputes, not only of their direct followers, but also of their more distant kinsmen. Sir Robert Gordon, tutor of Sutherland, had a dispute with the earl of Caithness in 1612 which was originally intended to be resolved by arbitration by some privy councillors who were 'indifferent and newtrall freinds' to both parties:

Bot the mater was thought so intricat and tedious by the freinds (who were then imployed in some more weighty bussines concerning the commounwealth) that they resolved to write unto the marquis of Huntly, desireing him to tak some paines in setleing these debates and controversies, seing the bussines did so neirlie concerne him.[61]

This also serves as a reminder that, by the early seventeenth century, government was not just about the allocation of resources and rivalries among the elite. It also involved 'more weighty bussines concerning the commounwealth', to which the Sutherland–Caithness dispute had to take second place.

Clientage did not have to operate through official channels of authority such as those which allowed the admiral to appoint deputes; it could cut across all formal boundaries. It was not in the job description of John Spottiswoode, archbishop of Glasgow, to

---

[58] *RPC* viii. 77, 85.   [59] *APS* iv. 440–1, c. 22.
[60] W. Fraser, *Memorials of the Family of Wemyss of Wemyss*, 3 vols. (Edinburgh, 1888), i. 197.
[61] Gordon, *Sutherland*, 318–19.

interest himself in the farming of the customs, but in 1609 he impressed the king by promoting a new syndicate to take over the tack (i.e. lease) of the customs, paying an extra £20,000 of duty.[62] His client was a leading member of the syndicate, James Inglis, who was also provost of Glasgow—a post in the archbishop's gift. Spottiswoode promoted a suit for Inglis in 1618: 'it wil encourage the honest man to labour his majesties benefit in the customis and other thingis, qhairof he wes a great instrument before'.[63]

The effectiveness of the patron's clients in their posts could thus affect his own political standing. The suggestion that in the early seventeenth century 'the Scottish nobles had too little to do' surely overlooks the efforts that many put into the task of recruiting and maintaining clients.[64] The grandee Lennox was secure in his position, but he was probably embarrassed by his subordinates' misdeeds, and it may be no coincidence that a challenge to the authority of his court was mounted by the burgh of Edinburgh in 1611.[65] Spottiswoode, with only loyalty and industriousness to recommend him, had to prove his worth by a constant flow of solid achievements; any mistakes would be seized upon by his rivals.

A vivid picture of the role of clientage in political faction-fighting emerges from the story of the rise and fall of Sir Archibald Napier of Merchiston (later Lord Napier), especially as told by himself. Although the treasurer, the earl of Mar, 'could not well brooke a colleg', Mar's enemies persuaded the king in 1622 to appoint a treasurer depute; Napier got the job by becoming a client of Mar's chief rival, the marquis of Hamilton. Mar and Napier then had to work together, but in 1628 Napier overreached himself by proposing to take personal charge of financing a planned royal visit. In October, there was a frantic race from Scotland to the royal court between Napier and Mar's own client,

---

[62] *RPC* viii. 589–90, 810–13; cf. *LP James VI*, 120–2.

[63] Spottiswoode to John Murray of Lochmaben, 2 Sept. 1618, *Eccles. Letters*, ii. 581. Spottiswoode may have felt in a good position to ask for things at this time, since in this letter he reported his success in getting the Five Articles of Perth through the general assembly. On Inglis as provost (appointed in 1609), see G. Eyre-Todd, *History of Glasgow*, 3 vols. (Glasgow, 1931), ii. 177. Cf. Spottiswoode to Sir James Sempill of Beltrees, gentleman usher of the privy chamber, 3 May 1612, W. Fraser, *Memoirs of the Maxwells of Pollok*, 2 vols. (Edinburgh, 1863), ii. 58–9.

[64] Donaldson, *James V–James VII*, 300. For a general survey of the mechanisms of client networks, see G. Lind, 'Great friends and small friends: Clientelism and the power elite', in W. Reinhard (ed.), *Power Elites and State Building* (Oxford, 1996).

[65] *Edin. Recs.* vii. 296–8.

Sir James Baillie of Lochend, receiver of rents: Baillie got there first, and although both claimed to have come off best in their interviews with the king, Mar's view—that the treasury could not stand the cost of a visit—prevailed. Napier clung to office, but was now relatively friendless and in 1631 had to resign.[66]

While client networks extended into the highest reaches of the court, they also served to carry the administration into the localities. It was here that the nourishing bounty of taxes, fees, gratuities, and kickbacks was to be obtained, flowing gradually up the system to refresh its upper branches. This is well illustrated in the machinery for collection of direct taxes on ecclesiastical benefices.[67] Whenever there had been taxes, some kind of network must have emerged in order to collect from each of the hundreds of benefice-holders. But from the mid-1580s, a semi-permanent network of regional collectors and sub-collectors was constructed by Archibald Primrose, clerk of the taxations. Snowdon herald is found as a regional collector, with Lyon king of arms (normally the heralds' superior) as his sub-collector. They were paid by being allowed to keep 12 d. in the £ of their receipts (and some collectors also exacted illegal collection fees from taxpayers). How did regional collector and sub-collector divide up this sum? No doubt they came to an agreement. As for Primrose, he had a separate fee from the gross tax receipts, but it is not hard to imagine him taking a rake-off from the subordinates whom he appointed.[68] But while they owed their employment to him, he, of course, also owed his position to the usefulness of the machinery that he had built up. The earl of Nithsdale, collector of the tax of 1625, was 'compellet to use Archibald Primrosse'.[69] This point also reminds us once

[66] *Memorials of Montrose and his Times*, 2 vols., ed. M. Napier (Maitland Club, 1848–50), i. 8–9, 29–64; HMC, *Mar & Kellie*, ii. 245–6; M. Lee, *Government by Pen: Scotland under James VI and I* (Urbana, Ill., 1980), 212–13; id., *The Road to Revolution: Scotland under Charles I, 1625–1637* (Urbana, Ill., 1985), 85–6. Napier's account attempts to convey the impression that he made his way by the favour of the king alone.

[67] J. Goodare, 'Parliamentary taxation in Scotland, 1560–1603', *SHR* 68 (1989), 23–52, at pp. 36–8.

[68] He was once accused of paying his own debts from the taxation, though such accusations from political rivals were common: earl of Kellie to earl of Mar, 19 Dec. 1622, HMC, *Mar & Kellie*, ii. 147.

[69] Spottiswoode to Nithsdale, 4 Apr. 1626, W. Fraser, *The Book of Caerlaverock: Memoirs of the Maxwells, Earls of Nithsdale, Lords Maxwell and Herries*, 2 vols. (Edinburgh, 1873), ii. 74–5.

more of the role of the nobility: the official collector of each tax was usually a noble, and his fee was several times that of Primrose.

We are often told that the absolutist state was bureaucratic. This is true enough, but bureaucracy was not what it is today. It was more patrimonial, and lacked many of the features of a modern bureaucracy.[70] Weber's 'ideal type' definition of a bureaucracy could be summed up as a professional hierarchy with clear functions and command structure, and with a separation between the official and the post.[71] The latter requirement was certainly not fulfilled, for many offices were treated as property. The clerk register in 1612 had the right to appoint his own deputes.[72] The clerks of session, meanwhile, also had property in their offices, so that the clerk register was not to appoint more than three clerks without the existing clerks' agreement.[73] As for function: in the lower reaches of the administration, clerks probably fulfilled fairly well-defined functions, but they did not necessarily act personally. Even in 1680, it was not clear whether the servant of the treasury clerk was primarily his own servant or a 'public servant', though there was no doubt that he did a lot of the treasury clerk's routine work.[74] Senior administrators could share or transfer functions easily enough: treasurer and treasurer depute had to work out their own *modus vivendi*, while both treasurer and lord advocate could act as public prosecutors. The officers of state were ordered to agree on the demarcation of their duties in 1592.[75] Many projects were initiated from outside government and adopted by it, not planned centrally from the start.

Another topic often discussed in this context is that of corruption. Neither clientage nor even nepotism were necessarily corrupt: they could become so, but so could other systems.[76] When offices were not hereditary (and most were not), it is easy to imagine that a son might succeed his father if he showed signs of ability, and not otherwise. He had, at any rate, had the best

---

[70] The classic discussion is G. E. Aylmer, *The King's Servants: The Civil Service of Charles I, 1625–1637* (London, 1961).

[71] M. Albrow, *Bureaucracy* (London, 1970), 44–5.   [72] *RPC* ix. 443–5.

[73] *APS* iv. 695–6, c. 114.

[74] A. L. Murray, 'The Scottish treasury, 1667–1708', *SHR* 45 (1966), 89–104, at p. 95.   [75] *APS* iii. 562–3, c. 41.

[76] The classic exposition of the issues for England is J. Hurstfield, *Freedom, Corruption and Government in Elizabethan England* (London, 1973), pt. III. See also L. L. Peck, *Court Patronage and Corruption in Early Stuart England* (London, 1990).

possible chance of learning the job, at a time when administrative jobs had to be learned through practice. Archibald Primrose (not the clerk of taxations) was granted the post of clerk of the privy council for life, in succession to his late father James, 'by whom he was instructed in knowledge of the procedures of the court of the privy council'.[77] Many jobs did not have to be done in person: hereditary sheriffs had deputes. There was some corruption, of course. One notorious lord of session, John Graham of Hallyards, was guilty of bribery and forgery, and yet was not removed (he was killed in 1593 in a feud with one of the enemies he had made). Graham's appointment, in 1583, seems to have been a political pay-off rather than nepotism: he had performed a valuable service by presiding as justice depute at the trial of the former regent Morton in 1581.[78] This could have happened in any age.

Most accusations of administrative corruption related to the taking of inordinate fees by, for example, the keepers of the seals and their staff. Maximum rates were set down in 1597, and again in 1606, 1609, and 1621: there were to be no extra fees such as 'chalmer fies' or 'drink-silver'. The effort was not entirely successful; in 1609 'the formair abuse, scafferie, and extortioun is not onlie renewit bot rissin to a fer gritter heicht'.[79] This was, however, inevitable when administrative staff were expected to live on their fees, and was not the kind of corruption which necessarily led either to administrative inefficiency or judicial partiality.[80] On the whole, we should take things as we find them and not assume that this was an *unusually* corrupt age. It was recognized that corruption could occur, particularly in men such as the justice clerk, but there were those who hoped to minimize corruption in his office:

If he quho is to be enclosed with assysors, (who for the most ar rud and ignorant) depending much on the clerc his information, if he, I say, be not a sound conscientious man, and free of baise bribrie, he may prove a pernitious instrument, and be the cause that iniquitie may be committed . . . young men, and men of great clannis, are most dangerous for that place.[81]

---

[77] *RMS* ix. 976.

[78] G. Brunton and D. Haig, *An Historical Account of the Senators of the College of Justice* (Edinburgh, 1836), 191–4; Brown, *Bloodfeud*, 66. He was related to the earl of Montrose, but Montrose was a minor figure.

[79] Skene, *DVS*, s.v. feodum; *RPC* vii. 164–77; *APS* iv. 408–9; 616–23, c. 19.

[80] Hurstfield, *Freedom, Corruption and Government*, 151–2.

[81] Alexander Colville, justice depute, to Lord Annan, 20 Dec. 1622, *Memorials of Montrose*, i. 20 n.

The continued role of the hereditary nobility, and the patrimonial nature of administration, are linked to the fact (obvious enough, but perhaps still calling for comment) that the European absolutist state was almost always an absolute *monarchy*. In theory, a centralized sovereign state could have been run as (for example) a parliamentary limited monarchy, or even a republic; in practice, this rarely happened. Absolute monarchy was taken by commentators to be natural. The chains of individual dependence that permeated the administrative structures, and that indeed animated them, found their most natural expression with an individual at the top of the chain. Parliaments in Scotland, as elsewhere in Europe, tended to hamper the full development of absolutism; parliament was never suppressed in Scotland, partly because it was useful in the initial stages of the construction of the new polity (especially in the 1580s), and partly because thereafter it was too strong. But after the 1580s it was more of an obstacle to the monarchy than a useful tool, and eventually found the scope of its activities curtailed.[82]

It might have been possible to go further in this clientage-based system, and to make more administrative posts heritable. This would have created something akin to the French *noblesse de robe*, a hereditary caste of local judges and other royal officials.[83] Such officials were answerable to nobody but the crown—although, secure in their position, they often acted independently of the crown too, and could oppose it at times.[84] Any involvement of educated, propertied laymen can be described as a *noblesse de robe*, but this is not a helpful usage of the term. What we have in Scotland, as in England, is the *ad hoc* recruitment of members of the landed

[82] J. Goodare, 'Scottish politics in the reign of James VI', in id. and M. Lynch (eds.), *The Reign of James VI* (East Linton, 1999, forthcoming).

[83] There has been debate on the question of whether there was a *noblesse de robe*, usefully reviewed by R. R. Zulager, 'A Study of the Middle-Rank Administrators in the Government of King James VI of Scotland, 1580–1603', Ph.D. thesis (Aberdeen, 1991). The interpretation offered here places less stress than does Dr Zulager on status and method of ennoblement, but otherwise his conclusions are broadly followed.

[84] Governments recognized that the sale of offices caused them problems; they only resorted to it *faute de mieux*, mainly in wartime. J. Brewer, *The Sinews of Power: War, Money and the English State, 1688–1783* (London, 1988), 19–21. A positive view of the practice in its French heartland, but making it clear that the practice was driven by war finance, is provided by W. Doyle, 'The sale of offices in French history', *History Today*, 46/9 (Sept. 1996), 39–44.

elite as servants of the crown.[85] These men were the sons of ordinary lairds and nobles, they would normally themselves hold freehold land, and their own sons would return to merge into the landed elite (at a higher level, it was hoped) with no special status. The significant change was the supersession of the clergy in the royal administration, as they were replaced by educated laymen.[86] The very fact that these laymen did *not* hold their offices heritably made it essential for them to acquire land for their sons, while their clerical predecessors, if they had had sons at all, had been more likely to seek benefices for them.

Scotland did, in fact, have a hereditary class of judicial officials: the hereditary sheriffs. They were in one sense an embarrassing medieval survival, but their continuation until 1747 suggests that they were at least *some* use to *someone*. They were not really a French-style *noblesse de robe*, because the French officials purchased their offices, specially created for the purpose, from the crown, and often paid an annual tax, the *paulette*, for the right to retain them heritably. They wanted the offices for the fees attached to them. Their existence had much to do with the circulation of money in particular channels. This was less so in the Scottish heritable jurisdictions, which were extensions of traditional territorial power rather than offices of profit: the main profit to be reaped from a hereditary sheriffship was in surrendering it to the crown for cash. Nevertheless, the administrative characteristics of the heritable jurisdictions were growing, while they were declining as engines of lordship. Sheriff courts had to implement the new statutes and collect the new taxes, whether the sheriff held his post heritably or not.[87]

Not only was the nobility still necessary in an absolutist state, but it was still a *landed* nobility; power was often still based on land, professional administrators notwithstanding. Land yielded not just money (in the form of rent), but also power (in the form of lordship or jurisdiction over tenants), and status (in that only a landed elite was truly respectable). This was why land in England (and, probably, Scotland too, though the subject has not been

---

[85] Cf. W. Fischer and P. Lundgreen, 'The recruitment and training of administrative and technical personnel', in C. Tilly (ed.), *The Formation of National States in Western Europe* (Princeton, 1975), 489.

[86] J. Wormald, *Court, Kirk and Community: Scotland, 1470–1625* (London, 1981), 67–71.

[87] Goodare, *Government*, ch. 8.

investigated) was valued at a price that gave a lower monetary return to capital than other forms of investment.[88] In early seventeenth-century Scotland, the influence wielded by lords through jurisdiction was probably waning, as changing patterns of landholding undermined the cohesiveness of the baron court, and as the expansion of centrally controlled institutions encroached on its autonomy.[89] There also seem to have been fewer prominent disputes directly about control of land; instead more is heard of faction struggles over influence at court. It was those with office or influence who were acquiring the land—through royal grants, influence in lawsuits, marriages arranged at court, or even purchase for cash.[90]

Although the flow of patronage was generally from crown to nobility, the nobles and courtiers could be expected to reciprocate in an emergency. One of the main measures of royal belt-tightening in the fiscal crisis of 1620–1 was an attempted freeze on pensions.[91] The king's first instinct, when he sought to raise money for his foreign policy late in 1620, was to call a convention of the nobility and ask them to contribute—though the ungrateful wretches then refused to do so without the other estates, and a parliament had to be called.[92] Similarly, the church had to display gratitude for royal patronage: Archbishop Spottiswoode in early 1621 volunteered the suggestion that the church should levy a heavy tax upon itself.[93]

So long as landed power was privileged, there could be no more

---

[88] L. Stone, *The Crisis of the Aristocracy, 1558–1641* (Oxford, 1965), 151–65. A. Offer, 'Farm tenure and land values in England, c.1750–1950', *Economic History Review*, 44 (1991), 1–20, demonstrates that the argument to the contrary of R. C. Allen, 'The price of freehold land and the interest rate in the seventeenth and eighteenth centuries', *Economic History Review*, 2nd ser. 41 (1988), 33–50, is mistaken.

[89] Goodare, *Government*, ch. 8; W. Makey, *The Church of the Covenant, 1637–1651* (Edinburgh, 1979), 182; cf. Beik, *Absolutism*, 13.

[90] This is a vast subject, but see esp. K. M. Brown, 'Aristocratic finances and the origins of the Scottish revolution', *EHR* 104 (1989), 46–87, at pp. 66–70, and Zulager, 'Middle-Rank Administrators', ch. 5; also M. M. Meikle, 'The invisible divide: Lords and lairds in Jacobean Scotland', *SHR* 71 (1992), 70–87. Professor Brown's forthcoming study of the nobility in this period will be of great value here.

[91] See Ch. 4 below.

[92] Goodare, 'Scottish parliament of 1621', 30–1. In 16th-cen. Germany there seems to have been far more systematic financing of the princes by their nobility, usually through loans: H. Zmora, 'Princely state-making and the "crisis of the aristocracy" in late medieval Germany', *P & P* 153 (Nov. 1996), 37–63.

[93] Spottiswoode to John Murray of Lochmaben, 9 Jan. 1621, *Eccles. Letters*, ii. 644–5.

than a subordinate role for finance. But money was more useful than before, because there was more of it around generally, and because there were more things that could be bought with it— including land itself. So men with money had to be offered a role. They could even take over some of the functions of government, though (as with the nobility) this had to be under controlled conditions.

It has been proposed by I. A. A. Thompson that a significant variable in the structure of the early modern state is how far it contracts out its activities. A medieval agrarian monarchy, he suggests, has a simple life: it runs its own warfare and collects its own taxes. Many states in early modern Europe, however, can be found farming their taxes, and contracting out the recruitment (and even command) of their armies. The choice was a difficult one; the Spanish monarchy oscillated between *administración* (direct management) and *asiento* (contracting) under Philip II, preferring the former in principle but finding the latter more convenient in hard times, before sinking helplessly into the arms of the contractors during its long seventeenth-century decline. England, by contrast, used contractors extensively in the early seventeenth century, but the successful abandonment of customs farming in 1671 led to the triumph of the directly managed system. France continued to use contractors, rather more heavily in periods of crisis; there was a shift in the seventeenth century from foreign to domestic contractors.[94] In general, contracting may be a transitional phenomenon in the story of the growth of the state. The state has to reach a certain level of administrative and fiscal sophistication before contracting is at all likely; but contracting is a decidedly mixed blessing, a sign of fiscal weakness or overcommitment. Expanding states don't contract.

What stage had Scotland reached in this scheme of things? Step forward, Thomas Foulis, goldsmith, entrepreneur, and contractor extraordinary in the 1590s.[95] Foulis never rose higher in the

[94] I. A. A. Thompson, *War and Government in Habsburg Spain, 1560–1620* (London, 1976), 256–73, 283–7; R. Ashton, *The Crown and the Money Market, 1603–1640* (Oxford, 1960), ch. 4; C. D. Chandaman, *The English Public Revenue, 1660–1688* (Oxford, 1975), 28; J. Dent, *Crisis in Finance: Crown, Financiers and Society in Seventeenth-Century France* (Newton Abbot, 1973), ch. 5 and *passim*.
[95] For more details of what follows, see J. Goodare, 'Thomas Foulis and the Scottish fiscal crisis of the 1590s', in W. M. Ormrod *et al.* (eds.), *Crises, Revolutions and Self-Sustained Growth: Essays in Fiscal History, 1130–1830* (Stamford, 1999). Foulis is also discussed in Ch. 4 below.

formal administration than the posts of sinker of the irons in the mint, which he obtained at the outset of his career in 1584, and master refiner of the metals, an appointment received in 1592.[96] He also had a tack of the royal mines, and became a mining entre-preneur, developing the profitable lead-mine at Leadhills. Mean-while, he became indispensable to the king as a financier, making loans, discharging large payments on his behalf, and receiving a large measure of control over the English subsidy.[97] The pinnacle was reached when he became sole executive officer of a treasury commission in December 1597, effectively giving him full control over the royal revenues, 'and that because the king was in his debt'; but the king defaulted the next month, leaving Foulis with vast debts that were not paid off for decades, if at all. The royal finances offered richer pickings after 1603, and later contractors prospered. The greatest was William Dick, who began by lending to the crown, helping to finance the royal visit of 1617. He became tacksman of the profitable customs on wine in 1628; a further loan in 1631 helped to reimburse the marquis of Hamilton for his mil-itary expedition to Germany, and he received a tack of the rents of Orkney and Shetland.[98] Scotland, like England, but unlike Spain, was in the less vulnerable position of using *internal* contractors.

Along with this co-option of finance came new directions in fiscal policy.[99] Direct taxation became regular in the 1580s and 1590s, and its incidence continued to grow; it was levied annually in most years after 1606. But as well as this taxation, which fell on all the propertied classes in fixed proportions, there were new levies that endeavoured to avoid taxing land and to lay as much as possible of the burden on commerce. Wine imports were taxed in 1590, and imports for lords' households were exempt from this lucrative levy; all imports had to pay customs in 1597; customs rates were increased in 1611; annual rents (interest

[96] *RSS* viii. 1722; *APS* iii. 559, c. 31. He was briefly collector of the customs in 1597–8, but this may have been merely a prelude to receiving a tack of the customs: *RPC* v. 388; *APS* iv. 165.

[97] NAS, accounts of Thomas Foulis, 1594–5, E30/14 (the only one of several accounts to survive); J. Goodare, 'James VI's English subsidy', in id. and Lynch (eds.), *Reign of James VI*.

[98] NAS, comptroller's accounts, 1616–17, E24/35, fo. 26ʳ; 1628–9, E24/46; 1630–1, E24/48, fo. 24ʳ.

[99] For details of this, see Ch. 4 below.

payments and annuities) were taxed after 1621. This last measure was blatant class legislation, since the nobility were notorious debtors. Creditors could not legally pass the tax on to their clients, since interest rates were limited to 10 per cent.[100] However, this should all be set against the unusual position of the Scottish nobility, which they shared with the English but with few other states: nobles as such had no exemption from taxation. Even in England, the nobility were systematically undertaxed, which in Scotland they were not.[101]

If there was a single defining role for the nobility, it was as military leaders. After the fading of traditional war-making, based on landed lordship, it ought in theory to have been replaced by a professional state army. In practice, although the crown gradually managed to obtain a monopoly of political violence, Scotland never reached the stage considered essential for Continental absolutisms, that of having a standing army. Of course Scotland, with no foreign enemies or territorial ambitions after 1560, hardly *needed* a standing army; but having one would still have strengthened the state internally, so long as it could have been paid for.[102]

One factor possibly undermining habits of private war-making was the periodic recruitment of Scotsmen to serve in foreign armies. This took place throughout our period, but reached a peak during the 1620s. This put in place a tradition allowing recruitment for money, rather than because of an obligation based on lordship. Military discipline and regimental organization were far removed from the local lord's war-band. Nobles, too, served in foreign armies, as commanders of these recruits rather than as heads of their local followings. The fact that Scotland exported warriors rather than importing them is a sign that it was on the fringes of the emerging European state system. Monarchies at the core of the system recruited mercenaries: those on the fringes

---

[100] K. M. Brown, 'Noble indebtedness in Scotland between the Reformation and the Revolution', *Historical Research*, 62 (1989), 260–75. For inconclusive discussion of whether the legal limits were adhered to, see J. J. Brown, 'The Social, Political and Economic Influences of the Edinburgh Merchant Elite, 1600–1638', Ph.D. thesis (Edinburgh, 1985), 236, 258.

[101] Goodare, 'Parliamentary taxation', 28. For an overview of fiscal exemptions, see Bush, *Noble Privilege*, ch. 2.

[102] For military matters, see Ch. 5 below. The first peacetime standing army, of the 1660s, is discussed in Ch. 10 below.

supplied them.[103] To the great Continental military contractors like Mansfeld or Wallenstein, or (in England) Burlamachi, Scotland contributed a few small names like the third marquis of Hamilton; but Hamilton fought for Sweden, not for Scotland.

The Scottish state may have been a weak (although still genuine) version of absolutism for this reason, but even the strongest and most imposing absolutist state was manifestly unable to do just whatever it liked. This presents a challenge to historians: how to conceptualize and explain the state's limitations? Perhaps it was not 'absolute' at all? Such reflections have led some European historians to reject the concept of the absolutist state altogether. Unfortunately, therefore, if some historians of France have argued that the concept of the absolutist state is *generally* and *in principle* invalid, then a historian of Scotland who seeks to demonstrate the concept's applicability to Scotland must deal with the French-inspired counter-arguments. This means travelling some distance away from the details of governmental developments in Scotland, but readers who have doubts about absolutism may find the theoretical passage that follows helpful.

The most sweeping rebuttals of the concept of the absolutist state need not detain us long, since they are largely based on misrepresentations of the concept itself. We are told, for instance, that the rule of law continued and that the monarch was not an arbitrary tyrant; that monarchs consulted their influential subjects rather than issuing diktats; that they were not in practice all-powerful for various reasons, ranging from bureaucratic inefficiency to the foot-dragging of entrenched local elites.[104] None of these points are in dispute; they seem mainly directed against the concept of absolutism as arbitrary tyranny, and do not challenge the picture drawn here of a centralized monarchy acting in partnership with the nobility.

A more sophisticated suggestion, canvassed by more than one historian of France, is that the legislative sovereignty of the state is a red herring, and that the powers of the crown (for in France the crown alone was sovereign) had more to do with the

---

[103] V. G. Kiernan, 'Foreign mercenaries and absolute monarchy', in T. Aston (ed.), *Crisis in Europe, 1560–1660* (London, 1965). In Ch. 5 below, it is argued that not all the 'fringes' were alike, and that Scottish society was not particularly militarized by the recruitment process; but the broad distinction stands.

[104] N. Henshall, *The Myth of Absolutism* (London, 1992).

administration of justice. Thus David Parker argues that royal legislation was 'more concerned with the proper distribution of authority than with the assertion of monarchical sovereignty', while Roger Mettam makes a related point:

The historians of 'absolutism' have erroneously maintained that the right to legislate was a cornerstone of monarchical power in the early modern period. It is true that the king could issue new laws, but his right to do so did not feature among the arguments of even the most ardent royalist pamphleteers. They would all have agreed that the role of the monarch as the fount of justice was a principal aspect of his sovereignty, but they stressed that this was the ruler acting, not as law-giver, but as supreme mediator.[105]

Dr Parker's conception of 'monarchical sovereignty', however, seems to have more of a whiff of the jackboot about it than mine does. His paper is full of references to French kings saying that they could change the law, and doing so; so why not recognize this as 'monarchical sovereignty'? Because, we are told, many of the laws they made concerned the allocation of responsibilites to different subordinate authorities; because some of these authorities were considered to hold their jurisdictions as of right (but recall Austin's distinction between right and power; it is power that is relevant); and because decisions were made at the behest of political factions and client groups rather than as a pure assertion of the monarch's untrammelled will. This is all true, but it does not make legislation unimportant; it just demonstrates that it was done by the normal operation of the political process within the structure of the state. If that state is sufficiently centralized, so that the government is focused on the sovereign authority; if that authority acts in partnership with the nobility; and if those nobles' local landed power continues even while they are co-opted as courtiers at the centre: that is enough to make it an absolutist state in the sense used in this book.

As for Dr Mettam's 'monarch as the fount of justice': this had

---

[105] D. Parker, 'Sovereignty, absolutism and the function of the law in seventeenth-century France', *P & P* 122 (Feb. 1989), 36–74, at p. 45; R. Mettam, 'France', in J. Miller (ed.), *Absolutism in Seventeenth-Century Europe* (London, 1990), 48. Dr Mettam's paper also contains most of the points against absolutism recently mentioned, while Dr Parker wants to modify or refine the concept rather than abandoning it. Some critical comments by a French historian on Dr Parker are offered by R. Bonney, 'Bodin and the development of the French monarchy', *Transactions of the Royal Historical Society*, 5th ser. 40 (1990), 43–61, at pp. 44–5.

certainly been important in fifteenth-century Scotland, and it has
been argued that the meaning of the provision of 'justice' was then
so wide as to encompass 'nothing less than the maintenance of a
stable social and political order'.[106] In our period, people may still
have expected that a 'stable social and political order' would be
maintained by a monarch who administered justice impartially, listened to good and wise counsel, and practised at least some of the
Christian virtues. The monarch still did supervise the workings of
government, did pardon offences, and so on; indeed, more things
began to be done by the personal authority of the monarch in the
early seventeenth century.[107] But this appearance of 'justice' as
stable and unchanging may well be just that—an appearance. Even
today, most people tend to think of their government as *managing*
the status quo rather than as changing it; government actions are
seen as 'just' or 'unjust' in a static situation, rather than as moving
society in one direction or another. The desire for rulers to be personally virtuous continues, while their private lives are still scrutinized zealously in the hope of uncovering moral lapses. Can we
not concentrate instead on the state, and on the exercise of power?

This causes an immediate difficulty for those who argue that the
'monarch as the fount of justice' invalidates the absolutist state.
The argument relies on the idea that the state regulating the courts
was doing something qualitatively different from the state issuing
legislation. But legal judgements and the regulation of courts, as
described so well by Dr Parker and Dr Mettam, are just as much
laws—coercive commands backed by sanctions—as are statutes.[108]
If these commands are now issued by a sufficiently centralized
state . . . well, a similar point has already been made.

Moreover, absolutist thinking did *not* necessarily prioritize the
provision of justice. In early seventeenth-century England, people
agonized over whether the king could tax or legislate without parliament.[109] Here, legislation was important—as was taxation. The

---

[106] R. Mason, 'Kingship, tyranny and the right to resist in fifteenth-century
Scotland', *SHR* 66 (1987), 125–51, at p. 128.

[107] Goodare, *Government*, ch. 4.

[108] See Ch. 1 above. Dr Mettam's description of the king as 'supreme mediator'
is also suspect: royal courts *adjudicated* (coercively) rather than *arbitrating* (with the
agreement of litigants).

[109] There is a large literature on this, but see e.g. C. Holmes, 'Parliament, liberty,
taxation, and property', in J. H. Hexter (ed.), *Parliament and Liberty from the Reign
of Elizabeth to the Civil War* (Stanford, Calif., 1992).

critics of the concept of absolutism usually have little to say about taxes; it is a crucial weakness in their argument. The establishment of regular taxation fundamentally reordered the relationship between the central Scottish state and local propertied elites.

The chief difficulty, then, with critics such as Dr Mettam is that they overemphasize continuity with the late-medieval past. This book is not about whether the government of Louis XIV operated in essentially the same ways as that of Louis XI or Louis IX; but the line of thought that says it did would also, when applied to Scotland, suggest that the government of James VI was doing nothing new. The evidence presented in this book points in a different direction.

The Scottish state, in fact, became a legislative body of a new kind from the 1580s onwards. Some of the legislation of that decade has already been mentioned. The state became a dynamo, energetically reshaping the law in a more centralized and integrated framework. But if folk even today think that governments merely manage the status quo, even less did the sixteenth century have a world-view in which new, unprecedented problems would constantly arise and call for new laws. The people living through the decline of the Scottish bloodfeud, even if they recognized what was happening, tended to see it as the removal of an abuse rather than as a restructuring of state power; their values and outlook were traditional even if their actions were not. We need to understand their outlook, but this should not lead us to take their propaganda at face value; instead, we should pay attention also to their actions. It is not a matter of the crown's (or the state's) 'right' to legislate, but how often it did so in practice, and what happened as a result. James VI himself, who did more than any individual to uproot the bloodfeud (and did it as a matter of deliberate policy), still thought of kingship in traditional terms. Like Dr Mettam's 'royalist pamphleteers', he wrote of 'Justice, which is the greatest virtue that properly belongeth to a kings office', and advised: 'Hold no parliaments but for necessitie of new lawes, which would be but seldome; for few lawes and well put in execution, are best in a well ruled common-weale.'[110] With hindsight, it is clear that he did not take his own advice—and the evidence is all over his own statute book.

---

[110] James VI, *Basilicon Doron*, in *Political Writings*, 43, 21–2.

One characteristic of Scottish absolutism is close to what some of the critics mean by the term, though devoting just three paragraphs to it may be some answer to those critics. It involved the central institutions of government discovering their power, and sometimes exhibiting a tendency to authoritarianism and repression. Maitland may have been the man who, in Bodin's phrase, 'showed the lion his clawes'.[111] These institutions were now able to supervise the political life of the nation more regularly, moving at least some way beyond the occasional attacks on dissidence that had been normal hitherto. Perhaps they were more high-handed than a fifteenth-century lord riding out with his armed followers in pursuit of his 'rightful heritage', perhaps not; the point is simply that a more centralized state meant a different kind of government.

This was noticeable in the universities, as James Melville noted in the remark quoted as epigraph to this chapter; they may serve as an example. Late-medieval universities had been controlled—to the extent that they were controlled from outside at all—by the church.[112] The move by James VI's government to influence universities was largely repressive, and there was no integrated policy on them; when universities developed in our period, which they certainly did, it was through private or local initiative. Thus, new universities were founded by the burgh council in Edinburgh (1582); by the Earl Marischal in Aberdeen (1593); and—a short-lived foundation—by Alexander Fraser of Philorth in Fraserburgh (1592).[113] As for central government action, it began in 1578 when parliamentary commissions were appointed to reform the universities, apparently concentrating on removal of Catholics.[114] The St Andrews commission—if only after being prompted by the general assembly—produced a complete reform scheme in 1579, and much of it was implemented.[115] But the major positive influence on higher education at this time was Andrew Melville, successively principal of Glasgow University and of St Mary's College, St

---

[111] Jean Bodin, *The Six Bookes of a Commonweale*, ed. K. D. McRae (Cambridge, Mass., 1962), 109.

[112] J. Durkan and J. Kirk, *The University of Glasgow, 1451–1577* (Glasgow, 1977), 227.

[113] For Fraserburgh (then called Faithlie), see *RMS* v. 2117; *APS* iv. 147–8, c. 52.

[114] *APS* iii. 98, c. 5.

[115] *APS* iii. 178–82, c. 62; R. G. Cant, *The University of St Andrews: A Short History* (2nd edn., Edinburgh, 1970), 50–1.

Andrews, whose work owed little to any member of the government and who was, indeed, often in conflict with the government.[116]

It is this latter fact that led to more comprehensive government intervention—the drive to eradicate the political influence of Melville and his presbyterian supporters. This was apparent in the political struggle for control of the new college of Edinburgh in 1581–3, a struggle won by a conservative faction on the burgh council (backed by the government). In 1584, when Melville was exiled, the archbishop of St Andrews was said to be planning to 'supplant' his college of theology at St Mary's.[117] This anti-presbyterian regime, however, collapsed in 1585, and Melville returned. The general assembly inspected the statutes of the new Marischal College in 1593, and 'hes allowit, approwin and affermeit the same'; the university of St Andrews had its autonomy vindicated.[118] The universities were again unmolested until the anti-presbyterian offensive was renewed in 1596—to be sustained this time until 1638. In 1597, the bishop and two officers of state revised the statutes of King's College, Aberdeen. At St Andrews, Melville's removal as rector was effected 'by the king and commissioners, by a borrowed authoritie from a corrupt assemblie'; the commissioners of the general assembly were by now the king's creatures.[119] But the tendency of the church, too, to become a department of state must be left to another chapter.[120]

Finally, the absolutist state generated a characteristic political culture. People learned to obey the central government—and not just through fear; they also *used* the government, and sought to promote their interests through institutions focused on the crown. Historians have sometimes given the impression that absolutism meant the king *imposing* his will on recalcitrant magnates, or new laws *forcing* people to obey the state.[121] In fact, even when king or policy-makers realized what they were doing (which they often did

---

[116] Durkan and Kirk, *University of Glasgow*, ch. 14; J. Kirk, ' "Melvillian" reform in the Scottish universities', in A. A. MacDonald et al. (eds.), *The Renaissance in Scotland* (Leiden, 1994); G. D. Henderson, *The Founding of Marischal College, Aberdeen* (Aberdeen, 1947), 16–18.

[117] M. Lynch, 'The origins of Edinburgh's "toun college": A revision article', *IR* 33 (1982), 3–14; William Davison to Walsingham, 27 May 1584, *CSP Scot.* vii. 155.

[118] *BUK* iii. 802; *RPC* v. 58–60.

[119] *APS* iv. 153, c. 63; Calderwood, *History*, v. 651.   [120] Ch. 6 below.

[121] e.g. Lee, *Maitland*, 221. The term 'absolutism' is unfortunate because it seems to possess so many such connotations, but it seems better to continue with it, defining it more carefully, than to invent a new term.

not), absolutism was never a bare act of will, nor could it simply be legislated into existence. The acceptance by the political nation of the supremacy of legislation was itself an integral and necessary part of the absolutist synergy.[122]

As governmental structures became more elaborate, widening circles of men of lesser property and status were drawn into them. Sometimes, indeed (as with the universities), they found that the central authorities wore heavy boots and were not too particular about where they trod. There were also dissidents who had to be systematically excluded from power. But many people discovered new pathways leading to influence at the centre. Lairds were still the clients of nobles, and accepted as such by King James, but he did insist that they should have direct access to the crown, to curtail autonomous noble power. In the years when the bloodfeud—traditional, local power—was being eliminated, the privy council offered redress, or at least a sympathetic ear, to its victims.[123] Above all, more and more groups lobbied parliament—burghs, craft guilds, ministers—or pulled wires within it—nobles seeking private acts.[124] Parliament was not always a selfless servant of the absolutist state, and absolutism had a tendency towards purely monarchical power; but often enough, especially in the early years (the 1580s and 1590s), crown and parliament cooperated in enhancing governmental centralization.

So one cannot entirely avoid speaking of the absolutist state as if it were a static, complete entity, but it should also be seen as a *process*—one, moreover, which could never be completed, if only because history never comes to an end, and any social system will be cluttered with bits of its predecessors. The state was 'absolutist' not in the sense that everything in it was absolutist, but rather in the sense that it was regularly doing things that would make it more absolutist than before. Not just the government, but the political nation, participated in this process.

As a process, the absolutist state could be all sorts of things. A merchant paying higher customs duties imposed by the royal prerogative; an earl at court seeking the grant of a monopoly to repair

---

[122] For the argument that English government also developed in response to changes in political society, see G. Harriss, 'Political society and the growth of government in late medieval England', *P & P* 138 (Feb. 1993), 28–57.

[123] Goodare, 'The nobility and the absolutist state', 164; Brown, *Bloodfeud*, ch. 8.

[124] Goodare, *Government*, ch. 2.

his fortune; a laird wanting to build a bridge, and asking the privy council for permission to levy a toll to pay for it; a group of dissidents hesitating over whether they dared to petition parliament: all these exemplified the spread of a political culture of absolutism. To the extent that people's attitudes and responses to government followed such lines, it can be said that the absolutist state existed— and only to that extent. From a legal and constitutional point of view, such a state gradually became predominant over older forms of government in the 1580s and 1590s, extending and consolidating its position over the next few decades; but a broader view must also see the absolutist polity as being re-created every day in the actions of members of the political nation. Absolutism did not simply impose itself upon people; it was constituted through realignments in the body politic as a whole.

4

Finance

> I fand his hienes verry weill and affectiounedlie disposit to se
> yow satisfeit, bot at the thesauraris handis ther cowld na
> money be had.[1]

The Scottish state in search of cash was nothing if not enterpris-
ing. In the autumn of 1565, an army was being raised to crush the
rebellion of the earl of Moray: the queen summoned Edinburgh's
leading burgesses to hear an 'orisoun' on her need for loans to
pay for it. When this failed to inspire them to open their purses,
six of them were imprisoned 'to thole the lawis for certane crymes'
(probably they were to be accused of lending to the rebels), and
released only when they 'appoyntit with our soveranis' with a loan
of 10,000 merks from the burgh. John Knox alleged that there
were 'soldiers set over them, having their muskets ready charged,
and their match lighted', and even the most sober accounts of the
episode leave the crudity of this fiscal expedient in no doubt.[2]

A generation later came an attempt to borrow that was not so
much crude as extraordinary. The counterpart to Moray's rebellion in the 1590s was the armed resistance of the north-eastern
Catholic earls, and in July 1594 their relations with the government were deteriorating rapidly. At this point the king approached
the defiant earls through an intermediary, Lord Home: would they
lend him 10,000 crowns? The request was politely refused.[3]

---

[1] Thomas Bannatyne to Sir Lewis Bellenden of Auchnoule, 7 Apr. [1585], HMC,
Report on the Laing Manuscripts Preserved in the University of Edinburgh, 2 vols., ed.
H. Paton (London, 1914–25), i. 50.

[2] *Diurnal of Remarkable Occurrents That Have Passed Within the Kingdom of Scotland
... Till the Year 1575*, ed. T. Thomson (Bannatyne Club, 1833), 84; Knox, *History*,
ii. 169–70; cf. Captain Cockburn to Cecil, 2 Oct. 1565, *CSP Scot.* ii. 217. Threats
were followed by bribery, with the burgh being offered the superiority of Leith:
M. Lynch, *Edinburgh and the Reformation* (Edinburgh, 1981), 110–11.

[3] News from Scotland, 21 July 1594, *CSP Scot.* xi. 378; cf. K. M. Brown, *Bloodfeud
in Scotland, 1573–1625* (Edinburgh, 1986), 166.

These two episodes took place against very different backgrounds. Mary in 1565 needed to borrow only for a specific and rare occasion—warfare. Although she would not have been solvent with only her Scottish revenues, she had (as we shall see) a large income as dowager queen of France that removed most of her financial worries. But by 1594, there had been almost a generation of internal and external peace which had made no such demands on the crown's finances, and there was no need to borrow to raise an army—10,000 crowns from the Catholic earls would hardly have been spent on fighting them. King James needed the money because, unlike his mother, he could not make ends meet.

Intensified fiscal demands were both a cause and an effect of state-building in Renaissance monarchies, as new sectors of society were brought face to face with the state and its proliferating revenue collectors. More people were taxed, more often, and on a wider range of activities. In France, government revenues doubled in real terms in the early sixteenth century; the story was similar in Spain.[4] Another way in which 1594 differed from 1565 was that this process—perhaps belatedly compared to the core European states—was well under way. The gross revenue of the Scottish state was increasing, at least slowly, in real terms for most of our period, despite tribulations and temporary setbacks. The fiscal administration was also becoming more sophisticated. By 1594, a recognizable financial sector, able to provide the crown with a range of banking services, had developed. And yet the crown still had to resort to outlandish contrivances.

This chapter will look first at some of the ways in which the finances could be managed, either on the revenue or expenditure side, in order to bring revenue and expenditure closer together in the long term. The second half of the chapter will look at short-term measures—borrowing and other forms of crisis management which were all too common and necessary, particularly in the years up to 1603. The evidence generated by the increasingly desperate crises of the 1590s will play a prominent part, so it needs to be borne in mind that this was probably the most difficult fiscal phase that the Scottish state ever experienced.

[4] M. Wolfe, *The Fiscal System of Renaissance France* (New Haven, 1972), 99–100; G. Parker, 'The emergence of modern finance in Europe, 1500–1750', in C. M. Cipolla (ed.), *The Fontana Economic History of Europe*, ii (London, 1974), 561.

For ordinary expenditure, the ordinary revenue was supposed to suffice. Traditionally, that revenue came largely from lands, in one of three forms: rents from peasants; rents from larger tenants who sublet to peasants; and feu duties, also mostly from larger tenants. Feu duties were a form of rent, but they were fixed in perpetuity, and unlike traditional rents they gave the possessors heritable security of tenure. Traditional tenures were steadily being converted to feu-ferme tenure during the sixteenth century.

Other familiar sources of revenue in 1560, mostly much smaller, were profits of justice (accruing irregularly from justice ayres), and feudal casualties from the crown's tenants in chief, such as wardships (in which the crown sold the right to administer the estates of minors). There were also customs duties, which were levied on most exports but not on imports; these had formed an important branch of the revenue when first introduced in the fourteenth century, but had since stagnated. The mint sometimes produced a small profit. Finally the government could raise additional extra-ordinary revenues from parliamentary taxation, falling on lands and on burghs; this was a rare expedient.

Apart from the introduction of feuing of crown lands (a decidedly mixed blessing in the long run), the Scottish fiscal system in 1560 was one to which few changes had been made for a long time. Because the crown had been able to meet its needs and even fight wars, there had been little pressure to change it. But by the 1580s, at least, the ordinary revenue no longer met the crown's needs. Inflation was eroding fixed rents and duties; the relative decline of the £ Scots caused difficulties for the crown, which made many of its purchases abroad; warfare was more expensive (not that there was much of this); the royal court was more expensive, needing to keep up with fashions elsewhere; and courtiers themselves were making more demands on the revenues. So we see a highly active fiscal policy.

Expenditure could not be planned in the long term, though the Octavians (the famous reforming exchequer commissioners of the late 1590s) tried to do so. The pressure to spend was so great as to engulf anything that could be raised and more; any limitation of expenditure was largely unplanned and entirely short-term, arising simply through insolvency. The system was income-driven—what was raised was spent. The accounting system did not allow advance budgeting; the function of the traditional exchequer, a largely passive body which met annually to receive accounts, was to prevent fraud. Under the charge and discharge accounting system, items were recorded at the point when liability was incurred rather than when the transaction actually took place; this meant the inclusion in the accounts of income that had not yet been collected and expenditure that had not yet been paid out.[5] If this gave each account something of the character of a budget, it was not one that could be used to plan ahead.

A second planning disadvantage of the accounting system arose from the Chinese walls that separated the financial officers. The establishment of a permanent exchequer in 1584 was a step towards more active fiscal planning.[6] However, it was still hard to distribute pressure evenly through the system: in the early 1590s, when the treasury was staggering ever deeper into deficit, the comptroller's accounts on occasion showed a small surplus. In 1597–8, when Walter Stewart held both offices, it must have been easier to transfer funds between the accounts—though by this time it was the comptroller's account that needed aid.[7] The problem was largely solved in 1610 when the two offices (and the two more minor ones of collector and treasurer of new augmentations) were combined permanently. The accounts continued to be kept separately, but were now run from a single office.[8]

If long-term fiscal policy thus ignored expenditure, there was nevertheless a tendency to realign expenditure towards more generally acceptable ends. It is impossible to consider expenditure in detail here, but trends on spending were sensitive to the changing needs of the nobility who made or approved policy. What the nobles needed was an increase in cash handouts, particularly pensions.[9] This redistributive use of crown revenues might be popular

[5] A. L. Murray, 'The procedure of the Scottish exchequer in the early sixteenth century', *SHR* 40 (1961), 89–117; id., 'Notes on the treasury administration', *TA* xii, p. xviii; id., 'The Exchequer and Crown Revenue of Scotland, 1437–1542', Ph.D. thesis (Edinburgh, 1961), 7–9.

[6] The permanent exchequer was initially for judicial work only, but the administrative aspect of its work became more prominent after 1590: *APS* iii. 309, c. 26; 455, c. 49; A. L. Murray, 'Sir John Skene and the exchequer, 1594–1612', *Stair Society Miscellany*, i (1971), 126; Melville, *Memoirs*, 373, 391.

[7] *ER* xxii. 317, 408; xxiii. 191.

[8] HMC, *Mar & Kellie*, i. 65–6. Parliamentary taxation was not brought within this system, however; each tax was a separate event, with its own collector, who managed his revenues separately from those of the treasurer. Cf. *RPC* xi. 470–1, 483.

[9] K. M. Brown, 'Aristocratic finances and the origins of the Scottish revolution', *EHR* 104 (1989), 46–87, at p. 71.

with the politically powerful, but would lead to long-term problems
with others who had to bear an increasing proportion of the
burden. Nevertheless, actual cuts were unlikely in this branch of
expenditure—or in any other branch. The cost of the royal household, the focus of the administrators' fiscal concerns until 1603,
had an underlying tendency to grow in the 1590s because of the
king's marriage and growing family. There were occasional cuts, as
when the privy council achieved a reduction in household staff to
'farre less nomber then had been used' in May 1590.[10] But such
measures, essentially responses to crisis, were rare. Sir James
Melville was aware of the possibility of cuts in the household—one
of his brothers was master of the household, while another was
treasurer depute; but his advice to restrict the number of household officers to two per post was probably, like most good advice,
easier to give than to act upon.[11] It was politically necessary to have
a lavish court to maintain the king's status in the eyes of the world.

If there was little prospect of cutting expenditure, there was, in
theory at least, a good deal of scope for increasing income. Most
of the traditional sources of revenue were given over to inertia;
they had sustained the crown for centuries, but a new age was
dawning in which they faced unprecedented challenges. The
policy favoured in the late 1590s by the Octavians was the recovery of crown lands. These lands, after all, had been the mainstay
of the crown for a century and a half, reaching their greatest extent
around 1542.[12] What was needed, to combat inflation, was vigilant
and effective administration, which is what the Octavians could
offer. The line of attack was clear: exploit to the full the crown's
right to revoke lands granted out during minorities, by using the
archives to identify unpaid dues and former crown lands that were
being concealed from the comptroller.

But while the theory was obvious, the practice was much less
clear. Rents were stagnant; inflation on an unheard-of scale had
eroded them. But of course many people had a vested interest in
fixed rents—some of them influential. Moreover, while most alienation of crown lands had in the past been by means of freehold

---

[10] Robert Bowes to Lord Burghley, 31 May 1590, *CSP Scot.* x. 306.

[11] Melville, *Memoirs*, 380.

[12] Murray, 'Exchequer and Crown Revenue', 172; P. McNeill and R. Nicholson
(eds.), *An Historical Atlas of Scotland, c.400–c.1600* (Conference of Scottish Medievalists, 1975), 72–3, 185.

grants to tenants in chief, the preferred tendency in the sixteenth century was to retain the crown's superiority but to set the lands in feu. Feuars made cash payments, sometimes large, in return for becoming proprietors with only the obligation to pay a feu duty fixed in perpetuity. In the early sixteenth century this had done the crown little harm: feu duties were usually as much as the old rent if not more, and inflation was low.

The full contours of the disposal of crown lands have yet to be charted, but in the late sixteenth century, their feuing was clearly proceeding by leaps and bounds. Statutes encouraging it were passed in 1584 and 1587. In 1588 there was an attempt to link feuing with agricultural improvement: those taking feus of the crown lands in Fife and Strathearn were to be required to plant trees and orchards and to build houses and dovecotes. But it does seem that most feuing was simply a source of short-term cash. This trend, which was eventually to prove irresistible, was incompatible with the recovery of crown revenues from land. Lands granted out might well find their way back to the crown, but once feued, control had been lost for good.[13]

The government, however, was reluctant to accept the verdict of inflation. The seriousness of the determination to rejuvenate landed revenues is captured in a warning of a finance commission of 1592 that this should be 'na utherwiss bot according to law'.[14] The repeated revocations of crown lands formed an important component of the programme. With these, the crown took advantage of its position at the apex of the feudal pyramid to act as private individuals did in reclaiming lands by revoking deeds done in their minority. However, the monarch did not have to wait till the age of 21 as others did, nor were the grants revoked restricted to their own minorities. The first of many revocations of James VI's reign was made in March 1575 when he was 8, recalling all crown lands granted out since the death of James IV on the grounds that only parliament could alienate crown lands.[15] This tended to undermine the trend towards absolute landownership, and to create a fruitful field for intrigue and patronage. Those nominally

---

[13] *APS* iii. 349, c. 5; 439, c. 13; NLS, 'Concernyng the chekker and the kingis rentis', Adv. MS 34.2.17, fo. 121ʳ; Murray, 'Exchequer and Crown Revenue', 202–3.

[14] NLS, 'Concernyng the chekker and the kingis rentis', Adv. MS 34.2.17, fo. 127ʳ.

[15] *APS* iii. 89–90.

affected would have to wait until the comptroller's officials identified the crown's rights, and negotiations on a compromise settlement might follow. The outcome of those negotiations is invisible
from the statutes—only a systematic investigation of individual
cases could establish the result of the political trial of strength
between crown and other landlords. Occasional comments like
that of 1585 that the lands reclaimed by previous revocations had
been 'newlie impetrat and purchast of his majestie be inoportun
and unressonable suittis' perhaps signal a lack of confidence in the
bargain the crown was obtaining.[16]

The revocation statute of 1585 was seen as the most significant
from the vantage point of 1598, when its enforcement was still
hoped for. It was more draconian than those of 1584 and 1587,
having fewer individual exceptions. It also contained the king's
pledge not to regrant any reclaimed lands until his 'awin neces-
siteis' were provided for. Similarly there were parliamentary an-
nexations of lands to the crown; but these too, if they were to take
effect, would clog up the flow of patronage. The annexation of
1594 was limited in its scope: a companion act explicitly dissolved
it for the purpose of setting lands in feu to their existing tenants.
It was soon being predicted that exchequer reforms, if they led to
greater efforts to recover crown land, would 'crab' many important people.[17]

None of the revocations could touch feuars, whose titles were
rock-solid so long as they paid their slowly diminishing duties. But
there were efforts to increase revenue from existing feuars. There
was an order, probably in January 1598, to investigate feus in
Galloway and Lochmaben.[18] More seriously, the feuars of the Fife
crown lands were ordered in 1599 to pay increased feu duties,
based on a rental of 1487 that Skene had discovered. The feuars
successfully resisted; one of them, threatened with eviction, won a
case in the court of session, arguing that the 1487 duties had been
reduced again in 1499 and in any case had never been paid. This

---

[16] *APS* iii. 382, c. 20. For examples of manoeuvres over revocations in 1444 and
in about 1550, see HMC, *Manuscripts of the Duke of Athole and of the Earl of Home*, ed.
W. Fraser (London, 1891), 114–15; Gordon, *Sutherland*, 137.

[17] BL, copies of documents relating to the revenues of Scotland, Add. MS 24275,
fo. 16ʳ; *APS* iii. 307–10, c. 26; 439–42, c. 14; 307, c. 25; 347–8, c. 4; iv. 64–5,
cc. 13–14; Ashton to Bowes, 14 Feb. 1595, *CSP Scot.* xi. 535.

[18] BL, copies of documents relating to the revenues of Scotland, Add. MS 24275,
fos. 16ʳ⁻ᵛ.

decision was ratified by parliament in 1600.[19] If the duties had been increased before feuing, their legal defence would have been much poorer; the Octavians came too late.

As well as feuing, wadsetting of crown lands seems to have been escalating. Wadsets were temporary alienations in return for loans, probably betokening greater desperation than feuing: crown lands to the value of £1,000 were to be wadset in July 1587 when the comptroller's revenue could not maintain the royal household until his rents could be collected at Martinmas. By the early seventeenth century, as we shall see, the finances were healthier, and the question was how existing wadsets could best be redeemed. Skene wanted to make this a priority. In 1610 it was proposed to use a cash windfall from an escheat to redeem some wadsets.[20]

The question of crown lands was linked with the statute that squeezed the last drop of revenue from the medieval church. On the whole the beneficiaries from the dispersal of church property had been, not the crown, but the landed classes—the exception being the thirds of benefices in 1562—and with the Act of Annexation of 1587 the crown took over merely the empty shell of a once-rich ecclesiastical structure. The act annexed to the crown the superiorities of monastic and episcopal lands as these were no longer 'necessar nor proffitable'.[21] It was followed by a series of statutes in the early 1590s to make the annexation effective. A census of church lands and thirds of benefices was ordered in 1592, and it may have been this order that led to the creation of a register of the feu duties of the annexed church lands. If so it was outdated by 1599, when the comptroller was wanting another such register to be compiled. Registers of rentals and feus of church lands were also ordered by two 1597 statutes, perhaps following on from the inventory of crown land that Skene had compiled in 1595. The main problem was that revenues from these lands slipped through the crown's fingers, ending up, as usual, in the hands of secular lords. In 1592 and 1594 there were statutes limiting pensions granted from benefices, and ordering that no more church lands should be erected as secular lordships.

[19] *APS* iv. 251–6, c. 56.

[20] *APS* iii. 456, c. 53; *RPC* v. 550–1; Murray, 'Sir John Skene', 150; BL, copies of documents relating to the revenues of Scotland, Add. MS 24275, fo. 9ᵛ.

[21] *APS* iii. 431–7, c. 8.

However, none of these acts could be passed without conceding a host of exceptions.[22]

It was probably these problems with the Act of Annexation that led the finance commission of 1592 to tell the king flatly that 'your hienes rent is nevir the better'. Very little could be gleaned from the church after this final, meagre harvest, as shown by the order to mulct Coldingham and Kelso, two monasteries exempted from the annexation, to pay the royal guard. Less than 6,000 merks was expected from this source.[23] Thereafter revenues moved if anything back towards the church. James was already planning to annul the Act of Annexation, if possible in his next parliament, in January 1598; he described it as 'vile' in *Basilicon Doron*, and decided on grounds of ecclesiastical policy to restore what could still be found of the bishops' ancient revenues. There was an abortive move to do this in the 1600 parliament, and it was successful in 1606.[24]

A central aspect of fiscal management was the struggle for the royal signature. Who, apart from the king (who was largely a pawn in the struggle), controlled the application of the royal sign manual to official grants of land and other forms of patronage? A running battle over this question was waged between the royal court and privy council: between politicians concerned to distribute patronage to their clients, and administrators collecting the revenue. James VI's tutor, George Buchanan, sided with the latter, if there is any truth in one of the stories that collected around him. Tired of upbraiding the young king for lack of restraint in signing petitions and grants, he administered a practical lesson: one day, James discovered that he had signed a deed making his tutor king for a fortnight.[25] James may have been both careless and generous, but it is unhelpful to focus on his personal qualities; the struggle

[22] *APS* iii. 564, c. 44; NAS, registers of temporalities of church lands, *c.*1592, E49/2/1–2; *RPC* v. 553; *APS* iv. 132–3, cc. 15–16; A. L. Murray, 'The pre-Union records of the Scottish exchequer', *Journal of the Society of Archivists*, 2 (1960–4), 89–101, at p. 95; for the statutes of 1592 and 1594, see *APS* iii. 544, c. 13; 571, c. 55; iv. 63, c. 5; 66, c. 17; for some exceptions, see *APS* iii. 587–8, c. 90; iv. 38–9, c. 55; 94, cc. 97, 99.

[23] NLS, 'Concernyng the chekker and the kingis rentis', Adv. MS 34.2.17, fo. 127ᵛ; *RPC* iv. 755.

[24] HMC, *Manuscripts of the Duke of Hamilton*, 2 vols., ed. W. Fraser *et al.* (London, 1887–1932), i. 30; James VI, *Basilicon Doron*, in *Political Writings*, 27; Hunsdon to Cecil, 19 Oct. 1600, *CSP Scot.* xiii, II. 713; *APS* iv. 281–4, c. 2; cf. Ch. 6 below.

[25] I. D. Macfarlane, *Buchanan* (London, 1981), 448–9.

was endemic in the patronage system. Nor was it always a problem. In a sense the system maintained a creative tension between the courtiers and the administrators, and historians' sympathy for the latter's point of view is often misplaced. The crown needed both courtiers and administrators, just as it needed both to raise revenue and to distribute rewards.

This discussion must rely largely on administrative sources, but because administrators were partisans in the struggle, care is needed in evaluating their complaints about royal giving. Even Queen Elizabeth was castigated as 'too liberal' by her lord treasurer.[26] In Scotland the issue was not new; unregulated royal generosity had been claimed as a problem under James V and before. Sir James Melville thought that Mary was 'naturally liberall, more than sche had moyen'. The court of session ordered a chancery writer not to pass irregular royal signatures in 1566. In March 1567 there was a freeze on gratis dispositions of gifts, pensions, and tacks (i.e. leases).[27] But neither Mary nor her father had the serious money problems that James VI faced. If James VI was too liberal, it was not because he distributed rewards without obtaining political advantage, but because the demand for patronage exceeded the supply.

The chief weapon available to the privy council was to use parliament to make rules requiring either that the council itself should approve signatures, or that only officers of state should present signatures to the king, or sometimes both.[28] The most intense period for such activity was between 1578 and 1593. In 1578, a statute appointing a new privy council laid down detailed rules on grants of casualties and infeftments in lands: essentially, new or altered infeftments had to be considered by the council. Only renewals in which there was 'na thing changit bot the persoun quha salbe infeft' could go direct from suitor to king to treasurer, while the comptroller was authorized to set tacks only for up to five years and to renew kindly tenancies. The keepers of the seals were to pass no grants not following this procedure.

[26] F. C. Dietz, *English Public Finance, 1558–1641* (2nd edn., London, 1964), 32.
[27] R. K. Hannay, 'On the foundation of the college of justice', *SHR* 15 (1918), 30–46, at p. 32; Melville, *Memoirs*, 111; *Acts of Sederunt of the Lords of Council and Session* (Edinburgh, 1790), 9; BL, Royal MSS, 18.B.vi, fo. 231ʳ.
[28] 'Signatures' in this sense were warrants for grants under the privy seal or great seal, requiring to be signed by the monarch.

Financial officers were not to answer the king's precepts for cash payments without the council's approval. In 1579, a similar but simpler statute ordered that none but the financial officers should present signatures to the king: there were three attempts to enforce this in the next two years. This position was temporarily abandoned during the spending spree of the Lennox regime, a statute of 1581 on 'importune and untymous suitters' accepting that suitors could present their own signatures to the king so long as they did not demand an immediate answer. The 1579 position was restored in 1585.[29]

The growth of a permanent exchequer aided the administrators. The privy council handed over much of the responsibility for vetting signatures—and, presumably, for continuing the struggle to be allowed to vet them—to the exchequer in 1590. This arrangement was ratified, broadly, by several statutes of 1592 and 1593. In 1587 there were to be no parliamentary ratifications until the appropriate composition had been paid to the treasurer, while 'na thing subscrivit be his majestie' was to be valid unless signed also by the relevant officer of state, although nothing was said about how this was to be enforced. This can be compared with a statute of 1592 enacting despairingly that the parliamentary ratifications, of which there were a record number in this parliament, would not be valid without the treasurer's signature. A more practical measure, perhaps, was to tighten up on procedures in an attempt to eliminate antedated grants.[30]

There were no elaborate regulations on signatures for the next five years. The Octavians, who ran the exchequer between January 1596 and June 1598, simply made the king promise not to sign anything without their approval;[31] uniquely, while it lasted, their regime had the political muscle to enforce this. Their successors, however, had their power base not in the exchequer but in the royal court and indeed the royal bedchamber; they depended on being able to say yes to their clients, and could not afford to allow the exchequer or privy council to restrict this. In early 1599 there were orders that signatures should be passed through the seals and

[29] *APS* iii. 97–8, c. 4; 151, c. 32; *RPC* iii. 284–5, 326, 349; *APS* iii. 229, c. 39; 380, c. 16. A number of signatures survive from 1580 and 1581, endorsed 'Red, past, and allowit in counsall': *RPC* xiv. 349, 354–60.

[30] *RPC* iv. 551–2; *APS* iii. 444, c. 19; 560, c. 34; 562–3, c. 41; iv. 19, c. 18; iii. 457, c. 54, para. 14; 563, c. 42; 569, c. 51.

[31] *RPC* v. 757.

that the comptroller and treasurer of new augmentations should authorize all dispositions of annexed and erected church lands. Casualties were not to be granted out by the king but to be componed for—that is, to have a sum negotiated and paid in composition—in the treasurer's office. In June 1599 there was even an order that all who had obtained infeftments, remissions, legitimations, or other signatures were to pass them through the great seal by 1 August. Since there were fewer great seal charters registered in June and July 1599 than in the corresponding period in 1598, this can have had little effect.[32] The same might be said of all these measures, but it is hard to believe that all that effort was wasted. More detailed study would be needed to establish when, if ever, the administrators were able to establish control over royal giving. The impression given by the administrative measures is that patronage was relatively unchecked in the early 1580s, and in the 1590s except during the Octavian regime. Before then, the crown's healthier finances had made the problem less urgent.

All these failures, caused as much as anything by conflict between supporters of the Octavian and chamber approaches, must have been frustrating. So it must have been good to find an issue that all sections of the governing class could unite on: the customs. Skene thought that 'thair is na rent of his hienes propirtie quhairin his hienes is sa far prejugit as in the abuis of his hienes gret custumes'.[33] Perhaps, but this probably tells us more about the attitudes of the ruling class—who were landlords, not merchants—than about actual trading practices, for the most detailed investigation of the latter has uncovered evidence only of moderate customs evasion.[34] Probably the landed classes looked with a more censorious eye on customs fraud than on, say, those who concealed a wardship or evaded a revocation of crown lands.

Medieval customs were traditionally levied only on exports, at more or less permanently fixed rates. This, however, was coming to an end; in England, for instance, the customs had been restructured in 1558.[35] In Scotland, in December 1582 the convention of

---

[32] *RPC* v. 542, 552–3; *APS* iv. 180; NAS, treasurer's accounts, 1599–1600, E21/73, fo. 55[r]; *RMS* vi. 721–61, 919–48.

[33] Quoted in Murray, 'Sir John Skene', 145.

[34] J. J. Brown, 'The Social, Political and Economic Influences of the Edinburgh Merchant Elite, 1600–1638', Ph.D. thesis (Edinburgh, 1985), 165–8.

[35] Dietz, *English Public Finance*, 7. Scotland levied duty on imports from England but no other countries.

royal burghs had been forced to deny a 'senister report' that
customs were being evaded, and to offer under pressure to take
the customs in tack. A four-year tack of the customs was agreed in
March 1583, with the burghs paying £4,000 and 30 tuns of wine
per year. This was a defensive measure by the burghs: when the
tack was renewed in 1586, it was done only because the alternative
was higher customs rates. Despite efforts to improve collection
procedures, the burghs' collectors could not raise enough to break
even on the contract, and more than once the convention of royal
burghs had to tax its members for 'inlaik of the customes'.[36] Effectively, then, the crown had increased its income from the customs
by a roundabout method: the burghs had chosen to provide this
extra money through taxation on themselves rather than through
increased customs duties. Artisans and small merchants were subsidizing the large overseas traders; the smaller burghs generally
were subsidizing a few great trading towns.

This arrangement was too unusual to last, and the customs
returned to direct management in September 1589. This might
have been the time to raise the customs duties, something the 1587
parliament had asked the exchequer to consider. But by now
the government was concentrating on another, related objective:
placing duties on wine imports, probably the largest untaxed
element in Scotland's overseas trade. This measure had already
been taken in England in 1558 and in Ireland in 1569—in
Ireland's case it was almost the only fiscal change of this period.
Scotland's tax, introduced by a convention in July 1590, imposed
a duty of three crowns per tun of wine imported, less 10 per cent
for 'the lekkage'. Within months the tax was being demanded on
re-exports as well, and 'the boroughs withstood the order set
downe', with Dundee even being put to the horn (i.e. outlawed)
before the government relented. In the final agreement, negotiated in March 1591, the government agreed not to levy the tax on
re-exports, and to change the duty to £8 per tun. As part of the
deal, it was recorded that the king 'promittis the saidis burrowis
that the payment of thair customes sall not be alterit nor changeit
fra the forme that hes beine usit thir fourtie yeiris bygone sa long
as the said impost is liftit'.[37]

<hr>

[36] *RPC* i. 147–8, 152–4, 158–61; *ER* xxi, pp. lviii–lxii, 561–4; *RCRB* i. 207, 235.
[37] *RPC* iv. 416; *APS* iii. 455, c. 51; Dietz, *English Public Finance*, 306–7; S. G. Ellis,
Tudor Ireland: Crown, Community and the Conflict of Cultures, 1470–1603 (London,

When the traditional customs rates were finally raised in 1597, the burghs not surprisingly cast this promise in the government's teeth, but otherwise they could do little. Export duties rose dramatically, and completely new customs were imposed on imports. This was a striking success. The measure was first passed by a convention, and when parliament came to ratify it, what purported to be a transcript even added a new clause highlighting its class nature: landlords were allowed to import or export goods for their own use duty-free. In January 1601 the wine import tax went up from £7. 16s. (presumably the £8 of 1591 minus a leakage allowance) to £27. 16s. per tun; resistance to this duty led to its reduction to £21 the following October, and class privilege was maintained with the duty on wine for nobles' and lairds' households being only £7.[38]

This was followed by another carefully planned general increase in customs rates in 1612. The king announced that he had 'preferrit the mercheant estate to our awne benefeit' by failing to do so, because the existing rates had been set when prices 'wer ten to ane chaiper nor thay ar now'.[39] There may have been some truth in this, and the vast increase in customs receipts detectable in the early seventeenth century certainly arose partly because of a boom in trade in the century's first two decades. Nevertheless, the merchants tended to see things differently, and their protests were predictable. The western burghs refused to forget the events of 1597, still resenting having to pay customs on 'all thair wairis out and in' in 1615.[40]

The expanding fiscal power of the state was mainly used to exploit the merchants, not the landed classes. The state failed to lift the incubus of tradition from the land tax. Direct parliamentary taxation was a highly significant question for the government, and for taxpayers of all propertied classes. The government did achieve some success in imposing taxes which in the early 1580s were more frequent than before, and from 1588 were far heavier. However, there were many structural problems with the antiquated

1985), 174–5; *RPC* iv. 514; Bowes to Burghley, 3 Apr. 1591, *CSP Scot.* x. 494; *Edin. Recs.* v. 34; NLS, 'Concernyng the chekker and the kingis rentis', Adv. MS 34.2.17, fo. 2^v.

[38] *RCRB* ii. 19–21; *APS* iv. 118; *Edin. Recs.* v. 161; *APS* iv. 135–6, c. 22; *RPC* vi. 200–1, 291.

[39] *RPC* ix, pp. lxv–lxxxv, 584–5, 605–6; BL, copies of documents relating to the revenues of Scotland, Add. MS 24275, fo. 9^{r-v}.

[40] *Edin. Recs.* vi. 74; *RCRB* ii. 329; *HP* iii. 229.

assessment and collection system for direct parliamentary taxes on land, at first concealed but eventually only too obvious. The government suffered some embarrassing defeats (particularly in 1600) which crippled its hopes of using parliamentary taxes on a scale for which they had never been designed.[41] The only alternative was to continue along the lines begun in 1590s with even heavier exactions from commerce and finance—in particular the 1621 taxation of annual rents.

This tax was a levy on interest payments and annuities—an original and distinctive feature of the fiscal landscape of early modern Europe. It was devised by the earl of Melrose to bring within the tax net the 'welthier sort . . . neither being churchmen, landedmen, nor burgesses'—by which he probably meant particularly lawyers, but also anyone else with capital.[42] It was introduced just after the nobility had refused to tax themselves (without the other estates) to support James's foreign policy in late 1620 and early 1621.[43] Taxing creditors was attractive to an indebted nobility. The creditors were unable to pass the tax on to them, because loans were most commonly made at 10 per cent interest—the maximum legal rate. Although supposedly introduced to meet a crisis, the tax on annual rents continued to be collected until 1638.

The search for some such tax had a long history. Despite the growth of direct taxes, the real story of the early seventeenth-century revenue is the story of indirect taxes. The successful restructuring of the customs in 1597 pointed the way for the policy-makers, and from then onwards they were casting around for new indirect taxes. A convention in December 1599 was called mainly to revise parliamentary tax assessments. However, it also considered a novel proposal for a duty on sales of grain (16d. per boll), cattle (2s. each), and sheep (12d. each), reportedly to meet the king's need for £500,000. This was surely an exaggerated sum to expect from any tax, but the king believed that he might soon be embroiled in a war for the English succession. The scheme may have been presented not as an excise but as a tax or penalty on forestalling (sales outside official markets); Moysie described it

[41] J. Goodare, 'Parliamentary taxation in Scotland, 1560–1603', *SHR* 68 (1989), 23–52.

[42] Melrose to James, 29 Mar. [1621], *Melros Papers*, ii. 394–5.

[43] J. Goodare, 'The Scottish parliament of 1621', *Historical Journal*, 38 (1995), 29–51, at pp. 30–5.

thus, recording that it had been dropped after being 'mour-moured against'. It is hard, however, to imagine how a tax on fore-stalling (an illegal activity) could have been collected. The English ambassador was told that if ever imposed it would be sure to be resisted by force, so unpopular had it been.[44]

An earlier attempt to mulct the salt trade might have had far-reaching consequences. In 1575 a convention of estates authorized the crown to purchase set quantities of salt at set prices. This might have turned into a kind of Scottish *gabelle*, with the crown con-trolling the salt trade and taking a rake-off from it. There were 'col-lectouris maid in evirie towne quhair salt vas maid', presumably for this purpose.[45] However, these collectors cannot have lasted for long, for no more is heard of them.

Apart from this abortive experiment, the only taxes on domes-tic trade actually imposed in this period were on wine sales. The first attempt was made in 1601, and was none too successful. A levy of 12*d.* in the pint was ordered in January, at the same time that wine import duties were quadrupled, and a minimum price of 6*s.* per pint was set. A sales tax was something quite new, and it could have been highly significant if it had succeeded in putting new tax-collection machinery in place. But nothing could stop the vintners continuing to sell wine at 5*s.* per pint, presumably without paying the tax. By the end of the year it had tacitly been abandoned.[46] Efforts were renewed in 1608, when retail sales of wine (or rather, purchases by retailers) were taxed at £4 per tun. Initially the impost was levied in Edinburgh only, and for the benefit of the burgh rather than the crown; this seems to have blunted the edge of protests. However, the government saw this success as 'ane pre-parative to his majestie for obteaning to his majesties owne use the lyke of all the remanent borrowes', and it was extended to them in 1613. It did not, however, become a major money-spinner like the increased customs.[47]

[44] Ashton to Cecil, 16 Dec. 1599, and Nicolson to Cecil, 6 Feb. 1600, *CSP Scot.* xiii, I. 584; xiii, II. 622–3; Moysie, *Memoirs*, 165; *RPC* vi. 205–6. Cf. the contempo-rary French attempt to impose a 5% excise (the 'pancarte'): R. Bonney, *The King's Debts: Finance and Politics in France, 1598–1661* (Oxford, 1981), 50.
[45] *APS* iii. 93–4; Pitscottie, *Historie*, ii. 319.
[46] *RPC* vi. 269, 230, 513–14; Robert Birrel, 'Diary, 1532–1605', in J. G. Dalyell (ed.), *Fragments of Scottish History* (Edinburgh, 1798), 53–4.
[47] *RPC* xiv. 624; ix. 551–3, 741; *Edin. Recs.* vi, p. xliv; *LP James VI*, 120–2; *RCRB* ii. 404, 433. For local payments of the impost see *Dumbarton Common Good Accounts, 1614–1660*, ed. F. Roberts and I. M. Macphail (Dumbarton, 1972), 10, 17.

A different source of revenue was periodically tapped until 1603: foreign subsidies. The significance of Mary's dowry as dowager queen of France is only just beginning to be appreciated: 60,000 *livres tournois* (£30,000 Scots) annually was a fabulous sum, funding most of the queen's household officers and increasing her gross annual revenue by perhaps 50 per cent.[48] James VI was keenly aware of the possibility of Continental subsidies; when he tried to borrow from the Catholic earls in 1594, he probably hoped that they might prove a conduit for Spanish gold. Much diplomatic effort was expended, largely in vain, on the search for such funds.[49] Along with his Danish marriage, James did get a sizeable dowry which it took him some years to spend. He also believed that he had some kind of promise of military assistance from Denmark; in 1594 he tried to convert this into money, asking for a loan from the king of Denmark and the German princes, which would be invested in France and only cashed if he needed to fight for the English succession.[50]

But the main chance was closer at hand. The English themselves were prepared to spend money to establish or bolster a sympathetic regime in Scotland; when official Scottish policy was not sufficiently pro-English, the money went to nobles who were believed to be 'well affected'.[51] There had been intermittent payments from England to the Scottish government since at least the regency of Moray. A more regular subsidy began after the Anglo-Scottish treaty of 1586, since this recognized that the crown, rather than the pro-English nobility, was now the most appropriate channel for the management of Scotland. There were no fixed times of payment, and Queen Elizabeth kept the sum to be paid vague, increasing or decreasing it at will. It averaged a little over £3,000 sterling per year (about £35,000 Scots) for the period 1586–1601: after that, James briefly received an increase to £5,000 sterling. In real terms this was still not much more than half what Mary

---

[48] M. Greengrass, 'Mary, dowager queen of France', in M. Lynch (ed.), *Mary Stewart: Queen in Three Kingdoms* (Oxford, 1988), 172–5.

[49] R. S. Brydon, 'The Finances of James VI, 1567–1603', Ph.D. thesis (Edinburgh, 1925), ch. 4.

[50] *Warrender Papers*, ii. 48. The justification for this was that forces might be needed in winter, when the Danish ports would be frozen.

[51] K. M. Brown, 'The price of friendship: The "well affected" and English economic clientage in Scotland before 1603', in R. A. Mason (ed.), *Scotland and England, 1286–1815* (Edinburgh, 1987).

had received from France, but it was received by the impoverished Scottish government as a 'legion of angels'.[52]

There was, however, no guarantee that 'angels' would descend to help the Scottish crown out of crisis: a thought that may serve to introduce the second section of this chapter, on fiscal crises and their management. James VI learned early about the precarious state of his finances: one crisis struck just as he was beginning to take a role in government. Having made the first formal entry into his capital, he had to go on progress through Fife and Angus in the summer of 1580; 'this progresse was devised becaus the Lord Ruthven, treasurer, alledged the treasurie was exhausted'. It is surprising that these progresses did not become the regular money-saving events that they were in England for Elizabeth.[53] However, there were certain recognizable policies which were regularly adopted to stave off insolvency. In such circumstances it was no use waiting, Micawber-like, for something to turn up; action would have to be taken, in the words of a 1592 finance commission, 'befoir it cum to ower instant necessitie'.[54]

Most of the crown's income was inflexible; the most conventional sources of revenue, like crown lands, doubly so. But naturally expenditure fluctuated—and when it also had a tendency to run ahead of income, each crisis seemed more serious than the last. Suddenly, the crown badly needed a source of loans to tide itself over. Medieval Europe had had few sources of large loans, and larger states had tended to raise their loans on the international money market. In the last three decades of the sixteenth century, England, which had hitherto sought loans in places like Antwerp, made a decisive break with the past: the Elizabethan regime sought instead a relationship with the domestic financial sector.[55] Scotland seems never to have needed the Continental bankers, but on a smaller scale the Scottish government, too, now sought to tap domestic capital.

[52] J. Goodare, 'James VI's English subsidy', in id. and M. Lynch (eds.), *The Reign of James VI* (East Linton, 1999, forthcoming); William Asheby to Walsingham, 12 Sept. 1588, *CSP Scot.* ix. 614.

[53] Calderwood, *History*, iii. 462; L. Stone, *The Crisis of the Aristocracy, 1558–1641* (Oxford, 1965), 453.

[54] NLS, 'Concernyng the chekker and the kingis rentis', Adv. MS 34.2.17, fo. 127ʳ.

[55] R. B. Outhwaite, 'Royal borrowing in the reign of Elizabeth I: The aftermath of Antwerp', *EHR* 86 (1971), 251–63.

Traditionally, apart from the occasional forced loan like that raised from Edinburgh in 1565, most borrowing had taken place within the crown's accounting system. The financial officers, principally the treasurer and comptroller, were personally liable for the debts they incurred on the crown's behalf (the crown having also, of course, a liability to reimburse them): as a result they might have to bear deficits out of their own resources. They were rewarded for this—in fact, this was the principal service for which they were rewarded; and as late as 1561 the treasurership was reckoned a 'proffytable' office. Robert Richardson, treasurer at that time, had risen from the lowly post of treasurer clerk, but he left his sons as lairds.[56] This would have seemed bitterly ironical to the earl of Gowrie, treasurer in 1582, when a list of debts incurred in the crown's service was sent to the English government: Gowrie himself was overspent by £33,000, the treasurer depute by £6,000, the comptroller by £5,000, and the collector general by £4,000. Together with £3,000 owed to the captain of Dumbarton Castle, the crown's debts according to this report amounted to £51,000. Although it excoriated the duke of Lennox, whom it blamed for the shambles, the report seems actually to have underestimated the deficit: in March 1582 the treasurer's superexpenses alone were £45,377.[57] By May 1583, the treasurer's accounts recorded debts to the treasurer depute of £14,342, to the master of the mint of £5,082, and to Gowrie of £67,488.[58] Gowrie had to wadset his own lands to bear the burden of his office, claiming the interest payments in his accounts.[59] The system was getting out of hand.

The response, partly a sign of greater administrative sophistication, but partly betokening desperation in the face of crisis, was a growing distinction between administrators and financial entrepreneurs. Earlier financial officers, like Gowrie, had fulfilled the function both of administrator and of provider of reluctant credit. This continued; the treasurers in particular ran up enormous

---

[56] Randolph to Cecil, 17 Oct. 1561, *CSP Scot.* i. 560; G. Crawfurd, *The Lives and Characters of the Officers of the Crown and of the State in Scotland* (Edinburgh, 1726), 383.

[57] Advice for James VI, 1582, *CSP Scot.* vi. 240; NAS, treasurer's accounts, 1581–2, E21/62, fo. 180ᵛ.

[58] NAS, treasurer's accounts, 1582–3, E21/63, fo. 137ʳ. To add further irony, one of Gowrie's creditors was a son of his predecessor, Robert Richardson: *APS* iii. 400, c. 32.

[59] NAS, treasurer's accounts, 1581–2, E21/62, fo. 67ʳ.

deficits from the late 1570s on, with the comptrollers' deficits remaining relatively under control at least until the later 1590s. But these deficits were no longer the sole source of credit: a new breed of financier arose, which was to prove a source of loans on an unprecedented scale. Meanwhile, the making of policy tended to devolve upon officers who did not provide credit themselves.

The emergence of the new administrators can be traced back to the early 1580s, a seminal time for financial administration as in so many other fields. The first permanent exchequer was set up in 1584, eventually becoming an active administrative department with auditors who did not bear the personal liability of treasurer and comptroller. Their responsibilities can be illustrated by an exchequer report, in August 1585, on the work they had done in finding some rents to shore up the unstable finances of the royal household for the rest of the year. They observed sharply that the treasurer's latest superexpenses were 'greit and difficill to be spedelie relevit, gif it sall not be your hienes guid plesour to foirbeire for a tyme the subscryving of signatures gratis'.[60]

This first permanent exchequer was abolished in 1587—possibly a retrograde step from this point of view, particularly at a time of fiscal crisis.[61] But Secretary Maitland continued to draw upon financial expertise. In July 1587, he wrote to the exchequer outlining the desperate financial state of the royal household, and appointing a special commission of eleven to overcome the crisis and to discover a 'likelie and possible meanes' of paying the crown's debts before 'confirmatioun of confusioun' was reached.[62] One was David Carnegie of Colluthie, a future Octavian. Some of these commissioners did lend to the crown themselves—the advocate John Sharp of Houston, for instance.[63] But the sums were modest, and their money was less important than their administrative talent.

A new commission reported in 1592, stressing that drastic action was needed. To underline this, it suggested dismissing all the financial officers, and came down, as the Octavians were to do, in favour of recovering crown lands rather than imposing taxation.

[60] NLS, 'Concernyng the chekker and the kingis rentis', Adv. MS 34.2.17, fo. 174[v].
[61] *APS* iii. 455, c. 49.
[62] NAS, Maitland to the exchequer, 18 July 1587, PA7/1/3.
[63] M. H. B. Sanderson, *Mary Stewart's People* (Edinburgh, 1987), 25–6.

The commission advised involving parliament in the work of the treasurer by having a committee of three, one from each traditional estate, to authorize all grants of feudal casualties: this would prevent them being granted 'ower guid chaip' since parliament knew that the alternative was taxation.[64] An exchequer commission of January 1595 foreshadowed the Octavians in another way, by proposing to replace the financial officers with 'mene' men.[65] This commission may not itself have been effective;[66] however, the proposal for 'mene' financial officers suggests that the government had moved away from the assumption that the officers should be the major source of credit for the crown. While the Octavians in 1596 opted to take over some of the financial offices themselves, they did install one 'mene' officer, Henry Wardlaw, chamberlain of Dunfermline, in the new post of receiver general, responsible for the entire income not only of the former comptroller, but also of the treasurer of new augmentations (the officer who received the duties from church lands annexed in 1587), and of the mint.[67]

If Wardlaw was appointed for his administrative abilities rather than his wealth, this underlines the fact that the crown was increasingly looking elsewhere for loans. An entirely new type of financial entrepreneur would supplement and eventually overtake the established financial officers of the crown as a source of credit, and sometimes take over some of the latter's accounting functions too. The Reformation period had marked an end to the occasional presence in Edinburgh of Italian bankers; thereafter Scots took their place, leading to a veritable credit explosion in the early seventeenth century. Janet Fockart was a precursor of it: a merchant and moneylender who lent to the crown among others in the 1570s.[68] Unlike the new-style administrator, who made policy but bore no personal liability, the importance of the new-style entrepreneur was that he or she could put large cash sums on the line. Such people are less audible in the official sources, for they made

---

[64] NLS, 'Concernyng the chekker and the kingis rentis', Adv. MS 34.2.17, fo. 127ᵛ.

[65] Ashton to Bowes, 18 Jan. 1595, *CSP Scot.* xi. 515.

[66] M. Lee, *John Maitland of Thirlestane and the Foundation of the Stewart Despotism in Scotland* (Princeton, 1959), 284.

[67] *ER* xxiii. 134. Wardlaw went on to a long and profitable career in royal service.

[68] S. G. Checkland, *Scottish Banking: A History, 1695–1973* (Glasgow, 1975), 726–7; Brown, 'Edinburgh Merchant Elite', 239–42; Sanderson, *Mary Stewart's People*, 99.

policy only indirectly—by deciding either to lend or not; but by the 1590s this voice was listened to eagerly.

This was when the crown's credit management became more sophisticated, largely through the goldsmith and financier Thomas Foulis. His official position was a lowly one: he was sinker of the irons in the mint from 1584 to 1614. In this capacity he made a good many of the crown's coin and seal dies; but it was hardly this that gave him a towering position in fiscal policy during the 1590s. He came to act as a state banker, channelling large sums from a host of investors towards the needy royal coffers. In return he gained increasing control over the handling of various branches of revenue—the mines, the English subsidy, the mint, and the customs. He acted in effect as an informal financial officer of the crown, making his own accounts, and at his height he was handling a good deal more money than either of the main formal officers, the treasurer and comptroller. He briefly took over the actual management of all royal finances in December 1597, but in January 1598 the scheme collapsed—or rather, was destroyed by a deliberately engineered royal bankruptcy. This left Foulis and his then partner Robert Jowsie owing their creditors £160,522, and holding a worthless IOU for this amount from the crown. This sum amounted to about a year's gross crown revenue from all sources, and without the bankruptcy of 1598 it is hard to see how James VI could have survived financially until relief finally arrived in 1603.[69]

The royal household deserves a special mention in discussion of fiscal crisis management. From the point of view of the king, a crisis was essentially a time when 'thair is not quhyte nor beir, silver nor uthir rent, to serve his hienes sufficientlie in breid and drink, nor uthirwayes'.[70] There were two basic ways to keep him and his household from starving. The first was to prise some revenues away from any of the regular officers, usually the comptroller who had primary responsibility for household finance, and assign them directly to the master of the household. This was being done, for instance, as early as 1570–1.[71] The long-term result would be to cause worse problems

---

[69] J. Goodare, 'Thomas Foulis and the Scottish fiscal crisis of the 1590s', in W. M. Ormrod *et al.* (eds.), *Crises, Revolutions and Self-Sustained Growth: Essays in Fiscal History, 1130–1830* (Stamford, 1999).

[70] *RPC* v. 255. 'Quhyte'=wheat; 'beir'=bere (a form of barley). Cf. A. L. Murray, 'Financing the royal household: James V and his comptrollers, 1513–43', in I. B. Cowan and D. Shaw (eds.), *The Renaissance and Reformation in Scotland* (Edinburgh, 1983). [71] *RPC* xiv. 80–2, 105–7.

for an already hard-pressed comptroller. A variant of this was to divert other officers' expenditure towards the household, as when Adam Erskine, collector general, was charged to supply it in 1583, presumably at the expense of ministers' stipends.[72]

The second approach was to force the comptroller or other officers to undertake to supply the household for a specified period. John Seton of Barns, comptroller, and Robert Douglas, collector general, made such an undertaking in 1588, as did David Seton of Parbroath, comptroller, in 1592. But there were limits to what this could achieve. Sir George Home of Wedderburn, comptroller in June 1598, was forced to undertake to furnish the household from his revenues, giving this priority over payment of creditors. In February 1599 this came badly unstuck: under pressure to meet impossible obligations, Home absconded.[73] The farcical spectacle of a minister of the crown hiding from his master—and his creditors—shows how desperate the crisis had become.

A report on the household in 1591 recommended that all existing debts should be divided into old and new, so that those who were currently 'prime furnessouris' could be paid—while longer-standing creditors would have to wait. 'Furnessouris' made allowance for the crown's well-known habits by charging higher prices: the report remarked on the need to avoid having to buy supplies 'at darrer prices nor the commoun mercatt for want of reddy silver'.[74]

The nature of 'reddy silver' was itself in flux: the Scottish coinage of this period suffered a dizzying plummet in value, as a result of debasement undertaken largely in response to fiscal crisis.[75] It is true that inflation was a European phenomenon, and that some was caused by other changes such as population growth. Some Scottish inflation may have been imported: the government occasionally tried to argue that finer coins were leaking abroad, which may not have been entirely false in the late 1570s when debasement had just hit the French coinage.[76] But at a time when the

[72] NAS, treasurer's accounts, 1582–3, E21/63, fo. 126ʳ.

[73] NLS, 'Concernyng the chekker and the kingis rentis', Adv. MS 34.2.17, fos. 116ᵛ–118ʳ, 12ᵛ–13ʳ; *APS* iv. 166; *RPC* v. 525–6, 530–1, 550–1.

[74] NLS, 'Concernyng the chekker and the kingis rentis', Adv. MS 34.2.17, fo. 138r.

[75] C. E. Challis, 'Debasement: The Scottish experience in the fifteenth and sixteenth centuries', in D. M. Metcalf (ed.), *Coinage in Medieval Scotland, 1100–1600* (British Archaeological Reports, no. 45, 1977), 171 and *passim*.

[76] J. H. M. Salmon, *Society in Crisis: France in the Sixteenth Century* (London, 1975), 224–5.

Scottish currency eventually lost two-thirds of its value against the English, most inflation clearly had its roots in the government's desire to rake off quick profits from the mint.

This is not to blame the policy-makers. When, in 1572, towards the end of the civil war, the king's party were faced with troops to pay, debts of £30,000, and 'na money to be had . . . except only be the cunychouse', what could they do? Various rates of alloy were suggested, and the 'bassest' was inevitably adopted.[77] That was war, but even in peacetime the government could never escape, from about 1573 on, from the need to debase the coinage. The master of the mint became effectively another of the crown's financial officers, with the mint accounts recording their own independent (very miscellaneous) discharge—and, inevitably, their own super-expenses.[78] The story of the mint, indeed, epitomizes the way in which short-term expedients increasingly became a way of life for a semi-bankrupt state. The king's own view, in *Basilicon Doron*, is instructive: a fine coinage is desirable, he writes, because one day you might want to debase it.[79]

Life was commonly difficult and dangerous for state financial officers. In France they might easily end up on the scaffold, no doubt *pour encourager les autres*.[80] This was not a Scottish habit, though there was a shadowy plot early in 1580 to charge Sir William Murray of Tullibardine, comptroller, and Adam Erskine, collector general, with 'sudden reckonings' that might have led to their execution.[81] The main threat to Scottish officers was to their purses. In 1587, the treasurer was ordered not to pay out more than £20,000 a year, or no *supersedere* would be granted to protect him from his creditors. The discharge for 1587–8 turned out to be a worrying £23,821.[82] In 1601, the former treasurer Walter Stewart, commendator of Blantyre, had to accept an arrangement

[77] BL., John Acheson, 'Anent cunyie, ane ample discourse' (*c.* 1581), Add. MS 33531, fos. 251ʳ–258ᵛ. For the text of the statute, which is not in *APS*, see R. W. Cochran-Patrick (ed.), *Records of the Coinage of Scotland*, 2 vols. (Edinburgh, 1876), i, pp. cxlv–cxlvi.

[78] Challis, 'Debasement', 190; NAS, mint accounts, 1582–1615, E101/2.

[79] James VI, *Basilicon Doron*, in *Political Writings*, 30.

[80] R. Doucet, *Les Institutions de la France au XVIᵉ siècle*, 2 vols. (Paris, 1948), i. 175; Salmon, *Society in Crisis*, 75.

[81] Bowes to Burghley and Walsingham, 10 May 1580, *CSP Scot.* v. 418. In Aug. 1580, Murray had substitutes appointed for him on health grounds: *RSS* vii. 2470.

[82] *APS* iii. 456, c. 54, para. 1; NAS, treasurer's accounts, 1587–8, E21/66, fo. 115ʳ. The accumulated deficit at this point was £52,996.

for repayment of his superexpenses, incurred between 1596 and 1599, that would have left him still out of pocket in 1606.[83] Such examples were by no means exceptional; Home of Wedderburn could testify that much worse could happen.

If serving an insolvent and unreliable crown was full of tribulations, why did financial officers not resign? Sir Robert Melville of Murdochcairnie wanted to continue as treasurer depute in 1596 even when superexpended by £35,656.[84] The reason is that though there seemed no end to his mounting debts, he had a wolf by the ears and feared to let go. While he was in post, the king had to protect him more or less; but if he relinquished control of his sources of revenue, manifestly inadequate though these were to cover his current expenditure, he ran the risk of being flung to his creditors to be devoured. After he was forced out by the Octavians, he did receive some reduction in his debt: the king promised to pay him a derisory 2,000 merks, and his successor, Walter Stewart, paid him £3,333. More importantly, some of his debts to Robert Jowsie were transferred to the king himself (which cannot have been good news for Jowsie), and Melville ended up owing a mere £23,447. He also obtained an act of parliament the next year protecting him from his creditors, so it was they rather than he who suffered in the short run. He was a loser again in 1601, however, when the exchequer unilaterally cut £3,333 from the current treasurer's liabilities, and numerous creditors had portions of their debts repudiated. Melville lost £700, the biggest single sum from this dubious operation.[85]

Melville could be thankful that he was not ruined. The story of John Acheson, master of the mint, is a sad one that has been well told by Athol Murray. He took on some of Gowrie's treasury debts in the late 1570s when the mint was making large profits, only to find himself still responsible for these obligations after he had been removed from office and the income that went with it; he was warded for debt in 1581. He was promised action to recover the debts in 1587, but his heirs in 1594 were still unable to sue Gowrie's heirs: the actions of Gowrie's creditors were still

[83] *RPC* vi. 542–3.
[84] NAS, treasurer's accounts, 1593–6, E21/70, fo. 82^v; Nicolson to Bowes, 7 Jan. 1596, *CSP Scot.* xii. 112–13.
[85] NAS, treasurer's accounts, 1592–3, E21/69, fo. 227^r; 1593–6, E21/70, fos. 82^v, 198^v; *APS* iv. 147, c. 50; NAS, treasurer's accounts, 1600–1, E21/74, fos. 138^r–139^r.

suspended, so parliament suspended the actions of Acheson's creditors too.[86] Another financial entrepreneur who ended up in gaol was Robert Jowsie: while in London in 1599 he fell a victim to the king's English creditors. Thomas Foulis was blamed for failing to rescue him, but he himself was as much a victim of the fiscal system as his unfortunate partner.[87]

Foulis and Jowsie were capitalists whose aim, in providing financial services to the crown, was to make profits. But the main reason why most financial officers continued willing to serve an insolvent crown was that the reward, traditionally, was not monetary profit but political power. Without the treasurer or comptroller 'myght noe man gete no goodenes of the king', complained Lindsay's Poor Man.[88] And political power brought favourable opportunities to acquire property for themselves, their kin, and friends. The gifts and hospitality which the burgh of Ayr, for instance, regularly had to offer to the officers of state, testify to their influence.[89] Whether they would be protected after leaving office was essentially a political question: it depended how much they were still worth to those in power. One financial officer who has been studied in detail is Robert Barton, treasurer and comptroller in the 1520s. He left office in 1530–1 superexpended by £6,780; probably less than half of this was paid by the crown, and he narrowly escaped imprisonment at one point, but his office had helped him to acquire a landed estate, and he received favoured treatment over a revocation of crown lands.[90] Melville of Murdochcairnie received various grants and favours both during and after his period of office, ending with a peerage—even though he spent most of the 1610s at the horn for non-payment of a debt he had contracted in office.[91] These political rewards were less common for the newer financial entrepreneurs: although they moved in the inmost circles of government, it is hard to see Foulis and Jowsie as politicians,

[86] Murray, 'Treasury administration', pp. xxx–xxxi; *APS* iii. 495, c. 102; iv. 83, c. 67.
[87] James Elphinstone to Sir Robert Cecil, 28 Feb. 1599, and Cecil to Elphinstone, 13 Apr. 1599, *CSP Scot.* xiii, I. 410–11, 445–6.
[88] Lindsay, 'Thrie estaitis', in *Works*, ii. 5.
[89] *Ayr Accounts*, 141, 152, and *passim*.
[90] W. S. Reid, *Skipper from Leith: The History of Robert Barton of Over Barnton* (Philadelphia, 1962), ch. 13; Murray, 'Financing the royal household', 52.
[91] W. Fraser, *The Melvilles, Earls of Melville, and the Leslies, Earls of Leven*, 3 vols. (Edinburgh, 1890), i. 114; iii. 147; J. B. Paul (ed.), *The Scots Peerage*, 9 vols. (Edinburgh, 1904–14), vi. 98; *RPC* xi. 272–3.

which is perhaps why their paths and those of the Octavians rarely crossed.

It was asked earlier why financial officers did not resign. Perhaps what is most remarkable is that, despite the rewards of office, some did. The earl of Cassillis is a case in point. He agreed to replace Walter Stewart as treasurer in April 1599, but resigned almost immediately on hearing that his appointment had been engineered to mulct him of his wealth—or rather, that of his wife, Jean Fleming, Lady Thirlestane. Unfortunately he had already entered into bonds for payment of some of Stewart's obligations, and although he rushed to the court of session it seems that his abortive appointment left him considerably worse off. His successor, the master of Elphinstone, learned from the experience, refusing to take on any past debts with the office. The clumsiness of Cassillis's treatment left the king with no choice but to accept this.[92]

In times of crisis, then, financial officers and entrepreneurs were decoy ducks. They had been given impressive-looking powers and sources of income in order to make them convincing conduits through which the money, goods, and services of others could be channelled to the crown without the latter being burdened with payment immediately, if at all. These suppliers' normal remedy was to sue the financial officer with whom they had contracted, but all too often the officers would receive protection from their creditors.[93] The Cassillis episode was just a more squalid version of this approach. Equally squalid, perhaps, was the forfeiture of the third earl of Gowrie in 1600. The king owed Gowrie a vast sum dating back to his father's treasurership in the early 1580s—the figure of £48,063 was mentioned in 1594.[94] Forfeiture might have been considered to wipe this out. But Gowrie also owed the same sum to his own creditors; would the crown, in escheating his property, also take on his debts? The legal position was uncertain. The first earl had been forfeited in 1584, and his debts had clearly still been extant on the restoration of his heirs. But the 1600 parliament

---

[92] NLS, 'Historie of the Kennedyis', Adv. MS 33.3.28, pp. 92–3; *RPC* v. 548–50; Nicolson to Cecil, 10 Apr. 1599, and advices from Scotland, 8 June 1599, *CSP Scot.* xiii, I. 444, 496; Paul (ed.), *Scots Peerage*, ii. 476.

[93] This procedure seems to have emerged in 1581: Murray, 'Treasury administration', p. xlix. Examples can be found of *supersederes* of such debts being granted by the privy council, the exchequer, the court of session, and parliament: *RPC* iii. 340; *ER* xxii. 162; *Acts of Sederunt*, 33; *APS* iv. 147, c. 50.

[94] *Acts of Sederunt*, 21.

favoured only two of Gowrie's creditors, and not from the first earl's treasurership.[95] It looks as though, having sheltered ingloriously behind Gowrie for two decades, the crown was finally able to disown these ancient debts.

This discussion of crisis management has focused on the 1590s, because the crisis was then at its most serious. There were few really serious fiscal problems in the 1560s or even 1570s. The civil war of 1570–3 did not help, but it seems not to have created a long-term problem for the future, except perhaps in the currency debasement to which the king's party resorted after 1571. In the 1580s, we get the first signs of a state unable to pay its way, with a tendency to run out of money without warning; in the 1590s this became worse. Some policy-makers, particularly Maitland and later the Octavians, tried to cope by reducing expenditure, but after the removal of the latter in June 1598 this option was no longer available. The five years between 1598 and 1603 were thus the most fertile of any for new attempts to raise revenue—most of which failed, and all of which had serious political costs.

But after 1603, the fiscal position of the Scottish state was transformed by the departure of the royal court to England—borrowing a final 10,000 merks from the burgh of Edinburgh to pay for its journey.[96] The Scottish revenues no longer had to bear the court's cost; royal money was not sent south, and the household (apart from a skeleton staff retained in Scotland) was paid for entirely by the English. The king also obtained English resources to offer to Scottish nobles seeking patronage.[97]

There was one point at which Scottish fiscal autonomy might have been subverted. One of the stated reasons for the reimposition of Anglo-Scottish customs in 1611 was that, once the Scottish treasury had been restored to health with an infusion of customs revenue, it might 'supplie his majesties treasur and coffers in England yeerlie with the summe of 3000 libb. sterling' (£36,000 Scots). But later that year, when the council were discussing how

---

[95] *APS* iv. 245, c. 47. The question was not a straightforward one, as appears from later uncertainty about the crown's responsibility for the debts of the earl of Orkney, forfeited in 1615: council to James, 12 Dec. 1621, *Melros Papers*, ii. 439–40.

[96] *Edin. Recs.* vi. 3; cf. ibid. 23, 27, for attempts to obtain repayment in 1606 and 1607.

[97] Cf. a list of English gifts to Scotsmen between 1603 and 1610, totalling (in sterling) £10,614 annually in pensions, £88,280 in cash, and £133,100 in rights to old crown debts: BL, papers of Sir Julius Caesar, Add. MS 12497, fos. 155ʳ–156ᵛ.

to create a revenue surplus, noting that the king 'expectit that he suld haif sum money over', John Preston of Fentonbarns, lord president, commented: 'I wold thai[r] wer money, but it must not go to Ingland'. Preston's view prevailed; there were no regular transfers of money between the Scottish and English treasuries in the early seventeenth century.[98]

There were three results of all this for the Scottish finances. One result was that the state could now manage occasional large-scale operations successfully—the main one being the king's visit in 1617, which cost the treasury over £200,000. (James is sometimes criticized for failing to keep his promise to return to Scotland every three years, but from a fiscal point of view it was probably just as well he did not.) The visit was financed ultimately from taxation, but large amounts had to be borrowed, and they were repaid on time.[99] A second result was that payments to nobles and courtiers expanded—a development pregnant with political consequences.[100] The third result was that James could now pay some of his old debts; and this was a leading fiscal theme of the doing-nicely-thank-you years from about 1605 to 1620.

Several of these themes emerge in a letter to the king by Sir Gideon Murray of Elibank, the treasurer depute whose financial wizardry lay behind the successful supplying of the 1617 visit. In 1615 he tried to block a royal precept to pay £30,000 to the courtier earl of Abercorn:

Till the beginning of June the cofferis wer emptie, att whiche tyme the Witsonday terme brocht with it, of fieis, pensiones, and preceptis, a burding of thriescoir and tuelf thowsand poundis and abone, whiche hes keiped and will still keipe the cofferis emptie for a long tyme.

The 'pensiones, and preceptis'—regular and occasional gifts to courtiers—were by now the most prominent item of royal expenditure, and clearly the appetites of the likes of Abercorn might

[98] BL, copies of documents relating to the revenues of Scotland, Add. MS 24275, fo. 9^{r-v}; John Spottiswoode to [Sir James Sempill of Beltrees], 12 Oct. 1611, *Eccles. Letters*, i. 281–2.

[99] W. A. McNeill and P. G. B. McNeill, 'The Scottish progress of James VI, 1617', *SHR* 75 (1996), 38–51, at pp. 47–50. This was an Anglo-Scottish operation (most of the king's travelling was in England), and one aspect of this was a subvention to Scotland from the English exchequer of £3,000 sterling (£36,000 Scots): NAS, comptroller's accounts, 1616–17, E24/35, fo. 26^r.

[100] J. Goodare, 'Scottish politics in the reign of James VI', in id. and Lynch (eds.), *Reign of James VI*.

worry any financial officer. But Murray also noted 'the gud happ I have had to pay your majesteis debtis'. Things were not really that serious; Abercorn got his £30,000 in the end.[101] However, one of the reasons for this was that the payment of the king's debts had been belated and partial; it is worth looking at this further.

The biggest single debt was that to Thomas Foulis. It had been contracted between 1590 and 1598; about half of it was repaid between 1607 and 1611 from the proceeds of the tax of 1606. This was an unusually popular tax with one of the main taxpayers, the burgh of Edinburgh, 'becaus we wnderstude it was your majesties will [that it] was sett for outtreding of your majesties debts'.[102] Payments from this revenue silenced the most pressing of Foulis's creditors, and the remaining ones were less of a priority. So the flow of money to Foulis dried up during 1611. A few final crumbs were thrown in his direction in the early 1620s, but much of the debt was never repaid by the crown. On the other hand, the crown had allowed him to gain control of the Leadhills lead mine, which he had developed and made profitable; if he had to repay many of the royal creditors from the profits, that was the way things often were for those connected with the finances of James VI.[103] Similarly, the absconding comptroller, Sir George Home of Wedderburn, was left in 1604 with debts of £26,331, plus £9,000 interest. His son was still trying to extract repayment in 1633, as was his grandson in 1663.[104] Many people in early modern Europe made fortunes from their state's finances, but Scotland in the 1590s had been a particularly bad place and time to try to do so.

The Scottish state was not completely immune to fiscal crisis even after 1603. There was only one such crisis between then and 1625, but even one crisis displays the limits to the fiscal stability of the state; the issues it raises may form a suitable coda to this chapter. It took place in 1620–1, as part of the general *economic* crisis of the period.[105] From July 1620 there was a temporary freeze

---

[101] NLS, Murray to James, 15 July 1615, Denmylne MSS, Adv. MS 33.1.1, vol. viii, no. 32; *RPC* x. 380–1.

[102] H. James (ed.), *Facsimiles of National Manuscripts of Scotland*, 3 vols. (Southampton, 1868–71), iii, no. 86.

[103] For the Foulis debt, see Goodare, 'Thomas Foulis'.

[104] *RPC* vi. 598; HMC, *Report on the Manuscripts of Colonel David Milne Home* (London, 1902), 106.

[105] Cf. C. P. Kindleberger, 'The economic crisis of 1619 to 1623', *Journal of Economic History*, 51 (1991), 149–75, at pp. 161–3.

on the payment of pensions, which nominally continued until late
1621. In practice things were more complicated, because pensions
were not always paid regularly anyway, and because there was a
stream of exceptions to the freeze. In March 1621 the crisis
worsened, with the customs badly hit by the 'decay of the trade
and handling', and with landlords also suffering from low grain
prices.[106] But the pensions freeze seems to have carried the
finances through—not surprisingly, when they formed such a large
proportion of Scottish expenditure.

Relief arrived early in 1622, in the form of an instalment of the
new parliamentary tax voted in 1621. There had been a gap in the
collection of parliamentary taxation since 1618, and from then on
the government did its best to ensure that there would not be
another. The conventions of estates of 1625 and 1630, and the parliament of 1633, were all called to vote new taxes more or less at
the moment when the previous taxes were ending. With money
flowing in to the crown from parliament, and flowing out again to
courtiers, the pattern of financial relationships between the Scottish state and the political nation was more sharply drawn in the
latter years of James VI than it had been for a long time before.

This chapter can be concluded, and the next one introduced,
by briefly noting the biggest event that did not happen in early
seventeenth-century Scotland. One reason for the unwonted stability of the Scottish state's finances between 1603 and 1625 was
that it never had to fight a war. No doubt this was a good thing for
other reasons besides the treasurer's peace of mind, but there is
little doubt that serious warfare would have placed intolerable
strains on the fiscal system. Why this was so, we shall now see.

---

[106] HMC, *Mar & Kellie*, i. 90–5, 99–103, 106; council to James, 29 Mar. 1621,
Melros Papers, ii. 396–7.

5

Warfare

In respect the kings of Scotland did not so abound in treasure and money to take up an armie under pay, as the kings of England did; therefore was the Scottish army wont to be raysed onely by proclamation, upon the penaltie of their breach of alleageance; so as they were all forced to come to the warre like snailes who carry their house about with them; every nobleman and gentleman bringing with him their tents, money, provision for their house, victuals of all sorts, and all other necessaries, the king supplying them of nothing.[1]

If Scotland's most notable military innovator, Robert Bruce, could have reviewed the royal armies of the early sixteenth century, he would have seen much that was familiar to him. An army of massed infantry wielding pikes, supported by heavily armoured cavalrymen, had fought at Bannockburn (1314) much as it did later, with less success, at Flodden (1513), Solway Moss (1542), and Pinkie (1547). The official musters known as wapinshawings had been known equally well in Bruce's time. And he would have nodded understandingly at the assumption of early sixteenth-century Scots that the army mustered in this way would be likely to find its theatre of war in the Borders and its foes in the English. Warfare treated as large-scale raiding of England was more than familiar to the king who used it to vindicate the independence regained at Bannockburn.[2]

He would also have noticed a few changes. There were now some firearms field and siege artillery, and handguns—which could be impressive, though they hardly dominated the battlefield.[3]

---

[1] James VI & I, speech to parliament, 1607, in *Political Writings*, 177.

[2] G. W. S. Barrow, *Robert Bruce and the Community of the Realm of Scotland* (3rd edn., Edinburgh, 1988), 66, 208–9, 236–7; A. Grant, *Independence and Nationhood: Scotland, 1306–1469* (London, 1984), 154–6.

[3] The Scottish army at Pinkie (1547) had hardly any handguns: D. H. Caldwell, 'The battle of Pinkie', in N. Macdougall (ed.), *Scotland and War, AD 79–1918* (Edinburgh, 1991), 74.

Discussion with James IV would have impressed upon him the growing significance of seapower, though Scottish efforts at sea ceased with James's death. In 1540, he would have been surprised at the statute 'that the army of Scotland be unhorsit except greit baronis'; the act's rationale was horses' destructiveness to crops, but it may also have reflected the general European trend away from cavalry in the previous half-century.[4] However, the traditional Scottish army had always had fewer cavalry than most, since Scottish agriculture was ill suited to meet heavy warhorses' massive demands for winter fodder.

Nevertheless, continuity rather than change would have been paramount. Above all, Bruce would have noticed little change in the way that the army was recruited, organized, and supplied. The early sixteenth-century army was indeed, as James VI described it, an unpaid mass levy. Bruce had won his victories with just such a force. But James, in 1607, spoke of it in the past tense. This may have been a little premature, but the sixty years before his speech had seen more changes in the way that the state's military capacity was deployed than the previous two hundred. It will be the primary task of this chapter to outline the changes that took place between about 1547 and 1601. In that period, the state became less willing to rely on the autonomous, unpaid forces of private lords, and sought to construct other forms of war-making. The focus will be on military structures, and there will be no effort to narrate the course of each military operation. The remainder of the chapter will deal with the period after 1601, when private war-making was decaying rapidly and there was scope for more innovations.

The changes began immediately after Pinkie. The Scots had reacted to their defeat at Falkirk in 1298 by turning to guerrilla warfare; in 1548 they turned instead to French assistance. That did not last, and in 1560 the Scots found themselves in the almost unprecedented possession of a government aligned with England. The result was to close off the sole avenue of external war for the Scottish state, which had neither to fight nor to mobilize for external war during the period covered by this book. Universal peace reigned.

Or did it? Despite the low-pressure military system made

---

[4] *APS* ii. 362, c. 22; J. R. Hale, *War and Society in Renaissance Europe, 1450–1620* (London, 1985), 47.

possible by the absence of external threats, there still remained a number of fields where Scots could kill and be killed to further the state's political ends. This was largely because they could also kill and be killed for many other reasons. The state lacked monopoly control of political violence for most of our period, when blood-feud was recognized as a legitimate means of settling disputes among the political elite. This created a structural instability in the state, since private feuds might escalate into small regional wars, and these in turn into rebellions against the state.[5] On the other hand, the interpenetration of private and public violence might work to benefit the state, when it could call on other lords to suppress dissident ones. Private violence may have been more common than public violence, but there was a continuum between the two. Moreover, public violence was usually deployed to try to suppress—and in our period to supplant—the private violence which it closely resembled.

The government would resort to violence only if provoked, of course. Depending on the level of provocation, there were different levels of response. The most basic was a simple response in kind: to encourage the armed following of a friendly magnate to batter the armed following of a dissident magnate. This had been going on for centuries, and could amount to little more than the crown betting on the winner in a regional conflict. Royal backing for such magnates sometimes conferred little advantage. The government was still sanctioning private warfare in 1594, when the earl of Argyll was sent against the rebel Catholic earls, meeting their forces at the battle of Glenlivet. Argyll lost. Far from lengthening the list of crimes for which the rebels had to answer, the battle helped to ensure that they were leniently treated in the eventual settlement, while Argyll, the crown's loyal servant, languished in disfavour.[6]

There is a sense in which almost all warfare in sixteenth-century Scotland was equally private. The crown did not expect to create an army from its own resources. It did have much the largest collection of artillery, as we shall see. There was also a royal

[5] As when the bitter Maxwell–Johnstone feud became by degrees a Maxwell rebellion against the crown in the 1580s: K. M. Brown, 'The making of a *politique*: The Counter Reformation and the regional politics of John, eighth Lord Maxwell', *SHR* 66 (1987), 152–75, at pp. 156–7.

[6] Roger Ashton to Bowes, 3 Dec. 1594, 29–30 Jan. 1595, *CSP Scot.* xi. 487, 523.

collection of infantry weapons, but for these the crown largely relied on weapons possessed by private individuals, and routinely stockpiled by burghs, magnates, and lairds. Still less could the crown raise men for its armies without the lords' cooperation: when in 1596 the 'haill gentilmen and frie halderis within the sherefdome of Edinburgh' and some other sheriffdoms were absent from the host, the absence of their tenants was taken for granted.[7] The ability of lords to raise private armies, both authorized and unauthorized, continued to manifest itself almost to the very end of the sixteenth century.

When lords' followings came together under royal authority, they formed a body known to medieval historians as the 'common army', an entity going back to pre-feudal times—though the continuities in military service between David I (1124–53) and Robert I (1306–29) are less germane to the present purpose than those between Robert I and James VI.[8] The 'common army', though a step up from the following of the individual lord, was still essentially a loose collection of lords' followings. It was described in 1599 as 'ane unskilfull and unarmed multitude'.[9]

Who served in the army? This question can best be pursued at local level. Lord Wharton, the English commander occupying Galloway in 1547, compiled a list of the local landlords and the fighting men they claimed to be able to raise. Dumfriesshire produced 46 names of lords (mostly lairds, some 'surname' groups, and one or two burghs), who claimed to lead a total of 5,970 men. The stewartry of Kirkcudbright had 7 lords and 771 men.[10] There was no information on how these men were to be equipped, but if two out of Scotland's two dozen shires could raise well over six thousand men, the Scottish common army was potentially very numerous.

Wharton's survey was only a paper exercise, raising the question of how much of the potential fighting strength could actually be mustered. The roll of the 'Valpynschavene of Conynghame', held in Irvine in 1532, listed all the lands in the bailiary from which service was due, and all from which it was received. There were

[7] NAS, treasurer's accounts, 1596–7, E21/71, fos. 73ᵛ–74ʳ.

[8] G. W. S. Barrow, *The Anglo-Norman Era in Scottish History* (Oxford, 1980), 161–8.

[9] *APS* iv. 188.

[10] H. Maxwell, *A History of Dumfries and Galloway* (Edinburgh, 1896), 178–80. Some prominent names were missing from the list, including Lord Maxwell and the laird of Johnstone, so these figures could be underestimates.

apparently 71 estates—more than in Galloway. But 47 estates were noted as absent; 17 attended but were not equipped for war ('nocht bodin'); only three were equipped, and two of those may have been individuals rather than lairds with followers.[11] The fighting strength of Cunningham, it seems, might be counted not in thousands but in tens.

According to Sir David Lindsay, the 'husbandmen and commons' went into battle 'formest in the front'. Armies seem to have been composed of the more prosperous peasants, led by their feudal superiors. Poverty bred no warriors: a government commission in 1567 worried that evictions were making people 'unhable to serve in the kingis weris'. In the Highlands, 'thame that labours the ground are commandit to remane at hame'. A predominance of richer peasants was assumed by the legislation codifying weapons requirements: in 1540 no service was envisaged from anyone poorer than a 'yeman'. 'Na pur man' (with under 20 merks in goods) was to serve on expeditions into England, by a law of 1456. In 1600 it was complained that recruits were 'for the maist pairt puir' and unable to equip themselves.[12]

The most important single document illuminating these issues at local level is the roll of the wapinshawing of the sheriffdom of Moray, mustered at the cairn of Kilboyack on 2 February 1596.[13] Like the Cunningham wapinshawing, this was a real exercise. The roll provides no evidence on absenteeism, but there is a great deal of detail on who was present, how they were recruited, and how they were equipped.

The first point shown by the roll is that men were mustered under their landlords' leadership. This was the assumption both in the Galloway survey and in the Cunningham wapinshawing too. Mustering by lords was the only kind of mustering there was, whether the service was private (as it presumably was in Wharton's Galloway survey: he wanted his six thousand men to fight not for the Scottish state but against it) or public.

The 900-odd men present in Moray had come in 11 groups: 8

[11] W. Fraser, *Memorials of the Montgomeries, Earls of Eglinton*, 2 vols. (Edinburgh, 1859), ii. 118–20. Four estates were not noted either present or absent. For the national order to hold this wapinshawing, see *ADCP*, 382.

[12] Lindsay, 'Thrie estaitis', in *Works*, ii. 247; *APS* iii. 45; W. F. Skene, *Celtic Scotland*, 3 vols. (2nd edn., Edinburgh, 1886–90), iii. 429; *APS* ii. 362–3, c. 23; 45, c. 3; *RPC* vi. 130–1.

[13] *RPC* xiv. 376–80.

headed by lairds, one by the bailie of the earldom of Moray, one by the bailie of the lordship of Urquhart, and one by the bailie of the barony of Kinloss which had been feued to a number of small men. Lairds came on horseback; they brought followings typically described as their 'heill kynne, freindis, and servandis' or as the 'men, tennentis, and inhabitantis of [their] landis'. A few of these followers were fully armed horsemen, but most were footmen with various levels of equipment—and apparently socially graded too.

Thus, John Grant of Freuchie brought 500 men, more than half the total present, describing 300 of them as 'fensabill men according to the custowme of his landis to defend within the cuntray and the schyris heirabut'. The remainder were clearly not expected to fight at all. But of the 300 'fensabill men', only 80 were equipped 'to pas to the kingis wyris'; half of these were equipped with jack (reinforced jacket) and two-handed sword, and half with bow, sword, and target 'according to the hiland custowme'. The 'custowme of his landis' thus divided the remaining 420, seemingly with some precision, into 220 with few weapons (who were expected to fight for the laird locally, but not for the king elsewhere) and 200 with even fewer weapons or perhaps none (who would do no fighting). Internal, local wars—bloodfeuds—and external, national wars—'the kingis wyris'—were differentiated.

Similarly Archibald Douglas of Pendricht brought 21 scantily equipped footmen—typically they had 'ane swirde, but [i.e. without] armour'—who would have been expected to fight, except that some were 'onabill of thair bodeis, and in extreme povartie'. This poverty seems only to have been relative, since he brought a further 16 who were non-combatants of lower social status: 'cotterris . . . nocht meit to beir armur, being onabill of thair bodeis'. There are clear signs in all this of a social level below which men were not expected to fight—because they could not afford weapons—nor encouraged to do so—because it was 'nocht meit'. And yet this lowest class was also the largest at the muster. Discounting the lairds themselves, the 900-odd men present were made up of 5 per cent horsemen, 18 per cent armed footmen, 34 per cent unarmed or lightly armed footmen, and 42 per cent non-combatants.

There are two possible explanations for the presence of these non-combatants. One is that an army needed support personnel. The Regent Moray's army in his expedition to the south-west in

1568 had 5,000 fighting men and 3,000 'boyes and yonge men that kept horses'—a similar proportion of non-combatants to the 1596 wapinshawing. But 4,000 of the regent's fighting men were 'horsemen in armour', and there were also 4,000 'cariage horses with victuallis'.[14] With so few horses at the 1596 muster (under 50 among 900 men), there would have been little for 'boyes and yonge men' to do. Nor were the non-combatants described as 'boyes and yonge men'. The second possible explanation is that some lords mustered their tenants willy-nilly, feeling that if they could not bring fighting men, then men who could not fight were still better than nothing. On the other hand, not all lords did this. David Brodie of that Ilk probably had more adult male dependants than the six he came with, for three of these were horsemen. The bailie of the earldom of Moray brought 160 men: 20 were horsemen, but 'the rest bot powir nakit men for the meist pairt', and these can hardly have been all the fighting men of the earldom.

The weapons of the earl's horsemen were not detailed, but there was no suggestion that they had firearms.[15] The weapons held by the best-equipped men, including the lairds themselves, were usually listed individually; they included only nine firearms. It is overwhelmingly clear from the roll—and the same conclusion was drawn at the time—that the Scottish common army was hopelessly ill-equipped by the standards of professional Continental armies. The wapinshawing of 1596 had been summoned as part of the preparations to resist a threatened Spanish invasion; it is just as well that the invasion never came.

What of those lords who were not at the cairn of Kilboyack at all? Only eleven groups were recorded, whereas the Cunningham wapinshawing had anticipated attendance from seventy-one. The Moray roll was silent on absenteeism, but the privy council complained immediately afterwards about 'a grite noumer of personis within everie sherefdome being absent'.[16] It is hard to avoid the impression that the lords who came did so, not because they were

---

[14] P. H. Brown (ed.), *Scotland before 1700 from Contemporary Documents* (Edinburgh, 1893), 205–6.

[15] During the bonny earl of Moray's feud with the earl of Huntly in 1591, his agent had ordered some hagbuts, but perhaps they did not arrive. Many of those at the cairn had taken part in the feud on one side or another, and one wonders how they remembered it: K. M. Brown, *Bloodfeud in Scotland, 1573–1625* (Edinburgh, 1986), 155.

[16] *RPC* v. 266.

obliged to, but because they wanted to. For their dependants, of course, it may have been different.

These regional figures can be used to construct national ones. The population had increased a good deal between the sixteenth century and Webster's pioneering census in 1755, but its distribution had probably changed less. So it is possible to use the regional *proportions* given by Webster to scale up our regional figures to the whole of Scotland. For the Galloway survey, this exercise gives a notional Scottish army of 140,000—quite close to the notional 100,000 suggested as a mid-sixteenth-century maximum by David Caldwell. However, as he points out, this is a figure for all able-bodied men. The largest army actually assembled, that for the Pinkie campaign of 1547, probably numbered about 22,000 or 23,000.[17] And if the political will to fight slackened, the musters would be less impressive to the warmongers. Scaling up the Cunningham wapinshawing produces a notional national army of about 1,000—which may indeed be about right for some of the more modest royal armies of the sixteenth century. Often only a small and erratic number of lords were willing to turn themselves and their tenants out for war. No doubt many would have personal incentives to do so—perhaps a desire to stand well with the king, or a feud with a member of the opposition. The common army was a congeries of individuals who served for very uncommon reasons.

One incentive for service that the government was patently unable to promise, in this traditional, decentralized, magnate-ridden army, was pay. The major European states had long been helplessly addicted to mercenary war-making, in which an ever-increasing dose was needed to gain the same result, and the side-effects—waste, rapine, even mutiny if pay failed to arrive—multiplied. The cost of the habit, too, proved disastrous, and was capable of bankrupting the greatest powers known. Fortunately, Scotland was not a great power, and although Scots travelled to

---

[17] *Scottish Population Statistics*, ed. J. G. Kyd (SHS, 1952); D. H. Caldwell, 'The use and effect of weapons: The Scottish experience', *Review of Scottish Culture*, 4 (1988), 53–62, at pp. 53–4; id., 'Pinkie', 73. The same exercise, when performed for the Moray wapinshawing, gives an improbably large notional army of 360,000. It can best be explained by suggesting either that Moray had a higher proportion of the Scottish population in 1596 than in 1755, or that some of those present (Grant of Freuchie being a likely possibility) had drawn some of their men from outside the sheriffdom. But it does suggest that there cannot have been substantial absenteeism at the wapinshawing.

fight overseas there was little possibility of establishing a standing army at home.

Inevitably, however, there were experiments with what some saw as a wonder drug, capable of curing all the political ills they knew— such as a potentially troublesome convention of estates at Holyrood in 1581. 'The utter gate of the Abbey Closse was keeped by Captain James Stewart, and some waged men . . . the nobilitie grudged to be thus controlled by him'.[18] Stewart, soon to become earl of Arran, and the nearest thing to a Francesco Sforza that Scotland produced, was the most successful of the mercenary captains who sometimes entered politics after a career of Continental soldiering. They attracted followings with experience of the same life, or aspirations to it. Contemporaries regarded their outlandish ways with horrified fascination. When Colonel William Stewart, captain of the royal guard, was offered the bribe of a 'velvet purse, with threttie foure-pund peeces of gold in it' by the commendator of Dunfermline, Stewart 'gave the 30 peeces to thrittie of the guard. Everie man bowed his peece, and caried it hanging at his knapskall or hatt all the way, as they came from Perth to Falkland; the purse was caried upon a speare point.'[19] The dark side of this lust for booty was shown in 1570, when Hamilton was sacked 'without commiseratioun or pitie' by mercenary troops—reportedly 'to pay the saidis horssmen and futemen thair wages with'.[20]

Apart from booty, what were these wages? In 1594, footmen were to be paid £8 per month and horsemen £24: similar to contemporary English rates of pay.[21] The proposed force—400 of each— would have bled the treasury white in no time. Dundee in 1588 gave pay of 40s. per month to 120 troops; this was only a quarter of the rate that the king proposed to pay, but it seems that the soldiers actually received it, while the royal troops did not.[22] When a full-scale field army was required, such elite forces would be only a nucleus, and the majority would be the 'common army' of lords'

[18] Calderwood, *History*, iii. 487.

[19] Ibid. 721–2.

[20] *Diurnal of Remarkable Occurrents That Have Passed Within the Kingdom of Scotland . . . Till the Year 1575*, ed. T. Thomson (Bannatyne Club, 1833), 192.

[21] Bowes to Christopher Sheperson, 17 Sept. 1594, *CSP Scot.* xi. 443; F. C. Dietz, *English Public Finance, 1558–1641* (2nd edn., London, 1964), 58. Wages for horsemen in the Borders were between about £9 and £17 per month in 1579: T. I. Rae, *The Administration of the Scottish Frontier, 1513–1603* (Edinburgh, 1966), 87.

[22] Dundee City Archive and Record Centre, Dundee council minutes, ii, p. 15.

conscripted followings.[23] One Border warden was promised 25 paid hagbutters (footmen with firearms), but was told that 'ye mon supplie the charge of horssmen be the service of the cuntrie [i.e. the 'common army'] and your feis and pensioun'.[24]

Even if unpaid, soldiers had to eat. Traditionally, they carried their food with them, or got followers to do so; their inability to purchase food on the way was a palpable handicap. Sir William Cecil noted in 1559 how 'the Scots of themselves, when they had a king of their own to aid them, never came into the field with more than fifteen days victual, neither could abide longer together, but were forced to return and change their numbers'.[25] There was a theoretical maximum of forty days for common army service, but even this was usually beyond the host's resources. The king in 1607 attempted to deny this: 'But neither is there any law prescribing precisely such a certaine number of dayes, nor yet is it without the limits of the kings power to keepe them together, as many more days as hee list.'[26] This was doubtful in theory, and wrong in practice. It is true that not all proclamations summoning the lieges in arms specified a period of service.[27] But explicit service for more than forty days is not recorded. Ian Rae's study of musters on the Borders shows that most summonses were for much less than forty days; twenty was the most common period.[28]

The number of days' service, and provisions brought, could be a matter of life or death, as the Regent Moray's expedition to the south-west in 1568 showed. The men were ordered to bring fifteen days' victuals. But on the eleventh day, 'there was a great hunger in the camp; for the Scottish pynte of wyne was at vii s. Scottyshe, and no breadde to be hadde. Some dyed for hunger in the campe.'[29] It was not an impressive performance from the man who would later be remembered as the 'Good Regent'.

Paid soldiers could buy their own food. Later in the century

[23] For the use of paid soldiers as a nucleus of the Border defences in 1482, see *APS* ii. 139–40, cc. 7–10.

[24] NAS, earl of Arran to Sir Thomas Kerr of Ferniehurst, 11 Feb. 1585, Lothian MSS, GD40/2/9, no. 75.

[25] *State Papers and Letters of Sir Ralph Sadler*, 3 vols., ed. A. Clifford (Edinburgh, 1809), i. 381.

[26] James VI & I, speech to parliament, 1607, in *Political Writings*, 177.

[27] For one that did not in 1589, see *Registrum Honoris de Morton*, 2 vols., ed. H. Cockburn (Bannatyne Club, 1853), i. 158–9.

[28] Rae, *Scottish Frontier*, 135.   [29] Brown (ed.), *Scotland before 1700*, 205.

there were signs that armies were using money. The one occasion when the Regent Morton was more keen than the Edinburgh magistrates on holding down bread prices in the town was when English troops were quartered there during the siege of the castle.[30] That was an English force, but a Scottish royal army, in Peebles in 1592, complained that it was no match for the 'indiscreit handling' it received from profiteering local burgesses supplying provisions. Having encouraged merchants to supply the army, there is no evidence that the Scottish authorities took the next step: arranging for their own deliveries.[31] Another aspect of armies' eating habits was illustrated in February 1602. The annually proclaimed Lenten fast was suspended in Dumfries, where the army was quartered; the doughty warriors (or at least their doughty leaders, who included the king) wanted meat.[32]

With the possible exception of the royal guard, Scotland's rulers were never allowed to become addicted to mercenary troops. Procedures to levy paid troops existed only in an *ad hoc* form, and there was no equivalent to the English system of lords lieutenant to coordinate recruitment.[33] They could use such troops when friendly lords and the common army were inadequate to the situation, but they did so sparingly, raising small forces to solve immediate problems and dispersing them when money ran out. Even this could be quite effective: no private lord, for instance, could match the few dozen professional soldiers periodically deployed in the Borders in the later 1570s.[34] By the 1590s, the dissident earls of Huntly and Bothwell had entered the mercenary game; but they were exceptional, not only in being the last private lords ever to challenge the crown directly, but in having access to foreign funds (Spanish and English respectively) to do so.[35] It was a game that the state could always win in the long run.

[30] Morton to council of Edinburgh, 2 May 1573, *CSP Scot.* iv. 556.
[31] NAS, treasurer's accounts (Leven & Melville), 1590–2, E22/8, fo. 180ᵛ. Cf. C. S. L. Davies, 'Provisions for armies, 1509–1550: A study in the effectiveness of early Tudor government', *Economic History Review*, 2nd ser. 17 (1964), 234–48, at pp. 234–5.
[32] NAS, treasurer's accounts, 1601–4, E21/76, fo. 115ʳ.
[33] C. G. Cruickshank, *Elizabeth's Army* (2nd edn., Oxford, 1966), 23. For an example, see W. Fraser, *The Annandale Family Book of the Johnstones, Earls and Marquises of Annandale*, 2 vols. (Edinburgh, 1894), ii. 11–12. Cf. Brown, 'Making of a *politique*', 157–8, for the context and (small) significance of this.
[34] G. R. Hewitt, *Scotland under Morton, 1572–1580* (Edinburgh, 1982), 134.
[35] Brown, *Bloodfeud*, 251; Melville, *Diary*, 315.

Once it had deployed friendly magnates, the common army, and mercenary troops against rebel forces, the Scottish government had played every card in its hand. It did, however, have a joker up its sleeve: English support. The English had been trying since the 1540s to establish a friendly regime in Scotland by force of arms; they had succeeded in 1560, and the potent arsenal at Berwick proclaimed that they were not resting on their laurels. On four more occasions an English force crossed the Border to shore up the 1560 settlement: in 1570 (twice), 1573, and 1588. In 1570 the English captured Home and Fast castles and garrisoned them until the 1573 settlement. In 1588, English siege guns from Carlisle helped to crush Lord Maxwell's rebellion.[36]

As well as being prepared for various levels of military mobilization, the crown tried to maintain a permanent military establishment. Royal castles abounded, and when they were as strong as Edinburgh, Blackness, Stirling, or Dumbarton they were a significant military presence.[37] No new castles were being built, and some of the existing ones had an unfortunate tendency to fall down. Edinburgh and Stirling Castles (which were also palaces) were kept in reasonably good repair. But even at Edinburgh, where the siege of 1573 had been followed by major repair works, it was reported ten years later that 'adjacent to the said new yett thair is twentie scoir of fwttis or thairby off the wall fallin downe', and 'upone the vest syde . . . the w[all] is fallin downe to the lenthe of fowrescoir of fwttis or thairby'.[38] The surviving accounts of the master of works record repair work mainly on palaces; the castles were not a priority.

The contents of castles—artillery and professional garrisons—were as important as their fabric. The new bronze cannon of the late fifteenth century were important both as siege and battlefield weapons, and their cost made them in effect a royal monopoly—helping to differentiate the military power of the crown from that of the magnates. Having imported its earliest cannon, the Scottish crown began to create the infrastructure to manufacture its own.

---

[36] R. Pollitt, 'The defeat of the Northern Rebellion and the shaping of Anglo-Scottish relations', *SHR* 64 (1985), 1–21, at pp. 9–12, 19; Moysie, *Memoirs*, 68.

[37] These four had their revenues guaranteed during the military-minded Arran regime in 1584: *APS* iii. 352, c. 9.

[38] *Accounts of the Masters of Works*, 2 vols., ed. H. M. Paton *et al.* (Edinburgh, 1957–) i. 310–11; Hewitt, *Scotland under Morton*, 147–8.

The cost was high, however, and Scotland dropped out of the gun-founding race in 1558.[39] Six field pieces were deployed against a rebel army in 1565, establishing the prestige of a genuinely royal army. On the other hand, the Regent Moray's expedition to the south-west in 1568 seems not to have used artillery much, if at all. Although it captured a dozen or so fortified houses, it did so by negotiation. The state was still participating in the traditions of kin-based private warfare, in which few of the leaders risked their lives, and the fighting would be ended by a compromise settlement.[40]

Still, the gunnery establishment was kept up. Though a small one, it was a constant drain on resources, unlike an army which was summoned only when needed.[41] However, there was no attempt to convert it into a garrison. Usually there were half a dozen gunners (occasionally only one), plus a handful of smiths and wrights.[42] This was not going to form the nucleus of a regular army, in the way that some states' garrisons came to do. Nothing in Scotland could compare with the five-hundred-strong English garrison at Berwick, to look no further.[43]

A higher priority was the royal guard. Mary established a per-manent guard early in her personal reign—the first such force for some decades.[44] Buchanan followed Aristotle in treating this guard, which he described as 'foreign mercenaries to overawe the citi-zens', as an acid test of a tyrant. He omitted to mention that Mary's guard consisted of 19 archers, all Scots. The pretext on which Buchanan said they were introduced, a 'vain show of courtly mag-nificence, and the custom of foreign kings', was probably the real reason. Foreign kings had certainly been setting a fashion for such guards in the late fifteenth and early sixteenth century. Scotland

---

[39] D. H. Caldwell, 'The royal Scottish gun-foundry in the sixteenth century', in A. O'Connor and D. V. Clarke (eds.), *From the Stone Age to the Forty-Five* (Edinburgh, 1983).

[40] Randolph to Cecil, 27 Aug. 1565, *CSP Scot.* ii. 198; Brown (ed.), *Scotland before 1700*, 201–6. The expedition did take artillery: *TA* xii. 130.

[41] Hale, *War and Society*, 46–8. In 1567 the queen's arsenal (housed in Edinburgh Castle) contained one double cannon, six single cannon, four culverins of various sizes (plus an English gross culverin 'auld and rottin'), and miscellaneous light artillery pieces: HMC, *Mar & Kellie*, ii. 21–7. There may also have been some cannon at Dunbar Castle. [42] *TA* xii. 13, 20; xiii. 125–6.

[43] On Berwick, see L. Boynton, *The Elizabethan Militia, 1558–1638* (London, 1967), 127. For the importance of garrisons see P. Contamine, *War in the Middle Ages*, trans. M. Jones (Oxford, 1984), 165.

[44] Early in the reign of James V there had been a fairly permanent guard of ten halberdiers: *ER* xiv. 285, 350, 459; xv. 91.

had nothing to match the force of 2,550 French guardsmen, and even the 150 English yeomen of the guard formed a more effective tripwire to distance the crown from political turbulence.[45] The Scottish guard, moreover, had an evanescent quality: after Mary's deposition, there were never adequate funds to ensure that it could actually be kept in being.

There is no record of a permanent guard during the minority of James VI.[46] But from 1580 onwards, the young king was no longer immured in Stirling Castle, and a guard was seen as part of the equipment of monarchical rule. The pro-English party in Scotland regularly pressed the English government for funds for a guard. Those less committed to the English 'amity' (such as the king's favourite, the duke of Lennox) took the same line, hinting that if England did not pay, France might. However, no foreign funds had been received when a guard of thirty horsemen was finally recruited, with Lennox as captain, in March 1582.[47]

When Lennox was overthrown by the pro-English Ruthven Raid in August 1582, the new regime planned to recruit a guard of its own, but the king persuaded them to desist. The English at last funded a guard in September, with at least one payment of £1,000 sterling (£9,000 Scots), apparently doled out gradually over the next few months by the English ambassador. The post-Ruthven regime in July 1583 ceased to be willing to ask the English for such funds. Nevertheless, in September there was talk of increasing the guard to 200 horsemen and 100 footmen; the coinage was debased for this purpose.[48]

With many competing claims on the treasury, the guard's

---

[45] George Buchanan, *The Art and Science of Government Among the Scots (Dialogus De Jure Regni Apud Scotos)*, ed. D. H. McNeill (Glasgow, 1964), 58; id., *The History of Scotland*, 6 vols., ed. J. Aikman (Edinburgh, 1830), ii. 393–4; *RSS* v, p. 556; *Accounts of the Collectors of Thirds of Benefices, 1561–1572*, ed. G. Donaldson (SHS, 1949), 118–19; 'The archearis of our soverane ladyis gaird, 1562–1567', *Maitland Miscellany*, i (1840), 26–36; Hale, *War and Society*, 137.

[46] There was conceivably a guard in 1575, when a law against carrying firearms made an exception for it (an earlier law in Dec. 1567 had not done so): *APS* iii. 84–5; 29–30, c. 23.

[47] HMC, *Salisbury*, ii. 284; Bowes to Walsingham, 5 Apr. 1580, *CSP Scot.* v. 390–1; *RSS* viii. 714; W. Fraser, *The Lennox*, 2 vols. (Edinburgh, 1874), ii. 325–7. An earlier order to levy a guard in 1581 was probably not carried out: *RSS* viii. 124. Cf. also the curious appointment in 1581 of Alan Coutts as colonel for life 'of all armeis of men of weir levied or to be levyed at any time heirefter': *RSS* viii. 274. No more is heard of this.

[48] *Warrender Papers*, i. 150–2; *CSP Scot.* vi. 184–5; Bowes to Walsingham, 9 July, 13 July and 23 Sept. 1583, *CSP Scot.* vi. 531, 539, 619; Calderwood, *History*, iii. 674, 761–2.

continuity would have been aided by an independent source of revenue. Funding from England was never as regular as the Scots hoped, and strings were always attached.[49] Arran's government produced an important scheme to establish the guard with its own hypothecated domestic revenue, as the college of justice had— and, like the college of justice, from church revenues. A statute of 1584 ordered the establishment of a force of forty gentlemen, 'hable, honest, and weill horssit and having sum reasounable levingis of thair awin', to be paid £200 per year each. Parish and episcopal benefices were to pay the first year's fruits, and all new benefice-holders were also to pay 20 per cent of their income towards it; the monasteries were to pay the 'portions' of all monks who had died since 1560 or who should die thereafter. This scheme was never fully implemented; there are no further references to payments from parishes and bishoprics, and at least some monks' portions were granted elsewhere. But a commission of £140. 6s. 8d. was paid to the officials collecting the 1583–4 portions; if this commission was at the same rate (12d. in the £) as was paid to tax collectors, they would have brought in £2,800, allowing the monks' portions to fund seven of the forty planned guardsmen for two years.[50] This may well have been the highest point reached by the scheme, but in 1587 there was a new effort: the collector of the portions was replaced and several gifts of portions made elsewhere were revoked. There were further such measures in 1595 and 1597, but their effect is unclear.[51]

Some kind of guard was maintained for most of the rest of the 1580s, at heavy cost: £3,527 was found, a part payment of arrears of wages, in June 1586, and 20,000 merks was assigned to the guard from the small barons' taxation in April 1588. If the latter sum was the guard's pay for two years, it would have paid for about thirty-three guardsmen at £16. 13s. 4d. per month (the rate paid in 1584).[52] In April 1590, a new guard of 100 horsemen and 100

---

[49] For the extent to which the guard was funded by the English in the late 1580s, and the political costs of this, see J. Goodare, 'James VI's English subsidy', in id. and M. Lynch (eds.), *The Reign of James VI* (East Linton, 1999, forthcoming).

[50] *APS* iii. 298–9, c. 13; *RSS* viii, pp. x, xix; NAS, treasurer's accounts, 1585–6, E21/64, fo. 127ᵛ.

[51] *RPC* iv. 134; v. 239; *APS* iv. 115.

[52] NAS, treasurer's accounts, 1585–6, E21/64, fo. 145ʳ; *RPC* iv. 274. If the guardsmen were intended to be decorative as well as fighters, they might cost more. Mary paid her archers (who served quarterly in rotation) between £70 and £100 per quarter: 'Archearis of our soverane ladyis gaird'.

footmen was recruited, provoking complaints. But by May 1591, this unusually large guard seems to have evaporated, and the king's desire to re-establish it was being thwarted by lack of funds. In 1592 it had been reconstituted, but not paid—a mutiny over pay was quelled with difficulty.[53]

In early 1593 the schemes for a royal guard became entangled with the demand to raise forces against the dissident Catholic earls—and this led the church to become involved. A convention of estates in January offered to pay for a guard: the burghs for footmen, the landed classes for horsemen. The burghs contributed £1,000 to pay 100 footmen for a month. In March, the order went out that *presbyteries* should organize a 'voluntare' collection from 'all noblemen, barronis, and landit men'. It was 'voluntare' only in a limited sense, since people could be outlawed for non-payment.[54] The church's attempt to rally the landed classes had only patchy success. The presbytery of Edinburgh, which coord-inated the scheme, wrote to other presbyteries in March 1593 'anent payment of the kingis gard'. Lists were circulated of 'the cheif nobilmen, barrones, and gentilmen of name and habilitie . . . with sic a proportione of money noted with everie ane of tham as utharis of lyk qualitie hes alreddie delyverit'. However, the col-lection went badly—'far less is done nor might have bene perfor-mit'. The barons and gentlemen of Lothian made a contribution, but those of St Andrews did not, and in the presbytery of Glasgow they objected that 'the actioune wes meir civile, and thairfoir thai thocht it nocht pertinent to the ministrie nor thair calling'.[55] By April, the government had perhaps given up; it was thinking of holding justice ayres to raise the cash for 50 light horsemen.[56]

In July 1593, a new guard had been raised of 100 footmen and 50 horsemen, paid for by courtiers and not the king.[57] This may

[53] Moysie, *Memoirs*, 82; Bowes to Burghley, 29 Apr. 1590 and 26 May 1591, *CSP Scot*. x. 283, 520; Calderwood, *History*, v. 146.

[54] *RPC* v. 55–6; *RCRB* i. 392–3, 407; *CSP Scot*. xi. 26; *BUK* iii. 810.

[55] NAS, presbytery of Edinburgh to other presbyteries, 20 Mar. 1593, GD149/265, pt. 1, fos. 13ᵛ–14ʳ; *Records of the Synod of Lothian and Tweeddale, 1589–1596, 1640–1649*, ed. J. Kirk (Stair Society, 1977), 55 (cf. Calderwood, *History*, v. 222); E. E. MacQueen, 'The General Assembly of the Kirk as a Rival of the Scottish Parliament, 1560–1618', Ph.D. thesis (St Andrews, 1927), 121–2; 'Extracts from the registers of the presbytery of Glasgow, 1592–1601', *Maitland Mis-cellany*, i (1833), 58–9.

[56] Bowes to Burghley, 19 Apr. 1593, *CSP Scot*. xi. 80.

[57] Bowes to Burghley, 30 July 1593, *CSP Scot*. xi. 704.

not have lasted long, since we find another new guard being recruited in April 1594: 'foure cornets of horsemen, and four hundreth footmen'. The general assembly was suspicious about this guard's godliness, and the English ambassador also worried about its sympathies with the Catholic earls.[58] The guard was, in fact, being used mainly in pursuit of the fugitive earl of Bothwell and his followers. Next month, during the riding of parliament, swords were drawn when they disputed the privilege of guarding the king with a contingent of Edinburgh burgesses.[59]

After all this activity, the guard for the second half of the 1590s was suddenly inconspicuous. Having subdued the Catholic earls by the end of 1594, and forced Bothwell into exile in 1595, the king was now more secure in his palaces. It is often said that James achieved personal security only by leaving for England in 1603, but his demands for a guard declined well before then. There was little or no royal guard for most of the rest of the personal reign. James may always have had a makeshift military force available: the guard in 1600 was said to consist of his household servants. The next year, an English envoy reported that although the king had no guard 'he relies upon the love of his people which he calls the true guardian of princes'. James could always make a virtue of necessity.[60]

The union of crowns opened a new era in the history of the royal guard. Before, its job had been to provide personal security for the king: now, it was free to roam the localities to enforce the will of the government. And the treasury could afford to pay it. So in July 1603, a new guard of forty horsemen was created. Its mission was to enforce hornings by arresting people who remained at the horn, under direction from the privy council.[61] The frequent references

[58] Calderwood, *History*, v. 295; *BUK* iii. 834; Bowes to Burghley, 18 May 1594, *CSP Scot.* xi. 337.

[59] Bowes to Cecil, 13 Apr. 1594, Bowes to Burghley, 21 Apr. 1594, *CSP Scot.* xi. 308-9, 319, Calderwood, *History*, v. 329-30.

[60] James Hudson to Cecil, 19 Oct. 1600, *CSP Scot.* xiii, II. 713; D. H. Willson, *King James VI and I* (New York, 1956), 91. In early 1603, Sir Robert Cecil offered personally to pay for a Scottish royal guard (whether with Elizabeth's connivance or not does not appear), but the scheme had still not been implemented when the queen died. James to Lord Henry Howard, n.d. [Jan. 1603?], *King James VI & I, Letters*, ed. G. P. V. Akrigg (Berkeley and Los Angeles 1984), 203; George Nicolson to Cecil, 1 Feb. 1603, *CSP Scot.* xiii, II. 1107; H. G. Stafford, *James VI of Scotland and the Throne of England* (New York, 1940), 208.

[61] *RPC* vi. 581-2, 584-5, 590-2.

to the guard's police activities in the privy council register suggest that it earned its pay.

Nevertheless, this pay amounted to over £13,000 per year, and there was another comparable guard in the Borders. By 1611, feuding had declined, and there was much less Border violence. The 'king's guard' was disbanded, though eight members of it were retained temporarily for the sole duty of arresting tax defaulters.[62] Meanwhile the Border guard was increased from twenty-five to forty men, and its theatre of operations expanded to cover the whole of Lowland Scotland; in effect the Border guard was transformed into a new 'king's guard'.[63] But there was less for it to do. After 1615 the privy council was no longer ordering the guard to rush hither and thither dealing with individual cases, and a final planned operation could be executed. The guard toured the country systematically, arresting the persistent outlaws (mostly in practice debtors) of each Lowland sheriffdom in turn.[64] The tour was completed in 1620; next year the guard was disbanded, on the grounds that the country had become sufficiently law-abiding not to need it. Scottish historians have often been 'king's friends' (in the phrase of K. B. McFarlane), and lamentations for the demise of this expensive weapon of royal authority have been frequent; but James's decision seems eminently reasonable.[65]

Wapinshawings[66]—practice musters—were a traditional feature of the common army. They form a neat counterpoint to the royal guard in the way that they evolved. They have already been discussed when their records illuminate the composition and recruitment of traditional military forces. But wapinshawings might also have served as a means of modernizing those forces. If warfare was to become an exclusively public pursuit, the state needed to construct a more emphatic distinction in the localities between its military forces and those of private lords. Short of creating a

---

[62] *RPC* ix. 189–90, 213, 226.   [63] *RPC* ix. 244–5, 279, 289–90.

[64] *RPC* x. 376–7, 425–6, 511; xi. 560–1, 565, 573–5, 583–4; xii. 24–5, 38–9, 176–7; cf. J. Goodare, *The Government of Scotland, 1560–1625* (forthcoming), ch. 8.

[65] *RPC* xii. 582–3. For a more balanced assessment than most, see M. Lee, *Government by Pen: Scotland under James VI and I* (Urbana, Ill., 1980), 207–9, where, however, the guard is regarded purely as a Border matter.

[66] The term is virtually always 'wapinshawing' (variously spelt from 'wapinschawing' to 'valpynschavene') in primary sources before about 1750. Only then, when the term had long been an antiquarian one, did the form 'wappenshaw' become common, and it is unfortunate that so many historians have preferred it. See *Oxford English Dictionary*, 2nd edn.; *Scottish National Dictionary*.

standing army, one of its most promising tools for this was the wapinshawing.

Traditionally, wapinshawings had four functions. They inculcated militaristic values; they established that men had an obligation to give military service, and defined who was to give it; they established an obligation for them to possess weapons; and they offered military training. In fact the last of these was probably extremely rare, and even legislators only mentioned it occasionally. Even the first three were not exactly common, because wapinshawings themselves were not regular events. But they had the important attribute of being controlled exclusively by the crown and its lieutenants; no private examples are cited in Jenny Wormald's study of lords and their followings, for instance. The earl of Huntly's breakaway northern administration used them in 1569, under commission from Queen Mary. Where there was no independent public authority, in the Highlands, there were no wapinshawings. However, the Moray wapinshawing of 1596, discussed above, shows that they still depended on a combination of public and private authority: landlords mustered their tenants and dependants. Even in the burghs, where no directly feudal hierarchy was involved, the wapinshawing attempted to reproduce the traditional forms of the social order, as the Glasgow merchants and craftsmen showed when they rioted over precedence in 1583.[67]

So wapinshawings had to be developed, and preferably in a way that placed more emphasis on direct links between fighting men and the state. What might be achieved is illustrated by what was happening in England. The ambitious fiscal-military survey of 1522 was still based on the 'quasi-feudal' principle of giving landlords responsibility for their tenants, but this was abandoned during the mid-sixteenth century. In its place was established the county militia, in which military service was demanded directly from individuals by agents of the state.[68] From 1573 onwards, there were 'special musters' at which military training was given—the origin of the trained bands. Men were paid to attend them, so they

---

[67] J. Wormald, *Lords and Men in Scotland: Bonds of Manrent, 1442–1603* (Edinburgh, 1985), 44, 91; Pitscottie, *Historie*, ii. 214; *Extracts from the Records of the Burgh of Glasgow*, 11 vols., ed. J. D. Marwick *et al.* (SBRS, 1876–1916), i. 102. For the unusual circumstances of the only known order for a Highland wapinshawing (in 1602), see *RPC* vi. 342–3; *CSP Scot.* xiii, II. 941–2.

[68] J. J. Goring, 'The general proscription of 1522', *EHR* 86 (1971), 681–705, at pp. 695–8; S. J. Gunn, *Early Tudor Government, 1485–1558* (London, 1995), 38–42.

became popular holidays. They were organized by lords lieutenant and their deputies in each county, assisted by justices of the peace and sheriffs. Reports had to be sent to the privy council, which scrutinized them with some care. When recruitment was needed for real armies, it tended to follow the same lines as the county musters, though there was reluctance to send the trained bands overseas.[69] The Scottish state was groping towards something similar, but it could not offer pay, and so had to accept the continued mustering of men by their local lords; eventually, however, it started trying to find ways round this.

An elaborate code of procedure for wapinshawings was enacted in 1540. There were to be wapinshawings in June and October every year in each sheriffdom, regality, and burgh. Weapons requirements were listed in detail for all down to the level of a 'yeman'. Lords were to give lists of their followers, with details of their weapons, to the sheriff, bailie of regality, or burgh magistrate, who would report them to the crown. The most striking requirement was for sheriffs to appoint drill captains in each parish, who would drill men in use of their weapons twice a month during the summer months. There is no evidence that any of this was regularly implemented, and the scheme for parish captains was almost certainly stillborn.[70] In 1552 there was an elaborate plan to raise an army for French service, not through parishes but through the tax assessment system; each 40 mcrks' land of old extent would recruit and equip one man. It would have been a striking modernization of the recruitment system, but was rapidly abandoned in the face of opposition.[71]

The scheme of 1540 was revived, with minor amendments, in 1575. This was during a period of return to normality after the unrest and civil wars of 1567–73; but it may also have been inspired by the establishment of the Elizabethan trained bands in 1573. However, the scheme for parish drilling was the one part of the

---

[69] Boynton, *Elizabethan Militia*, ch. 1; Cruickshank, *Elizabeth's Army*, ch. 2.

[70] *APS* ii. 362–3, cc. 21–7; cf. *ADCP*, 504. For the traditional duties of sheriffs at wapinshawings see *Sheriff Court Book of Fife, 1515–1522*, ed. W. C. Dickinson (SHS, 1928), pp. xli–xliii.

[71] *RPC* i. 129–32, 134–7; earl of Cassillis to Mary of Guise, 17 Dec. [1552], *Scottish Correspondence of Mary of Lorraine*, ed. A. I. Cameron (SHS, 1927), 363–4; *TA* x. 154. For the tax assessment system, and for another failed attempt at modernization by Mary of Guise in 1556, see J. Goodare, 'Parliamentary taxation in Scotland, 1560–1603', *SHR* 68 (1989), 23–52, at pp. 23–9.

1540 programme that was *not* revived. Instead, the Regent Morton put his faith in specially nominated local commissioners to convene the regular wapinshawings. But the government made no effort to proclaim the first of the projected wapinshawings in the localities, nor to communicate with its fifty-four commissioners either before or after it had been scheduled. The first wapinshawing of the series was held, but that seems to have been all.[72]

The most intense period for wapinshawings was between 1595 and 1600. This was just after the royal guard was sidelined, in 1594; the reason was that the state's political requirements from its licensed killers had changed. Up to the end of 1594, the king had been worried about the internal threat to his authority from dissident magnates, and his first priority had been the personal security that came from being surrounded constantly by a few dozen armed men. But in 1595 and 1596, the most immediate military threat to his regime came from the second armada currently being prepared by Spain; English and Scottish strategists agreed that the Spanish attack might come through Scotland. James thus desired not a small guard kept constantly in being, but the ability to raise an effective, full-size army when the time should come. This desire was intensified as the issue of the English succession became both more immediate and more complicated in the late 1590s; James and his advisers came to be convinced that they faced a possible war of the English succession. Their solution to this, too, was to prepare to raise a large army.

These strategic considerations resulted in another joint initiative of church and state, launched in November 1595. All ministers were ordered to persuade their parishioners that a Spanish threat existed, and to exhort them to prepare to resist it in arms. Then a general wapinshawing was proclaimed for 2 February 1596. Regional mustering-points against invasion were also designated. All this, it was announced, was a prelude to a regular system in which parish captains (appointed by sheriffs) would convene the subjects twice each month, 'to leirne and trayne them to gang in ordour and to beir thair wapponis'. To underline the religious nature of the cause, the general wapinshawing itself was preceded and followed by days of fasting.[73]

---

[72] *APS* iii. 91–2; *TA* xiii. 67–72; Pitscottie, *Historie*, ii. 321.
[73] *RPC* v. 233–6, 241–2; *CSP Scot.* xii. 66, 77; Nicolson to Bowes, 29 Jan. 1596, *CSP Scot.* xii 137; Robert Birrel, 'Diary, 1532–1605', in J. G. Dalyell (ed.), *Fragments*

The exercise had mixed results. The privy council complained immediately afterwards that those musters seen by the king had not come up to expectations in numbers or equipment, but the main concern was undoubtedly equipment. The report of the Moray wapinshawing (discussed above) attested to a substantial turnout, and the fact that a report was made at all was a notable innovation.[74] But the report showed all too clearly that the men of Moray had omitted to acquire the latest killing devices. It was this omission that the privy council would shortly set out to remedy.

The general assembly, meanwhile, was still keen on the idea of regular musters in parishes, in which men would be 'trainit up in the exercise of thair armes'. Indeed it now wanted the captains chosen by *kirk sessions*, rather than sheriffs.[75] This implied a radical restructuring of the common army, and it did not happen. 1596 was, in fact, the last year in which crown and church would co-operate over warfare. Such cooperation required strong leadership from the church nationally, since military training was far beyond the average kirk session's concept of its remit. The only possible sources of such leadership in girding the nation for an anti-Catholic crusade were the committed presbyterians, who had backed the 1596 wapinshawing with righteous fervour. However, the Edinburgh riot of 17 December 1596 caused a permanent breach between them and the king. By 1597, the government was actually censuring radical ministers for having organized 'moustouris and wapinschawings' and neglecting their parochial duties.[76] The Catholic threat itself receded after the second Spanish armada was scattered by a storm late in 1596.[77] There would eventually be a third, but it seems not to have generated so much defiant official flag-waggery.

---

of Scottish History (Edinburgh, 1798), 36. Four editions of the printed proclamation for the wapinshawing were issued: H. G. Aldis, *A List of Books Printed in Scotland before 1700* (2nd edn., Edinburgh, 1970), nos. 274, 283, 284, 284.5. For the king's suspicious response in 1594 to an earlier demand by the general assembly 'that the haill subjectes be chargeit to put themselves in armes', see *BUK* iii. 833.

[74] It seems to be the only report that survives, but others were certainly sent in, including one from Aberdeen: 'Extracts from the accounts of the burgh of Aberdeen', *Spalding Club Miscellany*, v (1852), 62–3. For the demand for reports, see NAS, treasurer's accounts, 1593–6, E21/70, fo. 194ᵛ.

[75] *BUK* iii. 860.

[76] Thomas Hamilton to John Lindsay of Balcarres, 21 May 1597, *Melros Papers*, ii. 612.

[77] R. B. Wernham, *The Return of the Armadas: The Last Years of the Elizabethan War with Spain, 1595–1603* (Oxford, 1994), 139–40.

The privy council's attention now shifted to the question of weapons and equipment. The wapinshawing of 1596 had shown that men could be brought together; now they needed to be made to buy weapons, since there was no likelihood of the state providing these itself. The direction things would take was clear. The legal obligation to possess weapons was a recognized concomitant of the obligation to provide military service; the council would specify what these weapons should be, and threaten to prosecute those who failed to acquire them. A captive market would thus be created for anyone who cared to enter the arms trade.

In 1598, Colonel William Stewart (a former captain of the guard) brought forward a scheme to require all to possess weapons, as a prelude to importing them. Sounded on the idea, the magistrates of Edinburgh replied cautiously that the burgesses would be content to be armed by the laws of the land. Undeterred, the privy council issued an order that every man was to be 'armit according to his rent', with details of the weapons that all the propertied classes were to possess. A date was set for a general wapinshawing in 1599, at which they would show that they had acquired the requisite weapons. This was ratified at the next convention of estates, but the convention also rejected a more radical proposal— probably the grant of a monopoly of weapons imports to Stewart or someone like him.[78]

In July 1599, however, another convention accepted this idea. The burgesses, it stated, had refused to import weapons (no doubt they could not afford the odium of dragging reluctant customers before the courts). A three-year monopoly of importing weapons was granted to Sir Michael Balfour of Burleigh. The privy council would help him force people to buy them, and he would receive half of the escheats of those convicted of refusal.[79] Balfour

[78] The convention of estates also passed an act making Monday into a 'pastyme day', to be spent by the lieges 'in useing and handling of thair armour and in uther lauchfull gaimes and pastymes procureing habilitie of body', but no more was heard of this. *RPC* v. 446–7; *Edin. Recs.* v. 212; *APS* iv. 160, 168–9, cc. 2, 13; Nicolson to Cecil, 1 July 1598, *CSP Scot.* xiii, I. 228. Imports were necessary because few materials of war were produced in Scotland. There were numerous 'dagmakers', but 'dags' (pistols) were mainly for private violence rather than battlefield use. D. H. Caldwell, 'Royal patronage of arms and armour making in fifteenth and sixteenth century Scotland', in id. (ed.), *Scottish Weapons and Fortifications, 1100–1800* (Edinburgh, 1981), 82.

[79] *APS* iv. 190. As a result, the general wapinshawing of 1599 lost its purpose. A wapinshawing was held in Edinburgh on 18 May 1599: *Edin. Recs.* v. 248. But the general one, originally set for 1 May, had in Apr. been postponed to 6 Aug.: *RPC* v. 551. It was eclipsed by Balfour's newly agreed scheme in July, and never took place.

undertook to import enough weapons for 2,000 horsemen and 8,000 footmen. Confusingly, when the proposed weapons were listed, they were divided, not into those of horsemen and footmen, but into heavier and lighter arms. The former consisted of corslet and Spanish pike, with helmet and other equipment; the latter of either musket, or light corslet and pike or sword. Earls were to have twenty stands of the heavier arms, lords ten, and lairds one for every fifteen chalders' or 1,000 merks' rent. Lairds with 300 merks' rent or more, and burgesses worth £500 in goods, were to have the lighter arms themselves. This army seems likely to have been mainly an infantry one, as both pikes and muskets were infantry weapons, and there was no official provision for cavalry; perhaps the government assumed that enough people would serve on horseback without prompting.[80] At any rate, Scotland had placed its legal requirements on weapons well ahead of England, where the position had been laid down by the militia statute of 1558. Although this had been regarded as outdated within a decade, it was never amended.[81]

Balfour bought the weapons in the Netherlands in the summer of 1600, carefully watched by English agents. One report credited him with the purchase of 6,000 corslets, 10,000 pikes, and 4,000 muskets and calivers; another, with having weapons for 10,000 men.[82] His attempts to make people buy them led to regular protests. Burgh magistrates were made to take responsibility for their citizens: Aberdeen was forced to take 45 sets.[83] Edinburgh, Dundee, and St Andrews had been exempted from the monopoly at the start, and many individuals later managed to obtain official suspensions of their obligation to buy. The scheme was far from completely successful—Balfour did not reach his target quantities,

[80] *APS* iv. 190–1; *RPC* vi. 546.

[81] Boynton, *Elizabethan Militia*, 61, 70. The statute required bows, bills, hagbuts, and almain rivets (light armour). In the 1580s and 1590s the Armourers' Company of London lobbied unsuccessfully to have it updated to corslets and calivers: I. W. Archer, 'The London lobbies in the late sixteenth century', *Historical Journal*, 31 (1988), 17–44, at p. 21. However, English practice kept ahead of the statutory requirements.

[82] Robert King to [. . .], Middelburg, 27 June/7 July 1600, HMC, *Salisbury*, x. 206; Ralph Winwood to Sir Henry Neville, Paris, 7/17 July 1600, *Memorials of Affairs of State . . . from the original papers of Sir R. Winwood*, 3 vols., ed. E. Sawyer (London, 1725), i. 229.

[83] *RPC* vi. 180–2; Aberdeen City Archives, William Kennedy's 'Alphabetical index to the first 67 volumes of the council register of the city of Aberdeen, 1398–1800', vol. i, pp. 24–5.

and he scarcely made his fortune. Many of the weapons were still
unsold in 1609. But it may well have achieved as much as could
have been expected.[84]

As well as providing weapons for the army he planned to have,
James was now beginning to try to extract pay for it from his subjects. After the wapinshawing of February 1596, he had already
begun to think of establishing a paid army of 6,000 men 'to be
maintained at the charge of 300 persons'. He was not consistent
over this, and a military discipline commission established in July
1599 noted that 'the povertie of the crowne and cuntrey is not able
to sustene wageit men under commandment'.[85] By early 1600, the
plan for a paid army had revived, and indeed expanded to 15,000
men. It was still to be provided by his most wealthy subjects, but
not to be mustered by traditional common army service. Partly this
army was for an expedition to the Isles, and partly in preparation
for the English succession. This scheme was clearly connected in
some way with the king's tax scheme of 1599–1600, when he
hoped that he might get a very large tax to pay for an army. How
the tax was to be assessed is not clear; the 'persons' who were to
pay may have been tax districts rather than individuals, both in
1596 and in 1599–1600. Few details were recorded before the
scheme was killed off by a convention of estates in June 1600.[86]

When James reached his understanding with Sir Robert Cecil
about the English succession in 1601, the pressure for warlike
preparations eased dramatically—which was just as well, since the
tax scheme of 1599–1600 had latterly been the centrepiece of the
king's plans. Scotland subsided into the unwarlike state that it had
perhaps preferred all along. Orders for general wapinshawings
returned after 1607, though there are few details of how well they
were complied with, and they were much less important than they
had been between 1595 and 1601.[87] A brief footnote to the story
of wapinshawings is necessary, however, to cover their importance
in the burghs.

Some burghs seem to have had fairly regular annual wapinshawings as part of their annual civic ritual. That in Glasgow was a

[84] *APS* iv. 188; *RPC* vi. 365; viii. 586.
[85] Bowes to Burghley, 24 Feb. 1596, *CSP Scot.* xii. 149; *APS* iv. 188.
[86] Nicolson to Cecil, 9 Mar. 1600, HMC, *Salisbury*, x. 59–61; Goodare, 'Parliamentary taxation', 43–5.
[87] Stafford, *James VI and the Throne of England*, ch. 7; *RPC* vii. 407, 414; viii. 78; x.
244–5.

remnant of the former Summerhill assembly, a consultative body which was downgraded as the burgh's government became more oligarchical. On the other hand, the 'vesying of the wappynis' in Peebles in May 1572 was clearly prompted by ongoing civil war. Wapinshawings were held in Aberdeen only when central government demanded them—in 1596, 1599, and 1600, but not again until 1607, when they once again became frequent. The burgh protested against a demand for a second wapinshawing in 1596.[88]

In June 1600, just before the rejection of his tax scheme, the king proposed to the burghs that wapinshawings should be held monthly. The convention of royal burghs agreed. In Glasgow at least the plan was actually implemented, and in March 1601 arrangements were made to provide military training—the king's dearest wish. Eventually, the burgh created what appears to have been an effective, trained militia in this way.[89] In Edinburgh, there were annual wapinshawings between 1598 and 1600, but not again until 1607—when they once more became annual events, and remained so until 1625 and after.[90] It is easy to think of townsmen as being less warlike than the armed followers of territorial magnates, but the urban wapinshawing is evidence against this idea.[91]

The outbreak in 1601 of what was obviously going to be a prolonged international peace for Scotland—it did in fact last until 1625—provides an opportunity to pause and take stock. The Scottish military system in the first quarter of the seventeenth century was a notably low-pressure one; how might it be understood in a broad comparative context?

[88] J. McGrath, 'The medieval and early modern burgh', in T. M. Devine and G. Jackson (eds.), *Glasgow*, i. *Beginnings to 1830* (Manchester, 1995), 32; *Charters and Documents Relating to the Burgh of Peebles, with Extracts from the Records of the Burgh, 1165–1710*, ed. W. Chambers (SBRS, 1872), 339–41; Aberdeen City Archives, Kennedy, 'Index to council register', i, pp. 637–9; 'Accounts of the burgh of Aberdeen', 62–3.

[89] *RCRB* ii. 83; *Extracts from the Records of the Burgh of Glasgow*, 11 vols., ed. J. D. Marwick *et al.* (SBRS, 1876–1916), i. 208–9, 218; D. Murray, *Early Burgh Organization in Scotland*, 2 vols. (Glasgow, 1924–32), i. 225–7.

[90] *Edin. Recs.* v. 219, 248, 270; vi. 30, 41, 51, 62, 73, 85, 99, 106, 128, 143, 159, 177, 189, 209, 221–2, 232, 243, 253, 269.

[91] This brief survey of urban wapinshawings is necessarily selective. Most printed burgh records have been printed only in extracts, which do not always include *regular* events like annual wapinshawings. A full investigation of MS records would shed further light on the subject, but is beyond the scope of this study. Towns' participation in traditional private warfare (which mainly seems to have taken place before 1600) is discussed by K. M. Brown, 'Burghs, lords and feuds in Jacobean Scotland', in M. Lynch (ed.), *The Early Modern Town in Scotland* (London, 1987).

One suggestive evolutionary scheme is proposed by Bernard Guenée, who has divided late-medieval recruitment into a number of broad phases. Although these stretch back some way before the period with which this book is primarily concerned, they provide some kind of perspective, especially since Scottish war-making may well have been in an earlier phase than that of some states. First came the strictly feudal army, composed of the king's feudal vassals and their own vassals. It was already more or less extinct by 1300. Next, typically in the fourteenth century, there was the mass levy (the French *arrière-ban*). All able-bodied men were called on to serve with weapons appropriate to their status; a proportion (selected by the government or by the locality) had to do so, while at least some of the others had to contribute money. The mass levy would sometimes be paid, though it might not be. Then there was the contract army of mercenaries, led by captains who were both commanders and entrepreneurs. At first these were often fully independent 'free-lance' companies, but by the sixteenth century the mercenary captain had to make a prior contract with a particular state. This led eventually to the full nationalization of armies; but while that was happening, there was also a further phase of really big contract armies during the Thirty Years War.[92]

In Scotland, for most of the sixteenth century, the recruitment system favoured by both lords and state was the traditional mass levy, in which 'all maner of man betuix sexti and sextene' were called upon to serve.[93] This was still in use for the Moray wapinshawing of 1596, but the deficiencies of such a force were all too apparent, and the government only tolerated it in the hope of turning it into something more effective. Efforts to achieve this were abandoned in 1601, when the immediate need for a large army vanished. Orders for wapinshawings ceased for some years, and the traditional common army began to rust away through

[92] B. Guenée, *States and Rulers in Later Medieval Europe*, trans. J. Vale (Oxford, 1985), 137–44. This classification is not the only possible one, but it provides a convenient way of making sense of the Scottish evidence. A more detailed but broadly compatible account is given by Contamine, *War in the Middle Ages*, 77–101, 126–37, 150–72. Whether the strictly feudal army had ever existed is doubted by S. Reynolds, *Fiefs and Vassals* (Oxford, 1994), 348–52 and *passim*.

[93] *APS* ii. 45, c. 3. Cf. the Second Statute of Westminster in England (1285). This called for military service from all men from 15 to 60 and specified their equipment—though it was more concerned with local peacekeeping than service in the king's wars: A. L. Brown, *The Governance of Late Medieval England, 1272–1461* (London, 1989), 93–4.

disuse. The government also ceased to tolerate the exercise of autonomous military force by lords and their followings—the local structure on which the common army rested. Bloodfeud went into decline. In 1606, the privy council ordered all iron yetts (gates) removed from houses in the Borders, and converted to 'plew irnis' in true biblical fashion.[94] The common army still existed on paper, though by 1607 the king was speaking of it in the past tense. It would still have been the only way to raise a really large Scottish army, but no such army was likely to be required so long as the connection with England was maintained.

Instead the Scottish state required more limited forces in the early seventeenth century. These forces now began to raised by a method that approximates to Professor Guenée's next stage: the contract army. This system called for military entrepreneurs, miniature Tillys and Wallensteins, to run the crown's warfare for it. They did not just command the troops; they managed their pay, drawing on their own financial resources to do so, and hoping to make a profit. They could not operate in sixteenth-century Scotland, with its unpaid armies, but once the tradition of unpaid service began to rust away, there was scope for the entrepreneur.

A good example is Lord Ochiltree's expedition to the Isles in 1608. Ochiltree, who had previous military experience in the Netherlands, was granted pay for 500 men, and had five captains, five ensigns, and ten drummers. As well as this modern-seeming military force, there was to be a traditional one composed of the followers of a number of individuals who were summoned to attend. Whether they did so is not recorded; governmental attention was given only to the regular troops, who were clearly the mainstay of the expedition. Ochiltree's entrepreneurial skills were more limited than his military ones; he accomplished his objectives in the Isles, but incurred extra costs and got his accounts in a muddle. It took five years before he and the privy council could agree how much he should be paid for what. The entire cost of the three-month expedition, plus the subsequent garrisoning of Dunyveg Castle, seems to have come to £38,000. Artillery and ships were also supplied by the English, at no charge to Scotland.

[94] *RPC* vii. 271.

Ochiltree seems to have made a loss on his contract, but this very fact suggests that he had hoped to make a profit.[95]

Another such contractor was the earl of Caithness, who commanded the army that suppressed the Orkney uprising of 1614. It might be thought that such an army would be recruited in Caithness and would need only to cross the Pentland Firth: not so. The expedition was largely assembled in Edinburgh, and preparations for it were well under way before Caithness took over command. Indeed he was appointed only because he happened to be in Edinburgh and volunteered his services. He did pick up 30 of his own men on the way to Orkney, and 200 in Orkney itself, but the 60 soldiers recruited in Edinburgh, along with cannoneers, wrights, and smith to work the two siege guns, were the core of the force. And it was paid by the crown, using the earl as an intermediary and manager.[96]

The same trend towards paid troops was visible in the recruitment of larger armies. Even before 1601, James had hoped to bypass the traditional common army. After that date, only one sizeable recruitment effort was made for the remainder of his reign, but it showed that his hopes had now been realized. This was the regiment sent in 1620 to aid the king's son-in-law, Frederick, Elector Palatine. It appears to have been Frederick who was expected to pay the regiment's wages (or perhaps England was); no Scottish sources refer to its payment. But it was recruited by the Scottish government, and so needs to be examined in as much detail as the limited evidence allows.

Recruitment took little or no notice of the landlord's kin, friends, and dependers, the familiar nucleus of the private army of the late-medieval lord. The first evidence of the recruitment process was the issue in April of letters to the landlords of the 'personis inrolled to be transportit', asking for them to be sent to Edinburgh. How the 'rolls' had been compiled is unknown, but suggests some kind of bureaucratic procedure. Another important point is that the lords were not expected to *lead* their men to

[95] *RPC* viii. 281, 590, 740; x, 68–70; *CSP Dom. 1603–1610*, 418; HMC, *Report on the Laing Manuscripts Preserved in the University of Edinburgh*, 2 vols., ed. H. Paton (London, 1914–25), i. 110.

[96] P. D. Anderson, *Black Patie: The Life and Times of Patrick Stewart, Earl of Orkney, Lord of Shetland* (Edinburgh, 1992), 113–17.

Edinburgh. The crucial point that demonstrates the eclipse of the common army is that no summons to the lieges was issued, as the traditional system would have required. The recruits were formally volunteers.[97]

Instead of seeking the lord's most prosperous tenants, the regiment concentrated on recruiting from the poorest classes of society—those who had been thought 'nocht meit' for warfare under the traditional system. This was possible because they were being paid and equipped by the state, instead of relying on their own resources. A proclamation encouraged vagrants to enlist with the regiment, promising them remission of the statutory penalties for vagrancy. Those borderers who were surplus to official requirements and had been marked down for transportation to the colonies were also invited to enlist. It is no surprise that some of these soldiers deserted after receiving their initial wages. Nevertheless, 1,500 troops, commanded by Colonel Sir Andrew Gray, did sail for Hamburg in late May.[98]

Gray himself, the regiment's commander, also merits attention. As the younger son of an obscure laird, he in no way resembled the territorial magnates who had usually commanded the traditional common army. He was a military careerist who had fought in Continental armies and had received Scottish patents for gunpowder manufacture—a rare and unsuccessful attempt to produce war materials in Scotland.[99] The successful raising of his regiment led him to seek further promotion, as hereditary muster-master of Scotland. He obtained a royal signature, but the council promptly quashed it, declaring that such a post should not be heritable. Gray reappeared in 1626 as a member of Charles I's council of war.[100]

The professional military officer, seeking employment from the state, had scarcely existed in Scotland before the early seventeenth century. There had been one or two in the royal guard, like Colonel Stewart. There were also members of the landed classes with specialist military experience, often obtained on the

[97] *RPC* xii. 255.   [98] *RPC* xii. 257–61, 272–3; Calderwood, *History*, vii. 444.
[99] *RMS* vii. 1635; *RPC* xi. 322. He had a connection with Sir George Hay of Nether Liff, clerk register and entrepreneur, to whom he sold some lands in 1606: *RMS* vi. 1737. For Gray's and other gunpowder patents, see *RPC* x. 284; xi. 275, 306, 319, 322; *RMS* vii. 1635. For imports of gunpowder even after the patents, see *LP James VI*, 319–20. Gray seems also to have recruited an *English* company in the early months of 1620: *CSP Dom. 1619–1623*, 125, 132.
[100] *RPC* xii. 292; *RMS* viii. 970.

Continent: William Meldrum of Cleish, whose 'douchtie deidis' were celebrated in verse by Sir David Lindsay; or Sir James Melville of Halhill, who wrote his own account of his soldiering. But neither Meldrum nor Melville gained or used their military experience in the service of their own sovereigns.[101] To that extent, Colonel Gray was a new phenomenon.

By Gray's time, the state had largely succeeded in establishing direct control over its armed forces. This had profound implications for the role of the nobility—a subject that can only be briefly touched on here. In the sixteenth century, lords had still commanded and recruited fighting forces from their own lands— forces that were primarily theirs personally, whether they fought in the name of the crown or not. Now this role was dissolving. In Spain, the role of the nobility in the military recruiting and command structure increased in the early seventeenth century— but this was a symptom of the degeneration of the Spanish state, no longer able to maintain the same degree of central control over its armed forces. In France, Richelieu was beginning the process of *abolishing* high, honorific military offices like that of constable, in order to prevent their aristocratic holders impeding royal control of the armed forces.[102]

Scottish counsels could be divided on the issue of heritable command, but the cancellation of Colonel Gray's patent indicates that the official feeling against heritability could prevail over pressure for it from those whose military skills may have put them in a strong bargaining position. The military governor of the proposed Leith fortifications in 1626 was to be not a 'heritable gouvernor' but 'removeable at pleasure'. Lord Spynie's commission as muster-master in 1626 was for life—a compromise between heritability and appointment at pleasure.[103]

Another role for the nobility was in military recruitment. This

---

[101] Lindsay, 'The historie of Squyer William Meldrum', in *Works*, i. 145–96; Melville, *Memoirs*, 21–35. Melville was a member of the military discipline commission of 1599 (*APS* iv. 188), but by then his military experience was over forty years out of date.

[102] I. A. A. Thompson, *War and Government in Habsburg Spain, 1560–1620* (London, 1976), ch. 5; C. Jones, 'The military revolution and the professionalisation of the French army under the ancien régime', in M. Duffy (ed.), *The Military Revolution and the State, 1500–1800* (Exeter, 1980), 38–9.

[103] NAS, minutes of council of war, 1626–9, PA7/2, no. 30a, fo. 12ᵛ; *RPC* 2nd ser. i. 293–4. Little is known of Gray's officers. B. G. Seton, *The House of Seton*, 2 vols. (Edinburgh, 1939–41), i. 365–6, names a few of them.

role continued, but it no longer conferred such extensive control over the recruits. The earl of Nithsdale, seeking recruits in 1627, was urged to get the privy council to divide up the sheriffdoms between different colonels by lot, 'with reservatione of such men as ar in your awin landis, and in the landis of your capitanes, and in thais menes landis quho ar oblissed and cautione for [en]listing of the compenies off your capitanes'. It was still easier to recruit in Nithsdale's own sphere of influence—his own lands and those of his clients; but this was not the only place for recruitment, and the council's permission was always needed. Influence and connections could be wielded *within* the council to get permission to recruit, but that was another matter.[104] Landlords never lost their role in recruitment ('Squire nagged and bullied till I went to fight', as Siegfried Sassoon wrote), and commanders were still drawn from the landlord class; but they now required the legitimate authority and material infrastructure that only the state could provide.

It helped if military commanders had high status. This was usually linked to possession of land, but the status itself mattered too. The very *name* of a high-ranking nobleman was useful, if one was available, to give a fighting force added credibility. Colonel Gray lacked a distinguished name, but the seventh earl of Morton eminently possessed one. He was the nominal commander of a Scottish regiment in the duke of Buckingham's expedition to the Ile de Ré in 1627. Contrary to what has sometimes been thought, he did not sail with the regiment himself; it was his name that counted.[105] Eventually, in the later seventeenth century, men would tend to acquire distinguished names (in the form of peerage titles) *because of* their military service commanding the state's troops, rather than being entitled to command through the *prior* possession of a title.[106] A large part of the ethic of the nobility had always

---

[104] Lord Ogilvy to Nithsdale, 22 June 1627, W. Fraser, *The Book of Caerlaverock: Memoirs of the Maxwells, Earls of Nithsdale, Lords Maxwell and Herries*, 2 vols. (Edinburgh, 1873), ii. 82–3; J. A. Fallon, 'Scottish Mercenaries in the Service of Denmark and Sweden, 1626–1632', Ph.D. thesis (Glasgow, 1972), 50–1.

[105] The expedition sailed from the Isle of Wight on 27 June 1627 and returned five months later; Morton was back in Edinburgh by 17 July. Sir James Balfour of Denmilne, *Historical Works*, 4 vols., ed. J. Haig (Edinburgh, 1824), ii, 158–9; *RPC* 2nd ser. ii. 16. Younger sons were more likely to serve in person: Fallon, 'Scottish Mercenaries', 39–40, 323.

[106] K. M. Brown, 'From Scottish lords to British officers: State building, elite integration and the army in the seventeenth century', in Macdougall (ed.), *Scotland and War*, 144–5.

been one of 'service', primarily meaning warfare; but such service had previously involved the lord in making his own troops available to the crown, rather than accepting a job in a professionally run state army.

One branch of warfare that was not obviously relevant to a landed nobility was war at sea. In the early years of the sixteenth century, appreciation of sea power had grown rapidly in Europe, and James IV had made a sustained effort to keep up with the great powers.[107] This was abandoned on his death, and the history of the Scottish navy was a complete blank for the rest of the century. Highland warfare used galleys, and Earl Patrick in Orkney had several ships armed with cannon.[108] Official Scottish war-making might involve the occasional requisitioning of merchant ships for the 'convoy and transporte' of Highland military expeditions;[109] otherwise it was restricted to terra firma.

England, however, came to see itself as one of Europe's leading maritime nations, and after 1603 it was natural that it would take account of Scottish waters in its operations. Iron ordnance was sent to Scotland in 1604 to furnish a ship; there is no trace of this ship in Scottish records, and it was probably English. The ship *Advantage*, burnt in Scotland in 1613, seems to have been English.[110] It may have been this event, together with the government's growing interest in the territorial waters of the state, that led to the acquisition of a Scottish warship in 1614, exactly a century after James IV's *Great Michael* had been sold to France. The new vessel was a more modest 40-ton Dutch-built ship, bought from its English skipper and owner, John Mason. It may have been the *Golden Fleece*, in which Mason had recently been attempting to collect assize herring duties from Dutch fishermen.[111] In 1619, the privy council decided to mothball the ship (now called the *Charles*). Ten days later, however, the ship was being made ready for another expedition on the assize herring duty. Its costs at this time were noted as £115 per month for the pay and allowances of four men and a

---

[107] N. Macdougall, ' "The greattest scheip that ewer saillit in Ingland or France": James IV's "Great Michael" ', in id. (ed.), *Scotland and War*.

[108] J. Dawson, 'The fifth earl of Argyle, Gaelic lordship and political power in sixteenth-century Scotland', *SHR* 67 (1988), 1–27, at pp. 4–5; Anderson, *Black Patie*, 45.

[109] *RPC* v. 475.

[110] *CSP Dom. 1603–1610*, 92; *1611–1618*, 217.

[111] NAS, disposition by John Mason to Sir Gideon Murray, treasurer depute, Edinburgh, 24 Aug. 1614, E90/1. For Mason and the assize herring, see Ch. 7 below.

boy.[112] In 1621 it was in poor condition, and repairs costing 2,000 merks were authorized. But in October 1621, during a fiscal crisis, the ship was ordered to England on the grounds that there was 'no more use' for it in Scotland.[113] This was the end of the Scottish navy for the time being.

Throughout, however, there had been English ships stationed in Scottish waters. Two of the six English guard ships were there in 1618.[114] The task of asserting the state's authority in Scottish territorial waters now devolved entirely on the English navy. It was a task it fulfilled only with difficulty in the summer of 1623, when Dutch ships and Spanish ones (Dunkirk privateers) frequented the harbours of Leith and Aberdeen, determined to fight one another. A squadron of four English ships was sent to enforce British neutrality.[115]

Although Scotland never became known for its maritime endeavours, it was a household name in European military circles as a market place for the hire of mercenary troops. How did this relate to the military power of the Scottish state itself? To answer this question, one must begin with Victor Kiernan's classic study of the use of mercenaries in early modern Europe. He postulates a twofold division. On the one hand there were the large, settled, territorial monarchies. They employed mercenaries because it was easier and safer than putting weapons into the hands of their own subjects. On the other hand there were the peripheral regions and states, often mountainous, always poor, which made a trade out of supplying experienced fighting men. They tended to display 'democratic' tendencies, although becoming 'politically stagnant' when vested interests arose in maintaining good relationships with regular employers. The *locus classicus* for this twofold division was the symbiotic relationship between the French monarchy and the Swiss federation. Scotland, like Switzerland, featured regularly on

---

[112] *RPC* xi. 593–4, 602–3; James Raith to Robert Abercromby, secretary to earl of Kellie, Holyrood, 25 June 1619, *CSP Dom. 1619–1623*, 56; NLS, Denmylne MSS, Adv. MS 33.1.1, vol. ix, no. 13a.

[113] *RPC* xii. 497, 530; James to earl of Mar, 1 Oct. 1621, HMC, *Mar & Kellie*, i. 101. The royal guard was also disbanded at this point. The ship left in May 1622, having been repaired at the expense of the Scottish treasury: *RPC* xii. 712–13.

[114] *Calendar of State Papers and Manuscripts . . . Venice*, 38 vols., ed. R. Brown *et al.* (London, 1864–1940), xv. 160.

[115] *CSP Dom. 1619–1623*, 583, 606; *1623–1625*, 13, 19, 20, 29, 43; *RPC* xiii. 33, 64, 97, 100–1, 117–18, 170, 181, 298, 791–2, 813–14.

the supply side of the mercenary contract. Was Scotland, too, a quasi-democratic federation of armed peasants?[116]

The answer, surely, is no. Switzerland provided a fully integrated military service to its clients, supplying experienced units of armed men ready to fight. Scotland supplied able-bodied men, but client states had to provide them with weapons, and usually also organize them into regiments.[117] No Continental state would have sent the men at the Moray wapinshawing into battle as they stood. Scotsmen certainly fought on the Continent in large numbers throughout our period. But they did not provide their own weapons, and probably did not bring weapons back with them when they returned. Indeed it is unlikely that many returned at all.[118]

Scottish recruitment patterns and military structures had more in common with England than they did with Switzerland. Policymakers in England tended to favour a militia of prosperous folk. There was some reluctance to arm the poor; evidence of fear of rebellion exists, but more immediate concerns were that poor people could not afford to buy weapons, and might not stay in one place long enough to be part of a regular system. By contrast, English armies sent overseas were regularly recruited from any riff-raff that could be found, with no more than pro forma misgivings.[119] The Scottish state was groping towards a version of something similar. The nearest equivalent to the militia—the system of wapinshawings—also relied on prosperous folk who could afford to buy sets of imported weapons. The fact that Scotland had no counterpart to the English county weapons depots

[116] V. G. Kiernan, 'Foreign mercenaries and absolute monarchy', in T. Aston (ed.), *Crisis in Europe, 1560–1660* (London, 1965); quotations at pp. 123, 130. For a brief summary of Scotland's exports of mercenaries, see I. R. Bartlett, 'Scottish mercenaries in Europe, 1570–1640', *Scottish Tradition*, 13 (1984–5), 15–24. A more detailed study is Fallon, 'Scottish Mercenaries'.

[117] The exception was the west Highland tradition of supplying mercenary troops to fight for Gaelic Irish lords: G. A. Hayes-McCoy, *Scots Mercenary Forces in Ireland, 1565–1603* (Dublin, 1937).

[118] Troops returning home are hardly mentioned in Dr Fallon's splendidly detailed case-study, although there are frequent references to officers returning home. Many Scottish units in Danish service were disbanded in 1629, and the men were provided with free quarters at Elsinore so that they could find passages home on Scottish ships; but many if not most of them entered Swedish service instead. See Fallon, 'Scottish Mercenaries', 240–6, 303–5. Hardly any Swedish recruits returned from the Thirty Years War, to judge from one local study: F. Tallett, *War and Society in Early Modern Europe, 1495–1715* (London, 1992), 218.

[119] Cruickshank, *Elizabeth's Army*, 26–30; Boynton, *Elizabethan Militia*, 107–13.

only underlines this point.[120] Meanwhile, Colonel Gray's regiment drew its recruits from the same fully Shakespearean riff-raff as in England.[121]

The Scotsmen fighting overseas did not, therefore, militarize Scottish society directly. But they, or at least their officers, probably helped to channel the latest military *ideas* back to Scotland— ideas which could then be adopted in Scotland's own military forces and structures. Apart from the transition to paid troops, the earliest and perhaps clearest such innovation was the adoption of regimental and company structures. Late-medieval armies, including the Scottish army up to at least 1565, had been organized in large 'battles' of several thousand men, but an increased emphasis on drill and manoeuvre broke these down into smaller units.[122] These can be glimpsed in the Scottish royal guard as early as 1594, when it has been seen to have included 'foure cornets of horsemen'. A related development was the adoption of a new and larger array of officers in the new regiments. These seem first to have appeared in the armies of the Dutch Republic in the 1590s— armies which included several Scottish regiments. The new officers included lieutenant-colonel, sergeant-major (in charge of drill), quartermaster, company chaplain, and company surgeon. Increasingly, regimental officers were appointed by the States General, thus allowing more state control; before, the regimental commander had appointed all his subordinates and had effectively had a free hand in organizing his regiment. In 1599 the Dutch army was also re-equipped with standardized weapons.[123]

Scotland's own regiments saw a partial implementation of these ideas. There is no information on Colonel Gray's officers in 1620, but Morton's regiment in 1627 did indeed have the new officers—lieutenant-colonel, sergeant-major, corporal, quartermaster, provost-marshal, surgeon, and chaplain, as well as twenty-two company captains. Each company was to have ten officers and eighty common soldiers. But Morton was to appoint all the commissioned officers, and also received discretion to have fewer,

---

[120] On these see Cruickshank, *Elizabeth's Army*, 112–13.

[121] In 1627, the privy council asked JPs and parish ministers to report the names of 'ydle and maisterlesse men' for recruitment purposes: *RPC* 2nd ser. i. 604–5, 689–93. Dr Fallon regards Scottish and English procedures for the recruitment of mercenaries as similar: Fallon, 'Scottish Mercenaries', 76.   [122] *RPC* i. 379.

[123] H. Dunthorne, 'Scots in the wars of the Low Countries, 1572–1648', in G. G. Simpson (ed.), *Scotland and the Low Countries, 1124–1994* (East Linton, 1996).

larger companies. This represented less central control than the Dutch had, but it was comparable to Swedish practice. The council of war, in its plans to import weapons at this time, echoed the Dutch in its new-found concern for standardization.[124] The old common army, to which men had brought their own motley weapons, was dead and buried.[125]

Did Scottish mercenaries fight also in English service? They had certainly fought for Queen Elizabeth. In 1589, for instance, James Colville of Easter Wemyss commanded a regiment of 1,500 men in English pay that fought on behalf of Henry IV of France.[126] One of the benefits that both states were sometimes urged to see in the union of crowns was that England would be able to draw on Scottish supplies of fighting men:

If to the hardiness of our constitution were added the military discipline of the English (in which I avow their equality with the ancient Romans, and the deficiency of ourselves, who through going into battle in reliance upon our personal courage alone have often experienced severe defeats): backed by English military discipline, I say, we need never fear the issue of any war in which we may engage.[127]

Yet there is surprisingly little evidence of Scottish soldiers in English armies after 1603. Negatives are hard to prove, but English regiments seem not to have used Scotland as a recruiting-ground.

[124] *RPC* 2nd ser. ii. 50–2 (the captains were to appoint their own subordinate officers); Fallon, 'Scottish Mercenaries', 46–8; NAS, minutes of council of war, 1626–9, PA7/2, no. 30a, fo. 2ᵛ. These innovations have not been gathered together under the heading of a 'military revolution', since consensus seems currently to be lacking even among the proponents of this concept as to what the 'revolution' essentially consisted of and when it took place. It seems safer at present to assume that there were significant developments in methods of state killing throughout the early modern period, though no doubt the debate will continue. See M. Roberts, 'The military revolution, 1560–1660', in id., *Essays in Swedish History* (London, 1967); J. Black, *A Military Revolution? Military Change and European Society, 1550–1800* (London, 1991); D. Parrott, 'The military revolution in early modern Europe', *History Today*, 42/12 (Dec. 1992), 21–7; J. Black, *European Warfare, 1660–1815* (London, 1994), ch. 1; D. Eltis, *The Military Revolution in Sixteenth-Century Europe* (London, 1995), ch. 2 and *passim*; M. Poe, 'The consequences of the military revolution in Muscovy: A comparative perspective', *Comparative Studies in Society and History*, 38 (1996), 603–18; G. Parker, *The Military Revolution, 1500–1800* (2nd edn., Cambridge, 1996), ch. 6 and *passim*.

[125] The common army was now used only against lawbreakers in the Highlands: e.g. *RPC* 2nd ser. v. 362–4, 465. This was armed policing of traditionally armed opponents, not interstate warfare.

[126] Moysie, *Memoirs*, 73, 78. Cf. F. Michel, *Les Ecossais en France, les Français en Ecosse*, 2 vols. (London, 1862), ii. 122–3.   [127] Craig, *De Unione*, 458.

England certainly did not employ actual Scottish regiments, which did not exist. The main English theatre of operations, the occupied Dutch cautionary towns, had no official Scottish troops. Indeed the return of peace in 1604 was probably more significant than the union of crowns; Scotsmen had fought for England so long as there was fighting to be done. Scottish forces did serve in Ireland after 1603, as there was still fighting to be done there. As before, these forces were recruited and officered in Scotland but paid by England.[128] Some foreign regiments recruited both in Scotland and in England, and Scottish timber was cut for the English navy.[129] But of Anglo-Scottish military cooperation under James VI and I there is little trace, probably because he worked hard to ensure that there was little fighting to do.

In 1625, Charles I dragged his kingdoms into a series of wars that Scotland at least had neither sought nor prepared for. Sir Patrick Home of Polwarth 'never saw this kingdom in worse equippage both for hors and armes. . . . Thare is not a craftisman to make a steal bonett in al the land lyk as quhen theyr wes no smyth in Israel. The God of Hosts must be our scheild.'[130] A full review of Scotland's war effort in the late 1620s would be beyond the scope of this chapter, but the outlines seem clear. The council of war regularly treated Sir Harry Bruce, general of the artillery, as the only person in the country with real experience and ability in organizing a war—and he had duties in England too.[131] A few regiments were raised in Scotland, but there was no special taxation (either central or local) for them, and overall the war effort was minimal. Given the low level of military preparedness in Scotland, it might seem that it could hardly have been otherwise. However, the real reason for the smallness of the effort was that there was no real threat to Scottish territory from the enemies that Charles had made. Those Scots who felt a commitment to the war were probably in a small minority. Their compatriots made a deliberate decision to kill time but little else.

Things were different in the 1640s, because the idea of fighting

---

[128] This is an under-explored topic, but see *CSP Dom. 1611–1618*, 219.

[129] Fallon, 'Scottish Mercenaries', 35; *RPC* viii. 234, 277–8, 552–4; *CSP Dom. 1603–1610*, 422.

[130] Home to Sir Robert Kerr of Ancram, 7 Dec. 1625, *Correspondence of Sir Robert Kerr, First Earl of Ancram, and his Son, William, Third Earl of Lothian, 1616–1649*, 2 vols., ed. D. Laing (Bannatyne Club, 1875), ii. 482.

[131] NAS, minutes of council of war, 1626–9, PA7/2, no. 30a, fos. 2^v–3^r, 4^v, 9^{r-v}.

to defend and promote the National Covenant attracted deep and widespread commitment. In military matters, little else had changed between 1625 and 1639; there was still 'no smyth in Israel'. As Edward Furgol points out, 'the Covenanters had to propel Scotland into the military revolution from a standing start'.[132] Weapons had to be imported, soldiers recruited and drilled, taxes raised, supply systems established, more soldiers recruited and drilled, more taxes raised—none of these being procedures to which the Scots were accustomed. And yet the effort succeeded. Unlike in the 1620s, people were determined to make it succeed. So successful was it, indeed, that it caused the deaths of perhaps 60,000 people (28,000 of whom were soldiers) in Scotland—something that the military machine of the previous reign could never have accomplished.[133] What the reign of James VI had achieved, then, was not the construction of a modern military force, but the demolition of an old one and the laying of some foundations to replace it. Although it was a 'standing start' in 1639, Scotland was at least facing in the right direction; half a century earlier, it would not have been.

[132] E. M. Furgol, 'Scotland turned Sweden: The Scottish covenanters and the military revolution, 1638–1651', in J. Morrill (ed.), *The Scottish National Covenant in its British Context* (Edinburgh, 1990), 137; cf. E. M. Furgol, *A Regimental History of the Covenanting Armies, 1639–1651* (Edinburgh, 1990), ch. 1.

[133] C. Carlton, *Going to the Wars: The Experience of the English Civil Wars, 1638–1651* (London, 1992), 212–13. These were deaths *in Scotland,* and do not include those arising from the extensive Scottish campaigns in England and Ireland.

6

Religion

> Forsameikle as sinne and iniquitie is and hes bein the caus of
> Godis heavie plaigues and judgmentis, and the caus of great
> desolatioun in kirk and politie within this cuntrie for laik of
> discipline and putting of the actis of the kirk, quhilk has bein
> meikle compleinit in tymes past, to dew executioun . . .

To anyone familiar with the records of the general assembly of the
church, this passage will at once evoke the Protestant church's per-
tinacious struggle to establish its authority and discipline within
Scotland. The general assembly was forever lamenting 'laik of discipline', which became almost a catch-phrase; the 'actis of the kirk'
show it working energetically to create structures of ecclesiastical
authority to tackle 'sinne and iniquitie'. But is this particular act
quite what it seems? It continues:

And siclyk that thair hes bein great ignorance of his sacred majesties royall
and supreme auctoritie in practiseing of forren and uncouth lawis con-
trair to the actis of parliament and secreit counsall maid thairanent; and
lykewayes that thair hes bein great desolatioun in the commoun weill,
truble, dissordour, injuries, and wrangis amongst the inhabitantis of the
land for laik of governement, administratioun of justice, and putting of
the samen to dew executioun . . .

This passage is, in fact, the preamble to a series of acts of the sheriff
court of Orkney and Shetland.[1] It is true that the author may well
have been James Law, bishop of Orkney, who was involved in all
aspects of the islands' administration at this time (1615)—their
'laik of governement' as well as their 'laik of discipline'. But this
should make us wonder, not just why a sheriff court sounds like
the general assembly, but also why a bishop sounds like the privy
council.

---

[1] *Court Books of Orkney and Shetland, 1614–1615*, ed. R. S. Barclay (SHS, 1967),
25.

Orkney could have been unusual, but at the other end of the country, the church of Selkirk was equipped with 'a thing they call the jogges, which is for such as offend but particularly women brawlers, their head being put through it, and another iron in their mouth, so abiding foaming till such time as the bailiffs please to dismiss them, it being in the time of divine service'.[2] Public penance during the church service could be administered not just by the church authorities, but also by the civil magistrates.

It is sometimes convenient to think of 'church' and 'state' as separate entities, but in fact 'laik of discipline' and 'laik of governement' were much the same problem. *All* governmental authorities were concerned about religion, if for no other reason than that it was seen as the basis of their own authority. Post-Reformation Scotland, moreover, developed a strikingly powerful and effective network of authority in religious affairs, involving not just kirk sessions, but also burgh councils; not just the general assembly, but also parliament. Many historians have treated the issue of conflict between 'church' and 'state' as a key organizing concept for this period. Although much can be learned from their works, it should not be allowed to overshadow the extent to which there was a *single* network of authority encompassing both civil and religious institutions in fruitful cooperation.

Instead, let us begin by asking simply: How did one rule a Protestant people in the sixteenth century? Or (a slightly different question): How did a Protestant government rule its people? There were no simple answers to these questions. State Protestantism could be reflected in anything from municipal efforts to keep the poor off the streets, to the apocalyptically inspired crusade that some envisaged against the Antichrist.

At parish level, the people first had to be instructed in their religious duties. The direct requirements for this were preaching and catechizing: preaching to expound the word of God, catechizing to inculcate it into the memory of individuals. Preaching and catechizing called in turn for a wider and deeper cultural shift: a shift towards a more firmly literate, educated, text-based, print-

---

[2] 'Account of a journey into Scotland', 1629, in HMC, *Report on the Manuscripts of the Earl of Lonsdale*, ed. J. J. Cartwright (London, 1893), 76. For similar action by the Glasgow burgh court see J. McGrath, 'The medieval and early modern burgh', in T. M. Devine and G. Jackson (eds.), *Glasgow*, i. *Beginnings to 1830* (Manchester, 1995), 34.

based culture. The ministers themselves were expected to be educated to a high level—normally university level—in order to give a sound, detailed, and intellectually satisfying exegesis of their text. Andrew Melville, principal of St Mary's College at St Andrews University and a leader of the radical reformers, believed that to deal with 'controversies' the ministers would have to know Greek and Hebrew, since trying to understand the finer points of the Scriptures from translations was 'practically foolish and impious'.[3] Their parishioners, too, or at least a significant proportion of them, needed some vernacular literacy. So an educational infrastructure was also needed, as was a printing industry.

To bring all this home to the people, parish communities needed to be reinvigorated. For this, the pattern of corporate worship was important, with communion services at or near Easter as the crucial ones to which ordinary folk would be expected to come; the Easter service itself was not new, of course, but the presence of a preaching minister may have given it new significance. In some ways the Protestant church actually made the creation of community more difficult: it terminated the function of parish fraternities; it ceased to offer opportunities for investment in the beautifying of the parish church; it even hoped to abolish burial services, though it had to compromise in response to popular demand for them.[4] Still, these drawbacks were offset by the power of the new preachers, as their Catholic opponents recognized: 'the communion and other services . . . are always the same, and have not such a harmful effect on those present as the sermons, which need to be refuted'.[5]

---

[3] Quoted in J. Kirk, ' "Melvillian" reform in the Scottish universities', in A. A. MacDonald *et al.* (eds.), *The Renaissance in Scotland* (Leiden, 1994), 298.

[4] Fraternities have been studied in England: see e.g. E. Duffy, *The Stripping of the Altars: Traditional Religion in England, 1400–1580* (New Haven, 1992), ch. 4. They are not mentioned by D. McKay, 'Parish life in Scotland, 1500–1560', in D. McRoberts (ed.), *Essays on the Scottish Reformation* (Glasgow, 1962), but there is much on pre-Reformation church furnishing in D. McRoberts, 'Material destruction caused by the Scottish Reformation', ibid. Before 1614 the communion service was often near Easter Day rather than on the day itself, but even for churches holding two or four communion services per year, the Easter one was most significant. On burial services, see *The First Book of Discipline*, ed. J. K. Cameron (Edinburgh, 1972), 199–200, and G. Donaldson, *The Faith of the Scots* (London, 1990), 71.

[5] C. Giblin (ed.), *The Irish Franciscan Mission to Scotland, 1619–1646: Documents from Roman Archives* (Dublin, 1964), 30. For the difference that a dynamic minister could make to a congregation, see M. B. Verschuur, 'Enforcing the discipline of the kirk: Mr Patrick Galloway's early years as minister at Perth', in W. F. Graham (ed.), *Later Calvinism: International Perspectives* (Kirksville, Mo., 1994).

As well as providing these services to the community, the church was also a disciplinary institution. Discipline could itself create community, as the godly folk of the parish strengthened their identification with the church through the visible contrast that it drew between them and the ungodly. Community, after all, implies conformity, and exclusion of those who fail to conform. Attendance at the communion service was often restricted to those who had received tickets in advance, tickets being granted to those who satisfied the church elders on basic religious knowledge and denied to those who had committed moral lapses.[6] If the lapses were serious, the offenders could also find themselves in further disciplinary trouble—which is what now needs to be examined.

'Discipline' was one of the three marks of a true church in the Confession of Faith of 1560, and the one that was most unusual in a European context.[7] By 'discipline' the reformers sometimes meant having an adequate church organization, but they usually meant coercion of ungodly members of the congregation—partly in the hope of reclaiming the offenders for God, but also simply to stamp out ungodliness. In pursuing the role of religion in government, we need to be alert to both senses of the term 'discipline'—the organizational structures, and the coercive attack on ungodliness; but the latter is inevitably prominent.

Coercive discipline was wielded against various types of people. There were the ordinary folk who danced on the sabbath or had illegitimate babies; these formed the staple business of all kirk sessions. There were also more ideological and challenging forms of ungodliness: witches, seen as an underground conspiracy against God and the community; committed Catholics, whose refusal to conform presented a problem that the government could never forget; radical Protestants, who in the early seventeenth century were coming to be identified (and to identify themselves) as dissidents within the state church. An individual parish minister or kirk session might well not be able, or willing, to tackle these problems, and they thus came to be matters for the higher authorities.

The key individual, nevertheless, was the parish minister, for without him neither kirk session nor higher authorities could

---

[6] I. B. Cowan, *The Scottish Reformation* (London, 1982), 144–9.

[7] G. Donaldson, *The Scottish Reformation* (Cambridge, 1960), 78–9; M. F. Graham, *The Uses of Reform: 'Godly Discipline' and Popular Behavior in Scotland and Beyond, 1560–1610* (Leiden, 1996), 39. The other two were correct preaching and correct administration of the sacraments.

operate. Who provided the ministers? The decision on appointment of ministers was an uncontentious compromise between lay
and ecclesiastical authority.[8] The difficult question was: who paid
for them? Local initiative from committed Protestants, plus some
government pressure, provided enough funds in the early years of
the Reformation to launch the new church successfully, particularly in the towns;[9] but it was always recognized that the church
would need to take over some resources from the old church.
Parish benefices existed from pre-Reformation times, consisting of
small parcels of land and rights to a share in the teinds (i.e. tithes).
Gradually during our period the benefices were allocated to
Protestant ministers. Meanwhile, ministers who lacked benefices
(initially the great majority), or whose benefice was inadequate,
had their stipends topped up centrally by the state. All benefice-
holders who were not ministers had to pay one-third of their revenues into a central, state fund, and a committee of the exchequer
was appointed annually to allocate ('modify') stipends. This gave
ministers an unexpected dependence on central government. As
part of this routine, for instance, the usual meeting of Stirling presbytery had to be cancelled in November 1587 'berassone the maist
part of the brethrein of this presbytery was in Edinburgh the said
day all waittein on the lordis modefearis of ministeris stependis this
yeir'. After 1607, responsibility for modification of stipends was
transferred to the bishops, who were also agents of the crown.[10]

The church did its best to recruit ministers, but shortage of
money and its own high educational standards meant that progress
was slow; only towards the end of our period, in the 1610s and
1620s, did most parishes have their own ministers.[11] Still, it should
not be assumed that the church only then became an effective

[8] For more details on this complex topic, see J. Kirk, 'The survival of ecclesiastical patronage after the Reformation', in id., *Patterns of Reform: Continuity and
Change in the Reformation Kirk* (Edinburgh, 1989).
[9] Id., 'Recruitment to the ministry at the Reformation', in id., *Patterns of Reform*.
[10] *Accounts of the Collectors of Thirds of Benefices, 1561–1572*, ed. G. Donaldson
(SHS, 1949), introd.; Knox, *History*, ii. 27–32; *Stirling Presbytery Records, 1581–1587*,
ed. J. Kirk (SHS, 1981), 295; Calderwood, *History*, vi. 688.
[11] M. Lynch, 'Preaching to the converted? Perspectives on the Scottish Reformation', in MacDonald *et al.* (eds.), *Renaissance in Scotland*, 306–14; W. R. Foster,
The Church before the Covenants, 1596–1638 (Edinburgh, 1975), ch. 8. Parishes
without ministers often had 'readers', qualified to read prayers and provide some
of the rites of passage but not to preach or (usually) administer communion; to
cover for this, many ministers had to take responsibility for several parishes.

institution; it had long since captured the commanding heights of the Scottish state, particularly the towns, and the strategic rural parishes of east-central Scotland. By the early seventeenth century, the parishes without ministers were mainly in the Highlands (where discipline did not become effective until long after our period) or more remote Lowland areas.[12]

Along with full-time, professional ministers went kirk sessions, the distinctive organs of the Scottish Reformation. They were committees of lay 'elders', mostly drawn from the propertied classes, whose authority derived nominally from the congregation but who were usually in practice self-selected. Kirk sessions were almost entirely new bodies; the courts of the old church had had nominal competence over some of the same offences, but their main concern had been with the marital and testamentary matters now dealt with by the civil commissary courts. Kirk sessions, by contrast, dealt with offences that nobody had been much concerned to punish before, or that had not existed before: adultery and fornication; breach of the sabbath; open resistance to Protestantism by Catholics. As newcomers to government, they themselves had to find a niche within the structure of existing authority in the localities. They did so with triumphant success.[13]

Scholars studying kirk sessions tend to contrast their effectiveness favourably with that of civil institutions: 'even by the early seventeenth century the Church was an institution equipped with a far more modern system of government than the State'.[14] The only authority that fell heavily on the common people, it is implied, was that of the kirk session. Here, some caveats are in order. Certainly, kirk session discipline had a striking impact in Scotland, but it was felt selectively, by certain categories of people only. The kirk session might not affect you much if you kept the sabbath and refrained from fornicating. On the other hand, the baron court

---

[12] For a local study in the late 16th cent., see F. D. Bardgett, *Scotland Reformed: The Reformation in Angus and the Mearns* (Edinburgh, 1989), ch. 5. For more on the Highlands, see Ch. 8 below. For the tendency to concentrate resources in towns, see J. Dawson, ' "The face of ane perfyt reformed kirk": St Andrews and the early Scottish Reformation', in J. Kirk (ed.), *Humanism and Reform* (Oxford, 1991), 491–4.

[13] Cf. J. Goodare, 'Scotland', in R. W. Scribner *et al.* (eds.), *The Reformation in National Context* (Cambridge, 1994).

[14] R. Mitchison and L. Leneman, *Sexuality and Social Control: Scotland, 1660–1780* (Oxford, 1989), 25; cf. Graham, *Uses of Reform*, 149–50.

might be deeply concerned about you if you committed assault or withheld your rent; even the sheriff court might have a word or two with you if you stole or killed. Many kirk sessions concerned themselves with assault too, and some even dealt with murder; but one can agree that kirk sessions were powerful institutions of government without jumping to the conclusion that they were the only show in town.

What we need, therefore, are better comparative studies of the scope and effectiveness of religious and civil authorities, especially in the localities. Studies of kirk sessions certainly show that they were effective in bringing discipline home to people—many of those summoned cooperated.[15] Unfortunately, none of these studies make comparisons with civil courts. The records of a baron court do not usually tell us about summonses, but we may well wonder whether the ordinary man charged with assault could evade its authority for long. The only study to compare kirk session and baron court argues that the latter was at least as effective.[16] As for central authority: although the records of the general assembly are full of appeals from lesser church courts, that does not mean that the assembly was a uniquely powerful central body. The central civil courts also heard many appeals from the localities.

The point, then, is not that ecclesiastical courts were more powerful or effective than civil ones. It is that Scotland was distinctive for having kirk sessions at all. Every European country had courts to punish assault, but few took seriously the repression of illicit sex.[17] That does not mean that kirk sessions were *all* that mattered, or even that they were necessarily *more* effective than other organs of government.

One issue that was immediately raised by the successful creation of kirk sessions was: who controlled them? Traditional local authorities were linked into existing hierarchies, and were ultimately answerable to the central government—or if they were not, as with

---

[15] Graham, *Uses of Reform*, 275; Foster, *Church before the Covenants*, 80.

[16] M. H. B. Sanderson, *Scottish Rural Society in the Sixteenth Century* (Edinburgh, 1982), 12–13.

[17] The English church courts, though not as ineffective as used to be suggested, hardly compare with the intense discipline seen in Scotland: M. Ingram, *Church Courts, Sex and Marriage in England, 1575–1640* (Cambridge, 1988); B. Lenman, 'The limits of godly discipline in the early modern period, with particular reference to England and Scotland', in K. von Greyerz (ed.), *Religion and Society in Early Modern Europe, 1500–1800* (London, 1984).

the heritable jurisdictions, that was a problem. If kirk sessions were not accountable either, that would be a bigger problem. For the first decade or two of the Reformation, the higher government of the church was unsettled, with conflicting tendencies and latent possibilities which did not all develop. During the 1570s, two rival forms of polity slowly crystallized: presbyterianism and episcopalianism.[18] Bishops had been largely eclipsed at the Reformation; by the time a Protestant episcopate began to take shape, in the 1570s, many ministers were coming to prefer the idea of oversight by presbyteries, committees of parish ministers. Bishop or presbytery might be equally capable of supervising the kirk session, but they had radically different implications for the government of the country. Presbyterians usually saw authority vested by God in the church (the entire community of believers): their view of authority was thus an ascending one. Conveniently, authority ascended to the ministers who articulated this view. King James, equally conveniently, saw authority as descending from him personally to the bishops whom he appointed, and from them to the parish ministers: 'the bishops must rule the ministers, and the king rule both'.[19] This conflict would not be easily resolved. Presbyterians made things worse by tending to adhere to George Buchanan's views on the election of kings, making civil authority ascending also.[20]

That the system of kirk session discipline needed to be controlled is suggested by the subversive potential of some of the doctrines that Scotland had embraced with such apparent fervour in 1559–60. Christianity itself contained elements and traditions that, were they to be taken seriously, might threaten the social order: the Sermon on the Mount, the epistle of James, the ideals of St Francis.[21] The First Book of Discipline (1560–1) professed to fear

---

[18] For two detailed but very different views of the polity of the early years, see Donaldson, *Scottish Reformation*, ch. 5, supplemented by id., *Reformed by Bishops* (Edinburgh, 1987); and J. Kirk, 'The superintendent: Myth and reality', in id., *Patterns of Reform*. See also D. G. Mullan, *Episcopacy in Scotland, 1560–1638* (Edinburgh, 1986), chs. 2–3.

[19] Spottiswoode, *History*, iii. 241. Presbyterians thought that power was exercised 'conjunctlie be mutuall consent of thame that bear the office and charge', i.e. the ministers: *The Second Book of Discipline*, ed. J. Kirk (Edinburgh, 1980), 165. Cf. Calderwood, *History*, v. 315.

[20] For James and Andrew Melville's reverence for Buchanan, see Melville, *Diary*, 121, 313.

[21] The 'Beggars' Summons', a Protestant manifesto of 1559, turned the friars' profession of poverty against them: *Source Book*, ii. 168–9.

that 'the papistical tyrannie shal onely be changed into the tyrannie of the lord and laird', and announced that 'as well the rulers,
as they that are ruled' should be subject to church discipline; Knox
waxed eloquent on the equality of rich and poor in the eyes of
God.[22] It was intended to apply godly discipline to all classes and
both sexes.[23] The more radical ministers modelled themselves on
the Old Testament prophets, regularly noting when any of their
leaders' prophecies came to pass. King James, by contrast, thought
that 'prophecie' had 'ceased in the world'—which was just as well,
since prophecy could be one of the sharpest tools for undermining the *status quo*.[24]

Control was also needed because reformers within the church
differed in their long-term aims and ideals. The most radical ministers—the presbyterians—aspired to create a fully godly society,
purged of outward sin and corruption, which would fit Scotland
to join battle against the Roman Antichrist in the coming last days
of the world. Such a vision prevailed among the presbyterian leadership, and underpinned their stress on doctrinal purity: they knew
that when the Lord had gone before the Israelites by day in a pillar
of a cloud, it had not been to encourage them to compromise.
More douce and respectable reformers, however, limited themselves to a narrower range, and to ideals that seemed achievable
within the existing structure of society. They were prepared to
settle for the administration of decent prayers, Sunday worship,
and rites of passage in every parish, together with the establishment of an obedient and ordered clergy, and the suppression of
witchcraft and Catholicism. In fact the less adventurous kirk sessions might find even witchcraft and Catholicism difficult targets;
some concentrated almost exclusively on fornication and adultery
among the lower orders.

The episcopalian leadership was often willing to take up the militant ideal of the crusade against Antichrist (so long as there were
no awkward foreign policy implications); but they were likely to
make it sound like a conventional war—and one in which Protestants agreed to compromise among themselves in order to unite

---

[22] *First Book of Discipline*, 156–7, 173; Knox, *A Letter Addressed to the Commonalty of
Scotland* (1558), in *Works*, iv. 521–40.

[23] Graham, *Uses of Reform*, ch. 7.

[24] Melville, *Diary*, 125 (an example of a prophecy coming true); Calderwood,
History, v. 290 (a subversive sermon using prophecy); James VI & I, speech to parliament, 1605, in *Political Writings*, 154.

against the common enemy, which was just what the presbyterians were not prepared to do. William Cowper, bishop of Galloway in 1614, could not comprehend why Protestants would choose to criticize their own regime rather than falling into line in the common anti-Catholic struggle. Arthur Williamson, who tells us about Cowper, also points to the intellectual distance between two reforming leaders of the first generation, John Knox and John Erskine of Dun, the one with universalizing concerns about the apocalypse, the other with particularizing worries over witchcraft in Angus.[25]

To enforce moral discipline, whether in a universal or particular way, the church had to possess jurisdiction over morals. The successful establishment of the first few kirk sessions as disciplinary bodies made it desirable to define exactly what their powers should be. A statute of December 1567 declared that the church's jurisdiction consisted in the preaching of the word of God, the administration of the sacraments, and (most relevantly for us) 'correctioun of maneris'. But it also noted that this was vague, and set up a commission to report back to the next parliament with proposals to clarify it. Nothing happened as a result, although the commission still existed in 1569 and a request of the general assembly for its 'jurisdictioun' to be 'separate fra that quhilk is civill' was referred to it. The assembly seems to have been seeking a clearly marked sphere in which it could exercise unrestricted or unsupervised power; but it did not get one. A new parliamentary commission of 1579 in similar terms was equally barren, and there matters rested.[26] Kirk sessions continued to wield extensive local power, but in the first two decades of the Reformation they varied greatly in how they did so, as individual groups of elders felt their way gradually forward. St Andrews, for instance, excommunicated people regularly—twelve in 1564 alone—whereas there were only two recorded excommunications in Aberdeen and none in the Canongate.[27]

All these disciplinary cases were on matters of prime concern to the kirk sessions, especially fornication and adultery. But the

[25] A. H. Williamson, *Scottish National Consciousness in the Age of James VI* (Edinburgh, 1979), 91–3, 55–9.

[26] *APS* iii. 24–5, c. 12 (1567); *BUK* i. 140, 146; *RPC* ii. 6–7; *APS* iii. 137–8, c. 7 (1579); Hope, *Major Practicks*, i. 25, citing the 1579 act.

[27] Graham, *Uses of Reform*, ch. 3. The Aberdeen and Canongate records survive only for a few years, but the variability of practice seems clear.

church also sought a broader field in which it wished to exercise the sole or primary authority. The general assembly went to the regent in 1571 with a shopping list of six jurisdictional demands. A few of them were in fields where the church already had a good deal of control, but wanted the boundaries more clearly drawn; most were matters which the church had allowed to slip through its fingers since the Reformation.[28] First, they wanted to be able to define religious doctrine. Currently this might have been thought to be the church's job, but the ratification of doctrine had pertained to parliament since 1560 and the statutory adoption of the Confession of Faith. Secondly, they wanted the power to admit ministers to benefices, and to suspend them if necessary. Currently, superintendents or commissioners could appoint ministers to *parishes*, but the benefices were in the hands of lay patrons. Thirdly, they wanted to be able to punish moral lapses, if necessary by excommunication; the church did have the power to excommunicate, but this was not based on any clear enactment, and later events would show that there were complications surrounding it. Fourthly, they wanted to judge legal cases involving ministers. The pre-Reformation church courts had been able to do this, but Protestant ministers had lost any special legal status and had to sue in the civil courts like anyone else.[29] Fifthly, they wanted to excommunicate people who withheld the revenues of church benefices. Currently the church had no jurisdiction over the property of benefices. Finally, they wanted jurisdiction over matrimonial cases, 'because the conjunctioun of marriages pertaines to the ministrie'. Currently, this was the province of the commissary courts, over which the church had no control. This shopping list is a fair conspectus of the limits of ecclesiastical jurisdiction. The limits remained the same thereafter, for the church's demands were ignored.

The failure to meet the church's broader demands was also a failure to define precise jurisdictional boundaries. This stored up the potential for conflict between church authorities and civil magistrates, as both sides recognized.[30] Conflict here was not entirely

---

[28] *BUK* i. 187.
[29] Balfour, *Practicks*, i. 28; M. Dilworth, *Scottish Monasteries in the Late Middle Ages* (Edinburgh, 1995), 22.
[30] Regent Morton to Robert Campbell of Kinzeancleuch, 23 Jan. 1574, *Wodrow Society Miscellany*, i (1844), 289.

inevitable, and in practice there was often compromise locally. But there were so many religious and political debates in later six-teenth-century Scotland that the church's jurisdiction was highly likely to become contentious. Problems might arise if discipline was used against the elite—or if failure to discipline the elite threatened to delegitimize the whole disciplinary system. One could not simply exempt the elite from religious authority, because the authorities usually agreed (at least in principle) that Catholics were subversive—and the Catholics who were most subversive, on the face of it, were the elite Catholics. Something had to be done about them—but what, and on whose terms? The trouble was that not *all* elite Catholics were subversive, or not all the time; some were at court and in high favour with the king. If, for instance, the church leadership wanted to excommunicate the earl of Huntly, while the king wanted to protect him (as happened more than once in the early 1590s), the stage was set for a jurisdictional contest between church and state. Should the state win, and should it establish an active supervisory role over the church, the result would be a church normally known to historians as 'Erastian'.

At this point we need to look in more detail at what the church actually did when it punished moral offenders. Its main sanction was penance. Offenders would be ordered to do public penance in church, usually for between three and twenty-six consecutive Sundays; they would usually also be fined, or briefly imprisoned, for instance for twenty-four hours. In theory they were supposed to display actual penitence for their offence. They would then be absolved. All this was usually done by the kirk session, although from the 1580s the presbytery might handle complex cases or recal-citrant offenders. One reason why people submitted to discipline is that the church had a further sanction in reserve—excommuni-cation; and although we have already heard a little about excom-munication, it is worth examining it more carefully. Who had power to excommunicate? For what offences? How was it enforced and supervised? Such questions go to the heart of the issue of how 'Eras-tian' the church was. This is usually discussed in the general sense of how far the church was subject to civil control or supervision— but to Erastus himself, an Erastian church was one in which *excom-munication* was subject to civil control or supervision.[31]

[31] J. N. Figgis, 'Erastus and Erastianism', *Journal of Theological Studies*, 2 (1901), 66–101.

Excommunication—exclusion from contact with the church and civil society—was pronounced against serious offenders who refused to submit to church discipline. A statute of the Reformation Parliament ordered church jurisdiction on excommunication to be transferred to a temporal court, no doubt the projected commissary court.[32] This might have been a logical sequel to the routine use of excommunication by the pre-Reformation court of the bishop's official, the ancestor of the commissary court; but it did not happen. The commissary courts became such secular bodies that it would have been inappropriate. Their existence, rather than weakening the church, seems to have strengthened it by allowing ministers and kirk sessions to specialize in what they did best—moral discipline. None of the Continental Protestants whose ideas underpinned the disciplinary system (Oecolampadius, Bucer, Calvin) had envisaged the church overseeing contracts or testaments, the areas in which the commissary courts specialized.[33] So excommunication remained with the church. Initially an individual minister (usually with kirk session) could excommunicate, but once the presbyterian system was in place it was the presbytery which normally took the responsibility. After 1610 all sentences were supposed to be confirmed by the bishop, and the number of excommunications dropped sharply.[34]

The sanction of excommunication was often enough to bring offenders to submit to the church and do penance. But it was always assumed that excommunication might have to be followed by further sanctions from the civil authorities. Before the Reformation, excommunication might be followed by putting to the horn after forty days, and this was renewed by a statute of 1573.[35] The attitude of local civil authorities was thus important. The Edinburgh council ruled in 1571 that it would enforce excommunication with banishment.[36] The church was dependent on secular

---

[32] Robert Keith, *History of the Affairs of Church and State in Scotland, from the Beginning of the Reformation to the Year 1568*, 3 vols., ed. J. P. Lawson and C. J. Lyon (Spottiswoode Society, 1844–50), i. 325. This statute was omitted from *APS*: cf. J. Goodare, 'The Scottish parliamentary records, 1560–1603', *Historical Research*, lxxii (1999, forthcoming).

[33] Graham, *Uses of Reform*, 71.

[34] Foster, *Church before the Covenants*, 100–5. Alan R. MacDonald, who has examined many of the presbytery records, has kindly pointed out to me that this rule was not always adhered to.

[35] *APS* iii. 76*, c. 14; cf. Balfour, *Practicks*, ii. 564.

[36] *Edin. Recs.* iii. 283. Cf. Graham, *Uses of Reform*, 49–64, for other early disciplinary ordinances.

power in many guises, not all of them official ones. The presbytery of Glasgow in 1593 had to negotiate with Sir William Livingstone of Kilsyth, who seems to have held no public office, 'anent sum ordour to be tane with excommunicat and inordinat persones within the said lardis boundis; requeisting the said lard to put to his helping hand for redressing of the misbehaviour of the saidis persones, that the censures of the kirk striken aganis thame may be feirit be thame'.[37]

All this support from the civil power—if it was forthcoming—was no doubt welcome, although it underlines the church's lack of full independence. However, the civil authorities might get a little *too* involved with ecclesiastical sanctions. In August 1567, the newly appointed Regent Moray was adopting a quasi-ecclesiastical role himself: he ordained Mr Thomas Beanston, tacksman of the priory of Pittenweem, to do penance for an unspecified offence in the parish church of Anstruther, on the stool of repentance 'as custum is'.[38] That was very unusual, though it reminds us how fluid were the power structures of the Protestant church in its early years; more common, but equally worrying to some in the church, were secular attempts to regulate whom the church could and could not excommunicate. If and when these attempts were rigorous and successful (and only then), Scotland did indeed have an Erastian church.

Before the Reformation, the crown had had no regular interest in these matters, although Balfour cited two cases in which it had intervened over excommunication of civil magistrates 'wrangouslie or inordourlie'.[39] Local civil authorities might regulate excommunication—at least in towns, where the kirk session was usually an adjunct to the burgh council, and possessed neither the power nor the intention of taking an independent line. In 1579, a burgess of Edinburgh and his wife complained to the privy council that the ministers were about to excommunicate them for no good cause; the ministers and the *bailies* of Edinburgh were ordered to desist by the privy council.[40] If the *bailies*, not the kirk session, were

---

[37] 'Extracts from the registers of the presbytery of Glasgow, 1592–1601', *Maitland Club Miscellany*, i (1833), 60.

[38] HMC, *Sixth Report, Appendix* (London, 1877), 643. Moray may have been acting in his capacity as commendator of the priory of Pittenweem, but the point remains: he was no minister. [39] Balfour, *Practicks*, ii. 565.

[40] *RPC* iii. 239. For the relationship between burgh council and kirk session, see M. Lynch, *Edinburgh and the Reformation* (Edinburgh, 1981), 38–45. Further research in rural local records might shed further light on this subject.

regarded as having responsibility for excommunication, this shows
how far the church was already Erastian in a local sense; what is
unusual about this case is that the privy council saw fit to become
involved, for central government had not as yet had much to do
with excommunication.

As with other aspects of church–state relations, this began to
change with the Black Acts of 1584. We shall hear more about
these acts later, but by one of the acts, parliament cancelled an
excommunication directly—that of Robert Montgomery, archbishop of Glasgow, by a commissioner of the general assembly. The
act explained that excommunication was within the jurisdiction of
the crown, since excommunicates were 'debarrit from all civill
societie and benefite of his hienes lawis'; it also asserted the right
of king and privy council to cancel future excommunications.[41]
Erastus would have approved.

However, this hard line could not be maintained after the fall,
in 1585, of the Arran regime that had passed the Black Acts. In
the late 1580s and early 1590s, the crown sought to conciliate the
church leadership. In 1587, the king seemed willing to negotiate
with the assembly, or at least resigned to the necessity of doing so,
when he wanted two excommunications cancelled.[42] Compromise
was still the theme in 1595, when power to enforce excommunication was given to crown commissioners in parishes (a scheme
which in the event never left the drawing board). The idea seems
to have been that they would *support* the kirk sessions, rather than
supervising or superseding them.[43]

From the late 1590s onwards, however, the era of compromise
was at an end. The privy council is now found intervening more
actively in the work of presbyteries, to tell them whom they might
excommunicate, whom they *must* excommunicate, and especially
whom they were not allowed to excommunicate.[44] Two issues were
of particular concern to the government (for different reasons):
adultery and Catholicism.

Disputes over adultery arose through the dual nature of the
offence, both ecclesiastical and statutory. Twenty-six weeks' public
penance was one thing: a death sentence was another. Could a conviction before the kirk session or presbytery lead to a criminal

---

[41] *APS* iii. 311–12, c. 31.   [42] *BUK* ii. 700–1.   [43] *RPC* v. 200.
[44] Cf. P. G. B. McNeill, 'The Jurisdiction of the Scottish Privy Council,
1532–1708', Ph.D. thesis (Glasgow, 1960), 33, 60–1.

prosecution being brought before the court of justiciary? The two jurisdictions used different procedures, so could an offender be found guilty in one and innocent in the other? The court of justiciary had an assize to determine guilt or innocence, while the members of the church courts performed that function themselves. As a defender, one was not required to testify on oath before the court of justiciary.[45] But before the presbytery one would probably be ordered to do so—and those who refused could be excommunicated. This issue of dual jurisdiction arose for several offences, and the general assembly had asserted in 1575 that the church had prior, or at least independent, power in this area.[46] There was a special problem with adultery, because statutes of 1563 and 1581 had prescribed the death penalty for 'notour adultery' without succeeding in giving a clear definition of this crime. However, if a presbytery excommunicated someone for adultery this would, under the terms of the 1581 act, make the adultery 'notour', and would also furnish strong evidence of guilt to the court of justiciary.[47]

The problem with Catholicism was similar—again, hearing of mass was both an ecclesiastical and a statutory offence—but more linked with politics. The king was in principle willing to take strong action against Catholics, but he wanted to be able to make exceptions when he chose—first for certain favoured nobles and courtiers whose loyalty or at least quiescence he could rely on, and secondly for *any* Catholics at times when he was pursuing a sensitive foreign policy. The national presbyterian leadership, who understood this well, periodically picked up the weapon of excommunication of leading Catholics as a means of putting pressure on the king.[48]

And there was a further jurisdictional issue. James reminisced to the English house of commons in 1621 that

the puritan ministers in Scotland [did] bring all kinde of causes within the compasse of their jurisdiction, saying, That it was the Churches office to judge of slander, and there could no kinde of crime or fault bee committed, but there was a slander in it, either against God, the king, or their

---

[45] Hope, *Major Practicks*, ii. 189, 252, 260–2.   [46] *BUK* i. 343–4.

[47] *APS* iii. 213, c. 7 (1581); ii. 539, c. 10 (1563). The main dual offences were adultery, breach of the sabbath, fornication, usury, incest, hearing of mass, resetting of Jesuits, and witchcraft; the last four, like 'notour' adultery, carried the death penalty in certain circumstances.

[48] e.g. the process against the countess of Huntly begun on 4 Jan. 1597: NAS, Edinburgh presbytery minutes, CH2/121/2, fo. 97ᵛ.

neighbour. And by this meanes they hooked in to themselves the cognisance of all causes.[49]

This was exaggerated, but not fancifully so. The general assembly asserted in 1587, for instance, that it was slanderous for someone to attend church services while at the horn, even if the horning was for a civil offence: this would have allowed them to wield ecclesiastical discipline over those at the horn. The presbyterians aspired to 'separat everie soule from their slanderous knowne sinne', including 'murtherers, theeves, usurers, or not payers of their debts', whether the civil magistrate proceeded against them or not—though they pointed out that if the civil magistrate did his duty there would be fewer such offenders to excommunicate.[50] 'Slander' was a broad concept, and it could be incurred by those who failed to punish offences as well as the original offenders. The general assembly declared in 1590 that 'great slander lyis upon the kirk throw manifold murthers, notorious adulteries, and incests', and decided that summary excommunication of the offenders was necessary 'upon the notoritie of the cryme' (in other words, simply upon report of it) because they 'schifts from place to place' to prevent regular proceeding against them. The synod of Lothian and Tweeddale approved this policy next year, and issued admonitions against all 'murthereris' at the horn as a preparative to excommunicating them.[51] Summary excommunication of this kind was one of the earliest issues to become contentious. The king asked the general assembly in 1595 that 'summar excommunicatioun, without any citatioun, be alluterlie abolischit'. It was suspended in 1598.[52]

The privy council seems first to have drawn a distinction between crime and slander in December 1598. The presbytery of Hamilton got into trouble for proceeding against a woman for fornication with a man who, she claimed, had abducted her against her will and from whom she had since escaped to marry another man. The council remitted the action for the fornication, and for 'sklander,

---

[49] James VI & I, *His Majesties Declaration . . .* , 1621, in *Political Writings*, 257.

[50] *BUK* ii. 691; Calderwood, *History*, v. 593–4.

[51] *BUK* ii. 776; *Records of the Synod of Lothian and Tweeddale, 1589–1596, 1640–1649*, ed. J. Kirk (Stair Society, 1977), 33. The records usually refer to 'slander', but 'scandal' is also found, and seems in this context to mean the same thing. Both could also be used in the modern sense of defamation of one individual by another, with which the church was also concerned.

[52] *BUK* iii. 852, 947.

giff ony may be', to the commission of the general assembly (a body of hand-picked ministers coordinating royal policy on the church). The council discharged the presbytery from proceeding against the woman's brother for 'revessing' because of his part in rescuing her from the abductor: this was a criminal charge pertaining to the justice court only.[53] Such interventions soon multiplied; by March 1600 the general assembly was complaining that they were hampering the work of the church. The king promised that the privy council would hear complaints about excommunication only if the complainer first registered a pledge to recognize the presbytery's jurisdiction, but that did not halt the advance of conciliar supervision.[54]

The issue of dual jurisdiction came into sharper focus when it was linked with the church's practice of proceeding by oath of the defender. A man complained to the privy council in May 1600 against the presbytery of Hamilton. They were accusing him of incest, summoning him to give his oath on the truth of the charge, and threatening to excommunicate him for refusal to do so. 'Seing the cryme of the awne nature is capitall, importing the hasard and perrell of his lyffe, the said complenair can not be haldin to gif his aith thairupoun.' The privy council decided for the complainer, ordering him to find caution to submit to trial in the court of justiciary and discharging the presbytery from any further action in the meantime.[55]

In 1605, a woman was being pursued for adultery by the presbytery of Paisley, and complained to the privy council. Sir Thomas Hamilton's notes bring out her argument well once his syntax is digested:

She could not be compelled to sweare upon her awin turpitude, nather could thay proceid to sik ane precognition as, gif she wer acquit be thame, sould not be ane liberation to hir from farder persute before the justice; and [which], gif she wer forced be the presbiterie to grant and mak her repentance, wald be ane necessar cause to fyle [i.e. convict] her be ane [criminal] assyse.

The presbytery 'alleged that be the act [of 1581] maid anent notour adulteraris the kirk had power to urge the pairties to purge thameselfis be thair aithis, and gif thay failled, to excommunicat

[53] *RPC* v. 509–10.
[54] *BUK* iii. 951–2; cf. A. R. MacDonald, 'Ecclesiastical Politics in Scotland, 1586–1610', Ph.D. thesis (Edinburgh, 1995), 207–8. [55] *RPC* vi. 108–9.

thame'. But the council found for the complainer; the presbytery could neither compel her to give an oath nor excommunicate her for failing to do so. Hamilton regarded it as a precedent.[56] Shortly afterwards, the presbytery of Dalkeith was hauled before the council in a similar case; they put up a spirited and sophisticated defence, but the privy council decided that the church could proceed against the complainer 'for tryell of the sclander of the said adulterie . . . allanderlie'—not the adultery itself. Subsequent cases on the issue were decided in the same way.[57]

Early in 1609 the king wrote to the bishops discharging all proceedings against those excommunicated for capital crimes. While pointing out that they had no authority to cancel excommunications, they promised to do their best. In June 1610, as part of the general restoration of diocesan episcopacy, they were empowered to confirm all excommunications.[58] Meanwhile, the final precedent had been established on the issue of dual jurisdiction, in July 1609. The presbytery of Dalkeith alleged that they could try a woman for witchcraft: it was 'idolatrie' and 'apostasie', which surely fell within the church's jurisdiction. The council agreed that if someone *confessed* to these offences the presbytery could inflict ecclesiastical censures,

bot, gif thay deny it, the kirk hes no power to tak tryell or to judge of the fact and of the guiltines of the pairtie, because thay have onlie power to try what is idolatrie or heresie, and the tryell wha is ane idolater or heretik is onlie competent to the criminall juge and to the assyse.[59]

This position, highly restrictive to the church, became accepted practice thereafter.[60]

---

[56] A similar action by the woman's alleged partner followed: he claimed additionally that the presbytery could not proceed by witnesses (who were anyway 'husseis, fellows and bairnes'), and that the case ought to be heard either by the justice court or by the commissaries of Edinburgh. Again, the decision went against the presbytery although they were represented to argue their case. *RPC* vii. 52, 130; cf. 119–20 for a similar case.

[57] *RPC* vii. 146. A presbytery might obtain a decision in its favour if the complainer failed to compear when summoned, however. *RPC* viii. 193, 198, 381; xiii. 108–9; xiv. 564, 619; 2nd ser. viii. 326.

[58] Bishops to James, n.d. [shortly after 4 Apr. 1609], *Eccles. Letters*, i. 194; *BUK* iii. 1096.

[59] *RPC* xiv. 612. For the woman's subsequent trial (and renewed acquittal), see 'The trial of Geillis Johnstone for witchcraft, 1614', ed. M. Wasser and L. A. Yeoman, *SHS Miscellany*, xiii (forthcoming).

[60] Cf. Sir George Mackenzie of Rosehaugh, *The Laws and Customes of Scotland in Matters Criminal* (Edinburgh, 1678), 89. This does not mean that the church's evidence carried no weight in the civil courts. In 1626, the court of justiciary accepted

These controversies had related to the jurisdiction of the church, but the privy council also began to act periodically as a straightforward appeal court. In 1601 the council agreed with a complainer that the presbytery of Cupar had no evidence to justify excommunicating her, and ordered them to desist. Similarly, in 1605, the privy council ordered an investigation into a complaint by an excommunicated person, 'and in the mentyme ordanit the excommunication to cease'.[61] These decisions were taken even though it was accepted that the church had jurisdiction in these cases; the privy council's objection was that it had no evidence, and the council was establishing its right to review church cases on the evidence.

Excommunicating Catholics was rather like excommunicating adulterers. It was decided in 1604 that a presbytery could proceed against a Catholic for the *slander* of having resetted (i.e. harboured) Jesuits and attended mass, but not for the *fact* of having done so, the latter being a criminal offence.[62] The difference was the highly political nature of Catholicism. In 1603 and 1604, the commission of the general assembly began to intervene to restrain presbyteries from excommunicating leading Catholics.[63] The background was probably the king's pursuit of a negotiated peace with Spain. In February 1605, the king ordered presbyteries and synods not to excommunicate noblemen until they had informed the commissioners of the general assembly (who would in turn inform the king). The presbytery of Aberdeen thus had to halt proceedings against the marquis of Huntly and his wife. Sometime between then and November 1607, this order was tightened up, and all ecclesiastical proceedings against noblemen were to be handled by the privy council: ministers were merely to give information to the council.[64] This certainly did not mean that Catholics, noble or otherwise, were to escape persecution; it did mean that the persecution was controlled by the government.[65]

a 'publict confessioun maid befoir the presbiterie of Edinburgh' as sufficient evidence to convict a woman for infanticide: *Selected Justiciary Cases, 1624–1650*, 3 vols., ed. S. A. Gillon and J. I. Smith (Stair Society, 1953–74), i. 47. But it was the court of justiciary that made the decision to convict; it was in no sense ratifying a decision of the presbytery, which is what the church had wanted.

[61] *RPC* vi. 272; vii. 60.   [62] *RPC* vii. 6–8, 16.
[63] MacDonald, 'Ecclesiastical Politics', 123–4.
[64] *RPC* vii. 19–21, 178, 466–7; viii. 5–6.
[65] For the difficulties which Catholics, even prominent ones, could sometimes face, see *RPC* x. 839–40; xii. 448; John Maxwell to Sir John Maxwell of Pollok, 11 Nov. 1629, W. Fraser, *Memoirs of the Maxwells of Pollok*, 2 vols. (Edinburgh, 1863), ii. 206–7.

One final case may be cited in order to draw a line under this issue. In February 1604 the council *ordered* the unwilling presbytery of Ayr to excommunicate Thomas Kennedy of Drummurchie and his accomplices, who had been put to the horn as murderers in a notorious feud.[66] Erastianism could hardly have been carried further.

So far, the question of power in religious matters has been considered as a question of jurisdictional boundaries. The church might possess a jurisdiction over certain matters that was independent of the state—or it might not, and indeed after 1584 probably would not. We can go on from there to enquire whether the church as a whole was a department of state. The Catholic controversialist John Hay asked Scottish Protestants in 1580:

Quhether is the generall assemblie subject to the king, and sould be called in his authoritie, or nocht; Gyf it be subject, quhy refuse ye your statuts to be examined be his counsell? Gyf ye say it is not subject, quhy deny ye that to the king of Scotland, quhilk your brethrene of Ingland grantes wnto thair quene?

Well might he ask. Later he partly answered his own question: 'in this poinct ye remain as yit in difference, and dissention amangs your selves'.[67] Historians have generally agreed with him, although they have also had their own 'difference, and dissention' about what exactly the relationship between church and state was. The pope's authority had been abolished in 1560: did that make the monarch head of the church, and if not, who or what was its head? The Catholic Mary, obviously, never claimed the headship of a church that she tolerated in practice but regarded as illegitimate. The general assembly as a result gained much practical experience of running its own affairs, a situation that it found congenial; but it still aspired to a positive relationship with a godly prince.

Meanwhile, there was nobody in Protestant Europe more confident in his own role as godly prince than James VI. So relations should have been harmonious. Alas, they were not. But while much discussion of this has been illuminating, it has not always focused

---

[66] *RPC* vi. 603.
[67] John Hay, *Certaine Demandes Concerning the Christian Religion* (1580), in *Catholic Tractates of the Sixteenth Century, 1573–1600*, ed. T. G. Law (STS, 1901), 42, 64.

on the crown's legal powers as regards religion. The royal supremacy was fundamental to the English Reformation;[68] should we be discussing a royal supremacy in Scotland also?

Answers to this question can begin by noting that, as in England, there could be two views of the supremacy. Either it was a strictly *royal* supremacy, inherent in the monarch, or else it rested on parliamentary statute. G. R. Elton argued that the royalist interpretation was favoured by Henry VIII—the Act of Supremacy was certainly worded to admit, if not encourage, the view that it merely ratified his inalienable rights; but that successive parliamentary alterations (including Mary's inability to rid herself of the hated title, even reduced to an etcetera, without parliament) finally established that the Elizabethan supremacy was a statutory one. This is fair enough, but it takes us only to 1559. Elizabeth subsequently took the view that parliament's involvement in religion should have ended at that point, leaving religion as a province of the royal prerogative. By the 1590s, Richard Hooker's parliamentary concept of the supremacy had become subversive.[69]

In Scotland, it was parliament that in 1560 abolished the pope's authority and enacted the Confession of Faith. The crown could certainly present candidates to bishoprics and monasteries—even Mary did this. It could also present to parish benefices, though persons so presented were not necessarily ministers in the early years.[70] Other than that, James VI had no special ecclesiastical authority. Parliament, and not the crown, ordered in 1573 that benefice-holders refusing to subscribe the Confession of Faith should be deprived.[71]

Bishops after 1572 did have to take an oath acknowledging that the king was 'the only lauchfull and supreme governour of this realme, as well in things temperall, as in the conservatioun and purgatioun of the religioun'.[72] Under this it was James's duty, no doubt, to ensure that sayers of mass were punished according to the law (again, even Mary had done this), and that illegal abuses were

---

[68] See e.g. P. Collinson, *The Birthpangs of Protestant England* (New York, 1988), 9–11.

[69] G. R. Elton, *Reform and Reformation: England, 1509–1558* (London, 1977), 196–200; C. Cross, *The Royal Supremacy in the Elizabethan Church* (London, 1969), 35–7.

[70] Donaldson, *Scottish Reformation*, 150–5; Kirk, 'Survival of ecclesiastical patronage', 376–85.

[71] *APS* iii. 72, c. 3.   [72] *BUK* i. 220.

eliminated from the church; but it was equally his duty, as head of the judicial system, to ensure that the correct weights and measures were maintained and users of false ones punished. Weights and measures were no part of the royal prerogative; the king supervised them, but did not control them personally. The Confession of Faith was sanctioned, and Catholics punished, by the same authority that fixed the size of the grain firlot: parliament.

But parliament could transfer some of its day-to-day authority to the crown. This, indeed, was the practical basis of the Elizabethan royal supremacy: it was the *crown* that had the (statutory) right to regulate the church. And this began to happen in Scotland in the 1580s, not long after the leading ministers in the general assembly had adopted an uncompromisingly presbyterian programme. The 'King's Confession' adopted in 1581 was perhaps part of this trend; the basis of its authority was monarchical rather than ecclesiastical or parliamentary or even conciliar. It was adopted first by the royal household, whereupon the king personally ordered its subscription throughout the realm. However, the presbyterians were not worried by this, because they welcomed its comprehensive renunciation of Catholic doctrine (which, they audaciously claimed, included episcopacy).[73] The discord of this period is sometimes described as a struggle between church and crown; it could also be interpreted as the church leadership tending to favour one side in the political faction struggles of 1578–85, making the church politically vulnerable when the other side were in power. And in 1584 the other side (in the form of Captain James Stewart, earl of Arran, and his ex-Marian cronies) were in power with a vengeance. Thus the Black Acts were passed.

The angry presbyterians who so labelled the legislation of May 1584 never said exactly which of the many statutes were black, or even grey. To summarize the most significant ones briefly: royal authority was asserted over the church generally; all jurisdictions and assemblies not approved by parliament (presbyteries, and perhaps also the general assembly, were implied) were discharged; the crown, through bishops and commissioners, could deprive ministers for a range of specified causes; and the authority of

---

[73] Calderwood, *History*, iii. 501–6; Melville, *Diary*, 87; cf. *Source Book*, iii. 32–5. The privy council did not meet on the date of the order, 2 Mar. 1581: *RPC* iii. 361–2. The Confession supplemented that of 1560, noting that it had been 'stablished and publictly confirmed by sindrie actis of parliamentis'.

bishops in their dioceses was asserted. This combination gave the crown comparable powers to the Elizabethan Act of Supremacy, and indeed in places was more detailed.[74] A gap was filled by a further act, in August 1584, imposing an episcopalian oath on all ministers, readers, and university and college teachers.[75]

The Black Acts thus had two related, but distinct, strands: one favouring episcopacy, the other the royal supremacy. The distinction becomes clear when we realize that only the episcopalian programme was repudiated on Arran's fall in 1585—and even that mainly tacitly. The parliament of 1585 restored the dissident ministers who had fled from Arran's regime, but repealed none of the Black Acts despite being pressed to do so.[76] A conference between ministers and royal commissioners in 1586 agreed that presbyteries should be restored to a central role; bishops, although retained, were to be answerable to them and to 'senats' (selected ministers acting like cathedral chapters), while these in turn were to be answerable to the general assembly.[77] From then until 1591, bishops were steadily elbowed aside in the key matter of appointment of ministers; presentations by the crown, in the parishes in which it was patron, were supposed to be directed to bishops for them to give collation, but an increasing proportion were directed to presbyteries instead. The episcopalian oath of 1584 was replaced by an anodyne one. The bishops also lost many revenues by the Act of Annexation of 1587.[78]

Much of this was ratified by the Golden Act of 1592, which explicitly ratified the existence of general assembly, synods, presbyteries, and kirk sessions, gave presbyteries powers of excommunication, and directed that presentations of ministers should (as was already beginning to happen in practice) be directed to them and not to bishops. It repealed the act of 1584 giving authority to bishops (c. 20), but otherwise the structure of royal supremacy was left in place; in particular the act on royal authority (c. 2) was not repealed

[74] *APS* iii. 292–4, 303, cc. 2, 4, 5, 20; 1 Eliz. I c. 1, quoted in Cross, *Royal Supremacy*, 126–31.
[75] *APS* iii. 347, c. 2. On the conflict that followed, see A. R. MacDonald, 'The subscription crisis and church–state relations, 1584–1586', *RSCHS* 25 (1993–5), 222–55, and Williamson, *Scottish National Consciousness*, 66–8.
[76] *APS* iii. 395–6, c. 24; Calderwood, *History*, iv. 450–65.
[77] Calderwood, *History*, iv. 491–4.
[78] Donaldson, *Scottish Reformation*, 217–19; MacDonald, 'Ecclesiastical Politics', 185–9.

but given some meaningless qualifications. The crown also had the right to summon general assemblies.[79] Still, the church was by now clearly presbyterian, and the few surviving bishops had lost almost all authority. Given that the presbyterian leadership tended to favour a separation of church and state—the famous doctrine of 'two kingdoms', to which we shall return—the church's polity may look as if such a separation had been established. Perhaps it had, but only to the extent that the presbyterians possessed the political initiative, and were able to establish a day-to-day freedom to do what they wanted without asking the king's permission. Such a position was never complete and always precarious, and if the crown were able to rally political support for an Erastian interpretation of the existing legislation, it might easily be reversed.

And after the crisis of December 1596, this is what happened. Between then and 1612, the crown advanced inexorably to overturn presbyterian dominance. In 1597 the general assembly was induced to recognize royal authority more fully, and a crown-appointed 'commission' of the assembly was set up to coordinate ecclesiastical policy. In late 1598, *Basilicon Doron* declared the king's intention of re-establishing bishops to govern the church. He began appointing bishops in 1600 and the complement was filled by 1606, though initially they had few ecclesiastical powers. At the same time, he began gerrymandering and then postponing the general assembly. In 1606, parliament restored bishops to their lands and confirmed their place in parliament, while a blatantly rigged 'general assembly' agreed that the bishops were to be moderators of synods (an 'act' seemingly achieved by falsifying the minutes of the meeting), while moderators of presbyteries were to be permanent and answerable to bishops. This reversed the ascending principle of authority on which the presbyterian structure had hitherto been based. Between 1607 and 1609, the synods were forced to accept episcopal control, often in the teeth of fierce resistance; many presbyteries also had to accept 'constant moderators', though some escaped and were allowed to continue electing moderators. Bishops began to supervise stipends (1607) and commissaries (1609). In 1610, another nominated general assembly gave bishops full ecclesiastical powers in their dicoeses—powers to induct ministers to benefices, to deprive ministers, and to

---

[79] *APS* iii. 541–2, c. 8.

confirm all excommunications. Finally, this was confirmed by parliament in 1612, and a clause making bishops theoretically subject to the general assembly was deleted.[80] The bishops, though thus confirmed in their independence from the presbyterian church courts, were always subject to the civil power—crown and parliament. It might have been possible for them to argue that they held their offices *jure divino*, directly from God, but they never did so in our period. Instead they gloried in their subjection to the state, which they contrasted with the allegedly subversive claims to independence made by both presbyterians and Catholics.[81]

The last major changes to the church by general assemblies were a new confession of faith, adopted in 1616, and the Five Articles of Perth in 1618. The confession was inoffensive (probably because it was fully Calvinist), while the Five Articles were widely execrated. But even with the confession, critics objected to the gerrymandering of the assembly; they went on to claim that this deprived the Five Articles of all legitimacy.[82] Meanwhile, as with the Elizabethan supremacy, the crown also sought parliamentary legislation which would enable it to regulate the church without further reference to general assembly or even parliament. The clearest example of this is James's attempt, in 1617, to have parliament pass a statute allowing him to regulate the church by edict, with advice of the bishops and selected ministers. The resulting protest caused the king to withdraw the proposal, though with bad grace—it was, he said, 'a thing no way necessary, the prerogative of his crown bearing him to more than was declared by it'.[83] At the

---

[80] These developments have been fully discussed—and debated—by MacDonald, 'Ecclesiastical Politics', chs. 2–5; Mullan, *Episcopacy in Scotland*, ch. 6; M. Lee, 'James VI and the revival of episcopacy in Scotland, 1596–1600', *Church History*, 43 (1974), 50–64; id., *Government by Pen: Scotland under James VI and I* (Urbana, Ill., 1980), ch. 3; and Foster, *Church before the Covenants*, ch. 2.

[81] Mullan, *Episcopacy in Scotland*, ch. 7 and *passim*. The concept of *jure divino* episcopacy was in theory compatible with the absolutist state, for Catholic states retained a *jure divino* papacy with little difficulty. Claims to *jure divino* episcopacy did surface briefly in 1669–70 (a period in which the conceptual development of the absolutist state was at its height in Scotland), but never took root: J. Buckroyd, *Church and State in Scotland, 1660–1681* (Edinburgh, 1980), 82–4.

[82] For the confession of 1616 see *BUK* iii. 1132–9; Calderwood, *History*, vii. 226–7; and (for its theology) J. Perry, 'John Spottiswoode, Archbishop and Chancellor, as Churchman, Historian and Theologian', Ph.D. thesis (Edinburgh, 1950), 14–17. For the Five Articles see, *inter alia*, I. B. Cowan, 'The Five Articles of Perth', in D. Shaw (ed.), *Reformation and Revolution* (Edinburgh, 1967).

[83] Spottiswoode, *History*, iii. 244–5; Calderwood, *History*, vii. 251–3.

end of his reign, it was clear that the state had full authority in the church—far clearer than it had been in 1560; the unresolved question was whether ultimate authority lay with crown or with parliament.

How does all this relate to the issue of 'two kingdoms' or 'one kingdom'? One cannot discuss religion and government in post-Reformation Scotland without confronting these two theories of the relationship of church and state. They provided radically different views of the way ecclesiastical authority was exercised in Scotland—or of the way it *ought* to be exercised: a small but crucial distinction.

The one-kingdom theory was simple. The king had (or ought to have) authority over all his subjects, and ruled the church just as he ruled the other institutions of the kingdom. His authority to do so was conferred directly by God. The two-kingdoms theory, characteristic of the presbyterians, was slightly more complicated. There were (or ought to be) two separate kingdoms: the secular one, in which the king ruled, and the spiritual one, in which Christ ruled and there was no earthly head. The presbyterians did have something looking rather like an earthly head of their church— the general assembly; but they saw it as different because its authority ascended from its constituent members rather than being conferred directly by God (or by the king).

So it was an important issue, on which contemporaries could disagree sharply. For example, it could only be a resolute believer in one kingdom who would argue that 'Sathan . . . hath persuaded to princes, rulers, and magistrates, that the feeding of Christes flock appertaineth nothing to theyre charge, but that it is rejected [i.e. devolved] upon the byshoppes and estate ecclesiasticall'. Conversely, the act ordaining that none of the 'ministeris of Godis word . . . sall in ony wayis accept, use or administrat ony place of judicature in quhatsumevir civill or criminall causis' has doubtless absorbed the view that there should exist two separate, parallel jurisdictions in church and state. The trouble is, though, that the first quotation comes from John Knox, while the second is one of the anti-presbyterian Black Acts of 1584.[84] To discuss the theory of 'two kingdoms' or 'one kingdom' is to enter a labyrinth of paradoxes.

---

[84] Knox, *Appellation . . . to the Nobilitie, Estates and Communaltie* (1558), in *Works*, iv. 485; *APS* iii. 294, c. 6.

It is the two-kingdoms theory that creates the most intractable conceptual problems. It might appear at first sight to be based on a formal equivalence between the sacred and secular kingdoms; but there could be no such equivalence. Both sacred and secular authority derived, it was agreed, from God. The Ten Commandments dealt both with matters that were purely spiritual—offences against God—and with matters that were mixed—offences against one's neighbour. Separating the two kingdoms, church and state, was also conceptually intricate when both consisted of the same people. Finally, when the secular authorities were conceded (as they were) a role in protecting the church, conserving it and purging it of corruption, who was to define what constituted corruption? If the Old Testament was anything to go by (and it was central to the reformers' view of godly rule), a devout king would defer to the prophets of God—the reformers themselves—on the matter. Once the reformers were in power in the church (as they were), this could have made it difficult for a king to exercise his allotted religious role.

The one-kingdom theory presents its own problems. If religious authority vested in the crown, did that give the king the right to administer the sacraments? The answer was no; only ordained ministers could do that. This seems a little odd, but at least the king did appoint the bishops who ordained the ministers. But why did the king have bishops?—because the primitive church had had bishops? If so, then perhaps the bishops were bishops by direct divine authority and not by the crown's will after all?

Further conceptual difficulties arise with both theories. Suppose that the king, or the presbyter, wanted to proclaim true beliefs or suppress false ones: they could not say (or even believe) that they had *chosen* to define those beliefs as true or false. Religious authority, in short, did not vest in the present religious authorities, or at least could not be said to do so.[85] In discussing *government* and religion, which we are trying to do in this chapter, are we pursuing a chimera?

---

[85] Protestants were inclined to appeal to the Bible here, but as a Catholic controversialist observed, 'it is maist fals that the vryttin vord can be judge of al controverseis ... it may nather heir the parteis, nor pronounce the sentence, quhilk tua thingis apertenis necessarlie to the office of ane lauchful judge'. Nicol Burne, *Disputation Concerning the Controversit Headdis of Religion* (1581), in *Catholic Tractates*, 147.

Most historians analysing these questions have concentrated on what contemporaries said on the subject.[86] This is useful and indeed essential, but has two serious limitations. First, contemporaries did not agree. Secondly, they rarely distinguished between what was the case and what ought to have been the case: they would be likely, for instance, to say that there *were* two kingdoms when they meant that, although there was only one, there *ought* to be two. This is so even for parliamentary statutes, since although the Black Acts made clear that there ought to be one kingdom, they were not necessarily enforced in full.

So since we can obtain a good idea from contemporaries of what the two kingdoms *ought* to have looked like, perhaps we can focus on that ideal for a moment, and then come back to see how far it corresponded with reality. Suppose that there had really been two kingdoms: what would the government have looked like?

There would have been, first of all, two parallel supreme bodies, parliament (civil) and general assembly (ecclesiastical). Parliament would have consisted of the secular rulers, the nobility, lairds, and burgesses; the general assembly would have consisted of the ecclesiastical rulers, the ministers, elders, and doctors: both acknowledging the nominal authority of the king, but probably not allowing him many practical powers (certainly not a veto on ecclesiastical legislation). Parliament would have legislated on secular matters, the general assembly on ecclesiastical ones. The general assembly would have had no need to trouble the secular authorities about funding for the ministry and allied functions (schools, universities, poor relief), since the ministry would somehow have obtained title to the property of the old church and, with it, financial independence.

There would, though, have been some overlap between the two jurisdictions. While it would have been clear that parliament did not legislate to *control* the church, it would have done so to *support* it. The church would have taken the lead in defining a range of offences, from adultery to usury, which were not only secular but

---

[86] The two essential works on this—propounding strongly contrasting interpretations—are G. Donaldson, 'Church and community', in id., *Scottish Church History* (Edinburgh, 1985), and J. Kirk, 'Minister and magistrate', in id., *Patterns of Reform*. Although what follows will adopt a third view, it could not have been written without the thoughtful guidance and detailed exposition that these two papers provide. The section on what 'two kingdoms' ought to have looked like is particularly indebted to Dr Kirk. See also R. G. Kyle, 'The church–state patterns in the thought of John Knox', *Journal of Church and State*, 30 (1988), 71–87, at pp. 79–81.

also (and primarily) biblical. It would thus have regulated marriage and divorce, and very likely crimes such as murder. Parliament, recognizing the church's competence, would willingly have passed its own legislation to add secondary civil penalties to the primary ecclesiastical ones. There would have been an independent civil sphere, consisting of matters on which the Bible offered no guidance, where the general assembly in turn would willingly have ceded primacy to parliament. This sphere would not, however, have extended to matters such as who the king's councillors should be or what foreign policy should be followed; it would have been agreed that both councillors and foreign policy needed to be godly, and that it was the church's role to keep them up to the mark. The state was not a *secular* 'kingdom'; it had to be godly too.

The primary requirement for the two-kingdoms theory, therefore, was that the general assembly be a body equal to, and parallel with, parliament. It has been claimed that this was so, but the evidence cited (that there was no appeal from general assembly to parliament, and that the general assembly also consisted of the three estates of the realm) does not support this.[87] There was no appeal to parliament from the court of session or the privy council either. Nor were the secular estates fully *represented* in the general assembly, which consisted largely of ministers; some lords, lairds, and burgesses came because they wanted to support the cause, but they did not have to.[88]

The general assembly did start life technically independent of (if not parallel to) parliament; the church courts operated without parliamentary sanction. This was not new, since it had been the case for the pre-Reformation church also. Moreover, as James Kirk has shown, most early Protestant leaders either thought in terms of two kingdoms, or at least did not hesitate to tell civil rulers not to interfere in the church.[89] But this did not last. In 1584 the Black Acts positively asserted crown authority over the church. Still more

---

[87] D. Shaw, *The General Assemblies of the Church of Scotland, 1560–1600* (Edinburgh, 1964), 20.

[88] The scanty evidence for the membership of general assemblies is investigated by MacDonald, 'Ecclesiastical Politics', 15–51. For more on the relationship of assembly and parliament, see J. Goodare, *The Government of Scotland, 1560–1625* (forthcoming), ch. 2.

[89] Kirk, 'Minister and magistrate'. Most of the evidence in this paper is drawn from the period before 1584, and Dr Kirk notes that James VI succeeded thereafter in establishing state control over the church—or at least in establishing 'a measure of acquiescence, compromise and outward conformity', although 'even a king endowed with such ingenuity was unequal to the task of stifling ideas' (p. 279).

decisive, because the church generally accepted its legitimacy, was the Golden Act of 1592. From then on, whenever the general assembly met, whenever church courts admitted and deprived ministers, or imposed penances and excommunication for breaches of moral discipline, they did so by a right conferred by parliament. The Golden Act, welcome as it was at the time, merely transferred the royal supremacy from episcopacy to presbytery.

Presbyterians were careful to claim that with the Golden Act, 'the king and estaitis takis not upoun thame to give the powir to the generall assemblie thair to convein, quhilk nethir thai nor the kirke ever thought it to be in thair handis, but in the handis of Christ Jesus allenirely . . . but onlie to ratifie and approve it, conforme to thair Christiane duetie by the auctoritie that God hes put in thair handis'.[90] But there were no such words as these in the act. It is more likely that king and estates *did* think they were giving the church this power, and that it was in fact parliament's command which made the system—presbyterian or episcopalian, as it chose—effective. However, effectiveness is a matter of practical political power, not just of words on the statute book. The royal supremacy was not simply a matter of specific statutes (like the Black Acts, or even the Golden Act) legitimately passed or not passed; indeed it was not ultimately a concrete thing that did or did not exist. It was a shifting political quantity measured by the crown's current ability to get its way.

Some historians have suggested erroneously that the two-kingdoms theory implied that parliament should not legislate for the church at all, and that the presbyterians' welcome for statutes in their favour (such as the Golden Act) was inconsistent from this point of view.[91] In fact, the two-kingdoms theory never required the *complete* separation of church and state that this would have entailed. All thinkers accepted that the state should legislate on ecclesiastical matters. What the presbyterians denied was that the state could legitimately lay claim to direct control of the church.

Thus, it would not have been acceptable for parliament to introduce newly invented articles of belief, such as an eleventh commandment. (Even the church would have claimed to be unable to do that.) But this still left a quite broad field for the civil power;

---

[90] Melville, *Diary*, 601; cf. Calderwood, *History*, vi. 352.
[91] e.g. J. Goodare, 'Parliament and Society in Scotland, 1560–1603', Ph.D. thesis (Edinburgh, 1989), 47; Donaldson, *Faith of the Scots*, 87–8.

parliament *could* enact the Confession of Faith, and could even offer to amend it: 'gif any man will note in this our confessioun any artickle or sentence repugning to Godis holie word . . . we . . . do promeis unto him satisfactioun fra the mowthe of God (that is fra his holy scriptureis) or ellis reformatioun of that quhilk he sall prove to be amyss'.[92] It was parliament that would decide. Formally this was declaratory law, since nobody suggested that God's law could be *made* in parliament; but this need not obscure the reality of parliamentary enactment.[93] Certainly the church did not enact it. As for the other desiderata of the two-kingdoms theory—the church's need for financial independence, or its desire for a power of veto (on grounds of ungodliness) over appointments of royal councillors or decisions on foreign policy—such a programme never came close to realization, even before 1584. One writer (probably the councillor John Lindsay of Balcarres) thought that the church should be able to 'admoniss and reproif' the secular magistrates 'with sic modeste or scharpnes as the caus requyris, to the exempill of the anciant prophetes';[94] but in the 1590s even this came to be curtailed.

It can be recognized, then, that the two-kingdoms theory was a fiction—or, to put it more charitably, an unfulfilled ideal. The ideal gained in attractiveness as it receded in attainability; indeed it was to some extent a posthumous invention. As late as August 1596, Andrew Melville could speak of the 'twa kings and twa kingdomes in Scotland' in the present tense, but after the crisis of December 1596, the presbyterians switched to the past tense. They began to lament the 'declyneing aige' of the kirk of Scotland', and demanded the restoration of what they came to believe had been a golden age of church liberty.[95]

I observed that this topic was full of paradoxes. So perhaps I could conclude it by undermining the distinction that I earlier said was essential—between whether people thought there *were* two separate kingdoms and whether they thought there *ought* to have been. What mattered, in the final analysis, was whether people

[92] *APS* ii. 526–7, c. 1. All Protestant confessions had a provisional status, but it was unusual for this to be so explicit: W. I. P. Hazlitt, 'The Scots Confession of 1560: Context, complexion and critique', *Archiv für Reformationsgeschichte*, 78 (1987), 287–320, at p. 296.
[93] For 'divine law' and 'fundamental law', see Ch. 1 above.
[94] NLS, Balcarres papers, Adv. MS 29.2.8, fo. 171ʳ.
[95] Melville, *Diary*, 370, 505–6.

acted as if there were two separate kingdoms. In their actions, they were guided both by what they believed was the case *and* by what they believed ought to be the case. For example, between 1592 and 1596, the period of clearest presbyterian dominance, even the king sometimes *asked* the church to do things when, if he had taken literally the supremacy in which he believed, he could have *commanded* them to be done. He acted in those cases as if there were two kingdoms, because he suspected that he lacked the practical power to do otherwise—even though he might believe that there was really (or ought to be really) only one.

A contrasting example is provided by the general assembly of 1618 that passed the Five Articles of Perth. Here, the king did command, and plainly had the power to get what he wanted: ministers who objected risked having their stipends reduced or worse; the royal guard was stationed outside the building. Small wonder that many voted for the royal programme even though most had misgivings about it. A few, of course, may have been committed believers in it. A third group stuck to their principles and voted against the articles; some would later go as far as disobeying them. But they were, nevertheless, passed; the claim to independent church jurisdiction had been, once again, rejected, and the existence of a single kingdom subject to the real authority of the king had received another practical demonstration. As a *claim*, however, the ideal of two kingdoms remained very much alive, and continued to guide many people's actions.

A third example may also help. When privy councillors were in church on a Sunday, they presumably thought of themselves as members of the church. When on Monday they had to face dissident ministers across the council table, and those ministers claimed a commission from the general assembly, the councillors behaved as if it was a question of 'us and them'. And so did the ministers, although the day before they had presumably regarded the councillors primarily as fellow-Christians. But there were not two real kingdoms in this example: the privy council had power, the dissident ministers (at least for the time being) did not.

So if people themselves ever made this conceptual separation when they governed, and if power was ever exercised by two bodies neither of whom in practice took orders from the other, and if those rulers involved both in church institutions and in state institutions ever recognized a separation between the two: to that extent, *and no further*, there were two kingdoms. As Gordon Donaldson plaintively put it:

It is all very well to speak about wearing two hats, and possibly an individual might take one view wearing his parliamentary hat and another view wearing his assembly hat. . . . Does the conflict between 'church' and 'state' resolve itself into a conflict between two hats?[96]

From this point of view, it seems that it does.

Turning from theory to practice, we can now look at some aspects of how the system of moral discipline was actually implemented in the localities, focusing on the relationship between the different institutions involved. The establishment of a disciplinary structure led to periodic friction, but on the whole the structure was fairly well integrated into existing networks of power.[97] Whether the system of moral discipline could create *community* (a question raised early in this chapter) may be left to others to answer; but it could certainly create *consensus* among the governing elite.

This consensus was strongest in what came to be the core area of business for kirk sessions and presbyteries: punishing illicit sex among the lower classes. All the authorities favoured this, and all kirk sessions put the bulk of their efforts into it. When the elders took time off from fornication and adultery and turned their attention to other things, they were often unable to maintain the same level of consensus. Persecuting Catholics, enforcing the sabbath, or exercising discipline of any kind against members of the propertied elite: these could stir up controversy or even resistance. But quite a few kirk sessions still did these things quite a lot of the time. They found that as well as encountering opposition, campaigns on these issues might also rally support. The more ideologically charged aspects of the disciplinary system, therefore, tended to foster conflict rather than consensus.

A kirk session or presbytery dominated by radical presbyterians would be particularly likely to rock the boat by pushing its authority into these contested areas. In the last two decades of the sixteenth century, the presbytery of Edinburgh put much energy into

[96] Donaldson, 'Church and community', 237.

[97] What follows are some general impressions based on a wide range of sources, but see esp. Graham, *Uses of Reform*; Mitchison and Leneman, *Sexuality and Social Control*; and M. Graham, 'The civil sword and the Scottish kirk, 1560–1600', in Graham (ed.), *Later Calvinism*.

attacking crypto-Catholics at the royal court, while the presbytery of St Andrews embroiled itself in local power struggles with less doctrinaire opponents both in the burgh council and in the presbytery itself. In both presbyteries, routine discipline suffered as a result.[98] But the exercise of power does not cease when it is contested; the fact that persecution of Catholics was controversial did not mean that Catholics were not persecuted.

The problems of the disciplinary system were essentially political; they were caused by disagreements over what punishments should be inflicted for what offences. Jurisdictional intricacies on their own would not necessarily cause problems. Earlier in this chapter we saw the privy council establishing its right to supervise disciplinary cases in the complicated dual offences of adultery and Catholicism. Most of the complaints were brought to the council by members of the elite; peasants arraigned for adultery usually had to accept their fate and do penance. And there were other offences, equally complicated in law, which in practice were punished without difficulty by the local authorities. Witchcraft is a prime example. Like adultery and (in Protestant eyes) Catholicism, witchcraft was a dual offence, both scriptural and statutory; but kirk sessions rarely had difficulty with it. To be sure, they learned that they could not punish witchcraft themselves—the one witchcraft case that came before the privy council during the struggle over excommunication showed this. But the kirk session could call in the civil authorities to execute the witch—and this is usually what they preferred to do. With adulterers or Catholics, the church wanted them to do penance; with witches, it wanted them dead. Because it could not inflict the death penalty, it *had* to call in the civil power. Indeed, unlike with the Inquisition in some Catholic countries, the real decision on an alleged witch's guilt or innocence was made by the civil power, while the church was confined to the earlier stages of gathering of information. But whatever the precise division of labour, the point is that witch-hunting was a consensual operation; conflict between civil and ecclesiastical authorities over witchcraft was possible in theory but rare in practice.[99]

One reason for the kirk sessions' success may be that traditional power structures in the localities contained gaps. Those authorities who had traditionally been in nominal charge of moral

[98] Graham, *Uses of Reform*, 184–201.
[99] C. Larner, *Enemies of God: The Witch-Hunt in Scotland* (London, 1981), ch. 9.

discipline were not up to the high standards that were now expected of them. Here, the new church courts could often move in and take over without anyone minding. Thus, once the general assembly had secured a statute banning pilgrimages in 1581, the presbytery of Stirling was still waiting for action eighteen months later against those visiting its local holy well. Lord Doune, steward of Menteith, had a commission to implement the law but was doing nothing, and the presbytery's representations to him produced no effect. So they took action themselves, 'to the glorie of God and executioun of the kingis majesteis lawis'. A series of pilgrims was hauled before the presbytery for breaking what the minutes later tended to describe as 'Goddis law' rather than the king's.[100] If by doing this the presbytery was encroaching on the local civil magistrate's jurisdiction, this may have been embarrassing for the latter, but no objection from Lord Doune is recorded. This was not a conflict, or even rivalry, between 'church' and 'state'; it was a church court filling a gap, probably to the satisfaction of parliament which had passed the law against pilgrimages. Nor was it an attempt by the church to take over everything. Stirling presbytery had clearly delimited objectives and rebuked the kirk session of Alva in 1583 for having 'mellit with civill thingis, namelie, anent trublance, castein of stouppis, and capitall crymis as stelling of yowis and peis'.[101] It was one of the church's strengths that it concentrated on what it did best.

The region around Stirling also furnishes a broader and more formal example of how civil authority and ecclesiastical authority were expected to intersect. In his visitation of the parishes of the Dunblane area in 1586, James Anderson, minister of Stirling, carried commissions both from the king and from the general assembly. He asked some questions from the general assembly, and some from the king. The assembly wanted to know about church attendance, communion, preaching, schools, church fabric, benefice, manse, and glebe, and its questions on discipline related to sabbath observance, Catholicism, witchcraft, superstition, blasphemy, adultery, and incest. The king asked about all these disciplinary things too, and about whether there were any excommunicants, plus some of the pastoral issues (whether the

---

[100] *Stirling Presbytery Records, 1581–1587*, ed. J. Kirk (SHS, 1981), 115–16, 120, 130. For more details see Graham, *Uses of Reform*, 170–1.
[101] *Stirling Presbytery Records*, 133.

ministers and readers were up to their jobs); he also wanted some people to volunteer to accept royal commissions for punishment of moral lapses.[102] This does not tell us what people said when Anderson arrived in their parish, but it does show that different forms of authority could coexist without giving overt evidence of conflict.

Other local records demonstrate long periods of uncomplicated cooperation. The sheriff court of Shetland is a case in point. Drunkards were to be fined £6 'ad pios usus' by the sheriff. One case of fornication was treated as purely civil: a seducer was ordered to pay damages to a woman's brother for 'spilling of her virginitie', and there was no mention of action by the kirk session. A woman was convicted of slander by the sheriff court, and the sheriff remitted her punishment to the church. The sheriff received caution that a fornicator would be presented to the presbytery.[103] Only the sheriff court's version of these Shetland cases survives, but the court gave every impression of regarding kirk session and presbytery as valuable helpmeets. Some of the compromises were idiosyncratic ones—civil damages for fornication, or the sheriff asking the kirk session to mete out punishment to someone convicted in his own court. What is more typical is simply the cooperation between the different authorities involved.

It might be objected that there were few ideologically committed presbyterians in Shetland to stir up trouble. But even in the storm-centre of St Andrews in the 1590s, there was local cooperation. Many sexual cases were apparently heard in the burgh court instead of the kirk session; if this was the result of a struggle over jurisdiction, evidence is lacking. Similarly, in 1594, an adulterer received both ecclesiastical and civil punishment, in a way that seems to have been routine.[104] In Aberdeen, 1606 was the year after the presbyterians had held a controversial and unauthorized general assembly in the town. The synod of Aberdeen gave two lists of grievances to the king; the second, headed 'In commonweill', related to feuds and carrying of firearms.[105] These were *grievances*,

[102] *Visitation of the Diocese of Dunblane and Other Churches, 1586–1589*, ed. J. Kirk (SRS, 1984).

[103] *Court Book of Shetland, 1615–1629*, ed. G. Donaldson (Lerwick, 1991), 116, 44, 106, 114.

[104] Graham, *Uses of Reform*, 213.

[105] 'Extracts from the manuscript collections of the Rev. Robert Wodrow, 1605–1697', *Spalding Club Miscellany*, ii (1842), 151–2.

and so inevitably challenging, but unlike the first set of grievances (on the church) they were not particularly confrontational. Rather they seem to have represented a genuine attempt to contribute to solving problems of common concern to church and state. Such episodes did not hit the headlines in early modern Scotland, but they should be recognized as regular occurrences.

So there was often cooperation, or at least pragmatic coexistence, between kirk sessions and civil magistrates—sheriffs, stewards, bailies, and the like. At other times there was conflict. But is this surprising? Sometimes there was cooperation between sheriffs and justices of the peace; at other times there was conflict. Was the conflict or the cooperation more significant? Historians discussing the relationship between church and state have tended to focus on the conflict, but this is probably most useful when discussing specific conflicts in the field of national politics. In early modern times, political struggles inevitably tended to acquire a religious dimension. It is not nearly so clear that conflict was common in the localities. For most purposes, the local courts of the church were simply another set of courts for the enforcement of the authority of the government.

A final example may illuminate the question of moral discipline and political consensus from a related quarter—focusing on a biblical vice to which many Scots succumbed, but from which very few indeed were redeemed by discipline and penance. This was usury. It has often been noted that the church never pursued usurers with the zeal which its own occasional pronouncements might have suggested. Michael Graham, attempting to exculpate it from the charge of hypocrisy on the subject, argues that 'some usury was necessary for the purposes of commerce, and there was no real consensus in favor of its elimination. Usury did not lead to disorder; bastardy, popular rituals, feuding and gambling did.'[106] No doubt; and the question of whether there was a consensus against gambling is a subsidiary one which need not detain us. The main point is that Dr Graham evidently thinks it impossible to defend the church from a strictly biblical standpoint. No presbytery, fearing that usury might call down the wrath of God upon the land, attempted to put Deuteronomy 24:19 into practice.

But Scotland did see an anti-usury campaign in the 1610s. It was

---

[106] Graham, *Uses of Reform*, 348.

conducted, not by the church, but by the privy council. Usury, like adultery, Catholicism, and witchcraft, was a dual offence, statutory as well as biblical; the statutory definition of it (admittedly foreign to the Pentateuch) was established in 1587 as the taking of interest in excess of 10 per cent. In 1611, Lord Balfour of Burleigh received a commission to implement the statute, which was then dormant; the main aim was to raise money. 'Dyvers inhabitants of burrowes' were 'callet before the lords of sessioun at the instance of the kings majestes thesaurer and advocatt and be the Laird of Burlie, for transgressing the acts of parliament maid [anent] annuells for debts for taking of mair nor ten of the hunder'; decreet having been obtained against them, they had to pay a composition to the treasurer or to Balfour. The campaign was particularly vigorous in 1612; it faded away in 1616–17 after the burgh of Edinburgh apparently reached an expensive agreement with Balfour and the king. Usury, it was noted early on, was 'condempnit boith by divyne and humane lawis', but the church was not involved at any stage.[107]

Moral discipline, then, was a multifaceted affair. The church courts were usually in the front line of the discipline campaign, but they did not inhabit a different universe from the civil authorities. The concern for 'order', noted by Dr Graham, lay at the heart of many governmental initiatives, both civil and ecclesiastical. Even when moral discipline was a matter, not merely of order, but of 'divyne lawis', these were not the exclusive property of the church but could be invoked by the civil authorities also. Dr Graham argues that usury was not prosecuted by the church because there was no consensus against it, which may be true; but his own work shows clearly that kirk sessions and presbyteries could sometimes prosecute other offences, such as Catholicism among the elite, for which consensus was equally lacking. The prosecution of usurers, against which the burghs protested loudly but for which there was probably tacit approval by aristocratic debtors, was no more consensual than the prosecution of Catholic noblemen; there was no *requirement* for any aspect of the discipline system to foster consensus, so long as it served the immediate interests of those in power.

[107] *RPC* ix. 218, 251–2, 283–4, 311, 348, 385–7, 398, 401–2, 404, 412, 424–6, 455–6, 631–3, 703; x. 170, 411, 586; xi. 44, 142; *APS* iii. 451, c. 35; *RCRB* ii. 325, 329; *Edin. Recs.* vi, pp. xi, 74, 86–90; *RMS* vii. 913.

It might be argued at this point that usury was prosecuted only by the civil authorities because the main aim in doing so was fiscal. But there was a fiscal element even in fines for fornication and adultery—they paid for much of the church's programme of poor relief.[108] If the church had adhered strictly to a biblical, rather than pragmatic, programme of discipline, it might have noted that the biblical penalty for adultery was not fines and penance but stoning to death.[109] Coercive discipline by kirk sessions, and coercive discipline by usury commissioners, were both pragmatic; they were, in fact, the same species. The various institutions engaged in the never-ending struggle to convert the Scots into sober, devout conformists were wielding power that sprang from a single network of authority, a network including ecclesiastical and civil strands which were not only woven together but also usually reinforced one another.

There was a revealing dispute in the privy council in 1620, which encapsulates several of the issues raised in this chapter. The councillors received a royal letter demanding renewed action against the dissident minister Robert Bruce:

Chancelour Seatoun said, it was not their part to judge in kirk maters: the bishopes have a Hie Commissoun of their owne to try these things. Secretarie Hammiltoun said, 'Will ye reasoun, whether his majestie must be obeyed or not?' Chancelour Setoun answeired, 'We may reason, whether we sall be the bishops' hangmen or not.'[110]

Hamilton's reply is not recorded, but he could have argued that it was indeed the council's job to be the bishops' hangmen, or at least (since high commission had no jurisdiction over life and limb) the bishops' gaolers and collectors of fines. This was much the same role for the state, *vis-à-vis* the church, as had been envisaged by Andrew Melville in the 1590s.

Or was it? At least the privy council had discretion to decide in 1620 what action to take (if any) over 'kirk maters'. It was

---

[108] Cf. Larner, *Enemies of God*, 56.

[109] Lev. 20: 10. Even if this was considered to have been abrogated by the New Testament (e.g. John 8: 1–11), the penances and fines of the Scottish Reformation were still nowhere in sight. The church did initially claim that all adulterers should be executed, but it never expected the state to agree, and soon ceased to insist on the matter: J. R. Hardy, 'The Attitude of the Church and State in Scotland to Sex and Marriage, 1560–1707', M.Phil. thesis (Edinburgh, 1978), 377–94.

[110] Calderwood, *History*, vii. 450.

answerable to the king, but not *directly* to the high commission. In 1624, Archbishop Spottiswoode was to be found lobbying the royal court to stop the court of session from suspending a horning that had followed on a decreet of high commission—which was, he exclaimed, 'in effect a subjecting of our decreitis to thair judicatorie, and the disannulling of the Commissioun, and authoritie of it'.[111] This may have inconvenienced the high commission, but the tone of Spottiswoode's complaint was sheer hyperbole. The church had to accept that in practice it was just one of a number of institutions wielding public authority; all were interlinked, and had to cooperate with one another. Together they made up the structure of the state.

People continued to argue about the relationship between ecclesiastical and civil institutions; but the two-kingdoms issue, as it had been debated in the days of Andrew Melville and James VI, ceased to be a genuine fault-line of conflict. The subordination of the church to the state that occurred between 1584 and 1612 was irreversible. Some form of Christian state, as an integrated whole, became an ideal for all parties, the two-kingdoms theory notwithstanding. Religious radicals knew that they had to *capture* the state, and could not bypass it. In the middle ages, by comparison, the ideal of reformers had been to rejuvenate the supranational Christian community through the institutions of the church directly, with the civil authorities being only distantly involved.

From the mid-seventeenth century onwards, the terms of the debate underwent a further shift. Religious radicals still invoked versions of the two-kingdoms theory, but they were never more than small and outspoken minorities. And so long as they remained so, they were not going to capture the state. In the meantime, the real debate was about whether they should be persecuted—or, to put the same thing in modern terms, how much religious *pluralism* the state should tolerate. Because religious unity within the state remained an ideal into the eighteenth century and even later, subsequent ecclesiastical debates could take a strikingly similar form to those of our period.[112] But without a solid conformity to the state church and disciplinary system by the bulk of the elite, and without a commitment to persecution of dissidents, the similarity was one of form only, and not of substance. Once

---

[111] Spottiswoode to earl of Annandale, 18 Nov. 1624, *Eccles. Letters*, ii. 769.
[112] The debates over the Disruption (1843) are a case in point.

toleration of Protestant dissidents became official, as it did in 1712 (and in practice from 1690), the state may not have ceased to be Christian, but it could no longer lay claim to the kind of godliness sought by Knox, Melville, and even James VI.[113] It was only in our period, when the church had become a department of state and could make a realistic show of being the national as well as the official religion, that the ideal of a fully godly state was ever achievable. It was not achieved, but it came closer to success than before or since.

[113] Cf. Ch. 10 below, and for an impressive synthesis of many of these matters as they relate to England, C. J. Sommerville, *The Secularization of Early Modern England: From Religious Culture to Religious Faith* (Oxford, 1992).

7

Territory

The kingdomes being firmelie knit together, and one government setled, in tract of time it is to be hoped that all the
inhabitants of this empire will be fashioned to the same
manners, lawes and language.[1]

A recurring theme of this book so far has been the increasing unity
and integration of the early modern state, moulded by a developing central authority. But there is more than one way to look at
this. What did central authority mean on Rathlin Island? This small
island in the North Channel, now part of Ireland, had always had
connections with the Irish mainland, but until the seventeenth
century it was also part of the old lordship of the Isles, which was
subject to the Scottish crown if to any at all. It was valued for old
extent, the Scottish tax assessment. The anomaly remained largely
unnoticed. In 1549 it was described as 'perteining to Irland', but
the English in the 1560s were discussing the need 'to take away
the Isle of the Raghlins from the Scots' (meaning the MacDonald
clan, not the Edinburgh authorities). A celebrated court case had
to be heard in 1617 to decide which kingdom Rathlin belonged
to.[2] Neither 'Scotland' nor 'Ireland' can have meant much to the
people of Rathlin before then. How seriously can one take the
authority of a state which had so little impact in its remoter regions
that its very existence was barely noticed by the inhabitants?

The sovereign state is a territorial state; it claims authority over
all the inhabitants of a given territory. The stronger the sovereign
authority, the more precise the unity and definition of the

[1] Robert Pont, 'Of the union of Britayne', *Jacobean Union*, 23.
[2] W. F. Skene, *Celtic Scotland*, 3 vols. (2nd edn., Edinburgh, 1886–90), iii, p. 439
and app. 3 (it is doubtful whether taxes were ever paid, however); *Monro's Western
Isles of Scotland and Genealogies of the Clans, 1549*, ed. R. W. Munro (Edinburgh,
1961), 49; W. Clark, *Rathlin: Its Island Story* (2nd edn., Limavady, 1988), 85,
111–17.

territory. The Rathlin case of 1617 was a small instance of sharpening territorial definition, but there was a long way to go before the state could hope to see all the Scots—in Robert Pont's words, quoted above—'fashioned to the same manners, lawes and language'. Few were as ambitious as he, even within Scotland (and Pont wanted to unify all Britain). Most commentators would have accepted some internal diversity in 'manners' and 'language', but the integration of 'lawes' was agreed to be essential, and in practice this meant harmonization of 'manners' at least to the extent of accepting the same attitude towards law and authority. Scotland, though a small country, was a country of unusual diversity—in geography, in institutions, and in peoples. This posed many problems for the state. How did it tackle these problems, and to what extent did it succeed?

The sixteenth-century Scottish state had the advantage that it was clearly a conventional monarchy, with no serious rivalry from any *completely* different form of political organization. Unlike in some regions of Europe, there were no city-states or federations of towns, no crusading orders or autonomous ecclesiastical principalities—the kinds of power structure that could make difficult materials for state-building. Actually there *was* a federation of towns: the convention of royal burghs, which looked after the collective interests of the leading Scottish towns. Still, these were *royal* burghs, internally self-governing in many ways, but not seeking to increase their autonomy at the crown's expense, and not a federation of independent towns like the Hanseatic League in Germany.[3] They had often tended to ally with the crown in order to maintain a distance from the magnates. The royal burghs are best seen as a distinctive component of central and local government, linked to the former through the burgess estate in parliament. They thought of their commerce in 1628 as uniting the nation territorially, extolling

that mutuall band whairin the being of all cuntreyis does subsist, which is the mutuall participatioun and exchange of these commodities quherof ilk severall pairt of the cuntrey does abound be itselff, God so of his providence provyding that eache one pairt does not afford all sort of commodities bot that one is served be ane uther.[4]

[3] T. Pagan, *The Convention of the Royal Burghs of Scotland* (Glasgow, 1926), 263; cf. H. Spruyt, *The Sovereign State and its Competitors* (Princeton, 1994), ch. 8.
[4] *RCRB* iii. 259.

Still, it was mainly crown and parliament, rather than commerce, that gave a focus to the nation. However, the sovereign state, with which we are concerned, is not the same as the nation. There had been a 'nation' or 'people' of Scotland long before a sovereign Scottish 'state' was formed. The Scottish people, in the Lowlands at any rate, had been conscious of being Scottish (and not English) since the Wars of Independence, if not before. This was a 'Scotland' that was an *ethnic community*, a political grouping with a conception of a common identity. Such ethnic communities, the antecedents or building blocks of early modern states, could be based on a defined territory, but their primary identity was likely to be that of a 'nation' or 'people' with a common name, a shared past, and some form of common political structure. The monarchy had long been important to the Scottish ethnic community, the territory rather less so. The Scottish origin-legends told of the 'Scots' migrating to their present territory from elsewhere (Ireland, Spain, or Greece), where they had already been 'Scots'.[5]

The sixteenth-century 'nation' was something which, although it was felt to exist at a certain level of reality, was never as homogeneous as those who were most committed to it would have liked. Scotland as a nation was a composite product of long development, and while some formerly separate peoples had fused together, others had drifted away. The semi-detached nature of the Highlands since at least the late middle ages—an issue that will recur—prevented Scotland from being a nation-state in Charles Tilly's terms, 'a state whose people share a strong linguistic, religious and symbolic identity'.[6] Few states, indeed, have ever achieved this, though some have done a good deal of damage by trying; while even today, many people believe that states are nations, or at least ought to be nations, rather in the way that people in the middle ages believed that the emperor was lord of the world.

The composite nature of 'Scotland' was partly a matter of

[5] D. Broun, 'Defining Scotland and the Scots before the wars of independence', in id. *et al.* (eds.), *Image and Identity: The Making and Re-Making of Scotland Through the Ages* (Edinburgh, 1998); A. Grant, 'Aspects of national consciousness in medieval Scotland', in C. Bjørn *et al.* (eds.), *Nations, Nationalism and Patriotism in the European Past* (Copenhagen, 1994); R. Mason, 'Chivalry and citizenship: aspects of national identity in Renaissance Scotland', in id. and N. Macdougall (eds.), *People and Power in Scotland* (Edinburgh, 1992). The ideas of Anthony Smith, who uses the term *ethnie* for such an ethnic community, have been influential: A. D. Smith, *The Ethnic Origins of Nations* (Oxford, 1986).

[6] C. Tilly, *Coercion, Capital and European States, AD 990–1990* (Oxford, 1990), 3.

geography. The heart of the state was the south-central belt of low-lying, fertile land, from Fife and Lothian in the east to Ayrshire in the west. To the south of this region, a range of hills, the Southern Uplands; further south, the low-lying coastal plains of Galloway in the west and the Tweed basin in the east. Beyond the central belt to the north, a long and forbidding series of central mountain ranges. Along the north-east coast there were coastal plains, some with fertile land like the Carse of Gowrie and the southern coast of the Moray Firth. There were few land routes into the Highlands, but the western Highlands and Isles—the old lordship of the Isles—formed a well-integrated region linked by sea transport. This region, deeply notched with lochs and firths, had little fertile land. The far north was low-lying but mostly not fertile, although Caithness and Orkney possessed a prosperous agriculture. Economically marginal regions were harder to govern because they produced less of a surplus to support a state infrastructure.

This geographical diversity was paralleled by cultural divisions which were recognized to pose distinctive challenges to rulers. A threefold division was most common, into Borders, Highlands, and Lowlands. Sir David Lindsay saw the people of the Borders as prone to 'reif [i.e. plunder], thift, murthour, and mischeif'. The Highlands were infested with 'sweir swyngeoris' (idle rogues), the clan elites, who caused 'unthrift, sweirnes, falset, povertie, and stryfe'. The 'law land' was troubled only by 'singulare proffect' (undue self-interest), although this was still enough to send the 'commoun weill' into exile.[7] This was very much a view from the Lowlands (Lindsay was from Fife), but it was the view shared by government. Both in the Borders and the Highlands, the state operated—if at all—in distinctive ways.

Territorial integration called for precise boundaries. The state's formal borders, at least, were capable of easy definition—or were they? One of the strangest statutes of sixteenth-century Scotland was enacted in England, 'at Twesilhauch in Northumbirland'.[8] The Anglo-Scottish land frontier lay in an upland region, difficult of access from the heartlands of the Scottish state, and inhabited by people whose self-sufficiency and bellicose propensities had often been encouraged by the state in times of war. The long peace of

---

[7] Lindsay, 'The complaynt of the comoun weill of Scotland', in *Works*, i. 33.

[8] *APS* ii. 278. This was made by James IV and his lords on 24 Aug. 1513, on their way to Flodden.

the fifteenth century led to some disengagement between the English and Scottish border communities, and early moves were made towards orienting them away from one another and towards their respective governments.[9] But although it was short and fairly stable, the frontier contained several large 'Debatable Lands', areas disputed between Scotland and England. Because neither state could establish a certain claim, it was hard for landlords to establish possession there—except the priory of Canonbie, 'a hous of prayers and newtre betuixt both the realmes'. From 1522 onwards, there were official attempts to fix an agreed frontier more precisely, attempts which denote increased governmental concern with the region. Many territorial ambiguities were removed, particularly by a treaty of 1552, although residual problems remained. In 1607, land grants were being passed through the great seals of both kingdoms.[10]

To the west, things were less clear. The Atlantic Ocean formed a natural western boundary, but Lowlanders often had only a hazy idea of what it contained in the way of 'Scottish' islands. Some late sixteenth-century maps showed an enormous but imaginary island, 'Hirtha', seventy miles across, to the north of Lewis beyond North Rona.[11] The ambiguous position of Rathlin, neither fully Scottish nor Irish, has already been noted. But the issue for the state was not just the frontier line itself, but also the people who lived near it. Here we must once again begin with the Border region, and then move on to consider the Highlands.

The 'Scottish Borders' are an incomplete concept without their inescapable corollary—the English Borders. The Anglo-Scottish frontier region formed a single homogeneous zone, fifty or sixty miles deep, with the frontier itself running through the middle. The zone was defined partly by topography—the Scottish west and middle marches in particular were separated by the Southern Uplands from the heartland of the state to the north—and partly

[9] A. Goodman, 'The Anglo-Scottish marches in the fifteenth century: A frontier society?', in R. A. Mason (ed.), *Scotland and England, 1286–1815* (Edinburgh, 1987).

[10] W. M. Mackenzie, 'The Debateable Land', *SHR* 30 (1951), 109–25 (quotation at p. 113); T. I. Rae, *The Administration of the Scottish Frontier, 1513–1603* (Edinburgh, 1966), 1–4, 21–2; *RPC* iv. 799–800; vii. 81–2; *APS* iv. 443–4, c. 28; NLS, council to James, 19 June 1607, Denmylne MSS, Adv. MS 33.1.1, vol. ii, no. 28.

[11] Royal Scottish Geographical Society, *The Early Maps of Scotland*, i (3rd edn., Edinburgh, 1973), map 4 and p. 18. 'Hirta' was the Gaelic name for St Kilda, but this was not St Kilda.

by patterns of travel and raiding—tenants of the English border barony of Gilsland in 1585 were required to have arms and a horse 'hable sufficientlye to beare a manne xx^{tie} myles within Scotlande and backe agayne'.[12] The people living in this zone knew about the frontier, but did not let it dominate their lives. In both the Scottish and the English marches they spoke the same language, shared many of the same customs and traditions, sang the same songs, and intermarried with one another despite sporadic official attempts to prevent this. The fact that Scots and English periodically raided one another did not cut across this essential homogeneity: after all, within the Border zone, Scots also raided Scots and English raided English.

The Border region had become the way it was because of the long tradition of Anglo-Scottish warfare. Consider what it was like to live in a late-medieval frontier zone. From time to time, relations between your king and the other king would deteriorate, and the enemy would come raiding over the Border. Your cattle and goods would be prime targets. Your own king would not have armed forces on the spot to prevent the incursion; if there was going to be defence, you would have to be prepared to do it yourself.

So Border society was militarized. Peasants and townsmen were armed, possessed horses for warfare, and were 'mair expert in ordiring a battell than utheris'.[13] Probably, as on the English side of the Border, this consumed much of their surplus product, so that less was available to collect as rent.[14] Moreover, the process of militarization was a two-way one. You were armed, not just for protection from the raids of the other side, but to go and raid them yourself when the opportunity offered or when prompted to do so by the government.

A society based on do-it-yourself defence (not to mention do-it-yourself attack) was not likely to be a law-abiding society. It was far

---

[12] Quoted in S. G. Ellis, *Tudor Frontiers and Noble Power: The Making of the British State* (Oxford, 1995), 97. Crossing the Border into Liddesdale, 'xx^{tie} myles' would take the men of Gilsland as far as Teviotdale or upper Eskdale, enabling them to strike at most of the Scottish middle march.

[13] John Leslie, *Historie of Scotland*, 2 vols., ed. E. G. Cody and W. Murison (STS, 1888–95), i. 10, 12.

[14] Ellis, *Tudor Frontiers*, 39–40. It is not clear how much actual military service was done: M. L. Bush, 'Tenant right under the Tudors: A revision revised', *Bulletin of the John Rylands Library*, 77 (1995), 161–88, at p. 183.

from being Hobbesian anarchy; there were unwritten customs, and codes of honourable conduct. But if political power grows out of the barrel of a gun, this meant that power in the Borders rested with the local military leaders—the heads of the kinship groups often known in the Borders as 'surnames'. Their local power was so great that it swamped most forms of authority derived from the central state. This comes out clearly in the work of Ian Rae, to whose study of sixteenth-century Border administration all subsequent scholars are deeply indebted. He distinguished between 'surname' groups, whose membership was stable and who were primarily farmers, and 'gangs' (a contemporary official term) who associated more opportunistically, and who were primarily raiders. It is the latter group who most often took the nicknames well known on the Border (Jock of the Side, Ill-drowned Geordie, George Burnfield alias Cutlug)—nicknames which in some cases seem almost to have replaced their surnames. Nevertheless, surname groups and gangs might overlap, and they differed in degree rather than in kind.[15]

All this made the Borders hard to govern. Cross-Border problems, such as crimes committed by Englishmen against Scots or vice versa, could be dealt with only by negotiation between the wardens at 'days of truce'; if Anglo-Scottish relations were bad, one warden or the other might refuse to cooperate. Far from being punished, the criminals would be encouraged. Then there would be retaliation, and violence would escalate. Nor, in such a climate, would the main Scottish surnames be willing to cooperate with one another in order to ease their warden's task. Administration in the Scottish middle march periodically collapsed through feuding between the Kerrs and Scotts, or among the Kerrs themselves. In 1584, Thomas Kerr of Ferniehurst was even granted exemption from the jurisdiction of his warden, William Kerr of Cessford, and allowed to conduct independent negotiations with the English—a remarkable admission of administrative failure.[16] Such episodes could not be blamed on the English directly, but the political structure of the Border region allowed them to happen. Bad Anglo-Scottish relations would make things worse (and relations certainly were bad in 1584). But this also offered a way forward; for with *good* Anglo-Scottish relations, no problem of Border government

---

[15] Rae, *Scottish Frontier*, 6–8.   [16] Ibid. 76.

was wholly insoluble.[17] The entire process that had created the militarized Border society was reversible.

Traditional Highland society was similar in some ways, but there were important differences. There were kinship groups—the clans—whose local military power was similar to that of the Border surnames.[18] The difficulties faced by central government in imposing its authority on the Highlands were thus similar to its difficulties in the Borders. But the origins and political dynamics of the clans were different. The Borders were a frontier zone between two states: the Highlands formed a free-standing political community. There was no state beyond the Highland Line, whether friendly or hostile.

This had several implications. First, there was no large alien garrison in (say) Doune, as there was in Berwick: no danger of a large modern army marching across the Highland Line to conquer the Scottish state. To that extent, the problem was less pressing than in the Borders. Secondly, the political structure of the Highland–Lowland frontier was asymmetrical. In the Borders, there were three Scottish marches, each with a warden, and three parallel English marches facing them. As a Scottish warden, you knew that your English opposite number might be uncooperative, or might be up to no good in your own march—but you might do the same to him. So you knew where you stood. As a royal lieutenant looking towards the Highlands, however, you saw the authority of the crown on your side of the Highland Line, while on the other side was the authority of—who or what? Individual chiefs and lords, who were supposed to be Scottish subjects (although they accepted little royal control in practice), and with whom it was difficult to conduct formal diplomacy.[19] When authority was so fragmented, where did you start? Did you have to negotiate with each individual chief? This is, in fact, how the late-medieval English lordship in Ireland was obliged to conduct relations with the larger world of local Gaelic lordships that surrounded it; but it was hardly satisfactory.[20]

---

[17] Ibid. 155–6.

[18] A. I. Macinnes, *Clanship, Commerce and the House of Stuart, 1603–1788* (East Linton, 1996), chs. 1–2; R. A. Dodgshon, ' "Pretense of blude" and "place of thair duelling": The nature of Scottish clans, 1500–1745', in R. A. Houston and I. D. Whyte (eds.), *Scottish Society, 1500–1800* (Cambridge, 1989).

[19] 'His majesties royall minde' was 'nocht habill to condescend to entir in onye condicions with sic peopill' in 1614: *HP* iii. 170.　　[20] Ellis, *Tudor Frontiers*, 37–9.

Instead of a state, beyond the Scottish Highlands was the larger Gaelic world of Ireland; the two have often to be considered as a single political unit. There was no state to unite them, but they did form a single cultural community. Political processes in this community, although decentralized, had much in common from Galway to Lewis.[21] The Scottish state, if it wished to govern the Highlands, had the same problem as in the Borders that it could hope to influence only the Scottish part of the region; dissidents could take refuge in Ulster. There was, of course, an English lordship in Ireland, but before 1602 it did not control the north. The Gaelic region of the British Isles could conceivably be seen (like the Borders) as a frontier zone between the Scottish state in the Lowlands and the English state in Ireland—but the zone was so large that little diplomacy could be conducted across it. English viceroys in Ireland could not negotiate with the Scottish government.[22] The Scottish Highlands and Gaelic Ireland were not really a fixed zone between two stable states. Both Scottish and English policy-makers thought rather of a broad western zone in which there were *no* fixed or stable political structures because the only inhabitants were savages. It was a conceptual wilderness, comparable to the frontier of nineteenth-century North America.[23] Such a frontier was an open one, offering opportunities for expansion.

Government in the Highlands was very different from government elsewhere in Scotland. The institutions and patterns of authority familiar in the Lowlands, and connected to the crown, were largely absent in the Highlands, though many were present in the Borders. This is a large subject; only some aspects of it can be discussed here, though the broad picture should become clear.

[21] For the beginnings in our period of a Scottish–Irish division in this Gaelic world see J. Dawson, 'The Gaidhealtachd and the emergence of the Scottish Highlands', in B. Bradshaw and P. Roberts (eds.), *British Consciousness and Identity: The Making of Britain, 1533–1707* (Cambridge, 1998). I am grateful to Dr Dawson for allowing me to read her paper before publication. For cultural relationships see also D. E. Meek, 'The Gaelic ballads of medieval Scotland', *TGSI* 55 (1986–8), 47–72.

[22] The exception, an embassy sent by Sir John Perrot in 1585, seems to have been unique: H. Morgan, *Tyrone's Rebellion: The Outbreak of the Nine Years' War in Tudor Ireland* (Woodbridge, 1993), 37, 53. Cf. J. E. A. Dawson, 'Two kingdoms or three? Ireland in Anglo-Scottish relations in the middle of the sixteenth century', in Mason (ed.), *Scotland and England*.

[23] Parallels between the native inhabitants of the Highlands and of North America were already being discussed: A. H. Williamson, 'Scots, Indians and empire: The Scottish politics of civilization, 1519–1609', *P & P* 150 (Feb. 1996), 46–83.

What we need to do is to look at some of the most important aspects of government one by one, to see how far both Borders and Highlands differed from the central Lowlands. In the process, light may be thrown not only on the peripheries of the state but also—by way of comparison—on its core.

One of the features of Lowland government which lowlanders took for granted was the extent to which it was carried out in towns. Government was often (indeed, primarily) based on rural landed power and client networks, but many of the actual decisions were taken in towns. Courts of all kinds were held in towns—sheriff courts, commissary courts, even baron courts if the baron had a burgh of barony. Just as towns were market centres for goods, so they were also centres for governmental commands; information on what the government was doing was made available there. Royal proclamations were issued in selected royal burghs. Putting outlaws to the horn was done in the head burgh of the sheriffdom.

But in the Highlands, there were virtually no towns at all.[24]

Because there were towns all over the Lowlands, some of them were close to the Highlands, and functioned as frontier posts facing the region. Highlanders would probably come to them when they needed to—for trade, and also as an occasional link with the state. Thus in 1587 it was ordered that any summonses to 'ilismen, hielandmen, or borderaris in brokin cuntries' should be issued in the 'heid burrowis of the nixt schyris in the Lawland'. When the government wanted to communicate with *all* the 'clannis of the Hieland' in 1552, it sent a messenger to issue a proclamation in Elgin and Inverness.[25] Probably some Highland chiefs did actually go to Inverness from time to time, or send their agents, rather as today's crofters go there for shopping trips. Surviving records of the Mackintoshes and Chisholms—clans near to Inverness—include several extract decreets of the local sheriff court and a few of the commissary court; the chiefs made contracts in the town; and some at least of the hornings issued in Inverness against them reached their destination, though this is not to say that they

---

[24] The only active royal burgh within the Highlands in the 16th cent. was the tiny Rothesay: P. G. B. McNeill and H. L. MacQueen (eds.), *Atlas of Scottish History to 1707* (Edinburgh, 1996), 231–3. Tarbert was active as a sheriff's seat only, and the sheriff (the earl of Argyll) obtained tax exemption on the grounds that the inhabitants would not obey him: G. S. Pryde, *The Burghs of Scotland: A Critical List* (Glasgow, 1965), no. 42; NAS, decreets in the taxation of 1594, E62/1, fo. 81^r.

[25] *APS* iii. 456, c. 52, para. 2; *TA* x. 92.

were necessarily obeyed.[26] But these were the most accessible clans; the sheriffdom of Inverness also nominally included the Western Isles.

What the chiefs did not do—either they did not want to, or were prevented—was to play an internal role in these towns' political life, in the way that many Lowland lords expected. Chiefs did not become provosts of burghs. The names mentioned in the charters of late medieval Inverness were entirely Lowland ones, and clansmen were not allowed to become burgesses.[27] A study of burghs' participation in lords' feuds hardly mentions any highlanders' involvement, the one exception being the occupation of Inverness in 1593 by Alastair MacDonald of Keppoch during a feud with Lachlan Mackintosh of Dunachton.[28] It is true that Scottish burghs tried to be independent from *all* rural lords if they could; but they did elect noble provosts quite often, and it seems that they were willing to relate more closely to Lowland than to Highland neighbours. The traditional Highland way of life was not an urban one, and clan government itself functioned with no reference to towns.

There *were* towns in the Borders, pointing up the greater amenability of this region to government based on paperwork. The two clusters of small towns—in the Tweed basin, centred on Selkirk, and along the Solway coast, focused on Dumfries—meant that borderers were never too far from a place where they could, if they chose, find out what the government was up to. Towns were also mustering-points for military incursions into the region by the government. There may have been some antipathy between towns and borderers.[29] One system of Border government used remote country sites in medieval fashion—the 'days of truce' held on the Border line itself, at traditional open-air locations. Even then, days of truce were sometimes held in frontier towns—Jedburgh, Kelso, Dumfries, Alnwick, or Carlisle.[30]

---

[26] See various examples in *The Mackintosh Muniments, 1442–1820*, ed. H. Paton (Edinburgh, 1903), and *Inventory of Chisholm Writs, 1456–1810*, ed. J. Munro (SRS, 1992).

[27] G. S. Pryde, 'Scottish Burgh Finances before 1707', Ph.D. thesis (St Andrews, 1928), 17–18.

[28] K. M. Brown, 'Burghs, lords and feuds in Jacobean Scotland', in M. Lynch (ed.), *The Early Modern Town in Scotland* (London, 1987), 110.

[29] As there was in England: Ellis, *Tudor Frontiers*, 68.

[30] Rae, *Scottish Frontier*, 50–2, and map showing the meeting-places at pp. x–xi. For medieval open-air courts (an alternative to holding them in castles), see *Sheriff Court Book of Fife, 1515–1522*, ed. W. C. Dickinson (SHS, 1928), p. xviii.

The primary agents of rural local government were the sheriffs. Sheriffs' seats were almost entirely in the Lowlands; they functioned fairly normally in the Borders, but the only sheriffdoms fully in the Highlands were Argyll and Tarbert in the west. The sheriff of Inverness seems normally to have ignored the vast Highland area over which he had jurisdiction. When the earl of Huntly was appointed sheriff in 1509, it was thought a daring move to send sheriff deputes to remote places like Kingussie, Inverlochy, Tain, Dingwall, and Wick. Justiciary courts for the north-west Isles had to be held in Inverness in 1629, although it was on the wrong side of the country and outside the justiciar's area of jurisdiction.[31] The difficulties faced by sheriffs when they ventured into the Highlands are illustrated by the lands of Glenelg. Alexander Macleod of Dunvegan had possessed the estate for twenty years without permission from the state, or from the nominal proprietor, Lord Lovat, when in 1527 the sheriff of Inverness was ordered to put a stop to this. The signet letter to him admitted 'the dyfficultie to put your said rolment to execution becaus the said Alexander MakCloid duellis in the hieland quhair nane of your officers dar pass to poynd him for dred of thair lyvis without invocatioun of oure liegis and thair assistance as is alledget'. The sheriff was ordered to assemble a posse of the 'liegis' to enforce the law. This was not the way that sheriffs routinely governed—and it did not work.[32]

The extent to which Highland local government relied on baron courts is unclear, but may have been substantial.[33] Baron courts derived their origin from the crown, and from a feudal system which had only incompletely penetrated the medieval Highlands, but they were also engines of lordship of a kind that was familiar enough to Highland society—extensions of the lord's patriarchal authority. It can even be argued that Highland chiefs were more likely to use baron courts than their Lowland counterparts, because of the weakness of public jurisdictions such as that of the

---

[31] D. Gregory, *History of the Western Highlands and Isles of Scotland, 1493–1625* (2nd edn., London, 1881), 105; HMC, *Sixth Report, Appendix* (London, 1877), 623–4.

[32] *The Book of Dunvegan*, 2 vols., ed. R. C. Macleod (Third Spalding Club, 1938–9), i. 68–72. The Macleods still possessed Glenelg in 1608: *RMS* vii. 119.

[33] B. Lenman and G. Parker, 'Crime and control in Scotland, 1500–1800', *History Today*, 30/1 (Jan. 1980), 13–17, at p. 13; D. Sellar, 'Barony jurisdiction in the Highlands', *Notes and Queries of the Society of West Highland and Island Historical Research*, 16 (Sept. 1981), 22–6. For early Highland baron courts, see G. W. S. Barrow, *The Anglo-Norman Era in Scottish History* (Oxford, 1980), 137–9.

sheriff.[34] The government demanded in 1608 that the chiefs in the Isles should renounce the rights of jurisdiction which they had allegedly usurped. The Statutes of Iona (1609) seem to have assumed that island chiefs would have baron courts. The final clause required that contraveners of the Statutes should be arrested by the 'barroun and speciall man within quhais boundis the contravenair makes his speciall residence', whereupon he should be produced before the ordinary judge. This seems to have been a warning to the chiefs not to use their courts to punish all offences indiscriminately.[35] On the other hand, it is not clear that they *were* using their courts in this way; surviving baron court records from the fringes of the Highlands seem no different from Lowland ones in the powers they exercise.[36]

However, if the baron and regality courts with surviving archives are plotted on a map, they fall almost entirely in the Lowlands, with an almost complete blank for the Highlands and relatively few for the Borders too.[37] There were a few prominent regalities on the Highland Line, such as those of Atholl and Sutherland; some of the courts located on the edge of the Lowlands probably possessed jurisdiction over Highland areas, though the fact that people had to leave the Highlands to seek justice in them is itself significant. The overall pattern is striking; what is less clear is what it means. What we do not know is how representative these surviving court records—a minority of those that once existed—are. There are two possibilities. Either the records of Highland and Border courts have perished disproportionately, or else there were never so many courts there. The first explanation is likely for the Borders, since the proportion of baron courts known from other evidence in the middle march is comparable to that for the whole of Scotland.[38] The extreme rarity of surviving baron court records

[34] P. Hopkins, *Glencoe and the End of the Highland War* (Edinburgh, 1986), 17.

[35] *RPC* viii. 737; ix. 29–30. Cf. J. Goodare, 'The Statutes of Iona in context', *SHR* 77 (1998), 31–57, at p. 53. Leslie used the term 'special men' to refer to local magnates generally: *Historie*, i. 45.

[36] e.g. the Glenorchy baron court book in *Taymouth Book*, 352–90; that of Belladrum (1637–8) in 'A miscellany of old Highland records', ed. A. MacDonald, *TGSI* 43 (1960–3), 1–10, at pp. 9–10; 'Extracts from the baron court books of Menzies', ed. W. A. Gillies, *TGSI* 39/40 (1942–50), 103–17.

[37] I have done this with the list of baron and regality courts in P. Rayner *et al.*, *Handlist of Records for the Study of Crime in Early Modern Scotland* (List and Index Society, 1982). Many of the archives are later, but we can assume that most of the courts to which they relate were also functioning in our period.

[38] *Court Book of the Burgh of Kirkintilloch, 1658–1694*, ed. G. S. Pryde (SHS, 1963), p. xlii; Rae, *Scottish Frontier*, 16.

in the Highlands suggests that such courts were never common; but it may be that courts were possessed mainly by the greater chiefs, so that a small number of them might still have covered a large area.

The church was a vital agency of local government. In the Borders it seems to have functioned much as in the central Lowlands, although its achievements were more limited by poverty.[39] There was a fair sprinkling of ministers and readers appointed to Highland parishes from the early years of the Reformation, but whether they did much beyond officiating at baptisms, marriages, and burials is doubtful. Evidence as to whether they could speak Gaelic is inconclusive—some could, others could not—but what is more important to *government* is that there is virtually no evidence of kirk sessions. It was the kirk sessions who provided the dynamism of the Scottish church as an institution of government.[40] The three known presbyteries (Ardmeanach, Argyll, and the Isles) emerged late and remained shadowy bodies.[41] Also important, particularly in the presbyterian system, was the leadership provided by well-paid urban ministers; no Highland ministers were urban, and precious few were well paid. Protestant highlanders may well have felt that the church met their religious needs, even though it did not operate in the ways regarded as conventional in the Lowlands.[42] But the possibility of using the church for social control—to eradicate, as the king put it, 'that bipast savaigenes and barbaritie', and to plant 'civilitie, oure obedyence, and trew religioun (the onlie meane to preserve both)'—was absent.[43]

This is why there was almost no witch-hunting in Gaelic areas. Highlanders certainly believed in witches, but some of their distinctive beliefs—particularly the 'evil eye', the possessor of which caused *unintended* harm to others—were never adopted or

---

[39] I. B. Cowan, *The Scottish Reformation* (London, 1982), 175–9; S. Adams, 'James VI and the politics of south-west Scotland, 1603–1625', in J. Goodare and M. Lynch (eds.), *The Reign of James VI* (East Linton, 1999, forthcoming).

[40] J. Kirk, *Patterns of Reform: Continuity and Change in the Reformation Kirk* (Edinburgh, 1989), ch. 6. Dr Kirk takes a more positive view of the church's Highland achievements, perhaps because he focuses on what *was* achieved. His para. on kirk sessions states that 'each minister could expect support from his elders' (p. 477), but evidence for the actual functioning of a kirk session in any Highland parish in our period is lacking.

[41] McNeill and MacQueen (eds.), *Atlas*, 390. There were 50 presbyteries overall in 1607.

[42] J. Dawson, 'Calvinism in Gaelic Scotland', in A. Pettegree *et al.* (eds.), *Calvinism in Europe, 1540–1620* (Cambridge, 1994). [43] *RPC* viii. 743; cf. Ch. 6 above.

seriously confronted by Lowland witch-hunters. The institutions and structures that were required for a witch-hunt were absent, except in frontier towns (such as Tain and Rothesay) possessing kirk sessions.[44]

A broad picture is already emerging from this review of patterns of government. The Borders were part of the state structure, although with numerous differences because of the strength of their local lordships: the Highlands were not. In the remaining fields of government where it is possible to search for patterns, the Borders need not be mentioned because they scarcely differed from the rest of the Lowlands. The differences—and some were striking—lay in the Highlands alone.

The legal structure of the Highlands in the sixteenth century was not clearly differentiated from the Lowlands, though what they had in common was more evident in theory than in practice. Ancient Gaelic laws had supplied many of the forms of medieval Scots law, but the late-medieval expansion of a distinct Gaelic law in the lordship of the Isles had led to a divergence from the law of the Lowlands. This trend was reversed after the forfeiture of the lordship in 1493. A terse statute of 1504, commanding the use of Scots law rather than Gaelic law in the region, dealt a serious blow to the structure of Highland legal administration. Until then the laws had been administered by the brieves, hereditary judges in many islands. Only one brieve survived (in Lewis) in the sixteenth century, and there is little evidence of Lewis brieves acting as judges, though they did still perambulate lands.[45] Traditional Highland officials like the brieves were alien to the Scottish state and could not be employed by it. Sir John Skene in 1597 puzzled over the jurisdiction of the *toiseachdeor* of Kintyre: was he a species of bailie, a coroner, or what?[46]

Most officials were more familiar in the Lowlands than the Highlands. There is evidence of local commissaries in Skye and Iona, at

[44] C. Larner, *Enemies of God: The Witch-Hunt in Scotland* (London, 1981), 8, 80; 'Witchcraft in Bute, 1662', *HP* iii. 14. Tain was not itself in the Highlands, but witches from its Highland hinterland were tried there.

[45] *APS* ii. 252, c. 24; W. D. H. Sellar, 'Celtic law and Scots law: Survival and integration', *Scottish Studies*, 29 (1989), 1–27, at pp. 3–4; D. S. Thomson, 'Gaelic learned orders and literati in medieval Scotland', *Scottish Studies*, 12 (1968), 57–78, at pp. 57–61; W. Matheson, 'The Morisons of Ness', *TGSI* 50 (1976–8), 60–80, at p. 73 (the Morisons were the brieves of Lewis).

[46] Skene, *DVS*, s.v. tocheoderache. He was in fact a coroner, though details of his office remain obscure: Sellar, 'Celtic law and Scots law', 9–11.

least; but they seem not to have been actively supervised by central government. The only early commissary mentioned in the register of the great seal is that of Argyll—who was the earl himself. The Isles lacked a commissary in 1622.[47] Commissaries' main job was to register testaments, and no such registers survive for the Highlands before 1670—in marked contrast to the abundant registers for Orkney and Shetland.[48] As for notaries, although some were based in lairds' households, most seem to have been urban, making this one of the services provided by the frontier towns.[49] Few notaries operated in the Highlands, and again they were semi-detached from central government; none are listed in the central register of admissions.[50]

The main traditional function of government was to regulate the possession of land. Clans did not need the state for this, but they sometimes used it—unlike in Gaelic Ireland, where hardly any chiefs had parchment titles.[51] Lowland lords were obliged to use law and parchment, but they sometimes vindicated their titles with the sword also. These two systems thus overlapped, and could in places on the Highland–Lowland frontier be quite similar. A general overview like the present one must discuss 'Highlands' and 'Lowlands' as two distinct systems, which is how contemporaries generally saw them; but this black and white picture did have shades of grey.[52]

An overview of the highlanders' use of paperwork suggests that their separate identity was reinforced by a general aloofness from the routine business of administration of landed society. To take one perhaps minor Sutherland clan, the Gunns: throughout the sixteenth century, not a single member of the clan was mentioned

[47] *Collectanea de Rebus Albanicis* (Iona Club, 1847), 7; *RMS* iv, p. 1166; *RPC* xiii. 21.

[48] F. J. Shaw, *The Northern and Western Islands of Scotland: Their Economy and Society in the Seventeenth Century* (Edinburgh, 1980), 7–9.

[49] J. Durkan, 'The early Scottish notary', in I. B. Cowan and D. Shaw (eds.), *The Renaissance and Reformation in Scotland* (Edinburgh, 1983), 37; J. E. Thomas, 'Elgin notaries in burgh society and government, 1540–1660', *Northern Scotland*, 13 (1993), 21–30; J. Dunlop, 'Gunpowder and sealing wax: Some Highland charter chests', *TGSI* 44 (1964–6), 41–60, at pp. 44–5.

[50] J. Bannerman, 'Literacy in the Highlands', in Cowan and Shaw (eds.), *Renaissance and Reformation*, 219–20; *Protocol Book of John Foular, 1528–1534*, ed. J. Durkan (SRS, 1985), pp. ix–x.

[51] Macinnes, *Clanship*, 5–6.

[52] For more on this, see J. Goodare and M. Lynch, 'The Scottish state and its borderlands, 1567–1625', in eid. (eds.), *Reign of James VI*.

in the great seal register.[53] This bureaucratic invisibility would be very unusual for a landed Lowland family. We can also look at it geographically by sheriffdom, through the payment of composition for charters in the treasurer's accounts. Two typical accounts for the early part of our period—those for 1562–3 and 1565–6—reveal that composition was charged on a total of 204 charters. Of these, the three sheriffdoms covering most of the Highlands—Inverness, Argyll, and Bute—mustered five, two, and two charters respectively. These figures may understate the Highland contribution slightly, but the small and remote Lowland sheriffdom of Wigtown alone had seven charters.[54] To take another example, based on surnames: the great seal register for the period 1580–1593 contains 2,360 charters, and only three of them mention people called MacDonald.[55] Beyond the Highland Line, hardly anyone participated in the business of the state.

This aloofness from traditional government was carried over into the growing additional functions of the late sixteenth-century state. The increase in the amount and frequency of taxation was one of the most significant developments of this period. The Highlands seem to have escaped this. Of the 117 disputed cases arising in 1594–6 from the tax of 1594, none involved highlanders.[56]

Hardly any highlanders attended parliament, the political forum of the Scottish nation. They could not do so as peers, for virtually none held peerage titles. They could not do so as burgesses, for there were virtually no burghs. They could do so as shire commissioners—but only for two shires in our period, Argyll and Bute. The other shires containing Highland areas (mainly Inverness, Perth, and Dumbarton) were usually represented by lowlanders. There were hardly any monastic commendators, so that effectively left two or three bishops. Moreover, most of the highlanders who

[53] *RMS* ii–vi, per indices. The one mention of the clan was collectively, as rebels at the horn: *RMS* iv. 1128. The register is not a complete record of all charters, even those of the crown, and the highlanders' use of patronymics sometimes led to their appearing under other names. On the other hand, it included witnesses and other participants, and was not restricted to feudal proprietors.

[54] *TA* xi. 119–32, 259–79. Highland charters may be slightly understated here because some other sheriffdoms (such as Perth and Aberdeen) had Highland regions, and because estates in the west Highlands tended to be large. On the other hand, most of the charters in Inverness, Argyll and Bute were granted to people with Lowland names.

[55] *RMS* v, per index, s.vv. McConeill, McDonald.

[56] NAS, decreets in the taxation of 1594, E62/1.

did come to parliament, whether as nobles, bishops, or shire commissioners, belonged to just one clan—the Campbells.[57] They were highly untypical. Campbells deliberately sought a dual role, operating both as Highland chiefs and as Lowland lords and courtiers. By the early seventeenth century, when state intervention in the Highlands became more regular and intense, they would collaborate with this and seek eagerly to seize the lands of other clans. They, and the Mackenzies (who adopted a similar role in the 1590s), were the exceptions to the rule of non-participation.

Highlanders did sometimes fight for the Scottish state—but only when they wanted to, not because they had to. At the battle of Pinkie in 1547, there were 'wpoun the right hand and wing the earl of Argyle and all the wast hieland men of Scottland, and on the left hand Makclaine, Makcloud, and Makenze witht all the haill Yillis men of Scotland'. Only two years earlier, many of those 'on the left hand' had been negotiating with Henry VIII to provide an army of 8,000 men to fight on the other side. In the fifteenth century, the lords of the Isles had fought against the kings of Scots more often than for them; they acknowledged the kings' nominal overlordship but had no thought of being part of a unitary Scottish state machine.[58]

Highland chiefs who did use the government's machinery could find themselves disadvantaged because of who they were. Lachlan Mackintosh of Dunachton received a commission of fire and sword in 1579 to implement a horning against James Dunbar, sheriff of Moray. Dunbar complained that this was unjust: Mackintosh was 'a chiftane of ane hieland clan, the tennentis and servandis of sindrie landislordis, and he and they gevand litill gude obeydience to ony ordinar law and justice, and in respect thairof the mair unmeit to have commissioun'. This was no doubt special pleading, but Dunbar rightly thought that it strengthened his case before the privy council.[59]

[57] M. D. Young (ed.), *The Parliaments of Scotland: Burgh and Shire Commissioners*, 2 vols. (Edinburgh, 1992–3), ii, app. 2. Apart from the Campbell earls of Argyll, the only Highland peers in the 16th cent. were the Frasers, Lords Lovat. They were joined in the early 17th cent. by the Mackenzies, who became Lords Kintail and then earls of Seaforth, but even then the Highlands largely missed out on the inflation of the peerage.

[58] Pitscottie, *Historie*, ii. 96; *Letters and Papers, Foreign and Domestic, of Henry VIII*, xx, II, ed. J. Gairdner and R. H. Brodie (London, 1907), nos. 294–5; J. Bannerman, 'The lordship of the Isles', in J. M. Brown (ed.), *Scottish Society in the Fifteenth Century* (London, 1977), 214–16.   [59] *RPC* iii. 91–2.

This overview of participation in government has suggested that the political and administrative distinctiveness of the Borders was modest, a matter of degree only. Surname groups in the Borders wielded a great deal of practical power, but the conventional state institutions of the central Lowlands were also present, although in a weakened and sometimes modified form. But the Highland political community was excluded—or held itself aloof—from the 'Scottish' (effectively Lowland) political community. Most of the Highlands saw no government proclamations; no members of parliament, general assembly, or convention of royal burghs; no privy councillors; no sheriff courts; no justice ayres; no royal visits; no wapinshawings; no commissions of justiciary; no presbyteries or kirk sessions; no customers. It is hard to think of any normal activity of central government that regularly crossed the Highland Line.

The reasons for this are complex and doubtless multifarious, but seem to lie in the political and cultural identities of the Borders' and Highlands' elites. Borderers could be fully accepted into the life of the Scottish nation, if they chose to participate. If highlanders did the same, they soon came up against the long and elaborate Lowland cultural tradition of denigration of highlanders.[60] One important component of Scottish identity—pride in not being English—could be a more immediate matter for borderers than anyone else. Johnny Armstrong, the local hero whose ballad was quoted in Chapter 2, was remembered by borderers as hostile to the English and fiercely proud to be Scottish, even though he had been executed for insufficient loyalty to James V.[61] Highlanders might see themselves as in some sense 'Scottish', but because they tended to perceive English and Lowland Scots alike as 'Saxons', they had difficulty identifying with this key aspect of Scottishness. Their 'Scottish' identity had to be maintained in parallel with their Gaelic identity, and for most purposes it was the latter that counted. Highlanders never repudiated their allegiance to the king of Scots, but they maintained the tradition that they had been dispossessed of the Lowland part of 'Alba' ('Scotland') by 'Saxons'. Their allegiance thus had an irredentist flavour, legitimizing raids on the Lowlands which were properly Gaelic territory. It certainly

[60] D. Murison, 'Linguistic relationships in medieval Scotland', in G. W. S. Barrow (ed.), *The Scottish Tradition* (Edinburgh, 1974), 79–81.

[61] F. J. Child, *English and Scottish Popular Ballads*, ed. H. C. Sargent and G. L. Kittredge (London, 1904), no. 169.

did not make them the king's *obedient* subjects, either in their own minds or in the king's mind. Even the unusual poem to the earl of Argyll on the eve of Flodden, characterizing the English enemy as the 'Saxons', was marked by pan-Gaelic solidarity, hoping for assistance from Gaelic Ireland.[62] Highlanders were not welcome members of the Scottish body politic; being fully Scottish meant being Lowland Scottish.

Highlanders were also distanced from government because it was not conducted in their language. They spoke Gaelic, while government used Scots. In a sense this is an obvious and basic point which hardly needs elaboration; modern nationalists often base their claims to statehood on the possession of a distinctive language, while multilingual states generate regular criticism for their treatment of linguistic minorities. You cannot be governed effectively if you do not understand what the government is telling you to do; still less can you participate in the governing process.

But for whom is all this a problem?—for you, or for the government? Today it may well be a problem for both; in the sixteenth century, it depended on what you, or the government, wanted to achieve. If the highlanders had wanted (as we may do today) to participate in government, the linguistic divide would have been their problem. If the government could not make them do what it wanted, it would have been the government's problem. The main sixteenth-century problem was the latter one. Highlanders did not want to participate in the business of the Scottish state, they wanted it to leave them alone. Lowlanders, indeed, may sometimes have felt the same way, but they could not realistically expect to be left alone and so had to participate. By coming to parliament, for instance, they were recognizing the legitimacy of the state, while hoping to influence it. Highlanders had a realistic chance of ignoring it.

The way forward for the state, therefore, was to place the highlanders in the same position as the lowlanders—where they could (perhaps) participate, but had to obey. This could be achieved only by coercion. If it succeeded, and the normal processes of government were extended to the Highlands, official business would be

---

[62] J. MacInnes, 'Gaelic poetry and historical tradition', in L. Maclean (ed.), *The Middle Ages in the Highlands* (Inverness, 1981), 144–50; R. Mason, 'Chivalry and citizenship: Aspects of national identity in Renaissance Scotland', in id. and N. Macdougall (eds.), *People and Power in Scotland* (Edinburgh, 1992), 56.

conducted there in Scots. The language of the people would be submerged; officialdom would interact only with people speaking its own language. In many cases they would not speak it very well, as it would be their second language—but while this might prevent them participating, it would not prevent them obeying. This was what happened in Galloway and Carrick, where the common folk spoke Gaelic as late as the 1560s, but the elite spoke Scots and were a normal part of Lowland Scottish society.[63] If there was a language problem in Galloway and Carrick, it was the people's problem and not the state's problem.

In earlier centuries, if the written language of government had differed from the spoken language of the people (even the political elite), this had not been a problem for anyone. In the middle ages, literacy had been a technical skill which rulers did not have to possess personally (just as cabinet ministers today do not have to understand computer programming, however much the routine business of government depends on computers). There had been less written government, and more of what there *was* had been conducted in Latin, which was as familiar in the Highlands as in the Lowlands. (There were, indeed, no Highland documents in the vernacular at all; the traditional written language of the Highlands was classical common Gaelic, an exclusively literary language used also in Gaelic Ireland, rather than Scots Gaelic.) But now, the expansion of the written and printed word made this increasingly difficult. Lowland government's shift from Latin to Scots was not the problem; the Gaelic learned orders could translate from either language. The problem was that regular translation was no longer practical. There were simply too many documents. More government was a matter of parliamentary statutes, tax demands, royal letters under the signet, and litigation in the court of session—all in Scots. These new laws, policy initiatives, and procedures had to be grasped immediately and in depth by anyone who made decisions. They were the very stuff of government—and a lord who was not personally familiar with their details was at a disadvantage.[64]

As government expanded, and as its influence in the Highlands

---

[63] J. MacQueen, 'The Gaelic speakers of Galloway and Carrick', *Scottish Studies*, 17 (1973), 17–33; C. W. J. Withers, *Gaelic in Scotland, 1698–1981* (Edinburgh, 1984), 25, 38–40.

[64] This transition is analysed for medieval England by M. T. Clanchy, *From Memory to Written Record: England, 1066–1307* (2nd edn., Oxford, 1993), ch. 7 and *passim*.

grew, this disadvantage came to be felt by many Highland chiefs. Gregor MacGregor of Glenstrae, chief of the MacGregors during their disastrous feud with the Campbells of Glenorchy (1562–70), was illiterate in Scots and letters had to be written in his name.[65] And yet the MacGregors lived in the Highland–Lowland frontier zone, where there was more bilingualism, and where private authority-documents like rentals were proliferating alongside public ones—also in Scots. The humble and anonymous chaplain who compiled the Scots 'Chronicle of Fortirgall' may well have been a MacGregor.[66] The area where there was least literacy in Scots was the Isles, the area most remote from government influence.[67] Moreover, the government was not going to offer them any concessions in coping with Scots documents. At the interface between two language groups, business is normally conducted in the language of the dominant group.[68]

This was not just a matter of language in the sense of a technical skill (bilingualism) to be mastered; it was also an aspect of culture and identity, and the way in which language influenced attitudes to politics. The Scottish state was hostile to Gaelic not so much because of the language itself, as because it believed the people who spoke it to be savages. To be acceptable to the state they would have to cease being savages, which from the Gaels' point of view did not mean acquiring a new technical skill so much as *abandoning* the culture which they in turn believed to be superior to that of the Lowlands.[69] They would prove reluctant to do this—unlike the sixteenth-century Welsh elite, who adopted a dual cultural identity along with bilingualism. The proceedings of the council in the Marches of Wales were in English. There may have been interpreters; bilingual attorneys gathered much business. This did not

---

[65] M. D. W. MacGregor, 'A Political History of the MacGregors before 1571', Ph.D. thesis (Edinburgh, 1989), 339.

[66] R. H. MacDonald, 'Estate of Chisholm: Surviving rental lists of 1665 to 1871', *TGSI* 53 (1984–6), 58–136, at p. 61; *Taymouth Book*, 111–12. This was also the region in which Gaelic verse began to be written using Lowland Scots orthography, in preference to classical Gaelic forms: D. E. Meek, 'The Scots-Gaelic scribes of late medieval Perthshire: An overview of the orthography and contents of the Book of the Dean of Lismore', in J. D. McClure and M. R. G. Spiller (eds.), *Bryght Lanternis: Essays on the Language and Literature of Medieval and Renaissance Scotland* (Aberdeen, 1989).   [67] Bannerman, 'Literacy in the Highlands', 216.

[68] P. Trudgill, *Sociolinguistics* (Harmondsworth, 1974), 133.

[69] Cf. D. Stevenson, *Alasdair MacColla and the Highland Problem in the Seventeenth Century* (Edinburgh, 1980), 17.

prevent Wales from being assimilated into the structure of the English state, and even from preserving a large measure of cultural autonomy as it did so.[70] James VI, who soon afterwards came to rule over the Welsh without finding any fault with their Welshness, would have been happy enough to rule over a multilingual, or multi-ethnic, state, so long as all the ethnic groups within it had the same regard for his sovereign authority.[71] The point about highlanders was that they manifestly had no such regard.

At least nobody *else* was able to claim any sort of sovereign authority in the Highlands; the late-medieval lordship of the Isles was no more. It had used the sea to integrate its territory—the Isles themselves, much of the western coast of Scotland, and the northern coast of Ulster. The lords of the Isles had been dynastic princelings, and in the mid-fifteenth century had also held the north-eastern earldom of Ross. They might have been putting themselves in a position to erect a sovereign state. A later tradition related that Alexander, Lord of the Isles (*c.*1423–49), 'proposed to refer the decision of the controversy about the Isles to the arbitration of foreign princes', suggesting that he saw his lordship as somehow equivalent in status to the Scottish crown. He was indeed traditionally styled 'Rex Insularum'. But the lordship of the Isles, like the duchy of Burgundy, was one of history's might-have-beens; forfeited by the Scottish crown in 1493, the unity of the lordship was destroyed. Despite several rebellions in the early sixteenth century, it could never be revived.[72]

Still, the main strength of the system of Gaelic lordship in the Highlands was not its adherence to the lordship of the Isles—the political network centred on the Council Isle in Loch Finlaggan—but its roots in *local* society. Highland chiefs could rule happily without any higher authority at all. It would be wrong to think that the marginalization of the Highlands was because of any internal 'decline' in Gaelic areas. Much of the sixteenth century probably

[70] P. Williams, *The Council in the Marches of Wales under Elizabeth I* (Cardiff, 1958), 82–3; G. Williams, *Renewal and Reformation: Wales, c.1415–1642* (Oxford, 1987), 266–78, 332–57.

[71] G. D. Owen, *Wales in the Reign of James I* (Woodbridge, 1988), 2, 111; cf. Ellis, *Tudor Frontiers*, 74.

[72] 'History of the Macdonalds', *HP* i. 38; Bannerman, 'Lordship of the Isles'; A. Grant, 'Scotland's "Celtic fringe" in the late middle ages: The MacDonald lords of the Isles and the kingdom of Scotland', in R. R. Davies (ed.), *The British Isles, 1100–1500* (Edinburgh, 1988).

saw consolidation and even expansion in power for Gaelic lord-ships in Scotland and Ireland.[73]

Scotland and Ireland: these were meaningful terms in Edin-burgh, but less so the closer one approached to the supposed div-ision between the two. In John Carswell's mind when making his Gaelic translation of the Scottish service book in 1567 were 'we, the Gaels of Scotland and Ireland'.[74] The possession of a name is a vital marker of an ethnic community. Just as there was a Scottish 'nation' or ethnic community, so there was a Gaelic one. To the Gaels, the political division between Scotland and Ireland was alien and artificial, imposed by two non-Gaelic groups for which they used the common names of 'foreigners' or 'Saxons'. Their name for themselves, 'the Gaels', gave them an ethnic identity making them a free-standing political community—if the 'Saxons' would let them; they were reluctant to consider themselves 'Scottish', although the exigencies of being governed might oblige them to do so. George Buchanan noted that 'the ancient Scots' (the Gaelic-speaking Highlanders) 'do not . . . at present acknowledge the name of Scots'.[75] The Gaels' collective identity was deeply rooted in a sense of shared genealogy—one of the most potent coagulat-ing forces for ethnic communities before the age of the modern nation-state; it was not, however, based so firmly on attachment to a specific territory.[76] And the land that the Gaels inhabited was a development site for someone else's state-building.

We are concerned with a state, then, with its roots in the Low-lands. But we should not make the mistake of regarding the Lowland state as the norm, and the Highland community as the exception to that norm. On the contrary, the Highlanders' atti-tude to government was rather like the attitude that *everyone* had had to central government in medieval times, when it had impinged on people's lives more rarely. In the late sixteenth century, such an attitude gradually ceased to be tolerable to the

---

[73] M. Lynch, 'National identity in Ireland and Scotland, 1500–1640', in Bjørn *et al.* (eds.), *Nations, Nationalism and Patriotism*, 111–12.

[74] *Foirm na n-Urrnuidheath: John Carswell's Gaelic Translation of the Book of Common Order*, ed. R. L. Thomson (Scottish Gaelic Texts Society, 1970), 179–81.

[75] George Buchanan, *The History of Scotland*, 6 vols., ed. J. Aikman (Edinburgh, 1830), i. 124.

[76] R. A. Dodgshon, *From Chiefs to Landlords: Social and Economic Change in the Western Highlands and Islands, c.1493–1820* (Edinburgh, 1998), 32–4; cf. Smith, *Ethnic Origins of Nations*, 48–52.

state authorities. If there was a 'Highland problem' for the state, it was because the state had changed.

The threefold division between 'Borders', 'Lowlands', and 'Highlands' may have been complex enough for the Scottish state, but it did not exhaust the regional complexity of its territories. At the furthest extremities of the domains of the crown were the Northern Isles. Orkney and Shetland had been acquired by the Scottish crown only in 1468–9, and in unusual circumstances— given as pledges by Christian I of Denmark in lieu of the cash dowry promised when his daughter Margaret married James III. It was always open to the Danes to offer to pay off the dowry and redeem the islands; they made such an offer in 1560, for instance. However, the Scots showed no intention of returning the islands, and the Danes did not press hard. James VI's marriage to Anna of Denmark was arranged in 1589 without the 'mater of Orkney' causing difficulties.[77]

The intricacies of sovereignty in Orkney and Shetland were recently examined in detail by Gordon Donaldson. He argued that sovereignty was not transferred from Denmark to Scotland in 1468–9, for the agreement did not provide for such a transfer. Instead, sovereignty was acquired gradually thereafter by prescription and administrative integration. Since, he claimed, this process was completed only after 1707, the provocative implication was that the United Kingdom had sovereignty over the islands but Scotland did not.[78] His point about the acquisition of sovereignty being a gradual process is well taken, but it should be set in a different conceptual framework. Sovereignty was not, indeed, transferred in 1468–9: not, however, because Christian I may not have intended to surrender it, but because (in the sense in which this book uses the term) it did not then exist. Neither Denmark nor Scotland were then sovereign states. Professor Donaldson conflated medieval and modern concepts of sovereignty. Using the latter concept alone, we should not be thinking of the Northern Isles being exchanged between otherwise unproblematic unitary states, but of a process of state *formation* in which *all* the diverse territories of the state came gradually to be subjected to a unified central

---

[77] T. Riis, *Should Auld Acquaintance Be Forgot: Scottish-Danish Relations, c.1450–1707*, 2 vols. (Odense, 1988), i. 17–18, 33, 263–5; *Warrender Papers*, ii. 35–48.

[78] G. Donaldson, 'Problems of sovereignty and law in Orkney and Shetland', *Stair Society Miscellany*, ii (1984).

authority. The way in which this happened for Orkney and Shetland is interesting—the abrogation of the Norse laws in 1611 is rightly seen as a landmark (and is surely the *terminus ad quem* for Scottish sovereignty over the islands, 1707 being far too late a date)—but they were merely two among many localities that were made to move from the centre of their own world to the periphery of a much larger one.

Although Orkney and Shetland were peripheral components of the Scottish state, they nevertheless became *real* components of it. As the state became more centralized, what happened to the general relationship between centre and localities? While the state's relationship with Orkney would be affected by the exigencies of travelling between Edinburgh and Kirkwall, the issue of 'centre and localities' was not primarily one involving travel. 'Centre' and 'localities' were not different places; centralization happened *in* the localities, since everywhere was a locality. Centralization, to the extent that it happened in our period, did not primarily mean more men travelling from Edinburgh to tell Orcadians what to do. It meant a change in the structure of authority so that folk *on the spot*—those who exercised authority, and those who obeyed it—began to behave in ways approved in Edinburgh. They did more of the same things that were done by folk in other 'localities', attending the same courts, observing the same statutes, and paying the same taxes. Distinctive local government continued to exist, applying itself to particular local issues; but more of the business of government came to operate in the same way throughout the territory of the state.[79]

The dynastic aspects of kingship and lordship also affected the ways in which Scotland's disparate territories coalesced. Centrality and marginality in the late medieval kingdom were not necessarily matters of physical distance. Decentralized lordship could be exercised over long distances, and yet fail to be effective in regions close at hand. Even Lowland areas that we might imagine to be fully within the structures of the state could in fact be marginal. One such was in Ayrshire, where the ancestral lands of the royal Stewart family had in the early fifteenth century been erected into a 'principality' for the eldest adult son of the king.[80] Parliament in 1490 enacted that the tenants in chief of the principality should

---

[79] J. Goodare, *The Government of Scotland, 1560–1625* (forthcoming), ch. 5.
[80] W. C. Dickinson, 'An inquiry into the origin and nature of the title Prince of Scotland', *Economica*, 4 (1924), 212–20.

only be 'haldin to compere and ansuer in parliament and justice airis . . . ay and quhill that our soverane lord haf a sone that suld be immediate betuix the king and thaim'.[81] If they had a feudal lord with his own courts (the bracketing of parliament and justice ayres is instructive), they need not come to parliament. Nothing could be further from the idea of parliament as a sovereign law-making body for the whole country.[82]

It was a long time after 1490 before the principality had a prince: not until 1619, in fact. But the creation of Prince Charles as prince of Scotland gave him few rights of jurisdiction, nor was the act of 1490 exempting his tenants from parliamentary attendance mentioned. Charles was allowed to manage his estates, but it seems that here, as in creating him prince of Wales, James minimized his jurisdiction and political influence.[83] By 1619, the state had become a more unitary one in a way that had not been envisaged by the dynastic state of a century earlier.

To the extent that the ruling dynasty had interests well beyond Scotland, this too blurred the definition of the state. In the late middle ages, that dynasty can be seen acting like any other feudal ruling family; no great magnate family then was merely national. This feudal internationalism was sometimes a solvent of states, as the process of dynastic inheritance allowed (or obliged) rulers to assemble unlikely collections of provinces with divergent traditions and governmental structures. Shepherding such unwieldy assemblages in one direction, should the ruler wish to pursue anything so ambitious as a common policy for all of them, might end in revolt, or even in separation or collapse.[84] With this in mind, the French promise to grant the county of Saintonge to James I looks little different from the creation of the fourth earl of Douglas as duke of Touraine; Douglas, who actually received his French lands, was perhaps doing better than the king.[85] In the fourteenth

---

[81] *APS* ii. 221, c. 17. 'Ay and quhill' = until.

[82] Just as the principality was separate from the kingdom, so a queen dowager might have her own administrative structure, parallel to that of the king. Mary of Guelders had her own exchequer between 1461 and 1463: *ER* vii. 47, 161.

[83] *RPC* xii. 7–8, 57–62, 248–9, 277–9; P. Roberts, 'Wales and England after the Tudor "union": Crown, principality and parliament, 1543–1624', in C. Cross *et al.* (eds.), *Law and Government Under the Tudors* (Cambridge, 1988), 127–33.

[84] J. H. Elliott, 'A Europe of composite monarchies', *P & P* 137 (Nov. 1992), 48–71, at pp. 51–2; cf. A. M. Rao and S. Supphellen, 'Power elites and dependent territories', in W. Reinhard (ed.), *Power Elites and State Building* (Oxford, 1996).

[85] M. Brown, *James I* (Edinburgh, 1994), 110, 47–8.

century, Robert I and David II had been strongly identified with the survival of the Scottish nation, but once this was no longer threatened, their successors, the early Stewarts, came more to resemble another baronial clique. The captive James I, as a client of Henry V in France in the early 1420s, even acted against what Scots fighting there regarded as the national interest. James III made some efforts in 1473 towards asserting his dynastic claim to the duchy of Guelders, which was of no relevance to any but a small section of the military class.[86] If the nation was not the state, neither was the dynasty the nation.

If James III's interest in imperial kingship has often been noted, so have the hopes of his successor to lead a crusade. Talk of crusading was the small change of European diplomacy, but James IV seems really to have meant it, and pursued his project over many years. This surely indicates an archaic attitude to Europe, seen as a unified Christendom, and a distancing from the emerging idea of a Europe of sovereign states. The revival of crusading has been seen as the last hope for universal papal monarchy; those fifteenth- and sixteenth-century popes who were most keen on maintaining or reviving this political role (rather than concentrating on their immediate concerns as Italian princes) sought energetically to place themselves at the head of a crusade.[87]

In the early sixteenth century, the ambitions of the dynasty regained something of a national flavour, only to lose it once more. The concept of the 'commonweal' emerged at this time: virtue, justice, and good governance were to be sought by, and on behalf of, the political community. It was a concept focused on the crown, although it was not just up to the monarch to take the initiative; it is striking how little Sir David Lindsay's 'King Humanitie' contributes to the reform of the community in the 'Satyre of the Thrie Estatis'.[88] James V concentrated on relations with France, which led

---

[86] S. I. Boardman, *The Early Stewart Kings: Robert II and Robert III, 1371–1406* (East Linton, 1996), 61–2 and *passim*; Brown, *James I*, 21–4; D. Ditchburn, 'The place of Guelders in Scottish foreign policy, c.1449–c.1542', in G. G. Simpson (ed.), *Scotland and the Low Countries, 1124–1994* (East Linton, 1996), 70–1.

[87] A. Macquarrie, *Scotland and the Crusades, 1095–1560* (Edinburgh, 1985), 107–13; P. Prodi, *The Papal Prince: One Body and Two Souls: The Papal Monarchy in Early Modern Europe*, trans. S. Haskins (Cambridge, 1987), 176–7.

[88] R. A. Mason, 'Kingship and Commonweal: Political Thought and Ideology in Reformation Scotland', Ph.D. thesis (Edinburgh, 1983), 68–70 and *passim*; C. Edington, *Court and Culture in Renaissance Scotland: Sir David Lindsay of the Mount* (Amherst, Mass., 1994), 139.

to what proved eventually to be a dead end (though it might have worked out differently)—dynastic union with France. But he was very much a Scottish monarch pursuing Scottish interests, and his break with England towards the end of his reign was seen on both sides of the Border in national terms.

Mary never abandoned her personal French connection, but both she and James VI pursued the aim of union with England. This was equally dynastic in form, although unlike Saintonge or Guelders (but like France) it could be said to be in the interests of the nation. But the predominant element in the union of 1603 was dynastic, not national; if Scots and English welcomed it (and not all did), it was largely because of the enhanced status of their king. Only a few sycophants or eccentrics yearned to become exclusively or even primarily British.[89] As for the king himself, the moment he gained his new dual throne, he could no longer for that very reason identify his interests with those of either one of his realms singly, and the custody of Scottish national interests lay open to be claimed by a non-monarchical body—the presbyterian movement within the church.[90]

This brings us to the question of Scotland's relationship with England. It is clear enough that the Scottish state in our period stood in a dependent relationship to the separate state of England: a satellite state from 1560 to 1603, a component of a dual monarchy thereafter. It was, nevertheless, formally independent and fulfilled the criteria for sovereignty laid down by John Austin. Its subjects were in the habit of rendering obedience to it, whereas its sovereign was not in the habit of rendering obedience to the stronger neighbour. These criteria are not absolute; as Austin stressed, there is a conceptual continuum, rather than a sharp divide, between sovereign and non-sovereign states.[91] Scotland, as a satellite state, was certainly more dependent than some, but it makes more sense to regard it as basically sovereign. Queen Elizabeth was not in the *habit* of telling Mary or James what to do, nor did they *habitually* obey her. She certainly intervened from time to time to modify Scottish political arrangements to suit English

---

[89]　B. P. Levack, *The Formation of the British State: England, Scotland and the Union, 1603–1707* (Oxford, 1987), 189–90.

[90]　Lynch, 'National identity', 133–5.

[91]　J. Austin, *The Province of Jurisprudence Determined*, ed. W. E. Rumble (Cambridge, 1995), 168, 172–5. This aspect of his theory of sovereignty has been neglected. See Ch. 1 above.

interests, but this was done irregularly, and less as a command than as an act of ostensible friendship. She did not make the French mistake of sending an army of occupation to Scotland. Instead, Anglo-Scottish 'amity' became a powerful code-word for the promotion of a pro-English party within Scotland in the 1560s and 1570s. Friendship, of course, does not have to be between equals in power, or even between equals in status. When, in 1586, Elizabeth made the king himself the channel for her management of Scotland, she took care to ensure that her assistance (particularly financial assistance) to James was such as to oblige him to reciprocate by pursuing approved policies. But although this was a great success, it was achieved not by the issuing of regular, formal, and lawful commands, but by persuasion and indirect leverage.[92]

This, of course, is a necessary argument, for were it to be maintained that Scotland had already mislaid its sovereignty during the reign of Elizabeth, this would leave little or nothing for the union of crowns to accomplish. The union of 1603, dividing-line of so many textbooks and syllabuses: nobody could allow it to fade in significance, least of all for the question of national sovereignty. Or could they? It can be argued that even the transfer of royal authority to Westminster was not a fundamental transformation of Scotland's sovereign status. There was, indeed, a change, but it was of degree only. The sovereign authority was not the crown alone but the crown in parliament. Parliament contained no Englishmen.[93] Day-to-day public authority, too, was still exercised by the king of Scots through his Scottish executive officers. While there was an Anglo-Scottish court employing some British iconography, at least until 1625, there was little or no assimilation in the personnel of the administrative systems, or the habits and attitudes of the nobility. There remained two separate political elites. The court as a whole (both in Scotland and in England) was merely more distanced from political society.[94]

---

[92] G. Donaldson, *All the Queen's Men: Power and Politics in Mary Stewart's Scotland* (London, 1983), chs. 3, 5, 7; W. Ferguson, *Scotland's Relations with England: A Survey to 1707* (Edinburgh, 1977), ch. 5; J. Goodare, 'James VI's English subsidy', in id. and Lynch (eds.), *Reign of James VI*.

[93] In 1621, three Englishmen holding nominal Scottish titles were present by proxy in parliament, but the government, although hard-pressed, did not dare to use their votes: J. Goodare, 'The Scottish parliament of 1621', *Historical Journal*, 38 (1995), 29–51, at p. 49.

[94] Goodare, *Government*, ch. 2; K. M. Brown, 'The Scottish aristocracy, Anglicization and the court, 1603–1625', *Historical Journal*, 36 (1993), 543–76.

There remains, though, the issue of the dual or composite 'British' monarchy. 'Britain' was not alone in its composite status; most of the major states known to us as 'Spain', 'Poland', or even 'France' were in fact collages of smaller units. It has been persuasively argued that the asymmetrical authority exercised by their governments should be treated as a phenomenon in its own right, not simply as a disappointingly incomplete version of unitary state sovereignty.[95] This is certainly so, particularly since composite monarchies displayed such endless variety that each one needs individual consideration. That should not, however, lead us to abandon the concept of sovereignty; on the contrary, it is an essential tool for comprehending the complexities of the dynastic union—ever mindful of Austin's dictum that sovereignty need not be absolute. The question is: *how* sovereign was the state? But there needs to be a prior question—which state?—because we are asking not just about Scotland but also about Britain. Scotland was still largely sovereign, even after the dynastic union; but in a few areas, the shadowy outlines of a British state began to be detectable. Indeed, we are asking also about England, which was much more than a shadowy outline. If (to express the matter in not-quite-meaningless figures) Scotland was only eighty per cent sovereign after 1603, who had the other twenty per cent—England, Britain, or a combination of the two?

This distinction, between England and Britain, can illuminate the nature of the composite monarchy as it affected Scotland. If people in Scotland were in the habit of obedience to *England* (even just part of the time, or on some matters) then Scotland, to that extent, was a *colony*: it was governed, to that extent, by a foreign power. But if the Scots obeyed a government of *Britain* (to the extent that such a thing existed) then Scotland, to that extent, was a *junior partner*: it was governed, to that extent, by a polity in which Scots themselves participated.

Scotland was not a colony to any significant extent. There was *some* English influence, certainly, as there had been before 1603—and there was not necessarily *more* influence after 1603. But it continued to be exercised through diplomacy and compromise, not command. Both before and after 1603, Scotland and England

[95] J. Robertson, 'Empire and union: Two concepts of the early modern European political order', in id. (ed.), *A Union for Empire: Political Thought and the British Union of 1707* (Cambridge, 1995), 3–4.

were largely separate polities. Like it or not, they were neighbours and had to live with one another. This did not mean that they would be friends, or even that it was in their interests to be friends, but it did mean that they could not ignore one another. Many decisions taken in Westminster would be bound to affect Scotland in any age, and sometimes the Scots would also affect England. The two polities thus had to maintain contact; they had to discuss matters of mutual concern; and they had, on occasion, to modify their policies—to compromise—in the interests of maintaining good relations with their neighbours. This is what diplomacy is about. We tend to think of diplomacy as a process of negotiation between fully separate, fully sovereign powers, and that is one aspect of it; but in this context it is simply a process of compromise between neighbouring polities with interests sometimes similar, sometimes conflicting. English policy-makers asked themselves, 'What will the Scots think?' much as they asked, 'What will the French think?' Thus the English negotiators on the Spanish match in 1623 were concerned about the Scottish government's attitude towards persecution of Catholics, and had to discuss it with the Scottish bishops.[96] The very *similarity* of English and Scottish interests since 1560, with their governments sharing a common and sometimes embattled Protestantism, made them work together. England, being the more powerful state, had the upper hand in this relationship, which is why we can speak of Scotland as a satellite state; but a satellite state is not a colony. Arm's-length manipulation is not automatic or total control. As well as greater power, England also had greater problems (particularly in Ireland), and played for higher stakes. It sometimes had to compromise in response to the expressed interests of the Scottish government. This had been so before 1603, and it remained so thereafter.

As well as this English influence, there was also some British influence in Scotland. England could persuade and negotiate, but British government was a matter of command—at least to the extent that Britain existed, which was, however, not very much. Given that the embryonic British state was a composite *monarchy*, one should look for British influence in the fields in which the monarch had most influence—the fields covered by the royal

---

[96] *CSP Dom. 1623–1625*, 57. For the diplomatic model of 'British' policies in the 16th cent., see H. Morgan, 'British policies before the British state', in B. Bradshaw and J. Morrill (eds.), *The British Problem, c.1534–1707* (London, 1996).

prerogative. Policies on the coinage and the customs were effectively British, not Scottish, after 1603. It would be tempting to add foreign policy to this list, since this was one field which both Scots and English allocated to the prerogative. Scots were certainly interested in foreign affairs—there were celebrations in Edinburgh, just as in London, when Prince Charles returned from Spain in 1623 without having married the Infanta Maria.[97] Many Scots were also in military service abroad. However, mercenaries served for pay. They mainly served Protestant states, but like Charles's marital affairs this points up the extent to which foreign policy was governed by religious policy. The church has often been cited as an area for 'British' policy-making, but this seems to have been overstating the case.[98] Moreover, the royal prerogative did not have free rein in the Scottish church; much policy-making had still to be done by parliament—and even by the general assembly of the church. One cannot entirely ignore 'Britain' in the early seventeenth century, but it did not impinge much on the Scottish experience of being governed.

There is one further point. The analysis of composite monarchy as a system of government 'in its own right' should not necessarily entail treating it as a *stable* or *unchanging* system. It may have been normal in early modern Europe, but it was not unproblematic. J. H. Elliott has argued that composite monarchy was in fact a recurrent problem of governance. Most composite states were hampered by recalcitrant provinces; most of their rulers at some point entertained schemes for closer union. Some of these schemes took effect, some failed; some composite states were eventually integrated more closely (although rarely until after our period), others disintegrated. Should any really active, 'reforming' government emerge in a composite state, closer union would tend to appear on the agenda. No Spanish statesman was as active in promoting a 'Union of Arms' among Spain's many provinces as the count-duke of Olivares; how many other statesmen were as active as Olivares in *any* area of policy? A passive government could live with diversity and disunity, but a dynamic one would find it hard to tolerate.[99]

[97] Calderwood, *History*, vii. 580.
[98] J. Morrill, 'A British patriarchy? Ecclesiastical imperialism under the early Stuarts', in A. Fletcher and P. Roberts (eds.), *Religion, Culture and Society in Early Modern Britain* (Cambridge, 1994).
[99] Elliott, 'Composite monarchies'; id., *The Count-Duke of Olivares: The Statesman in an Age of Decline* (New Haven, 1986), ch. 7.

The union, then, was not a static and accomplished fact; it was a dynamic situation in which *more* union might be sought from time to time, both as an ideal in its own right and as a practical solution to specific problems of governance. Such changes were made by the consent of the Scots, or at least by what passed for consent in the mind of James VI. Thus there were periodic political manoeuvres to facilitate a *future* union. This future union could have been accomplished either through amalgamation, or through incorporation of Scotland into a greater England; the issue never arose during James's reign, though it seems clear that neither he nor his English advisers envisaged incorporation of Scotland. There were worries in May 1603 that James might subvert the Scottish nature of the court of session, 'now the only ornament off this land', by retaining some of its members in London, but no more was heard of this plan.[100] The Scottish privy council protested in 1608 against the summoning of four Scotsmen before the English privy council; they successfully countermanded the summons and warned the king that any repetition would 'greatlie exasperat' the Scots.[101] James chose the bishop of London to officiate at the consecration of his Scottish bishops in 1610; had he employed one of the English archbishops, it would have implied a possible subjection of the Scottish church to the English.[102] The dynamic instability of the regal union would cause several problems, and contribute to many others, later in the seventeenth century; but for whatever reason—skill or caution on the king's part, luck, absence of other pressing issues—moves for closer union had not overwhelmed the political agenda by 1625.

The 'British' issue—it was also a Scottish issue—which led to the most striking practical results in the reign of James VI and I was the issue of colonization. All the best and most fashionable monarchies in this period were acquiring colonies in order to add lustre to their crowns. Scotland scrambled on this bandwagon in the 1620s, not without difficulty, with the foundation of Nova Scotia. This was a new extension of the imperial ideal: 'empire' not as full powers within as an enlarged territory, often acquired by conquest. Both Scottish and British rhetoric was deployed to legitimize the

---

[100] Lord Fyvie to James, 30 May 1603, *LP James VI*, 56.

[101] *RPC* viii. 34–5, 489–90.

[102] W. R. Foster, *The Church before the Covenants, 1596–1638* (Edinburgh, 1975), 29. Many of these matters are discussed further in J. Wormald, 'The creation of Britain: Multiple kingdoms or core and colonies?', *Transactions of the Royal Historical Society*, 6th ser. 2 (1992), 175–94.

colony and to encourage settlement. Nova Scotia was chartered under the Scottish great seal, but the original nominal conquest of the territory had been by the English; the council of New England surrendered its claim to the territory to allow the king to make the grant to Nova Scotia's Scottish founder, Sir William Alexander of Menstrie.[103]

The colony was promoted very much as a court venture, which occasionally gave it a British flavour. Alexander himself was a prominent courtier, and it was through court circles that the capital for the project was mobilized—through the characteristic device of the sale of baronetcies. The Scottish trading community, by contrast, maintained a studied indifference towards the colony. The very full proceedings of the convention of royal burghs during the 1620s did not even acknowledge its existence.[104] Nova Scotia became a fully British issue when a 'Company of Adventurers to Canada' was formed in 1627. This company arose from a successful English privateering raid which stimulated the interest of investors. It was intended to help develop the Nova Scotia colony, and Alexander was a member, but the company's own patent was apparently an English one; its other members were English merchants and it operated from England.[105]

In contrast to the Nova Scotia venture—nominally Scottish, actually in part English—stood another, more substantial project that was nominally English but actually in part Scottish. This was the plantation of Ulster. Parallels between the Indians of the New World and the Gaels of Scotland and Ireland were already evident in the sixteenth century, as colonists irrupted into the lands of both.[106] The Ulster plantation was far more popular than the call to settle Nova Scotia, and the support for it extended well beyond the court. Indeed, the 77 initial Scottish applicants for lands in 1609 included no noblemen (though there were some nobles' sons); most were lairds or burgesses or their sons. The nobles came

---

[103] G. P. Insh, *Scottish Colonial Schemes, 1620–1686* (Glasgow, 1922), ch. 2; M. Perceval-Maxwell, 'Sir William Alexander of Menstrie (1567–1640), earl of Stirling, Viscount Canada and Lord Alexander of Tullibody', *Scottish Tradition*, 11/12 (1981–2), 14–25; D. Armitage, 'Making the empire British: Scotland in the Atlantic world, 1542–1707', *P & P* 155 (May 1997), 34–63, at pp. 47–9; cf. Elliott, 'Composite monarchies', 59–60.   [104] *RCRB* iii. 96–330.
[105] W. R. Scott, *The Constitution and Finance of English, Scottish and Irish Joint-Stock Companies to 1720*, 3 vols. (Cambridge, 1912), ii. 320; Insh, *Scottish Colonial Schemes*, 75–8.   [106] Williamson, 'Scots, Indians and empire'.

in only in 1610, when responsibility for recruitment was transferred from the Scottish privy council to the royal court. Scottish officialdom thereafter had little to do with the project. Nevertheless, by 1625, Ulster had been settled by about 8,000 adult male Scots. Possibly some went to Ulster *instead* of to America, weakening the transatlantic colonial effort, though it was argued at the time that the Ulster scheme's evident success would encourage other Scottish colonial efforts. The Ulster plantation, as a scheme coordinated from Westminster and Dublin, helped to integrate Scottish adventurers into a British framework.[107]

Territorial integration was happening both internally and externally: both through the incorporation of autonomous regions, and through the aggressive assertion of more precise boundaries. After about 1609, we find a new aspect of this: a concern for the state's territorial waters. The importance of sea power had grown enormously in the sixteenth century, with the establishment of the Spanish and Portuguese overseas empires. The Dutch thought in the early sixteenth century that their fleet (and thus the Emperor Charles V) might be developed to become 'master of the sea'.[108] Queen Elizabeth had never claimed the sovereignty of the seas around her realm, and had on the contrary asserted the freedom of the seas to all, so as to justify raids on Spanish colonies; but the English claimed territorial waters early in the reign of James I. It has been argued that James brought the idea from Scotland, as part of his traditional Scottish right to the assize herring, a levy on the herring fisheries, though this was just one among several causes. The new claim to jurisdiction over territorial waters was directed against the large Dutch fishing fleet—not to ban them altogether but to extract licence payments from them.[109]

---

[107] *RPC* viii, p. xcii; M. Perceval-Maxwell, *The Scottish Migration to Ulster in the Reign of James I* (London, 1973), 96–7, 311–12.

[108] J. D. Tracy, 'Herring wars: The Habsburg Netherlands and the struggle for control of the North Sea, ca. 1520–1560', *Sixteenth Century Journal*, 24 (1993), 249–72.

[109] T. W. Fulton, *The Sovereignty of the Sea* (Edinburgh, 1911), chs. 3–5, esp. pp. 124–5, 152–3, 165–81. Much of what follows is based on this. See also J. D. Alsop, 'William Welwood, Anne of Denmark and the sovereignty of the seas', *SHR* 59 (1980), 171–4. There was a reference in 1540 to 'our soverane lordis north seis' in connection with a dispute over a fishing vessel captured 'out of the se beside our soverane lordis north ile callit the Fire Ile [i.e. Fair Isle]', but no special jurisdiction over those seas was mentioned, the question being whether the nationality of the vessel was covered by letters of marque: *ADCP*, 496–7.

From the outset, the campaign had a British flavour. After a few years of discussions, it was launched with an English royal proclamation in 1609, banning foreign ships fishing 'upon any of our coasts and seas of Great Britain, Ireland, and the rest of the Isles adjacent' without obtaining licences, obtainable in London for England and Ireland, and in Edinburgh for Scotland.[110] The Dutch objected that the assize herring had never been levied in many Scottish waters, particularly those of the Northern Isles; James promptly sent two warships to do so.

Once things settled down and became more routine, there seems to have been more involvement of the Scottish government, and less was heard of 'Britain'. In 1612, the Scottish privy council commissioned Captain John Mason of the ship *Golden Fleece* to collect the assize herring in the Northern Isles. The burghs of Fife complained about this exaction, not omitting to disparage Mason as an Englishman, but the authority under which he operated was Scottish. In 1618, there was a Scottish proclamation, 'conforme to the law of nationis', prohibiting Scots from fishing within sight of the Faeroe Islands, while on the same day the privy council battened down the hatches in readiness to demand duties from Dutch fishing-boats in Orkney and Shetland waters. In 1619, another northern expedition was charged with extracting at least *some* money from the Dutch: the amount did not matter, so long as the claim was recognized.[111] All this effort achieved little, beyond annoying and inconveniencing the Dutch; but it shows just how far the Scottish, and indeed British, authorities had travelled in regarding themselves as ruling over an integrated kingdom with defined boundaries. It is surely no accident that Rathlin, with which this chapter began, was allocated to a kingdom in 1617.

Scotland changed its shape in the sixteenth and early seventeenth centuries. This could be seen visibly as the mapping of the country progressed. Late medieval maps had been sketchy, inaccurate, and rare. As late as 1513, Scotland could still be depicted with an east–west orientation. By 1595, a series of mainly

---

[110] *Stuart Royal Proclamations*, i (1603–1625), ed. J. F. Larkin and P. L. Hughes (Oxford, 1973), no. 98.

[111] *RPC* ix. 377, 531–2; xi. 328–30, 439–40, 462–3, 603, 605–9. Mason sold his ship to the state in 1614: Ch. 5 above. In 1615, apparently as a reward for his Scottish services, he became governor of Newfoundland: *Dictionary of National Biography*.

Continental map-makers had established the outline of the coast in all but a few Highland details, and accurately located the main Lowland towns, rivers, and hills.[112] More detailed still was the survey of Scotland undertaken by Timothy Pont in about 1585–95. Pont's manuscript maps showed most settlements, churches, bridges, mills, and the main houses of lairds. The prominence given to the latter—even the number of storeys was indicated—suggest that in many ways what Pont was mapping was a landscape of power. There was some official and ecclesiastical interest in publishing the maps in the early seventeenth century, and it was eventually achieved by publication of revised versions in Amsterdam in 1654.[113] The Scottish government's cartographical efforts, although limited, were comparable to efforts in England. The English government mapped Ireland, strategically sensitive, more efficiently than it did its own country.[114]

The full implications of all this are as yet hard to assess. What we need to understand is not just how well the country was mapped, but how the received meaning of maps evolved in a state that was becoming more concerned with territorial precision. To understand this evolution fully we would need to know more about late-medieval concepts of territory—about how people made decisions about distant places when they knew so much less about topography. There were certainly some roads in medieval Scotland, and although their condition may have declined in the late middle ages, they perhaps retained an importance as known *routes*.[115] Probably some people made it their business to remember topographical information, even (and indeed especially) before it was written down. Certainly this could be done on a small scale, and much of the actual travelling on the government's behalf was carried out by people who worked in one locality that

[112] Royal Scottish Geographical Society, *Early Maps*, i. 3–29.

[113] J. C. Stone, *The Pont Manuscript Maps of Scotland* (Tring, 1989), 5–14.

[114] P. Barber, 'Maps and monarchs in Europe, 1500–1800', in R. Oresko *et al.* (eds.), *Royal and Republican Sovereignty in Early Modern Europe* (Cambridge, 1997), 91–2. For French and English military interest in maps of Scotland see E. Bonner, 'The recovery of St Andrews Castle in 1547: French naval policy and diplomacy in the British Isles', *EHR* 111 (1996), 578–98, at pp. 582–7; J. E. A. Dawson, 'William Cecil and the British dimension of early Elizabethan foreign policy', *History*, 74 (1989), 196–216, at pp. 197–8.

[115] G. W. S. Barrow, 'Land routes: The medieval evidence', in A. Fenton and G. Stell (eds.), *Loads and Roads in Scotland and Beyond* (Edinburgh, 1984).

they knew well.[116] But it would be harder to do this on a national scale. Travellers could find their way in strange parts by asking directions from one settlement to another, and relying on traditions of hospitality—a workable, but rudimentary method.[117] Just as the administrative developments of our period often led to greater centralization of power, so the new territorial precision may well have meant more sophistication in the organizing of topographical information. The distances to different places were known, as were the times taken to communicate with them. Scottish policy-makers now had the opportunity to think strategically about their own country, in terms of space and time.

Timothy Pont's project was supported actively by his father, Robert, a leading ecclesiastical statesman whose ideas on the cultural implications of Anglo-Scottish union were quoted in part at the head of this chapter. Robert Pont also had strong views about borderers and highlanders in particular. The borderers: 'theeves, I say, and assassinats . . . not having learned, nor enduring labour and husbandrie (although their ground be rich and fitt for seed)'. Then there were

the wild and savadg Irish of the English dominion, and of the Scottish ilands the Hebridiani, or Æbudiani, who for the most part are enemies also to tillage, and weare out their dayes in hunting and idleness after the maner of beasts. These dout lest the English and Scottish once formed into one bodie, that they by force shal be made subject to the lawes, when as before for every light and trifling matter, as you would say for the wagging of a straw, they were readie to flie out and to ayde one another in their wicked defections. And if happely by any sleight or stratagem they were hemmed in or empaled, the Irish embarqued themselves for the Scotish iles, and these Hebridiani with their complices had a foorth into Ireland.[118]

Fortunately, thought Pont, the union of crowns would put a stop to this. His strategic vision is as noteworthy as his determination to eradicate all forms of regional particularism within the emerging British state. As it turned out, a fully British state was not created

---

[116] One example is the messenger Charles Murray, whose itinerary in central Scotland is examined by M. H. B. Sanderson, *Mary Stewart's People* (Edinburgh, 1987), 135–42.

[117] Cf. N. Ohler, *The Medieval Traveller*, trans. C. Hillier (Woodbridge, 1989), 79–89.

[118] Pont, 'Of the union of Britayne', *Jacobean Union*, 21–2.

for another century, and even then Ireland was excluded. Nor were the 'Hebridiani' as easy to assimilate as Pont hoped. Nevertheless, the late sixteenth and early seventeenth centuries saw a series of remarkable Scottish attempts to extend state power into the Borders and Highlands. The story of these attempts deserves its own chapter.

8

The Borders and Highlands

> Oure soverane lord and his thrie estatis convenit in this
> present parliament, considering the vicked inclinatioun of
> the disorderit subjectis, inhabitantis on sum pairtis of the
> Bordoures foiranent England, and in the Hielandis and Ilis,
> delyting in all mischeiffis, and maist unnaturallie and cruel-
> lie waistand, slayand, heryand, and distroyand thair awin
> nychtbouris and native cuntrie people, takand occasioun of
> the leist truble that may occur in the inner pairtis of the
> realme, quhen thai think that cair and thocht of the repress-
> ing of thair insolence is onywayes foryett, to renew thair maist
> barbarous cruelties and godles oppressionis: ffor remeid
> thairof . . .[1]

Scottish policy-makers left the world in no doubt that they
regarded the Borders and Highlands as a problem. The preamble
to this statute (of 1587) made it clear what they thought the
problem was, which helps us understand the 'remeid' they provided. The problem was the local people. They were wicked (which
in a lapsarian world one might consider irremediable), godless
(which might be ameliorated by establishing a preaching ministry), barbarous (here the likely solution was educational), and
'disorderit'—for which the answer was to make them feel the heavy
hand of the state. This chapter, like the statute itself, will concentrate on this last aspect of the problem.

Older histories usually suggest that the problem ('lawlessness')
was the same in both regions, and with government statements like
this one, it is easy to see why. Not only does the statute make it
clear that the state's idea of 'order' differed more radically from
that of the local people than it did in the heartlands of the state;
it also indicates a common approach to the two regions by that
state—an approach dictated by the interests of the 'inner pairtis

[1] *APS* iii. 461, c. 59.

of the realme'. Although parliament was supposed to represent the whole country, it had no qualms about typecasting *all* highlanders and most borderers as wicked (and wicked in much the same way). Although they comprised between a third and a half of the Scottish population, their point of view on this went unheard.[2] Policy for the Borders and Highlands was not made by, or for, or even in consultation with, the local people—even the local elite; it was imposed upon them from outside. And although the Borders and Highlands were two distinct regions, it was very much the same general policy for both.

But that was 1587. In the previous century—or even in the previous decade—a common approach would have been much less evident. There was a long tradition of active policy-making for the Borders, while it was only in the 1580s that a common Highland and Border policy was adopted. Before then, governments rarely saw the aloofness of Highland clans as a problem that had seriously to be tackled; Lowlands and Highlands had a tacit agreement to ignore one another. Scottish rulers occasionally deplored the fact that highlanders were wild, uncontrollable, and liable to raid the Lowlands. The pope was told that some Scottish clergymen had to 'defend against the raids of the highlanders', while others unfortunately had to live 'among the unruly Highland Scots'.[3] But the government did not conceive of all this as a 'problem' to the extent of feeling that a *solution* had to be found. Highlanders were like bad weather; they had to be coped with, but nothing could be done to change them.

Scottish governments thus paid only fitful attention to the Highlands. James IV, who successfully forfeited the lordship of the Isles in 1493, was perhaps the exception. He visited the Isles twice and was familiar with the Gaelic language. It was in his reign that a prototype 'general band' (on which more in a moment) was deployed in Highland Perthshire. Norman Macdougall doubts, however, whether even James IV had a sustained interest in promoting policies for the Isles.[4] This may be an overly negative assess-

---

[2] The scanty evidence on population is assessed by I. D. Whyte, *Scotland before the Industrial Revolution: An Economic and Social History, c.1050–c.1750* (London, 1995), 112–16.

[3] *Letters of James V*, ed. R. K. Hannay and D. Hay (Edinburgh, 1954), 32, 115. Cf. *ADCP*, which has even less on the Highlands.

[4] N. Macdougall, *James IV* (Edinburgh, 1989), 100–5, 115–16.

ment, but certainly the most characteristic governmental attitude towards the Highlands at this time was that of the dog in the manger. The Scottish state could not control the Highlands itself, but it could ensure that nobody else—neither the native lords of the Isles, nor any foreign power—would be able to do so.[5]

It was in this spirit that James V voyaged from Leith to the Western Isles in 1540. The voyage was a publicity stunt without detectable consequences, except that it did stake out the king's claim for all to see.[6] As late as the 1570s, George Hewitt's study of the regency of Morton has a whole chapter on the Borders, but hardly finds it necessary to mention the Highlands.[7] The Highlands and the state could readily ignore one another. In James VI's minority, the state did not yet have an active 'Highland problem', nor indeed did the Highlands yet have a 'state problem'.

This can be confirmed by a glance at the statute book. Statutory attention to the Highlands before 1581 was negligible. Statutes of 1455 and 1458 called for justice ayres to punish 'sornouris or oppressouris of the kingis liegis': sorners (from Gaelic *sorthan*, free quarters) were fighting clansmen who were maintained by the exaction of free board and lodging from the common folk.[8] It seems likely that the justice ayres were intended to punish the extension of these exactions to lowlanders. Calps—Gaelic death duties taken by clan chiefs from subordinates who acknowledged their lordship—were abolished in 1492 in Galloway, but left untouched in the Highlands.[9] That the arm of the law could not reach across the Highland Line was recognized in a statute of 1425 (re-enacted in 1450) requiring assythement (compensation) to be given before remissions for slaughter were issued; it admitted that this could be applied only 'in the low landis quhare the scaithis done may be kende'.[10] Again this was not a Highland policy, rather the recognition that a Highland policy was something that it was impossible for a Scottish government to have.

It is sometimes said that sixteenth-century Scottish governments

---

[5] The policy of the 16th-cent. English state towards Ireland was similar in many ways: H. Morgan, 'British policies before the British state', in B. Bradshaw and J. Morrill (eds.), *The British Problem, c.1534–1707* (London, 1996), 66–7.

[6] The voyage of 1540 has been little studied, but see W. C. Mackenzie, *The Highlands and Isles of Scotland* (2nd edn., Edinburgh, 1949), 118.

[7] G. R. Hewitt, *Scotland under Morton, 1572–1580* (Edinburgh, 1982), ch. 7.

[8] *APS* ii. 45, c. 13; 51, c. 26. [9] *APS* ii. 214, c. 5; 222, cc. 19–20.

[10] *APS* ii. 8, c. 25; 34, c. 2.

did have a Highland policy: to rely on trusted regional magnates, mainly the earls of Huntly and Argyll, to keep the area under control.[11] But that exaggerates what Queen Mary (for instance) was trying to achieve in her dealings with these men. She took little interest in influencing what Argyll was up to in Lorne or Glenorchy; what she wanted—and usually got—was the service of his Campbells in the Lowlands. The same applies with greater force to the Gordon earls of Huntly, for they were a Lowland family themselves, though they made bonds with Highland neighbours like the Frasers, Camerons, and Mackintoshes.[12] In the Highlands, Huntly and Argyll were left to get on with their own self-aggrandizement unrestrained—even when royal powers were involved. Commissions to lease crown lands were not usually issued to magnates in their own localities, for fear of diminishing royal revenues, but Huntly and Argyll did receive such commissions in their Highland spheres of influence.[13] The crown could not think about the northern or western Highlands without involving the Gordons or Campbells in some way; but it rarely wished to do so. The active and interventionist Highland policy of the 1580s onwards was a new departure.

Border government, by contrast, had been an active concern for centuries. The region posed serious challenges to the Scottish state, but many of those challenges were different from the ones it faced in the Highlands. The local exercise of political power through militarized kinship groups—the 'surnames'—was quite like the Highland clan system; but it also bore more resemblance to the familiar pattern of Lowland lordship. The political elite of the Borders participated in Scottish politics at a national level—perhaps not as much as those in the central Lowlands, but enough to be noticed. No linguistic divide separated the Borders from the core region of the state. Finally, and most importantly for the present purpose, the administrative distinctiveness of the Borders arose not from under-government (as in the Highlands) but from

[11] One study describes it as a 'fatal policy', but no details are given: I. F. Grant and H. Cheape, *Periods in Highland History* (London, 1987), 107.

[12] J. Dawson, 'The fifth earl of Argyle, Gaelic lordship and political power in sixteenth-century Scotland', *SHR* 67 (1988), 1–27, at pp. 1–7; for the Gordons' bonds see J. Wormald, *Lords and Men in Scotland: Bonds of Manrent, 1442–1603* (Edinburgh, 1985), 278–303.

[13] T. M. Chalmers, 'The King's Council, Patronage, and the Governance of Scotland, 1460–1513', Ph.D. thesis (Aberdeen, 1982), 110–12.

over-government. The lack of local nerve-ends of government in the Highlands meant that the crown was relatively insensitive to unauthorized violence. By contrast, it displayed a marked touchiness towards similar events in the Borders, because there were so many royal agents there.

The distinctive executive machinery of the Borders had been developed to cope with the proximity of the 'auld inemeyis of Ingland'. The warden's traditional duties were to organize warfare against the English (as often offensive as defensive, although then as now warfare was often described as 'defence'), and in the meantime to act as a local diplomat, maintaining contact with his English opposite number and negotiating with him to resolve any disputes over which it was not thought appropriate to fight (while trying to stir up as much trouble as possible in the opposite march). Most of these disputes were about crimes committed by Scots against English folk, or vice versa. This, if nothing else, brought the warden into contact with the maintenance of law and order in his own march: in this field, however, he had to operate in conjunction with the sheriff. Sheriff courts were regularly active in the Borders, if the evidence of one sheriff depute's book from Dumfries is typical.[14] The warden was additional to the sheriff, and on the whole above rather than below him: he found it no easier to make contact with individual lawbreakers.

In our period, the Border wardens gained a growing responsibility for serious domestic crime. In the early sixteenth century, crimes committed by Scots against Scots had gone to the justice ayres. However, in the second half of the century, the warden's commission was generally issued together with a commission as justiciar, empowering him to try the four pleas of the crown (murder, robbery, rape, and fire-raising). Courts held in this capacity were sometimes hard to distinguish from normal warden courts; they were peripatetic throughout the march, and do not seem to have become regular events.[15]

One mechanism for internal Border government became familiar early in the sixteenth century: the general band. This was a requirement for the landlords in the area to find surety that they would be responsible for crimes committed by their tenants and

[14] T. I. Rae, *The Administration of the Scottish Frontier, 1513–1603* (Edinburgh, 1966), 13.
[15] Ibid. 64–6.

followers. This was a way of getting round the fact that the tenants and followers were unlikely to come into direct contact with the agencies of the state. Signatories bound themselves to hand over criminals to justice ayres within fifteen days of being required to do so—or, if the criminals 'beis fugitive', they would expel them and their families from their lands and enter other tenants. The band used the structure of feudal landholding, as those who were to sign it were normally 'his majesteis immediat tennentis'.[16]

The general band developed gradually, and its early history requires further investigation than can be attempted here. A possible English parallel was employed by Henry VII in Wales— the 'indentures of the Marches', whereby local lords and royal officials signed contracts to observe and enforce the rule of law.[17] It was probably not a specifically Border mechanism in origin. One early band was made in 1501 by the landlords of Highland Perthshire.[18] A version of the general band was mentioned in the Borders in 1504, but the introduction of the general band was attributed later to the reign of James V—perhaps because it became more common then. In 1524, with a need for 'stanching of thift throw all the realm and specialy in Liddisdale and apoun the bordouris', the Scottish government ordered a band for the Borders.[19] Various bands were mentioned during the personal reign of James V, in terms making clear that a form of general band was in operation.[20] In the wars of the 1540s, the idea of lords signing bands to be responsible for their tenants and followers merged with the idea of bands to resist English invasion; the general band quoted by Balfour, although mainly concerned with crime, also deals with resistance to England and clearly dates from this period. It seems to be the earliest band specifically to be called a 'general band'.[21] By then it had become a familiar device in the sixteenth-century Borders.

---

[16] *RPC* iii. 74; iv. 787–9, the text of a later general band.

[17] P. Roberts, 'The English crown, the principality of Wales, and the council in the Marches, 1534–1641', in Bradshaw and Morrill (eds.), *British Problem*, 120–1.

[18] W. Fraser, *The Red Book of Menteith*, 2 vols. (Edinburgh, 1880), ii. 303–5.

[19] *APS* ii. 286, c. 9; *Taymouth Book*, 213–14. A 'band' for the local 'lordis and fre-haldaris' to sign (apparently a predecessor of the general band) had been made for the sheriffdom of Dumfries in 1504, when the making of a similar 'band of the mydill bordour' was discussed: *APS* ii. 247, 248.

[20] Rae, *Scottish Frontier*, 118. More details of the general band are found at pp. 115–19.

[21] *APS* ii. 461; Balfour, *Practicks*, ii. 574–6.

Along with the general band, a similar policy in the sixteenth-century Borders was the exaction of hostages from suspect families. The head of the family, or his son, would be handed over to the authorities, and consigned to a more or less comfortable imprisonment outside the Border region, as a 'pledge' that the family would observe the laws and would rise in pursuit of criminals. Their keepers were trusted lords, often the social equals of the hostages who inadvertently received their hospitality. The system was not rigorously enforced, and when a hostage was wanted it was often found that he had escaped or departed. Nevertheless, increasingly elaborate administrative arrangements were made, such as a rota system for hostages (1569), a convoy system to transport them to their destinations (1575), and penalties on custodians who allowed hostages to escape (1575, 1587). It seems as though the system had some effect. 'The sole difference between the General Band and the pledge system was that the material security offered for keeping essentially similar promises was, instead of lands, goods and money, the life of a human pledge.' The giving up of a hostage was more drastic than signing a band, and the general band was probably much more common.[22]

So a policy had grown up of requiring Border lords to take responsibility for crimes by their tenants and followers, expecting them to present the malefactors to justice, allowing prosecution of lords for their followers' crimes if they failed to do so, and obtaining regular cautions from each lord to observe these requirements.[23] Of course it was possible to exact bands from anyone, anywhere, suspected of being likely to commit a crime; the privy council routinely took bands (acts of caution) from parties at feud, to the effect that neither they nor their followers would harm the rival party.[24] What was distinctive about the general band in the Borders was that *all* lords in the region were expected to sign bands, and that these bands were in force indefinitely. Lords were being shown that the state regarded the whole lot of them as likely

---

[22] This para. is based on Rae, *Scottish Frontier*, 119–23; quotation at p. 119. Cf. also a remarkable collection of bureaucratic forms of letters on Border hostages, compiled in 1577: NAS, GD149/265, pt. 1, fos. 12^r–13^r.

[23] These early local bands had no standard form. The 1576 band of Roxburgh was briefer and less specific in the duties it imposed on landlords. With it was filed a copy of the 'auld band of Roxburgh' (1552)—this text was the more usual general band: *RPC* ii. 548–52.

[24] K. M. Brown, *Bloodfeud in Scotland, 1573–1625* (Edinburgh, 1986), 45–8.

troublemakers. Thus, the stewart court of Annandale in the mid-sixteenth century assumed that lords would have made a band; if an offender failed to answer a court summons, his landlord was to be charged 'according to his band' to enter him, or failing that to evict him from his lands.[25]

On the whole these bands were simply imposed by the authorities, but the very act of signing a band (or entering a hostage) implied a modest degree of assent to the policy. The 'Band of Teviotdaill' of 1569, in which the inhabitants of the Middle March bound themselves to be obedient to the king and to be 'professit inymeis' to the 'thevis, inhabitantis of the cuntreis of Liddisdaill, Eskdaill, Ewisdaill, and Annanderdaill', went further; it was explicitly the product of consultation with the signatories, and some 'statutis anent the Middill Marche' were agreed with their 'avise'.[26] But although the general band was imposed coercively, the individual who had signed it was regarded as having made a personal commitment and could be punished for breach of it.[27] It was possible, but difficult, to refuse to sign, as David Home of Wedderburn tried to do in 1566, on the grounds that he and his surname 'wer nevir culpable of sik crymes' and that it 'redoundis to the sklander of his haill freindis'.[28]

Border policy in the later sixteenth century evolved within the framework of several separate trends. Most obviously, Anglo-Scottish relations ceased to be generally hostile in 1560. Then the Scottish state was attempting to impose its authority more effectively in the localities—including the Borders. Finally—though this was less a new trend than a continuing factor—the borderers themselves went on making trouble for the authorities in a way that the latter were beginning to find less tolerable. Ian Rae felt that there was no significant increase or decrease during the sixteenth century in the frequency of cross-Border raids or of raids within Scotland.[29]

[25] NLS, 'Ordour to be observit in the stewart court of Annandaill', in MS copy of Balfour's Practicks, Adv. MS 24.6.3 (3), fo. 244ᵛ. This passage is not found in the published version. The stewart court of Annandale, and the 'buik appoindt for the same', are mentioned in 1579: *RPC* iii. 79.

[26] *RPC* i. 651–3. This may also have occurred elsewhere, since the Regent Moray seems to have made a wider attempt to reinvigorate the general band: *Taymouth Book*, 213–14.   [27] *RPC* vii. 703.

[28] HMC, *Report on the Manuscripts of Colonel David Milne Home* (London, 1902), 45–6.

[29] Rae, *Scottish Frontier*, 220. The following discussion is much indebted to his ch. 9.

What this meant for the government of the Scottish Borders can be sketched briefly, as most aspects of it have been discussed more fully by other writers, particularly Dr Rae. The cessation of Anglo-Scottish warfare and the transformation of Scotland into a satellite state made less difference than might be thought, since it did not lead English and Scots to *trust* one another, and old traditions of military readiness were maintained to some extent. The general band ceased to mention military action against the English, probably around 1560 although too few dated bands are extant to allow the change to be traced exactly. Closer diplomatic contact gave the English ambassador in Edinburgh a prominent role, and he could supplement the local diplomacy of the wardens in efforts to resolve Border disputes. As more attention was paid to each case, an impression can be gained (and was sometimes gained at the time) of increasing instability in the Border region, but it was really a matter of increasing governmental interest. However, the English government was now less worried about *routine* crime, focusing more on headline-hitting incidents like the murder of Sir Francis Russell at a day of truce in 1585.

In the aftermath of the civil wars of 1567–73, the Regent Morton paid close attention to the Borders. He had several aims, including the cementing of good relations with England and the raising of cash from judicial fines; but his main concern seems to have been to inflict damage on former members of the defeated queen's party. There were nine judicial raids to the Borders between 1573 and 1580, from which Morton's former opponents suffered severely.[30]

The regime of Chancellor Maitland, in the late 1580s and early 1590s, seems to have been more interested in Border administration for its own sake, and efforts were devoted to devising new privy council procedures for this. It was then—in 1587—that the first statute was passed to tackle the problems of the Borders and Highlands together. Although important in the Highlands, in the Borders it had less impact as it mainly codified existing practices.[31] The regime was unfortunate in having to cope with the climax of the bitter Maxwell–Johnstone feud, which temporarily rendered the west march ungovernable, but political stability was generally maintained.

After 1603, the significance of the international frontier was

---

[30] Ibid. 196; Hewitt, *Scotland under Morton*, ch. 7; *TA* xiii, app. 2.
[31] *APS* iii. 461–7, c. 59; Rae, *Scottish Frontier*, 212.

reduced. The frontier itself remained, but English and Scottish governments could cooperate fully in destroying the local power structures that it had engendered. This required superior military force, which was duly deployed to subjugate the region. The first powerful Border commission after the union lasted from 1605 to 1607. It consisted of a judicial commission of five gentlemen from each side of the Border, and two military forces to execute their orders. On the Scottish side, it concentrated on bringing to justice those at the horn for criminal offences.[32] The activities of this and subsequent commissions down to 1612 are summed up in the comprehensive exoneration which Lord Cranston, latterly captain of the Border guard, received in that year for his service against disobedient borderers: he had been 'constranit in thair persute to mak a quyck despatche of a grite nomber of thame without ony convictioun or dome gevin aganis thame by ane assyse, and sometyme to beseidge thame in houssis and strenths, and to rais fyre and use all uther hostile persute . . . as the necessitie urged and occasioun wes offered'. This was declared to have been good service.[33]

The privy council was much less bothered about the Borders by 1618, when the king wanted the 'most notorious and leude personis' to be transported to Virginia. The council told James smoothly that there were none such at the moment, but if there ever were, they would let him know. Later in the year, a detailed set of royal regulations was promulgated: it repeated the requirements of sixteenth-century statutes for landlords to answer for their followers, but also envisaged a survey being made of the 'idill and insolent personis'. The regulations closed with a list of fugitives from the Border commissioners, comprising only thirty-two names.[34] For the government, although not necessarily for the local people, the problem had largely been solved.

Let us return to the Highlands, where an active policy began only in 1581. The best guide to this policy is the king himself. James VI's remarks on the Highlands form one of the most

---

[32] M. Wasser, 'The Pacification of the Scottish Borders, 1598–1612', M.A. diss. (McGill University, 1986), ch. 4.

[33] *RPC* ix. 305.

[34] Council to James, 13 May 1618, *Melros Papers*, i. 311–12; *RPC* xi. 440–7. Cf. council to James, 23 Mar. 1624, *Melros Papers*, i. 554–8. The warden of the west march in 1579 had had a list of names of 'inobeydient' persons, 'five hundreth or ma': *RPC* iii. 73.

frequently quoted passages in his much-quoted *Basilicon Doron*, but
that is no reason not to quote them again here—they are vital to
our understanding of the issue:

> As for the Hie-lands, I shortly comprehend them all in two sorts of people:
> the one, that dwelleth in our maine land, that are barbarous for the most
> part, and yet mixed with some shewe of civilitie: the other, that dwelleth
> in the Iles, and are allutterly barbares, without any sort or shew of civilitie.
> For the first sort, put straitly to execution the lawes made alreadie by me
> against their over-lords, and the chiefes of their clannes, and it will be no
> difficultie to danton them. As for the other sort, follow forth the course
> that I have intended, in planting colonies among them of answerable in-
> lands subjects, that within short time may reforme and civilize the best
> inclined among them; rooting out or transporting the barbarous and stub-
> borne sort, and planting civilitie in their roomes.[35]

So most highlanders are bad, but only some (the Islesmen) are
completely bad. All have on the whole to be subdued by force
('dantoned'), but some may learn to become civilized as a result.
There are two alternative approaches: either force them to become
civilized, or root them out and replace them with 'answerable in-
lands subjects'. Maurice Lee has remarked that there was 'no
coherent Highland policy in 1603'.[36] This is true in the sense that
the government was temporarily floundering, and unsure of how
to achieve its aims—but the aims themselves were clear and
coherent.

   The primary aim, of course, was to get the Highland chiefs to
submit to the authority of the state. James recognized that they
would not do this voluntarily: they would have to be coerced. The
question of how that coercion was mobilized—a question of
means, rather than of ends—was causing difficulties in 1603, as
Professor Lee points out: it was just then hard to rely on those traditionally cooperative regional magnates, the earl of Argyll and the
marquis of Huntly. But, as argued above, their traditional significance has been exaggerated. Moreover, in the 1590s the crown had
already sent one military expedition of its own to the Highlands,
and would later send others to great effect.

   Government policy also had a secondary aim: to open up the

---

[35] James VI, *Basilicon Doron*, in *Political Writings*, 24.
[36] M. Lee, *Government by Pen: Scotland under James VI and I* (Urbana, Ill., 1980),
10–12.

economic resources of the Highlands to exploitation by lowlanders. This is what James meant by 'planting colonies' of lowlanders, since the reason lowlanders went to the Highlands was for profit. Writing in 1598, James had in mind the recently launched project to colonize Lewis. This was probably one reason why he distinguished between the mainland and the Isles, with only the latter being 'allutterly barbares'. Recent feuds in the Isles, and the connection of many southern Islesmen with the ongoing war in Ulster, would also have given him a jaundiced view of the Isles. In fact, as the government's policy unfolded, it did not concentrate solely on the Isles, but attacked troublesome or vulnerable clans wherever they were found. One of the main targets, the MacGregors, lived on the south-eastern margin of the Highlands.

The programme in James's book rested on a series of statutes that had been enacted between 1581 and 1597. Why the government decided to take an interest in the Highlands in November 1581 is unclear; it may have been a long-planned administrative initiative, or it may have reflected immediate political rivalries.[37] At any rate, a statute of that date castigated Highland clans as 'companeis of wikit men coupled in fellowschippis be occasioun of thair surnames or neir duellingis togidder'. They were neither answerable to the courts nor to 'onie anc landislord'. If, therefore, there was evidence that a criminal had been supported or resetted by his clan, then it was lawful for the victim to 'apprehend, slay, and arreist the bodeis and guidis' of the criminal, or any member of the clan.[38]

This use of the law was remarkable, to say the least. The idea of commissioning the victim of theft to avenge himself upon the criminal by killing him, without a legal trial, would normally have been

[37] If it was the latter, it may have been connected with a breach at court between the king's favourite, the duke of Lennox, and the chancellor, the earl of Argyll, leading Lennox to favour 'Macintosh, his adversary' (Lachlan Mackintosh of Dunachton, captain of Clan Chattan): *CSP Scot.* vi. 94. If so, the measure was presumably intended as an anti-Campbell one—an ironical origin for government initiatives in the Highlands. No political developments in the Isles suggest themselves as having impressed themselves on the government at this time: D. Gregory, *History of the Western Highlands and Isles of Scotland, 1493–1625* (2nd edn., London, 1881), 218–19.

[38] *APS* iii. 218–19, c. 16. The act has often been overlooked, perhaps because it did not mention the Highlands by name, but it cited the 15th-cent. acts against 'sorners', who (as we have seen) were a Highland phenomenon.

regarded with almost as much unease in the sixteenth century as today.[39] Still more dubiety would have attached to the idea that the vengeance could be wreaked, not only on the criminal personally, but also on any member of his extended family. What would have been unacceptable in the Lowlands was all right for the Highlands, because highlanders were not felt to deserve the protection of the law. Later enactments on the Highlands would be less crude than this pioneer effort, but they would breathe the same spirit.

The next statute, that of 1587 on both the Highlands and Borders, was a landmark.[40] Its main thrust was to make landlords responsible for people on their lands who committed crimes—their own tenants, or anyone passing through. All landlords were to find caution that they would offer redress for such crimes, and administrative arrangements were made to check up on this. Victims of crime could demand redress from a clan chief, and if not satisfied within fifteen days could pursue that chief as if they held a commission of justiciary. Landlords were to be summoned every six months to answer for their dependants' observance of the laws. However, the act also recognized that some clans held no formal title from the nominal proprietor, who would thus be unable to hold them responsible for their behaviour; in those cases, the 'capitanes, cheiffs, and chiftanes' of the clans were to be brought to book. Such clans were supposed to enter hostages quarterly as pledges of obedience.

The statute's attempt to treat the Highland and Border regions as part of the Scottish state, while simultaneously treating their political elites as lawless and disloyal, led to some contorted reasoning. Non-resident landlords were exempted from having to take responsibility for their tenants. Such landlords actually made social control more difficult, both in the Highlands and in the Borders;[41] but they themselves could not be treated as part of the problem, precisely because they were *not* resident in the supposedly problem regions. And as for the only cases where the statute envisaged direct contact with the inhabitants, these were particularly

---

[39] Vengeance killings were sanctioned in the code of the bloodfeud, but these were to avenge a previous *killing*, not theft, and they had no explicit statutory authority.

[40] *APS* iii. 461–7, c. 59. The preamble is quoted as epigraph to this chapter.

[41] Sir Duncan Campbell of Glenorchy to earl of Morton, 16 Sept. 1591, *Registrum Honoris de Morton*, 2 vols., ed. H. Cockburn (Bannatyne Club, 1853), i. 178–9; Rae, *Scottish Frontier*, 17–18.

improbable ones. Those 'vagabundis' for whom their landlords refused to take responsibility were to compear individually at the head burgh of the sheriffdom and find caution personally to obey the law. All highlanders and borderers currently living in the central Lowlands were to return to their place of birth unless their present landlord would find caution that they would be 'lawland and obedient men'. Much of the act was unlikely to be implemented in full, but these clauses seem not to have been designed for any kind of implementation; they were either to allow landlords to avoid responsibility for people beyond their control, or to plug a logical gap in the act with verbiage, or both.

A convention of 1588, seeking to make progress in the implementation of the act, noted 'the difficultie quhilk trew men hes in seiking redres of thair skaithis', because the criminals were protected by their chiefs and landlords. These sometimes possessed their own jurisdictions, and the act related that they were 'constrenand the complenaris . . . to repair unto thame to thair accustomat placeis of courtehalding'. One might have expected the government to welcome the thought that Highland lords had courts and were prosecuting crime in them, but no: it was resented because of the 'unsure passage' to get to the courts, both for the complainers and for 'sic as knawis the treuth of the cryme, and ar meitast to be assisouris'. In fact, the government simply wanted an assize of lowlanders, and the assertion that it was they who 'knawis the treuth' was window-dressing. Instead of using Highland courts, the act enjoined complainers to come to Edinburgh, where the court of justiciary would summon the alleged offender and grant letters to the complainer to summon an assize. If the offender failed to compear within fifteen days, and if two or three witnesses testified to the truth of the accusation, decreet would be granted for the complainer to collect compensation from the chief or landlord.[42]

The aim of this was not to do justice, but to remove the administration of justice from the local elite. The usual idea that crime should be tried in the locality, with an assize of local men who knew

---

[42] *RPC* iv. 298–300. The policy of having an assize of lowlanders is evident in the 1609 trial for treason of Sir James MacDonald. The events for which he was tried took place in Askomull, but the assize contained no highlanders although its large membership included men from Wigtownshire and Caithness: 'Documents connected with the trial of Sir James MacDonald of Islay', ed. A. Matheson, *Transactions of the Gaelic Society of Glasgow*, 5 (1958), 207–22, at p. 221.

the facts, did not apply in the Highlands. An earlier, perhaps transitional example of this had occurred in 1574, when Angus MacDonald of Glengarry had been issued with a commission of justiciary to punish those of his tenants who had killed a Kinghorn fisherman: the assize was to be drawn from 'the marchandis and marynaris that first sall happin to arrive at Lochstrone or Lochcarroun at the nixt fischeing'.[43] They would trust MacDonald himself only with the job of hangman.

The act of 1588, moreover, was not interested in helping those victims of crime who would *not* have 'unsure passage' to the local court because they themselves lived in the locality. The people who were intended to benefit were *lowlanders* who had been robbed by highlanders; they now had an additional weapon to use both against the criminal and against the criminal's chief. The act infringed the jurisdiction not only of sheriffs but of lords of regality, and how this could have been squared with them (assuming that the legislators cared about Highland sheriffs and lords of regality) is unclear.

In a convention of 1593, the statute of 1587 was again reaffirmed as the centrepiece of policy, and letters were to be issued charging all Highland and Border landlords who had not found caution in its terms to do so. The convention seems to have regarded this as equivalent to the general band. It also tightened up by requiring that the cautioners be 'landit men in the Incuntrey'.[44]

In 1594 the act of 1587 was elaborated further, concentrating on a list—a very long list—of delinquent clans and surnames. The blame for their delinquencies was laid firmly upon the chiefs and lords, and a clear distinction was drawn 'be names and surnames, betuix thame that ar and desiris to be estemit honest and trew men, and thame that ar and escheamis nocht to be estemit thevis, reifaris, sorneris, and ressettaris and sustenaris of thift and thevis'. The act called for a 'roll and catologue' of all members of the delinquent clans and surnames, so that someone (usually their landlord) could be charged to find caution to answer for any crimes they might commit, and so that 'it may be understand quha

---

[43] *Collectanea de Rebus Albanicis* (Iona Club, 1847), 100–1. The idea that the assize should know the facts was still very much alive in 1587; it gradually faded in the following half-century, but this seems separate from its deliberate removal from Highlands and Borders. I. D. Willock, *The Origins and Development of the Jury in Scotland* (Stair Society, 1966), 197.   [44] *APS* iv. 39–40.

wilbe obedient and quha inobedient and fugitive'. The clans and surnames would also have to enter hostages for the obedience of the chiefs and lords. This in effect strengthened the general band, making it easier to bring chiefs and lords to book for their followers' crimes. As for any 'brokin men' for whom nobody would take responsibility under this system, they were to be outlawed, so that if any 'trew men' committed 'ejecting, spulyie, slauchter, fire rasing or uther alleagit violent deid' against them, the victims would have no legal remedy.[45]

The screw was tightened by parliament in December 1597, when a statute ordered all Highland landlords and chiefs to produce written titles to their lands before the exchequer by 15 May 1598, and find caution that they would pay royal dues and not molest lowlanders coming into the area to open up fishings and urban settlements. A companion act projected the building of three Highland towns—the future Stornoway, Fort William, and Campbeltown.[46] As far as is known, no chiefs complied with the act on titles, and some of them probably did not have the kind of parchment title that it would have recognized. At a stroke, their land titles had been invalidated—at least if the government chose to take that view. At any time it might suddenly discover that a recalcitrant chief had not registered his title and so ought to be forfeited.[47] Courtiers regarded the act as important: actual forfeitures were expected as a result of it.[48]

This sixteen-year programme was the most drastic legislative intervention in the Highlands since 1504. Its increasing detail allowed the state unprecedented scope for coercive initiatives. It also marked a more subtle shift of gear in the Borders, where the region's autonomous militarized polity was now seen merely as a problem to be solved instead of a troublesome but necessary buffer against English hostility.

[45] *APS* iv. 71–3, c. 37. Two further administrative measures in the act seem not to have taken effect. Justice ayres were to be held biannually in the Highland and Border sheriffdoms; and (in a possibly garbled clause) all royal officers and tenants in chief were constituted justices to try highlanders and borderers.

[46] *APS* iv. 138–9, cc. 33–4.

[47] This was done e.g. to Hector Maclean of Duart in 1610, on the grounds that his *father* had failed to register his title in 1598: *RMS* vii. 26. See the excuses of Sir Roderick Macleod of Dunvegan, in a letter to the king of 7 Jan. 1615, for why he had failed to register: *HP* iii. 174.

[48] J. M. Hill, 'The rift within Clan Ian Mor: The Antrim and Dunyveg MacDonnells, 1590–1603', *Sixteenth Century Journal*, 24 (1993), 865–79, at p. 871.

Why did the statutes treat both Borders and Highlands the same after 1587? Essentially it was because the government had difficulty in obtaining access to those who failed to observe the statutes. The special characteristic of laws for the Borders was the lack of expectation that lawbreakers would come into direct contact with the executive machinery—and this was also the problem in the Highlands. On the same day in 1592 that a commission of lieutenancy was issued against 'the laules brokin hieland men of the Clan Chattan, Clan Camroun, Clan Rannald, and uthiris', the privy council was hearing a complaint against James Kerr, brother of the laird of Greenhead, 'a Borderair and clannit man in the cuntrey, aganis quhome the ordinar forme of law can not have executioun'.[49] James in April 1587, just before the statute was passed, announced his intention to take 'some speciall paines' in Highland affairs as he had recently done in those of the Borders. As Allan Macinnes has persuasively argued, policies that had been developed and tested in the Borders were available to be applied to the Highlands.[50]

There was also some reverse movement, from Highlands to Borders, in terms of official attitudes. This is illustrated by usage of the word 'clan'. This was the Gaelic word for children or descendants, and Highland 'clans' were known as such to writers in Scots from at least the fourteenth century. The term could be used generally in fifteenth-century literature to mean a family (especially if it offered a convenient rhyme), but it did not enter the official vocabulary for describing Lowland kin networks. It was, however, used of Border families from at least 1516—where a description of a Border family as a 'hous or clan' suggests a writer who was conscious of having imported it from elsewhere.[51] The borderers, then, may have come to be seen in the early sixteenth century as being as wild and uncivilized as the highlanders. No

---

[49] *RPC* v. 19.

[50] James is quoted in Gregory, *Western Highlands and Isles*, 237; A. I. Macinnes, *Clanship, Commerce and the House of Stuart, 1603–1788* (East Linton, 1996), 50–1.

[51] *Dictionary of the Older Scottish Tongue*, s.vv. clan, clannit; *RSS* i. 2830; *RPC* vii. 711. The one writer to describe feuding Lowland families as 'clanned gentlemen', James Melville, may have been indulging in hyperbole—the people concerned were the Boyd and Cunningham students from Ayrshire at the university of Glasgow in 1578: Melville, *Diary*, 71. Another Ayrshire author restricted his usage of 'clannis' to the Borders: *A Chronicle of the Kings of Scotland*, ed. J. W. Mackenzie (Maitland Club, 1830), 113.

wonder that it was Border policies that the state used when it eventually decided to do something about the Highlands. After 1597, the law was in place, and the focus shifted to executive and military action. There had already, indeed, been administrative initiatives on the Highlands alongside the statutory ones discussed so far. Some of these early schemes can seem naïve. In 1596, Donald Gorm MacDonald of Sleat received a new charter, specifying that he was not to let North Uist to 'hielandmen' without permission.[52] This may be an early indication of the government's desire to colonize the Isles, but they must have realized that this was not the way to achieve it, since such clauses did not reappear.

Initially the main executive development was the extension of the general band to the Highlands. We have seen that imposing a general band was one way of getting lords to take formal responsibility for the crimes of their tenants and dependants. It had been developed early in the sixteenth century for use in the Borders, but could be used in any other area where government authority could not be expected to extend beyond the heads of the local ruling families. In the second half of the century, it was adapted for use in the Highlands—and indeed in remote areas of the Lowlands such as Caithness (1566) or Aberdeenshire (1576). The privy council could impose a general band on any area where authority was felt to be held in contempt—such as Orkney and Shetland in 1597–8, despite the earl's protests.[53]

The statute of 1587 took a similar approach to that of the general band, though it seemed uninterested in employing it directly. It mentioned the general band casually, as something assumed to be in force, in two of its minor clauses; but it did not elaborate on it, and some of its other provisions modified or duplicated it.[54] Still, acts of caution by unruly landlords became much more common after the statute. They could specify conformity to the general band, or to the statute, or to both.[55] In 1590, sixty-eight landlords were charged according to the act of 1587 to find caution to keep order in their lands and to repress broken (i.e.

---

[52] *RMS* vi. 472. A military expedition to the Highlands was then in preparation, and the charter was part of MacDonald's submission to royal authority.

[53] *RPC* i. 449–50; ii. 547–8; v. 436–7; P. D. Anderson, *Black Patie: The Life and Times of Patrick Stewart, Earl of Orkney, Lord of Shetland* (Edinburgh, 1992), 54–5.

[54] *APS* iii. 464–5, c. 59, paras. 14, 19.

[55] *RPC* v. 733, for examples of all three.

masterless) men. They were mostly lowlanders with estates on the Highland–Lowland frontier, plus a limited selection of Islesmen.[56] The general band of 1599 for the sheriffdom of Dumbarton was extended into the *regality* and dukedom of Lennox—possibly setting a precedent for encroachment into regalities.[57] There was also a trend towards extracting hostages, not just cautions, from Highland chiefs. The scale of this is unclear, but hostages were being taken from some chiefs, at least from time to time, in the last years of the century.[58]

A new general band was issued in 1602, and all Highland and Border landlords and chiefs were ordered to subscribe it and find caution to obey it.[59] But in the next few years, Border and Highland policy diverged again. The 1602 band was reissued in 1617 for the Borders alone—probably because the Highlands were now covered by other arrangements, particularly an agreement with the leading island chiefs in 1616.[60]

The general band brought further private bands into being. Normally only lords who were tenants in chief had to sign it, but once they had taken caution to be responsible for their followers, they realized that they were going to have to keep those followers in order. In 1595, nine lairds, followers of John Grant of Freuchie, took caution that they would keep 'guid reull' and submit their followers to justice: 'becaus the said Johne Grant of Frewquhye is actit in the buikis of consall as caution for thame for guid ordour keiping'.[61]

Just as official bands led to private ones in the Highlands, so official intervention there was leading to private intervention. The general band facilitated this. The earl of Argyll complained in 1595 that his tenants' creditors were invoking the general band to pursue him for their debts ('yea, sumtymes for materis of les importance nor ten pundis'), on the ground that the general band

[56] *RPC* iv. 802–3.

[57] W. Fraser, *The Chiefs of Colquhoun and their Country*, 2 vols. (Edinburgh, 1869), i. 175–6.

[58] *APS* iv. 179; 236, c. 33. Cf. Gregory, *Western Highlands and Isles*, 263.

[59] *RPC* vi. 435–6, and for the text of the band, 825–9.

[60] *RPC* xi. 215–19, 225–9. Traditionally, the most important Highland agreement has been considered to be the Statutes of Iona of 1609. That these have been inflated in significance is argued by J. Goodare, 'The Statutes of Iona in context', *SHR* 77 (1998), 31–57.

[61] W. Fraser, *The Chiefs of Grant*, 3 vols. (Edinburgh, 1883), iii. 185–6.

made him responsible for the tenants. The privy council agreed with him that the general band should cover only 'oppin reiffis' and suchlike crimes, not debts.[62]

Another continuous executive trend from the 1580s onwards was information-gathering. No longer would any part of the Borders or Highlands be *terra incognita*. Catalogues of clans, chiefs, surnames, landlords, and people at the horn were compiled with increasing assiduity. There was a particularly comprehensive effort in 1590, when a roll was drawn up 'of the names of the landislordis and baillies of the landis duelland on the Bordouris and in the Hielandis quhair broken men hes duelt and presentlie duellis'.[63]

The final example of executive intervention to be considered here was the construction of a secret service in the Highlands. In the early seventeenth century this operated for all the world as if the region was enemy territory. Secret agents would undertake missions to the Highlands to get identified resistance leaders 'putt out' (a euphemism for being arrested or killed) for rewards of 1,000 merks or so. Chancellor Dunfermline often achieved good results 'be sic privie moyennis for small soumis'.[64]

This policy offensive might have led to the creation of special institutions for the Highland and Border regions. The Tudors' deployment of the council in the North and the council in the Marches of Wales is familiar. The council in the Marches was an all-purpose body, functioning as a court of law in civil, criminal, and even some ecclesiastical cases, an administrative and policing agency, and a military command.[65] Another parallel might be the Irish provincial presidencies, introduced in the 1560s. They wore a distinctly colonial look. They failed as law-enforcement bodies for lack of local acceptance, but did not 'go native'; they stayed

---

[62] *RPC* v. 249–50; cf. vi. 174–5, and vii. 103–4, for later cases of this kind.

[63] *RPC* iv. 781–2. Several statutes also included such lists. Cf. the increasing topographical interest in the Isles discussed in Ch. 7 above. The government does not, however, seem to have promoted the actual mapping of the territory, as the Elizabethan government was then beginning to do in Ulster: R. Gillespie, *Colonial Ulster: The Settlement of East Ulster, 1600–1641* (Cork, 1985), 10–11.

[64] Dunfermline to Murray of Lochmaben, 9 Dec. 1614, *HP* iii. 172.

[65] P. Williams, *The Council in the Marches of Wales under Elizabeth I* (Cardiff, 1958). To put it more formally: it was a miniature privy council, court of star chamber, court of chancery and court of requests, and an extended lord lieutenancy, as well as exercising some of the functions of the court of high commission. It did not exclude the authority of the central bodies. Cf. R. R. Reid, *The King's Council in the North* (London, 1921).

under central control, maintaining their existence as garrisons collecting revenue.[66]

The clearest examples of such institutions for Scotland are the
short-lived council for the Borders and Highlands, lasting a year
and a half from June 1590, and later the series of commissions for
the Isles. The former body, effectively a subcommittee of the privy
council, was set up to implement the statute of 1587. It did some
work, but petered out—apparently because it was felt that more
could be achieved in the full council. The council did continue to
keep a separate register for its Border and Highland business; from
1590 onwards there was far more such business—especially for the
Highlands—than ever before. The commissions for the Isles, of
which the main one was established in 1608 and upgraded in
1609, were similar in their close connection with the council.[67]

While the council retained control at the centre, the main institutions at the front line were the lieutenancies. Traditionally, a
Lowland noble (or a Campbell in the west Highlands) would receive
a temporary commission with military and judicial powers. When
lieutenants were appointed for the Borders, they possessed broadly
similar powers to those wardens who (as had become normal during
the late sixteenth century) were also justiciars. The one formal difference was that lieutenants could grant remissions to convicted
criminals. Lieutenants in practice had greater authority because
more political and military weight was usually put behind their commissions.[68] However, they represented an intensification of normal
practice rather than a new departure. With the new-style Border
commissions of 1605 onwards, the lieutenancies faded out.

Highland lieutenants varied widely in what they made of their
powers, and most traditional commissions were more for the self-
aggrandizement of the lieutenant than for the extension of royal
authority as such. The only holders of lieutenancies before the
1590s were the earls of Huntly (in the north) and Argyll (in the
west).[69] A full study of how they used their authority would be

---

[66] C. Brady, 'Court, castle and country: The framework of government in Tudor
Ireland', in id. and R. Gillespie (eds.), *Natives and Newcomers: The Making of Irish
Colonial Society, 1534–1641* (Dublin, 1986), 39–40.

[67] *RPC* iv, pp. liii–lvi, 780–814; viii, pp. liii, 59–61, 737, 742–6; NAS, *Guide to the
National Archives of Scotland* (Edinburgh, 1996), 24. A separate council register for
business for the Isles was maintained between 1608 and 1623.

[68] Rae, *Scottish Frontier*, 104–11.

[69] The Earl Marischal, exceptionally, was a lieutenant in 1589, perhaps in connection with his role as an ambassador: *RMS* v. 1733.

desirable, but the impression given by the sources is that these traditional lieutenants were rather like regalities. Regional magnates *took* such powers in order to enhance their own authority and deal with local rivals; the crown did not grant them as part of a national strategy. The powers were backed up by the magnates' own forces, not those of the crown. This was clearly the case with the three commissions of lieutenancy (and two of justiciary) obtained by the earls of Argyll between 1475 and 1550.[70]

These traditional, magnate-controlled lieutenancies became rare in the Highlands during the 1580s and 1590s, though they did not become extinct: the marquis of Huntly and duke of Lennox received a joint one for the northern Highlands in 1599. They probably did little with their commission; at any rate they did not produce much paperwork for the council.[71] In the past they would not have had to do so, but the council was now keeping a close eye on devolved judicial powers. It even blocked a commission over the Highlands which the master of Tullibardine sought in 1610: the 'royall and soverane pouer of justiceairis', it advised the king, was 'onlie proper to your majesteis heich justice'.[72]

The lieutenants' judicial importance may have been declining. For the Tudors, the key difference between their special regional courts and the common-law courts was that the former had no local jury to be bribed or intimidated. In Scotland, the privy council (which had no assize) developed an extensive criminal jurisdiction over 'riot'; no other criminal court acted without an assize, but, as we have seen, the government had achieved the same effect as the English by removing the assize for Highland crimes to the Lowlands.[73] This may have eclipsed the lieutenants' courts, still held on the spot and needing local assizes.

Meanwhile, a new type of royal lieutenant emerged in the Highlands from 1596 onwards. He was not a regional magnate seeking additional judicial powers over his local rivals: he commanded a

---

[70] M. D. W. MacGregor, 'A Political History of the MacGregors before 1571', Ph.D. thesis (Edinburgh, 1989), 85–8. Cf. the extensive commission of justiciary received by John Grant of Freuchie in 1555, clearly giving him powers rather than responsibilities: Fraser, *Chiefs of Grant*, i. 130; iii. 116–17.

[71] *RPC* vi. 8–10. The intention was probably to combine Huntly's regional following with Lennox's political reliability. Huntly was censured for misconduct as lieutenant in 1601: *RPC* vi. 295–6.

[72] Council to James, 6 June 1610, *HP* iii. 119–20. For 'justiceairis', probably read 'justiciars' rather than 'justice ayres'.

[73] Reid, *Council in the North*, 261; Williams, *Council in the Marches*, 83; J. Goodare, *The Government of Scotland, 1560–1625* (forthcoming), ch. 6.

royal army invading the region. This new interventionism focused on the Isles. It was no mere effort at containment—a containment policy would have been more likely to build fortifications in Strath Tay or Menteith—but a deliberate effort to extend state power into the most remote regions of the kingdom.

The shifting and sometimes labyrinthine manoeuvres that resulted do not look like a coherent policy, but increasingly they were one. It is necessary to distinguish between strategy and tactics. The strategy was that of *Basilicon Doron*: to subjugate autonomous clan power to the power of the state, and to open up the Highland economy to trade and exploitation. The tactics were to pick off, or co-opt, the chiefs one by one, as and when the opportunity offered. Opportunities arose haphazardly, so the tactics can seem to lack any pattern. Tactics were further complicated by the need to deal with resistance, as uprisings might break out unexpectedly. But the strategic aim behind the numerous interventions in the region remained steady. The most important military expeditions by new-style lieutenants took place in 1596 (to Kintyre), in 1605 (to Kintyre again), and in 1608 (to Islay and Mull). These expeditions were effective; it is no coincidence that the MacDonalds were deprived of Kintyre in 1607 and of Islay in 1612.[74]

It is also no coincidence that the lieutenants from 1605 onwards possessed an additional power: to set feus and leases of crown lands.[75] One of the ideas behind the assault on Highland autonomy was that much of the land could be shown to be in some sense crown land. Once the traditional possessors had been persuaded of this novel idea—or dispossessed for failure to recognize it—the region could become a money-spinner. Highland farming may not have been wealthy, but it did produce an economic surplus for the chiefs, and there was increasing interest in transferring some of this to the crown.

The new claim to Highland rents in the late sixteenth century was not based on the crown's traditional Highland estates.[76]

---

[74] Gregory, *Western Highlands and Isles*, 263–9, 306–8; *HP* iii. 72–85; *RMS* vi. 1911. For a planned expedition in 1592 that did not take place, see NAS, GD149/265, pt. 1, fo. 11ᵛ. For more on policy-making in this period, see Goodare, 'Statutes of Iona'.

[75] *RPC* vii. 115–17.

[76] For these, and the limited revenue or control that the crown had over them, see C. Madden, 'The Finances of the Scottish Crown in the Later Middle Ages', Ph.D. thesis (Glasgow, 1975), 186, 259–60.

Instead it rested on the forfeiture of the lordship of the Isles in 1493. Some of the lands of the lordship had remained in crown hands for a while, but they were gradually leased out to the local chiefs for rents that were small and rarely paid, leaving little but empty titles. There had been periodic efforts to reverse this; some of James V's dealings with Islay suggest that he may have intended to replace the chiefs and become the landlord himself.[77] This was beyond the crown's powers even in the 1530s, when it was a major landlord elsewhere, and by the later sixteenth century the disintegration of the royal estates had made it quite impossible. What James VI hoped to do was to rake off some of the chiefs' surplus through rents and feu-duties charged on them. If the crown's power was great enough, it might even be able to get the lion's share of the surplus, leaving the local chief with little more than the position of a well-paid estate manager. This could not be done to an established chief, for whom the drop in status would be intolerable. But if that chief was forfeited, his lands could be offered to others. If the competition was strong enough, the price could be driven up. A full study of the crown's financial dealings with the Highlands would be a sizeable undertaking, but as a leading example, let us consider the forfeiture of Islay as a fiscal operation.[78]

Islay had been the heart of the lordship of the Isles. In the 1590s it was mostly in the hands of the MacDonalds of Dunyveg, who had risen to power in the early sixteenth century despite what has been described as 'a bewildering spate of charters, leases, cancellations and regrants' by the crown.[79] However, the gradual disintegration of the clan offered opportunities for others—including the crown, which already had nominal title to some lands on the island.[80] When Angus MacDonald of Dunyveg submitted to the crown along with his rival, Lachlan Maclean of Duart, in 1591, Maclean offered to take on the 'farm' of the crown's lands. Meanwhile the king wanted to exchange some lands with MacDonald, 'that the kings

---

[77] W. D. Lamont, *The Early History of Islay, 500–1726* (Dundee, 1966), 38–40.

[78] A broader survey of the rents extracted from island chiefs between 1610 and 1615 is offered in Goodare, 'Statutes of Iona', 45–6.

[79] Lamont, *Early History of Islay*, 30.

[80] The crown lands were leased to MacDonald for the probably nominal rent of £186: *ER* xxii. 23. For the landholdings on the island see W. K. McLean, 'The Maclean–MacDonald feud: Disputed landholdings in Islay in the sixteenth century', *TGSI* 56 (1988–90), 223–43.

landes may be drawen to lye togither'. Maclean and MacDonald
both came in the king's will for treason, and were ordered to pay
10,000 merks each 'and as much in yearly rent'.[81] This did not
happen; the crown did extract £6,000 each from them, but this
was as composition for all past rents (and not just in Islay), while
no further payments were made.[82] Sir James MacDonald (Angus's
son) offered £600 per year for Islay in 1599, which the privy
council at one time intended to accept.[83] By 1606 the crown had
managed to get Angus MacDonald to pay some more rent for Islay
and Kintyre, 'wnto the quhilkis', he wrote, 'I and my foirbeiris hes
bene kyndle tenentis'; but this payment was the fruit of the military expedition of 1605.[84] MacDonald was deprived of Kintyre the
next year. In 1609 he paid three years' arrears of rent, £3,000, for
his lands in Islay and Colonsay; again that was the year after an
expedition.[85] All this showed that money could only be extracted
from the chiefs under pressure—and military pressure was expensive. What was needed was a system whereby the money would
come in regularly.

No further payments are recorded from MacDonald. In 1612,
Sir John Campbell of Cawdor took on a tack of Islay, nominally
from MacDonald; Sir Ranald MacDonald of Antrim and Sir George
Hamilton of Greenlaw (who as brother of the earl of Abercorn had
a court connection) soon got the privy council to press MacDonald to redeem the tack in their own interests, leaving Campbell's
agent advising him ruefully to 'luik with quhom ye mell heirefter'.
Hamilton paid £2,500 per year for three years.[86] The MacDonalds
were formally and finally dispossessed after the uprisings of
1614–15, and the possibility of feuing both their and the crown's

---

[81] Bowes to Burghley, 13 Feb. 1591, *Calendar of Letters and Papers Relating to the
Affairs of the Borders of England and Scotland, 1560–1603*, 2 vols., ed. J. Bain (London,
1894–6), i. 376; same to same, 23 Feb. 1591, *CSP Scot.* x. 463–4; Richard Douglas
to Archibald Douglas, 12 Feb. 1591, HMC, *Salisbury*, iv. 89–91. Cf. E. J. Cowan,
'Clanship, kinship and the Campbell acquisition of Islay', *SHR* 58 (1979), 132–57,
at pp. 135–6.

[82] *ER* xxii. 117.

[83] *RPC* vi. 24–5. He also offered to remove the rest of his clan and bring in other
tenants.

[84] *HP* iii. 86–8. The amount is not recorded—there are gaps in the MS comptroller's accounts—but it may have been the same as in 1609.

[85] NAS, comptroller's accounts, 1609–10, E24/29, fo. 20ʳ.

[86] NAS, comptroller's accounts, 1611–12, E24/30, fos. 19ᵛ–20ʳ; 1612–13,
E24/31, fo. 25ᵛ; 1613–14, E24/32, fo. 22ʳ; *Book of the Thanes of Cawdor, 1236–1742*,
ed. C. Innes (Spalding Club, 1859), 225.

lands arose. Campbell renewed his bid for the island, offering 8,000 merks (£5,333) per year, plus an initial payment of £2,000; but the government bargained him up to £6,000 per year, which Lord Binning noted was 'far above any thing that any responsall man of qualitie did evir to my knowledge offer for it'.[87] They were helped to do so by Sir James MacDonald, son and heir of the old chief; he also offered 8,000 merks per year, with a possible increase to 10,000, in a desperate bid to recover his hereditary lands.[88] Mac-Donald was not a 'responsall man of qualitie', but both he and Campbell were forced to increase their bids by the knowledge that the government had a choice.

The crown's income from Islay had thus grown in stages, from occasional sums in the 1590s, to £1,000 per year (irregularly paid) by 1609, and finally to £6,000 per year (regularly paid) by 1615. How much of the Islay peasants' surplus remained in the hands of their new masters, the Campbells, is not known (the figure of £7,200 was mentioned later), but it was clearly a good deal less than the MacDonalds had received.[89] Campbell of Cawdor, indeed, had overreached himself financially. He lamented to the privy council in 1618: 'your lordschipis knowis upoun quhat hard conditionis I haif undertane the rycht and title of the landis of Ilay, and how I am subjcct in a grite yeirlie dewytie for the same'. Some time after that, his debts (amounting, it was said, to 100,000 merks) grew so disastrous that his kinsmen stepped in to persuade him to sell some land and commit the management of the remainder to his son.[90] Still, he continued to pay the Islay feu-duty, though with difficulty.[91] As a final, tangible measure to sum up the crown's increased influence in the Isles, £6,000 per year from Islay may be as good as any.

In the period covered by this book, the Scottish state saw a remarkable transformation in its attitude to its remoter regions. Traditionally, the Borders had been a buffer zone against a hostile

---

[87] Earl of Somerset to Sir Gideon Murray, 29 June 1614, *CSP Dom. 1611–1618*, 239; NAS, comptroller's accounts, 1616–17, E24/35, fo. 19ʳ; 1617–18, E24/36, fo. 24ʳ; NLS, Binning to Patrick Hamilton, 28 Sept. [1614], Denmylne MSS, Adv. MS 33.1.1, vol. v, no. 89.

[88] *HP* iii. 165. Cf. a similar offer by his half-brother in Sept. 1614: ibid. 150.

[89] Islay was said in 1627 to be worth over £600 sterling (£7,200 Scots) per year 'of frie rent, over and above the kingis rent and church rent': *Thanes of Cawdor*, 270–1.

[90] *RPC* xi. 624; *Thanes of Cawdor*, 254–5.   [91] *Thanes of Cawdor*, 249, 252.

English state, in which the usual governmental institutions and mechanisms operated in distinctive ways if at all, and in which there were also special ways of governing—and of coping with the occasional difficulties. The militarized Border region offered Scotland cut-price security against English attacks, and diplomatic cards to play in relations with England generally. Once England and Scotland decided hesitantly to be friends, as they did after 1560, the borderers faced redundancy. It took the two states a long time to be sure that friendship was what they really wanted; old habits died hard, and difficulties in Anglo-Scottish relations were still bound up with violence on the Border, as with the celebrated Kinmont Willie incident in 1596. When James wrote *Basilicon Doron*, the Borders were still a problem, but he correctly foresaw that after the union of crowns, 'they will be the middest of the Ile, and so as easily ruled as any part thereof'.[92] A good deal of government effort was needed to establish this, but the effort had succeeded by 1625.

Obedience on the Border had been achieved, moreover, without creating an unstable situation for the future. A few nameless borderers had been summarily banished, burned out of their homes, or executed without trial; but on the whole the Border elite had been converted to a new role rather than being expropriated, marginalized, or subordinated. Their tenants, similarly, had had to learn new habits—paying economic rents—and forget old ones—cattle-raiding—but were still in possession.[93]

In the Highlands, however, the state's achievements had been more complex, and less stable or complete. The region had been treated as a colonial province, in which government was carried out for the benefit of the core state, in which local elites were not fully integrated, and in which they did not wish to be.[94] Many of the Highland elite *had* been expropriated, marginalized, or subordinated, and the most important of them—MacDonalds, MacGregors, Macleods—were not likely to forget this in a hurry. But in the meantime, so long as the national political position remained stable, they could do no more than nurse their grievances.

[92] James VI, *Basilicon Doron*, in *Political Writings*, 25.
[93] R. A. Dodgshon, 'Agricultural change and its social consequences in the southern uplands of Scotland, 1600–1780', in T. M. Devine and D. Dickson (eds.), *Ireland and Scotland, 1600–1850* (Edinburgh, 1983).
[94] The issue of colonialism is discussed further in Goodare, *Government*, ch. 9.

After forfeiting the lordship of the Isles, James IV had annexed it not to the crown of Scotland but to the principality, so that charters issued for the Isles ran thereafter in the name of the king as administrator for the prince.[95] What if he or one of his successors (such as James VI, who did have a prince after 1594) had gone further, and created a devolved administration for the Isles, or indeed for the whole of the Highlands? The prince, or his representative, could have acted as a viceroy, maintaining the region at arm's length from the Scottish state. The region might have developed its own administrative structures and traditions, adapted to its special local circumstances. State formation might have taken place there relatively painlessly, at least at first; it could have used the Gaelic language, and perhaps fostered the kind of economic development in which highlanders themselves could have taken the lead. Of course, the kind of devolved state structure in which highlanders would have been happy might well have come into conflict with the centre eventually. Sooner or later, the Scottish government would have placed more demands on it, and it would have had either to adapt itself to those demands, or to resist—with an uncertain outcome.

These reflections may seem speculative, but that need not prevent some fruitful comparisons from being drawn. Devolved regions with local privileges were perfectly normal in the seventeenth-century absolutist state. The Spanish monarchy consisted mainly of such regions, and would indignantly have denied that it was a colonial power *vis-à-vis* (for instance) Catalonia. This province was in a different position from the transatlantic New Spain, which was definitely a colony; Catalonia was *privileged*, and was sometimes a nuisance to Madrid as a result. It was, to be sure, semi-detached, governed by a viceroy who limited the Catalans' access to the king; but limited participation meant also limited demands. Catalonia's government was conducted in the Catalan language, not in Castilian. Its separate traditions and institutions gave its political elite the capacity to stir up a great deal of trouble if the crown ever tried to align it with Castile. Similarly, France had its *pays d'états*, the provinces possessing their own *parlements*; such provinces paid lower taxes and were less responsive to central authority. And they worked. The story of Catalonia and the Spanish

[95] e.g. *RMS* vi. 174, 790.

monarchy is best known for having had an unhappy phase in the 1640s, but this was triggered under extreme pressure in a losing war; the French *pays d'états* survived comfortably in the body politic until 1789.[96] The English state, where provincial administrations in the North and Wales were aggressive agents of centralization, seems to have been unusual in this broader context of contented provincial diversity.

In the light of this, the point about the development of the state in the Highlands is that no halfway house emerged: no possibility of a devolved provincial structure making only limited demands and offering only limited participation. On the one hand, there was traditional Highland society, based on clan power and with little or no state structure. On the other hand, there was the Scottish state, with a place for kinship connections, but with the most significant governmental roles taken by parliament, privy council, exchequer, taxes, sheriff courts, and so on. Perhaps the disparity between the two was too great for a devolved Highland province to be created; one of the reasons that the Catalan province worked for as long as it did was that Catalonia was highly urbanized and possessed state structures of its own. However hard it was to control from Madrid, the royal government knew that in Catalonia it was dealing with social equals who governed in familiar and respectable ways. That was not so when the Scottish privy council summoned the Highland chiefs to Edinburgh; lowlanders and highlanders still had some values in common, but the restructuring of Lowland government had left a wide gap between them. Unless the clans were prepared to adapt themselves to accept state authority in its full form, they would be condemned to remain pariahs on the fringes of the state, perennially vulnerable to any new initiative which might reveal that authority in the Highlands was still being exercised in uncivilized ways.

Which, of course, it was. James VI did *not* assimilate the clans to the state; authority in the Highlands continued to be exercised by clans, and not by bureaucrats or garrison commanders. The chiefs had lost one area of freedom of action, but they were still—mostly—in place, and still to some extent able to interpose themselves between the people and the regular institutions of

---

[96] J. H. Elliott, *The Revolt of the Catalans: A Study in the Decline of Spain, 1598–1640* (Cambridge, 1963), ch. 4 and *passim*; R. Bonney, 'Absolutism: What's in a name?', *French History*, 1 (1987), 93–117, at pp. 109–13.

government. It remained harder to prosecute crimes in the Highlands, and only the really serious cases would come to court.[97] The state's achievement had been to some extent a negative one, comparable to the forfeiture of the lordship of the Isles a century earlier.

The foundations of at least one more constructive development had been laid. The expansion of Campbells and Mackenzies had been associated with expansion of the economy, and particularly a policy of plantation of towns in the Highlands. The practice of urbanization may have been a little more complex than the theory, but certainly the almost total absence of towns in the region was now terminating. There had been no creations of royal burghs, but several burghs of barony had received charters: Stornoway, erected for the Fife Adventurers (1607), soon taken over by Mackenzie of Kintail; Laggan, for Campbell of Cawdor (1614); and Gordonsburgh (later Fort William), for Huntly (1618). They had joined Argyll's fifteenth-century burghs of Inveraray and Kilmun, of which the latter at least existed only on parchment. When or how these legal creations became actual towns is less clear, but the legal creations are worth noting in themselves. Meanwhile another town, as yet without a charter, was tentatively taking shape at Campbeltown. More highlanders, perhaps, had now begun to settle in towns, at least in Inveraray.[98] The Highlands had certainly begun to see early signs of economic development, although generally by and for lowlanders or foreigners rather than themselves: fishing, the cattle trade, the iron industry.[99]

There was still a good deal of political violence in the Highlands at the end of James VI's reign. Clan feuds continued; the 'pacification' measures themselves were pretty violent; these measures in turn led to uprisings, more 'pacification', and so on. The state still had no regular military presence of its own in the Highlands,

[97] M. B. Wasser, 'Violence and the Central Criminal Courts in Scotland, 1603–1638', Ph.D. diss. (Columbia, 1995), 57–62.

[98] G. S. Pryde, *The Burghs of Scotland: A Critical List* (Glasgow, 1965), nos. 280, 295, 303, 151, 165; A. McKerral, *Kintyre in the Seventeenth Century* (Edinburgh, 1948), 37; A. I. Macinnes, 'Social mobility in medieval and early modern Scottish Gaeldom: The controvertible evidence', *TGSI* 58 (1993–4), 371–405, at p. 387; M. Lynch, 'National identity in Ireland and Scotland, 1500–1640', in C. Bjørn *et al.* (eds.), *Nations, Nationalism and Patriotism in the European Past* (Copenhagen, 1994), 131. For parallel developments in Ulster, see N. Canny, *Kingdom and Colony: Ireland in the Atlantic World, 1560–1800* (Baltimore, 1988), 48–9.

[99] Goodare, *Government*, ch. 9.

though it had proved that it could hit hard if it chose. Certainly, traditional clan society had used its weapons freely. Certainly, it was now advisable for a clan to seek permission from the state before sending round the fiery cross. But for the state's client clans, that permission was readily forthcoming—as, indeed, it had to be. The state-sponsored expansion of the Campbells and Mackenzies had created an unstable situation, in which they experienced a vulnerability unknown in earlier ages. The clans they had dispossessed saw clearly what had happened, and sought revenge. Still, the very fact that Campbells and Mackenzies had made so many enemies would be likely to keep them loyal—so long as the state showed itself willing and able to support them.

This should not, then, be seen as an outright failure from the state's point of view. It would have been one if 'pacification' had been the goal; but really the goal was state control. Campbells had been commissioned to seize MacDonald lands not because they would bring peace, but because they were politically reliable. They had brought the state's goal a step nearer, but only a step. They had proved willing to make some concessions to state authority: paying royal rents and taxes, respecting the Protestant church, participating in Lowland politics, and not intriguing with foreign powers. But they were still clans, and they still—unlike the Lowland nobility—possessed autonomous military power. The Campbells, and the other clans (mainly Mackenzies) who tried some of their tricks in the seventeenth century, had reached much the same position *vis-à-vis* the state as the Border lords of the sixteenth century.

This comparison between the seventeenth-century Highlands and sixteenth-century Borders would need to be qualified in several ways. The relevant one here is that, in their relations with the state, sixteenth-century Border lords were *all* Campbells. They all had deep roots in an autonomous political community that was hard for the state to influence; they all participated (more or less) in the national business of government. No division grew up in the Borders between collaborating, predatory lords and traditional ones. By 1625, such a division in the Highlands was more evident than ever. It meant that the clans had to take more notice of the state than before, and ensured that they would never be able to unite against it. And if even Campbells and Mackenzies had not been fully integrated into the structures of the state, still less had other highlanders been. Moreover, when other highlanders *had* come into closer contact with the state, they had rarely been given cause to welcome the experience. The 'Highland problem' created between 1581 and 1617 would long remain to trouble the state; and the parallel 'state problem' would long remain to trouble the Highlands.

9

State Power

As to the estate of this country since I can remember this 29 years it was never so calm and quiet as it is at the present. No man living can say he has either seen or heard tell of so great reverence, fear, and regard in this land to the authority, to the laws and to justice, as is at the present.... [The king] might now freely deal with every subject according to his merit, give the law not only to every one of us in particular but even to us all, if they were never so many of us, nor so great, would seem to be mutin or rebellious; the which was able to make obedience, peace, and justice to flourish and to bring wealth amongst us.[1]

The late sixteenth and early seventeenth centuries were a crucial phase in the formation of the Scottish state. It not only became a more fully sovereign state, but also developed a larger and more integrated network of public authority, able to enforce the will of the government. By about 1625, all Lowland Scots, even the formerly autonomous nobility and clergy, could now be expected not just to acknowledge the authority of the crown, but to obey the law of the state. That law, moreover, covered a wide and increasing range of activities.

Probably few of those involved had a conscious sense that these changes were creating something new, because of the intensely conservative formulas in which the newborn state was swaddled; but some did. James VI's chancellor in 1605, the earl of Dunfermline, was one of them. Even at a discount for hyperbole, Dunfermline's remarks above display a consciousness of solid achievement. Then there is James himself, whose 'vaunt' that he was the first monarch to govern Scotland with his pen is often

---

[1] Dunfermline to Cecil, 20 Apr. 1605, HMC, *Salisbury*, xvii. 149–50. The reference to 'this 29 years' may mean 'since my 21st birthday'.

quoted.[2] One need not attribute a great deal of the change to the king's personal initiatives, although his skills in political manoeuvre and his well-developed survival instinct helped to create the conditions for it. It was not primarily his own pen, but the pens of his administrators, that mattered. What mattered even more was that people were now prepared regularly to *obey* these administrators' written or printed commands.

This chapter will look in more detail at the concept of power: what it meant to issue commands and have them obeyed. Power may well be seen as something that governments have, or perhaps are in: who but they? However, countries do not just contain governments; they also contain powerful people. Not all the powerful people in early modern Scotland derived their power from the government. This book is not directly concerned with the 'government' of households by fathers, or of landed estates by landlords; these forms of the exercise of power were relevant to us only when they impinged on the public sphere. What matters here is *state* power. We should thus ask: how far was state power differentiated from other forms of power?[3]

The state faced problems in establishing its distinctiveness. Nobles and lairds were nobles and lairds before they became privy councillors, justices of the peace, or kirk session elders. They had status and power as landlords, and retained this status and power alongside their public roles. The public offices they held, at every level, tended to reflect existing hierarchies of status, with possession of the broadest acres conferring the most realistic expectations of the highest public office. They used their public positions to pursue private quarrels. Can the degree of differentiation between their private and public roles be assessed? This question

---

[2] Often by writers who imply or assume that he was referring to his governing at a distance after the union of crowns, but in fact James was drawing a contrast between government by pen and by the sword: James VI & I, speech to parliament, 1607, in *Political Writings*, 173.

[3] What follows on this subject owes much to M. Braddick, 'The early modern English state and the question of differentiation, from 1550 to 1700', *Comparative Studies in Society and History*, 38 (1996), 92–111. The 'public' sphere has been taken to be the classical one—the sphere of political participation, as opposed to a 'private' sphere of domestic life and non-political voluntary action in civil society. For this distinction, and for alternative definitions of 'public/private' (state/market economy, sociability/individuality, civil society/family), see J. Weintraub, 'The theory and politics of the public/private distinction', in id. and K. Kumar (eds.), *Public and Private in Thought and Practice* (Chicago, 1997).

should be tackled at all social levels—from those at the top, who mainly *exercised* power, to those at the bottom, who mainly *experienced* its exercise by those above them.

Most late-medieval governing had been done by people whose primary source of power was not derived from the state—the landed nobility. They were not magnates because they governed: they governed because they were magnates. Government did not grant them their powers, such as their hereditary sheriffships and regalities, as part of any coherent system or plan. Rather they *took* those powers, and used them for their own ends. The process of their doing so constituted much of what is recognized as government. Even royal government could be similar; Robert II, the first Stewart king, continued to rely heavily on the territorial estates he had had before his accession, and his influence was largely restricted to central Scotland.[4]

At the very top, there continued to be little differentiation. The private and public lives of monarchs overlapped; one of their main functions, indeed, was to live their private lives in public. James VI justified his main recreation, hunting, on the ground that it 'resembleth the warres'. Although he divided *Basilicon Doron* into chapters on a king's public and private life, he stressed that the latter had a public dimension. Strikingly, he included his advice about a king's marriage and family life in the *public* chapter.[5] His body servants might well wield political influence through their position. Private, personal affection was a legitimate motive for public favour to such men as Buckingham: James here was 'a man like other men, who did what other men did', as he informed the English privy council. On the other hand, he referred to the time he spent writing poems as his 'vacant houres'; unlike hunting or family life, versification was not in his job description.[6] For a king, publishing poetry was a more private exercise than begetting children.

The nobles had a similar mixture of public and private activities,

---

[4] S. I. Boardman, *The Early Stewart Kings: Robert II and Robert III, 1371–1406* (East Linton, 1996), 91–6. See also Ch. 2 above.

[5] James VI, *Basilicon Doron*, in *Political Writings*, 40–2, 47, 58. There was also a chapter on a king's duty to God.

[6] Quotation from R. Lockyer, *Buckingham: The Life and Political Career of George Villiers, First Duke of Buckingham, 1592–1628* (London, 1981), 43. James's second published verse collection was entitled *His Majesties Poeticall Exercises at Vacant Houres* (Edinburgh, 1591).

but they were more focused on their estates, which were more obviously their *private* estates. If they wearied of public life, they might go home and pull up the drawbridge (literally in some cases) to shut out the public world. But with estates came clients and juris-diction, the management of which were quasi-public matters. Disputes with neighbours and rivals, whether resolved through negotiation, through feud, or through the courts, were inevitably political. The leading nobles were expected to 'serve' the crown, and thus involve themselves in public life. However, they no longer *had* to do so. It would have been much more difficult for a lead-ing earl to keep out of politics in the fifteenth century. Further research is required to elucidate this point fully; a hereditary nobil-ity will have its share of incapable individuals, but only the extreme forms of incapacity will be recorded. The third earl of Atholl, whose temporary 'curius pallice' offered magnificent entertain-ment to James V in 1531, was wealthy but politically insignificant; but because he remains a shadowy figure, it is not certain that he had the capacity for a public career.[7] But the fifth Earl Marischal did choose to remain aloof from politics in the late sixteenth century, although he was probably the wealthiest peer in Scotland. That his aloofness was not due to incapacity is clear from the fact that he performed occasional weighty public duties, and took a keen interest in the college he founded in Aberdeen in 1593.[8] He seems simply to have preferred private life—or rather, civil society—to political participation.

In practice, therefore, it seems that government tended to become the full-time business of *some* of the nobles, while the others trusted them to get on with it. Again, further research is required to explain how this worked. How far was it a problem—either for the nobles themselves, or for the crown that sought their 'service'? The church does seem to have been disappointed in the nobility.[9] But mutual dissatisfaction of crown and nobility seems

[7] Pitscottie, *Historie*, i. 335–8.

[8] Virtually the only public duties he undertook were as ambassador to Denmark in 1589, and as commissioner to the parliament of 1609: J. B. Paul (ed.), *The Scots Peerage*, 9 vols. (Edinburgh, 1904–14), vi. 51–3. For his wealth, see K. M. Brown, 'Aristocratic finances and the origins of the Scottish revolution', *EHR* 104 (1989), 46–87, at p. 49.

[9] K.M. Brown, 'In search of the godly magistrate in Reformation Scotland', *Journal of Ecclesiastical History*, 40 (1989), 553–81. Professor Brown's forthcoming study of the nobility may well shed light on these questions.

mainly to have occurred in the 1590s.[10] On the whole, seventeenth-century Scotland did not suffer from a *general* aristocratic reluctance to pursue public careers.

Along with differentiation between private and public came specialization among the political elite. There was now a wider range of public roles on offer for the nobility. One could serve in the central administration, perhaps utilizing one's new-found legal expertise. The role of military officer beckoned for some, though in our period it was mainly foreign princes who sought the military services of Scottish noblemen. Some, seeking to develop entrepreneurial skills, sought royal patents and projects, like Lord Erskine's notorious patent for the regulation of tanning in the 1620s.[11] This, together with the retreat of Marischal and those like him into the private sphere, was an indication of society's increasing complexity.

The increasing involvement of lairds in public life was another reflection of this specialization. As education spread and the printing industry got into its stride, a broad literary culture grew up that was no longer focused on the royal court but had its own roots in people of lesser property. There were careers opening up to them in the practice of law—as advocates or writers to the signet in the central courts, or as legal 'writers' and other office-holders in the localities. In public administration, too, legal education was often useful. Other careers beckoned in the royal court itself, and in military service. In the localities, the establishment of kirk sessions gave the lairds wider scope than before for policing the morals of the common people; as justices of the peace, they could regulate markets, wages, and prices. The ministry itself, since the Reformation, became a prosperous professional group drawn from this same social stratum. This expansion of public roles for lairds and sons of lairds has led the sixteenth and early seventeenth centuries to be described as the period of 'the rise of the middling sort'.[12]

---

[10] J. Goodare, 'The nobility and the absolutist state in Scotland, 1584–1638', *History*, 78 (1993), 161–82, at pp. 166–70.

[11] *RPC* xii. 160–71, 177–83, 189–93; *Aberdeen Letters*, ii. 140–8.

[12] M. Lynch, *Scotland: A New History* (London, 1991), ch. 15. Lairds' involvement in government is discussed by R. R. Zulager, 'A Study of the Middle-Rank Administrators in the Government of King James VI of Scotland, 1580–1625', Ph.D. thesis (Aberdeen, 1991), ch. 3. For ministers see R. Mitchison, 'The social impact of the clergy of the reformed kirk of Scotland', *Scotia*, 6 (1982), 1–13, and W. Makey, *The Church of the Covenant, 1637–1651* (Edinburgh, 1979), ch. 7.

As differentiation between public and private increased, this had two effects. There was more of a distinctive public sphere, but also more of a distinctive private one. For the elite, marriage and estate management had traditionally been quasi-public matters, but now they became more private. Aristocratic marriage had been undertaken largely as an alliance between propertied interests, but now parental control was relaxed and a wider variety of personal motives came into play.[13] Men had traditionally had to give military service in person, but now they did not. They could still *choose* to fight personally—even the college of justice raised more than one regiment in the 1640s, apparently recruiting numerous junior and apprentice lawyers among its volunteers.[14] The way people worshipped had been a public, political act, but during the seventeenth century, religious pluralism increased and worship slowly began to be a private matter.[15] To sum up, then, there were three categories of activity: the wholly public; the wholly private; and activities that were both. Differentiation meant the reduction of this third category. The elite acquired more private life, and more exclusively public life.

The common folk, meanwhile, mainly acquired more public duties. Their sexual activities and magical practices were now regulated by the kirk session. Peasants' teinds were collected under a new statutory authority. Many of them acquired new landlords through the feuing movement, also regulated statutorily. They became taxpayers, not directly, but through lords passing on their own tax burdens to them—although in forms that probably looked like rent, and which were thus partly private. The only real forums for popular participation in government, the birlaw courts, were neither influential nor new in our period. The new experience for the common folk was to have a wider variety of specialized governmental bodies regulating their activities.[16]

---

[13] R. K. Marshall, *Virgins and Viragos: A History of Women in Scotland from 1080 to 1980* (London, 1983), ch. 3.

[14] E. M. Furgol, *A Regimental History of the Covenanting Armies, 1639–1651* (Edinburgh, 1990), 57–8, 124–7.

[15] See Ch. 10 below. Differentiation of social functions might also be elucidated by an analysis of the changing self-presentation of nobles and lairds in their religious setting, such as private pews and burial monuments. Cf. F. Heal and C. Holmes, *The Gentry in England and Wales, 1500–1700* (London, 1994), 335–41; J. G. Dunbar, 'The emergence of the reformed church in Scotland, c.1560–c.1700', in J. Blair and C. Pyrah (eds.), *Church Archaeology: Research Directions for the Future* (Council for British Archaeology, 1996).

[16] J. Goodare, *The Government of Scotland, 1560–1625* (forthcoming), ch. 10.

How powerful was the Scottish state in the late sixteenth and early seventeenth centuries? The expansion of the public sphere, and its extension downwards to the lower classes, were signs that the scope of government was expanding. However, quantifying power is a complex matter. Medieval governments could be fully capable of drastic action. They established burghs—sometimes on green-field sites, not just recognizing existing settlements. They were intimately involved in burgh administration—more so then than later, when the burghs won autonomy through feu-ferme charters. They reshaped the land law, perhaps inadvertently but still drastically, by introducing and then modifying pleadable brieves.[17] From time to time they recruited large armies. And so on. Medieval rulers could sometimes achieve *more* than the governments discussed in this book, or at least what they did achieve could be more dramatic. The celebrated states of antiquity, similarly, had occasionally built extraordinary monuments, or conquered and relocated entire peoples. Who could deny that the ancient Egyptian or Assyrian states were 'powerful'?

In medieval and ancient times, however, societies were simpler, and it was easier for rulers to lay their hands on the levers of power. When government has fewer enforcement agents, there tend also to be fewer countervailing centres of power. The sixteenth and seventeenth centuries had more complex social systems, which could sometimes impede the execution of the government's will. James VI himself was often limited in practice—sometimes more than his predecessors—by having to go through the proper channels. A king of the thirteenth or fourteenth century probably possessed the personal authority to cancel a noble's heritable jurisdiction, should he have wished; James believed he did not, at least not without the consent of parliament, which he knew he would be unlikely to obtain.[18]

So the question 'How powerful was the early modern state?' may be a vital one, but it cannot be answered as it stands. Power is not abstract: it is power to achieve a specific goal. To measure this

[17] E. L. Ewan, 'The community of the burgh in the fourteenth century', in M. Lynch *et al.* (eds.), *The Scottish Medieval Town* (Edinburgh, 1988), 228–30; H. L. MacQueen, *Common Law and Feudal Society in Medieval Scotland* (Edinburgh, 1993), chs. 4–7.

[18] The exception was a unique heritable justiciarship, cancelled by parliament in 1584: *APS* iii. 357–60, c. 24. For the royal cancellation of a regality in the 1360s see MacQueen, *Common Law and Feudal Society*, 56.

power, we have first to identify the goals to which it sought to direct itself.

In the early modern period, the goals of government were growing in number. It targeted an increasing variety of groups—to get them to modify their behaviour, or to seek their support for certain official activities, or (in extreme cases) to exterminate them physically. The following list of goals concentrates on ends, rather than means, and thus does not discuss the state's efforts to construct or reconstruct its own institutions. The list is not exhaustive, but it may bring out some of the patterns involved. The items are not given in order of importance—but neither is the order random.

1. Nobles and lairds were pressured to end their feuds and to submit their disputes to royal justice.
2. Catholics were persecuted after 1560.
3. All the propertied classes were called upon regularly to pay taxes, the proceeds of which were redistributed to a group of privileged courtiers. Government office-holding was to become a more important route to wealth, through receipt of state revenues and other privileges like monopolies.
4. The landed classes were occasionally required to provide fighting men for state service, while at the same time the towns were asked for money for this purpose.
5. Autonomous kin-groups in the Highlands and Borders were put under pressure to submit to royal authority.
6. Creditors and debtors had their relationship regulated with increasing sophistication.
7. Traders were put under pressure to use the official open market, and to refrain from clandestine or unregulated trading, in order to benefit consumers.
8. Tacksmen and titulars of teinds (that is, their lessees and lessors) were called upon to regularize their relationship with one another, and to provide higher stipends for ministers.
9. Presbyterians were persecuted after 1596.
10. Adulterers, fornicators, sabbath-breakers, and other moral transgressors were subjected to ecclesiastical discipline.
11. Vagrants were persecuted in an attempt to get them to accept masters.

12. Gypsies, in the same spirit, were banished from the country.

13. Witches were periodically hunted, and executed when found.

The first five goals on this list affected, in theory, all classes except the poorest, but in practice their success depended on the attitude of the elite. So long as the nobles did not object to taxes, there would be taxes: so long as Catholic magnates resisted conversion, Catholic lairds and lesser folk connected with them would do the same. Numbers 6 to 9 affected, broadly, the middle ranks of society. The few presbyterian nobles were excluded from power, but were not actively persecuted; indeed there was much less persecution of lay presbyterians than of lay Catholics, and heavy coercion of presbyterians was experienced mainly by the ministers. (Catholic nobles had a wide variety of experience: some were intermittently persecuted, but some—indeed some of the same ones— were intermittently admitted to the inner circles of the royal court, as presbyterians rarely were.) The final four groups targeted were largely lower-class.[19]

Most of these goals were new. The only ones that had been pursued with vigour before 1560 were numbers 4 and 7, and pre-echoes of numbers 6 and 11 can also be found. In the period 1560–1625, the goals of the state thus expanded dramatically. Moreover, the state obtained a monopoly in most of these fields; in medieval times, even the exercise of violence (number 4) had been shared with nobles who could use it independently of the state structure, while aspects of the regulation of trade (number 7) had also been a concern of church courts that were not answerable to the state. Achieving this monopoly was part of what it meant to become a sovereign state.

It may be asked how far the policies on this list succeeded. The broad answer is that they all succeeded, if only to a modest extent in many cases; policies that had no noticeable effect have been excluded from the list. To be sure, there were statutes passed with little more than symbolic intent, such as the sumptuary laws; there were also initiatives that failed, such as the crown's attempt in 1575

---

[19] Further details of those goals not discussed in this book will be found in Goodare, *Government*, ch. 10.

to create a controlling interest in the salt trade.[20] Here, however, we are discussing policies that made an impact. They did not necessarily have total success—Catholics were not eliminated, and neither were vagrants—but they formed a structure of coercion that could not be ignored. The range of effective state action had broadened dramatically.

Why did early modern states take this increased workload upon themselves? This is such a big question that it is almost impossible to answer, even schematically. Saying this does not make the question disappear, but only a schematic answer can be attempted here; it is for European historians to integrate the material presented in this book into their own general interpretations. There are several possible approaches, which would involve a discussion of such trends as the rise of Western individualism, perhaps linked to the impact of Protestantism, ideological ferment, and incipient religious pluralism; the growth of literacy and print culture; the spread of capitalism; or the increase in population, and the inflation that came with it, breaking down traditional structures. In these terms, even the rise of the sovereign state may seem like a dependent variable.[21] Perhaps we should not think of the state as initiating changes in the early modern period, so much as responding to them. In this view, the state expanded to meet needs that had previously been met in some other way, or to take advantage of new opportunities. New ideologies, new technologies, new economic resources and practices: all could be shaped into tools of power, and those tools could be used by the state.

These tools, moreover, can be identified. State power can be broken down into its component parts. There are three broad types of power—ideological, economic, and military. The driving force behind laws, commands, and other acts of political influence or coercion can largely be summed up as: Do this because it is right, or legitimate, or necessary for salvation; do it because you will be rewarded financially if you do; do it because you will be killed if you don't. Most states use all three types of power. Most of them also claim a monopoly of military power, while some also

---

[20] F. J. Shaw, 'Sumptuary legislation in Scotland', *JR* NS 24 (1979), 81–115; for salt, see Ch. 4 above.

[21] Cf. E. Gellner, *Plough, Sword and Book: The Structure of Human History* (London, 1988), chs. 4–5.

seek to monopolize ideological or economic power. On the other hand, no type of power—even military—has always been the exclusive preserve of the state, as the history of early modern Scotland testifies.[22]

Each type of power is exercised, whether by states or others, using specific and identifiable resources. Ideological power relies on ideas, and means to disseminate them; economic power, obviously, on money and productive resources; and military power on troops. Sometimes these resources are convertible into one another, as when money is used to pay troops, or propaganda is issued to encourage them to fight, or when the troops are used to enforce tax collection. However, the three forms are not *reducible* to a single 'ultimate' form of power. There do exist conceptual systems in which power 'ultimately' exists in just one form—either ideology (currently fashionable theories of power as 'discourse' are like this), or economics (some forms of Marxism posit an 'economic base' to society, leaving everything else as 'superstructure'), or military force (a common-sense view of the superiority of the swordsman to the moneybags or ideologue in a one-to-one confrontation can be extended inappropriately into a general principle of 'ultimate' military control). Such conceptual systems are often valuable, particularly in the analysis of specific societies in which one of the three forms of power happens to predominate; but they cannot provide the whole story, which is that power is three-dimensional.

It should be mentioned that this threefold scheme does not solve all our conceptual problems. Some state activities are harder to fit into it: in particular, what about the exercise of judicial power? To some extent it is ideological—a law court has to be recognized as legitimate. But it can also be economic, using its authority to re-allocate disputed resources. And it even takes on a military aspect when physical coercion is used to enforce the court's decrees.

[22] This classification owes much to M. Mann, 'The autonomous power of the state: Its origins, mechanisms and results', in J. A. Hall (ed.), *States in History* (Oxford, 1986). Cf. also id., *The Sources of Social Power*, i. *A History of Power from the Beginning to ad 1760* (Cambridge, 1986), 22–7, where it is stated that there are *four* 'sources' of power, because the state itself (though using the other three sources) forms a distinctive power source. This seems unnecessarily complicated for the present purpose. Comments on this, and a similar tripartite division of types of power into 'economic', 'normative' (i.e. ideological), and 'political' (involving violent coercion), are given by G. Poggi, *The State: Its Nature, Development and Prospects* (Cambridge, 1990), ch. 1. On law as command, see Ch. 1 above.

Perhaps there would be a case for seeing judicial power—the ability to settle disputes—as a category of power in its own right. This might also provide a route into a contractual view of some of the state's activities, to set against the common view of the state as generally coercive.[23] However, this chapter must evaluate the Scottish evidence, and cannot aspire to settle all these theoretical questions. State power is not a tidy concept, and there will always be loose ends.

What is particularly important for the present analysis is that power is not static or finite. Power resources—means of exercising power—tend to accumulate, as people seek to increase their power. But they do not necessarily accumulate *in the hands of the state alone*. The state *may* control them, but not always. Non-state groups may have money, and refuse to let the state have a share; persuasive ideas may arise that set limits to what the state should do. Or then again they may not. Power resources, once created, may be appropriated by the state, or they may leak away into civil society. The power balance between state and civil society varies, even though the sum total of power has a long-term tendency to increase. There are thus two questions which must be asked. What power resources are available in each of the three categories (ideological, economic, military); and how much of this power is in the hands of the state? These questions are easier to pose than to answer systematically, but it may help to bear them in mind in what follows.

An outline of the newly created power resources of the sixteenth century might run as follows. In ideology, there were vast strides. New, compelling systems of religious belief and practice were created, with Calvinism having particular resonance in Scotland. More secular ideologies included resistance theory and the divine right of kings, both of which saw much of their development work done in Scotland. The expansion of an educated laity went hand in hand with the growth of the legal profession, and the idea that disputes could and should be settled in courts of law. The economy was transformed by the expansion of population and the restructuring of landed estates, with feuing of land helping to create a more absolute form of property in Scotland. This was followed by the creation of large estates run primarily for cash returns, and by

---

[23] Cf. R. G. Holcombe, *The Economic Foundations of Government* (London, 1994), 54–61.

the growth of overseas trade. Population growth placed the common people in a weaker bargaining position *vis-à-vis* their landlords and employers, enhancing the ability of elites to extract resources from them. The state with its taxes had the prospect of sharing in this economic power. Military developments were many, both in the equipment of fighting forces (firearms) and their organization (drill and manoeuvre). Another striking technological development of the century, printing, was mainly of use in disseminating ideology, but printing was useful for decrees on taxation or wapinshawings as well as for sermons and legal treatises. Let us investigate the growth of these power resources one by one, beginning with ideological power.

The power of ideas is easily overlooked, even though it pervaded early modern society.[24] It is not enough to treat power as the mere exercise of will in a vacuum. Even if (as Justinian's maxim had it) what pleased the prince had the force of law, the prince's pleasure was determined in a number of practical contexts which might severely circumscribe his actions. Machiavelli's prince knew that he might wish to do a thing but find it politically unwise. And even the things he was likely to *wish* to do would tend to be shaped (even if he knew his Machiavelli) by what people around him were saying that he ought to wish to do, which in practice meant that his wishes would tend to conform to the dominant value-systems of the time. Princes who wished to distance themselves from Machiavelli, like James VI, had an even stronger sense of the limitations on what they *ought* to do, however much they insisted that their theoretical power was unlimited.[25] Power may reside in the will, but it is also present in systems of thought, culture, and belief.

So the power of ideas is not simply a power imposed from on high. On the other hand, not all ideas were powerful. Anyone can have ideas, but only some people can get their ideas disseminated in influential form. Wide dissemination was possible without the written word—folk-tales crossed continents; but folk culture, orally transmitted, was separate from the culture of the elite. Scottish folk culture had more in common with folk culture elsewhere in

[24] A recent book on state formation by Charles Tilly deals with military and economic power much in the way that the present chapter does, but has little or no discussion of ideas: C. Tilly, *Coercion, Capital and European States, AD 990–1990* (Oxford, 1990). For ways in which ideology relates to social action, see T. Eagleton, *Ideology: An Introduction* (London, 1991), ch. 2.

[25] Cf. Goodare, *Government*, chs. 2, 4.

Europe than with Scottish high culture.[26] Moreover, to carry authority, ideas had to be systematic. This needed writing, education, and usually printing. The main alternative to printing was the pulpit, the occupants of which also required education. Intellectuals and disseminators of ideas in civil society thus tended to have some connection with established power structures, and the ideas they circulated tended to endorse those structures.

This was perhaps especially so from the perspective of the common people. Although the political ideas that they heard from officials and church ministers were not the only ideas that the lower classes had, they were credible ones, and more systematic than possible alternatives. The rising tide of clashing ideologies that the sixteenth century experienced did not, by and large, overflow into areas that might have upset the position of the elite as a whole. The most that was proposed by ideological dissidents was the kind of realignment of power that would upset the balance within the propertied classes. Such ideas could still be dangerously subversive, of course, if they convinced enough propertied people. The point to note just now is that the power of ideas was not simply coercive—with ideas being dictated from on high—but neither was it simply subversive. Rather it involved a tacitly negotiated consensus between the thinkers, who produced the ideas, and the rulers, who used them. The site for these negotiations was a client–patron relationship, since thinkers sought patrons who would buy their ideas. The resulting consensus was not always happy or complete; the ideological disagreement between James VI and his tutor, George Buchanan, is an important case to which we will return.

In sixteenth-century Scotland, the traditional systems of thought, culture, and belief about the nature of government were aristocratic. Men with great estates, men with a host of kinsfolk and dependants, were the natural rulers. The chivalric ideal in its classic form—martial prowess, loyalty, courtesy, generosity—began to wear a little thin after the Reformation, but parts of it retained vigour and were adapted to new uses.[27] Loyalty, in particular, was a value that could be transferred from the feudal lord to the court patron, the royal dynasty, and even the state. The absolutist state

[26] D. Buchan, 'Folk tradition and literature till 1603', in J. D. McClure and M. R. G. Spiller (eds.), *Bryght Lanternis: Essays on the Language and Literature of Medieval and Renaissance Scotland* (Aberdeen, 1989), 3.

[27] For the chivalric virtues see M. Keen, *Chivalry* (New Haven, 1984), 2–11.

could almost be defined as a polity in which men were loyal to aristocratic patrons within a strong framework of central authority.

The basis and model for traditional ideas of loyalty was kinship. Kinship was embedded in social practices, and needed no elaborate discussion or debate. (Other ideas were much talked about but rarely acted on—including, as many preachers might reluctantly have conceded, many of the things that people were told to do in sermons.) Kinship operated in various ways. It provided solidarity for militarized groups, and stable transmission of landed estates. Bonds of manrent created quasi-kin relations of 'friendship' and alliance to extend client networks beyond kinsfolk; kinsfolk themselves did not need to make bonds to one another.[28] Clientage within state institutions was similarly based on acts of ostensible *friendship*, not necessarily the same as kinship but not opposed to it. Absolute monarchy drew on kinship ideas—but less so than earlier forms of power. Many of the values of kinship fed into the practice of the bloodfeud, which the state sought to suppress.

An aristocratic value-system nevertheless continued to favour a government that worked in the interests of the aristocracy. The special privileges of the leading nobility were their access to the royal court, and recognition for their client networks. Client networks, once demilitarized, could become a valued means of arbitrating on allocation of office and patronage. Territorial magnates retained their special position even after they lost the autonomous military power on which their pre-eminence traditionally rested. They no longer settled their followers' disputes directly, but they influenced the courts. Instead of military leadership, they provided leadership in politics and administration. Indeed they could still provide military leadership, so long as they did so in armies controlled by the state.

Those ideas of the pre-Reformation church that related to secular power were fully in tune with this kinship-based system. The central feature of the fifteenth-century church was the proliferation of prayers and masses for the dead. This meant many things, but one of them was very much to do with kinship. The prayers and masses were provided by living relatives, to assist and to placate

---

[28] J. Wormald, *Lords and Men in Scotland: Bonds of Manrent, 1442–1603* (Edinburgh, 1985), 76 and *passim*.

their ancestors.[29] How this related to power is not easy to trace, but it is worth pointing out that one of the most important functions of the church was to regulate marriage. Over this vital matter for kinship and inheritance, the church possessed wide discretion. Marriage was normally prohibited between couples related in the fourth degree of consanguinity (broadly speaking, those with a common great-great-grandparent), but papal dispensations were available to permit marriages up to the second degree (those with a common grandparent). This also allowed broad scope for annulments of unsuitable marriages—a process sanctioned and policed by the church.[30]

This was a matter of real power. Regulating marriage meant adjudicating on legitimacy, and thus on inheritance of property and title. This power could be put to remarkably direct use. In the political crisis of 1543, one of the means by which Cardinal Beaton wielded influence over the regent, the earl of Arran, was his ability to investigate the questionable legality of the marriage of Arran's parents.[31] After the Reformation, the prohibition on marriage was reduced to the second degree of consanguinity, and the dispensing power was abandoned. This drastically reduced the church's field of discretion—and thus its influence over kinship.[32]

As well as abandoning these traditional ideas, the new Protestant church was also creating new means of exercising power. By the time of the Scottish Reformation, events on the Continent had demonstrated that the Protestant movement could be socially subversive, but also that it could form working alliances with secular rulers. The movement sought such an alliance eagerly. With the support of these rulers, the Protestant leadership could credibly aim, not only

[29] G. Donaldson, *The Faith of the Scots* (London, 1990), 47–51. The living relatives would eventually use the Reformation to renege on their traditional commitments: cf. C. Richmond, 'The English gentry and religion, *c.*1500', in C. Harper-Bill (ed.), *Religious Belief and Ecclesiastical Careers in Late Medieval England* (Woodbridge, 1991), 143–4; J. Bossy, *Christianity in the West, 1400–1700* (Oxford, 1985), ch. 2.

[30] For full details of the system see William Hay, *Lectures on Marriage*, ed. J. C. Barry (Stair Society, 1967), 185–247; for examples of its operation see B. Seton, 'The distaff side: A study in matrimonial adventure in the fifteenth and sixteenth centuries', *SHR* 17 (1920), 272–86.

[31] M. H. B. Sanderson, *Cardinal of Scotland: David Beaton, c.1494–1546* (Edinburgh, 1986), 154, 165–6.

[32] For challenges subsequently posed for the *criminal* courts through the continued use of canon law, see W. D. H. Sellar, 'Marriage, divorce and the forbidden degrees: Canon law and Scots law', in W. N. Osborough (ed.), *Explorations in Law and History* (Dublin, 1994).

to have its own forms of doctrine and worship professed in churches, but also to inculcate its values into the hearts and minds of the people. Thus was born the ideal of the godly state.

How the godly state was to be achieved was hotly debated, particularly in Scotland where the Reformation was initially accomplished by a revolution against established authority. The names of three thinkers stand out in this debate: John Knox, George Buchanan, and King James VI. Their ideas were not entirely new (some components of them went back centuries), but what mattered was the way in which they were applied to the new conditions.[33]

Knox in the 1550s had to promote the Protestant cause in the face of committed Catholic monarchs. He appealed to the 'lesser magistrates' or the 'nobilitie and estates', who had a recognized position within the state and could thus legitimize resistance to the monarch. Buchanan's political works, published in 1579–82, took this further and immediately became key texts for Calvinist resistance theory. He based his ideas on earlier accounts of the magnates censuring and deposing unsuitable kings, particularly the history of Scotland by Hector Boece (1527). However, Boece had no consistent political vision, and the story he told was essentially a moral one in which degenerate kings met their just deserts. Exactly how they came to do so mattered little to him. Buchanan argued that the just deserts were meted out by the *estates*, probably drawing here on the ideas of his old teacher, the conciliarist theologian John Mair. Historians have tended to represent Buchanan as wanting the power of the crown limited by 'the magnates', omitting the point that it was the magnates *assembled in parliament* to whom he assigned the legal power to act. He also endorsed tyrannicide by an individual, but only once the tyrant had been denounced by parliament.[34] Buchanan thus came close

[33] For what follows, see in general J. H. Burns, *The True Law of Kingship: Concepts of Monarchy in Early-Modern Scotland* (Oxford, 1996), chs. 4–6; R. A. Mason, '*Rex Stoicus*: George Buchanan, James VI and the Scottish polity', in J. Dwyer *et al.* (eds.), *New Perspectives on the Politics and Culture of Early Modern Scotland* (Edinburgh, n.d. [1982]); id. 'George Buchanan, James VI and the presbyterians', id. (ed.), *Scots and Britons: Scottish Political Thought and the Union of 1603* (Cambridge, 1994); Q. Skinner, 'The origins of the Calvinist theory of revolution', in B. Malament (ed.), *After the Reformation* (Manchester, 1980); A. Williamson, *Scottish National Consciousness in the Age of James VI* (Edinburgh, 1979).

[34] J. H. Burns, 'Institution and ideology: The Scottish estates and resistance theory', Institute of Historical Research, Electronic Seminars in History (archived 29 July 1997 at http://ihr.sas.ac.uk/ihr/esh/estate.html).

to saying that the basis of the Scottish constitution was the right of parliament to elect and depose kings. Certainly this is what contemporaries widely understood him to be saying. Not only was this a high claim for the power of parliament, but it also launched the idea that parliament and crown could be rivals for supreme authority.

Both Knox and Buchanan wrote before the 1580s, a crucial decade for the transformation of the Scottish parliament into a primarily legislative body. Thereafter their ideas on this became, if anything, more relevant. They were taken up by later presbyterians, who fused them with their own concern to establish the Scottish church on a secure legislative footing. To do this they did not simply seek statutes in their favour (although they were never backward in lobbying for legislation), but also developed the idea of Scotland as a covenanted nation that had made a binding agreement with God. These early 'covenants', such as the anti-Catholic 'King's Confession' of 1581, were interpreted as permanent, corporate commitments. The covenanting idea developed to some extent in parallel with secular ideas of law and legislation, since both were inimical to ideas of kin loyalty as traditionally understood.[35]

The divine right of kings was promoted in Scotland by James VI himself or in association with him, drawing on Continental ideas and imagery. For James, it was a deliberate response to Knox, Buchanan, and the presbyterians. It exalted the authority of the state, and immunized it from human alteration. The crown was placed firmly above parliament, above the church, and above the magnates too. James advised his son to persuade the magnates 'to thinke, that the chiefest point of their honour standeth in striving with the meanest of the land in humilitie towards you and obedience to your lawes'. The laws were the king's laws, and James claimed to be sole legislator, saying (not entirely accurately) that parliament was merely an advisory body.[36] At the same time he sought supreme authority over the church, and spent much of his reign making church government more hierarchical and its worship more ceremonial.

These ideas all had implications for the social and political position of the nobility as the sixteenth century drew to a close.

[35] Williamson, *Scottish National Consciousness*, 64–81.
[36] James VI, *Basilicon Doron*, in *Political Writings*, 29; Goodare, *Government*, ch. 4.

According to Roger Mason, there were circulating by then no less than four alternative models of noble conduct. As well as a traditional 'feudal-baronial' nobility, based on martial and chivalric values, there were ideas of a 'civic humanist' nobility, imbued with classical virtues and promoting the welfare of the community; a 'Calvinist' nobility, espousing the cause of the Protestant movement; and an 'absolutist' nobility, dependent on the crown and serving in the central administration.[37] Some of these tended to overlap. In particular the absolutist ideal could absorb much of the chivalric ethos through notions of service and loyalty, while civic humanism and Calvinism worked well together.

If ideas about the nobility were in flux, ideas about religion were disputed with vigour and conviction. One result of this conflict was that the state could not rely on the church to preach ideas of obedience. The typical Sunday sermon as such does not survive, but there is no reason to think that it would have contained more on the subject of obedience than more widely reported or published products. Presbyterians preached forcefully about obedience to the laws, but this was not the same as obedience to the king. They were likely to demand that the king act to punish malefactors, and to threaten him publicly with divine retribution for backsliding in this task.[38] Far from welcoming this zeal for law and order, James regarded it as seditious and tried to suppress it. But he seems not to have been able to replace it with a strain of sermonizing that would teach subjects their place more directly. Two sermons preached in the royal presence by Bishop William Cowper in 1617 said much in praise of the king's qualities, but nothing on the subject's duty to obey him.[39] It seems that Scottish governments may have been unable to 'tune their pulpits' as successfully as Queen Elizabeth was said to do.

So a desire to promote loyalty and obedience was surely an important aspect of the drive by early seventeenth-century Scottish governments to revise the form of worship, through liturgy and ceremony. A weekly prayer for the king had been included in editions of the *Book of Common Order* since 1575, but its tone was uncomfortably monitory: 'kepe him farre of[f] from ignorance . . .

[37] R. A. Mason, 'Imagining Scotland: Scottish political thought and the problem of Britain, 1560–1650', in id. (ed.), *Scots and Britons*, 10–12.

[38] e.g. Calderwood, *History*, v. 129–30, 337–8.

[39] William Cowper, *Workes* (2nd edn., London, 1629), 782–3, 788–90.

so instruct him . . . that his humane Majestie always obey thy Divine Majestie in feare and dreade'. Revised draft liturgies from the 1610s onwards were more deferential.[40] The Five Articles of Perth (1618) introduced some important ceremonies into the church, notably the controversial requirement to kneel at communion. Unfortunately, the attempt to enforce the new worship produced dogged and intractable resistance, throwing the spotlight on the *lack* of loyalty and obedience possessed by many people.[41]

In the ideas that the church promoted among the common people, the exercise of power was more consensual. Through moral discipline, aspects of Protestant Christianity were enforced among the common folk—sexual morality above all, but also sabbath observance and sobriety. This system of values may not have inspired ready or willing compliance among those on the receiving end of kirk session discipline, but it *was* consensual among the elite, because it was semi-detached from more contentious aspects of religious ideology. It was not an essential component of the broad Protestant cosmic vision, because it could play little direct role in the apocalyptic conflict with Antichrist that was expected to occupy the Protestant powers in the approaching final days of the world.[42] What moral discipline could do was to give the leaders of the church—bishops and parish ministers—a local power base. They did so through an alliance with lairds as kirk session elders, who gained power that they valued in disciplining their tenants. To the extent that this local discipline was linked with the ideal of the godly state at national level, the attraction of Protestantism among the folk of lesser property was enhanced. This is one of the ways in which conflict over ideology occurred primarily within the elite—although the resistance to the Five Articles of Perth sometimes involved the common people too.

To the state, economic power basically meant taxes. The state in our period, particularly after about 1590, extracted a larger proportion of the country's resources than before, and its ability to reward its supporters was correspondingly increased. The fiscal

---

[40] W. McMillan, *The Worship of the Scottish Reformed Church, 1550–1638* (London, 1931), 61–2; Knox, *Works*, vi. 379–80; 'A Scottish liturgy of the reign of James VI', ed. G. Donaldson, *SHS Miscellany*, x (1965), 95, 100; G. Donaldson, *The Making of the Scottish Prayer Book of 1637* (Edinburgh, 1954), 141–2.

[41] P. H. R. Mackay, 'The reception given to the Five Articles of Perth', *RSCHS* 19 (1977), 185–201.

[42] Williamson, *Scottish National Consciousness*, 55–6.

developments of the reign of James VI have been discussed
in Chapter 4: they included the establishment of regular parliamentary taxation on land, the imposition of customs on imports,
the raising of the customs rates to unprecedented heights, and
the taxation of annual rents (interest payments and annuities).
The state's power had not only increased, but had become
more fully differentiated from other forms of economic power.
Together with the alienation of many revenues from land, this
added up to a fundamental transition from a 'domain state' to
a 'tax state'.[43]

It would have been too much to expect this new fiscal system to
function smoothly. The edifice of parliamentary taxation had been
erected on the foundations of outdated medieval assessments that
had never been designed for regular taxation. The customs were
more effective, particularly in the first two decades of the seventeenth century when trade was expanding rapidly. But this
expansion was not sustained, and after 1625 most official effort
was directed down the fiscal cul-de-sac of Charles I's revocation
scheme. This aimed to recover some landed revenues, but became
bogged down in delays and red tape.[44]

One way of illuminating the state's economic structure is to look
at its role in exercising authority over peasants. One of the main
originators of the concept of the absolutist state, Perry Anderson,
has described it as '*a redeployed and recharged apparatus of feudal dom-
ination*, designed to clamp the peasant masses back into their traditional social position ... a *displacement* of politico-legal coercion
upwards towards a centralized, militarized summit'.[45] This would
seem to represent a shift of coercive power from the private to the
public sphere, or perhaps a differentiation into private and public.
Professor Anderson's theory cannot be accepted as it stands,
because the reason he gives is the ending of serfdom and the com-
mutation of labour services, calling for new forms of coercive
control. In fact, most states in western Europe saw a gap of at least
a century between the decline of serfdom and the rise of the absolutist state; in Scotland it was as much as two centuries. In

---

[43] Cf. E. L. Petersen, 'From domain state to tax state', *Scandinavian Economic
History Review*, 23 (1975), 116–48.

[44] A. I. Macinnes, *Charles I and the Making of the Covenanting Movement, 1625–1641*
(Edinburgh, 1991), ch. 3.

[45] P. Anderson, *Lineages of the Absolutist State* (London, 1974), 18–19. Emphasis
in original.

seventeenth-century France, as David Parker has commented, all the authorities shared a 'firm understanding that matters pertaining to peasants should not be dealt with in the higher courts'. The seigneurial courts dealt with peasants' cases, and the central judicial machinery of the state was not routinely deployed to control the peasants, although peasant uprisings were suppressed by royal armies. Direct state intervention in French village life, bypassing the seigneurs, began only in the late seventeenth and early eighteenth centuries. But the French state had had *economic* power over peasants since 1439, through the *taille*.[46] In the fiscal sphere, narrowly defined, Professor Anderson's chronological scheme has a good deal to recommend it—at least for France, often regarded as the typical absolutist state.

Early modern Scotland took a different path from France, although arguably it was still absolutist. Landlords had to share *judicial* power over their peasants with the state—more so than in France—but retained their *economic* power. Kirk sessions began to enforce moral discipline directly on peasants in the late sixteenth century; magnates, who were not session elders, did not control this process, though it certainly helped if landlords cooperated in it. Lords were also supervised by the state in the operation of their own baron and regality courts. The lords' former monopoly of judicial power over peasants had been broken. But the state failed to tax the peasants directly, although there were occasional proposals to do so. The most notable was a scheme for a sales tax on grain, cattle, and sheep in 1599, which was blocked by the shire commissioners in a convention of estates.[47] Only in 1644, with the establishment of the excise, did the state acquire significant rural revenues that bypassed lords.

This may be related to the question of economic rivalry between lords and state. In France, although lords and state usually cooperated, some rivalry was inescapable, since the state sought taxes from peasants who were the lords' tenants. The heavier the taxes, the less surplus would remain to be collected as rent. In Scotland, extraction of taxation from peasants was done indirectly, *through*

[46] D. Parker, 'Class, clientage and personal rule in absolutist France', *Seventeenth Century French Studies*, 9 (1987), 192–213, at p. 204; H. L. Root, *Peasants and King in Burgundy: Agrarian Foundations of French Absolutism* (Berkeley and Los Angeles, 1987), ch. 2; M. Wolfe, *The Fiscal System of Renaissance France* (New Haven, 1972), app. 2.

[47] Ashton to Cecil, 16 Dec. 1599, *CSP Scot.* xiii, 1. 584.

the lords. Only after 1644 did the state tax the lower classes directly. As we shall see in Chapter 10, the excise was the mainstay of the state between 1661 and 1678, when there was little or no land tax. In this period, the state could have been a rival to landlords. However, any worry the landlords experienced at this was probably outweighed by their satisfaction at the reduction of the land tax. As in France, they knew that they needed the state. State taxes falling on their tenants were not ideal, but were preferable to taxes falling on themselves.

Taxation in the early modern period was often used to pay troops; so this can serve to introduce the third type of power, namely military power. Military coercion was important—not because the Scottish state acquired a large military machine, but because it acquired a small one that was directly under its own control, and because alternative sources of military power—the military followings of great lords—declined. The shift of military power from autonomous nobles to the state was one of the most momentous transitions of the early modern period. Scotland initially lagged behind most of its neighbours, achieving this transition only in the decades around 1600, but it caught up rapidly. By 1625 it had a military machine very much like those of its neighbours in structure, although much smaller in size.

Does the small scale of military development in Scotland indicate a failure in this area of state formation? Undoubtedly it does. Early modern states were organized for warfare first and last; the emerging European state system was fiercely competitive, and those lands that failed to vindicate their territory militarily, from Brittany to Hungary, risked losing their independence. Scotland did not need a large military establishment in the period 1560–1625 because it had already lost some of its independence— but this happened less spectacularly than in some states, and the consequences for the political establishment were less drastic. A brief phase of dependence on France was succeeded in 1560 by dependence on England, which was occasionally challenged but never overthrown. Within the English diplomatic stockade, the Scottish state lacked natural predators, and led a more tranquil existence than many. It did not aspire to foreign conquests within Europe, and those states that might have attacked it were mainly interested in doing so as a route to attack England. Scotland's low-pressure military system was possible because it was not designed for the full range of tasks that a seventeenth-century war machine might be expected to fulfil.[48]

The period between 1595 and 1601, when it seemed that Scotland might be invaded by Spain, or drawn into a war for the English succession, was the exception to this rule. It was then that the only serious attempts were made to convert Scotland's tattered collection of military traditions into a full-scale killing machine on Continental lines. Although the wapinshawings of the 1590s had their comic-opera aspect, and were never likely to achieve their primary purpose of fighting and winning a major war, they were not wholly ineffective; they formed part of a programme that finally eclipsed the traditional common army. Instead of private recruitment by lords of their own feudal followings, there would eventually be armies recruited by public authority and paid by the state. But only when armies were needed—which in the later years of James VI they rarely were.

So the rule that states were shaped primarily by armies did not always hold good. There certainly *was* a Scottish state, even though it had little of an army; other chapters of this book have shown that. It is conventional to assume that early modern territorial states succeeded largely through warfare, with the strong destroying and incorporating the weak. This could sometimes happen, but as Hendrik Spruyt observes, many small and weak states survived, particularly in Germany. While not denying that warfare contributed to the integration of the sovereign state, he also points to the role of diplomacy and of *systems* of states. Small states could be swallowed up by larger neighbours, but might instead be protected by them against third parties. Here it was important to have the same *type* of state as one's neighbours: it allowed efficient diplomacy. The Hanseatic League, which as a federation of towns was a different type of state, was constantly hampered in its diplomatic affairs, and was ultimately superseded by territorial states. Many of those states were small, but they were integrated into wider systems.[49] Scotland from 1560 to 1707 might be seen from this point of view as part of an English, or perhaps sometimes Anglo-Dutch, state system.

---

[48] See Ch. 5 above.

[49] H. Spruyt, *The Sovereign State and its Competitors* (Princeton, 1994), ch. 8. Cf. M. Braddick, 'State formation and social change in early modern England: A problem stated and approaches suggested', *Social History*, 16 (1991), 1–17, at pp. 6–7.

Just as general theories of state formation must be able to explain the German petty states as well as France, so they should take in states with modest military systems as well as those that felt constantly impelled to fight wars *à outrance*. Scotland's system of public war-making may have been diminutive, but in the early seventeenth century, private war-making was even less significant. Not only did the bloodfeud gradually fade away, but while it lasted it never adopted the latest military methods. Lords' followings remained small and lightly armed; in most feuds they were counted in tens, more rarely in hundreds.[50] Neither the royal guard nor the Border guard ever suffered any serious defeats in their campaigns to police Scottish elites between 1603 and 1621.

Within limits, then, Scotland's modest war machine was a success. Although the objectives of state violence were limited by Continental standards, such violence was deployed in our period in order to achieve a wide range of objectives—and the list began gradually to be lengthened in the early seventeenth century. From the Anglo-Scottish peace of 1551 up to the 1590s, the military force of the Scottish state was used only against internal rebellion, and the structural differences between the official and rebel forces were sometimes hard to detect. From then on, it could be used to suppress private warfare more assertively, and to promote state control in the outlying regions of the country. This was wholly successful in the Borders and in Orkney, and had some impact even in the Highlands. Paid royal troops, even a couple of hundred strong or fewer, were now very different from the forces they opposed; they had the latest equipment, while their opponents were lightly armed in traditional fashion.

Most significantly of all, military force was now regularly used to coerce those who failed to obey administrative orders, even if their disobedience fell well short of violent resistance. During an outbreak of plague in Edinburgh in 1597, the privy council granted a commission of justiciary to the burgh magistrates, allowing them to enforce quarantine regulations, and to impose a tax for 'ane ordinar force' to instil popular respect for their authority.[51] The Scottish war machine was never called on to repel foreign invasion, or to enforce the state's will on other states; it was not designed to

---

[50] The scanty evidence on size of followings is reviewed by Wormald, *Lords and Men*, 91–3. Occasionally, followings were counted in low thousands.

[51] *RPC* v. 411–12.

do so. But the royal guard was called on to collect the state's taxes; and this task *was* successfully accomplished.

However, even Scotland experienced some of the unwelcome side-effects of addiction to military force, despite the low dosages involved. All too often, European rulers found that maintaining their war machine itself forced them to make more demands of their subjects than was wise. James VI discovered this problem, to his fury and frustration, when his tax scheme in 1599–1600 was rejected by a convention of estates at heavy political cost to his regime. Charles I demanded military taxes at the outset of his reign, in 1625; he too was rebuffed. The convention of estates that did the damage this time was intractable on several other issues, but royal exactions lay behind most of them.[52] And behind royal exactions often lay warfare, actual or planned.

The power of the state had thus surmounted a number of obstacles in the reigns of Queen Mary and King James, and had reached a position of at least apparent stability by 1625. In the century after James's death, the Scottish state faced unprecedented challenges, and also gained some new opportunities. It will be the task of the next and final chapter to see how it responded.

---

[52] *APS* v. 175; Charles to council, 12 Feb. 1626, *The Earl of Stirling's Register of Royal Letters, 1615–1635*, 2 vols., ed. C. Rogers (Grampian Club, 1885), i. 18–19.

10

Perspectives on State Formation

Elizabeth ruled as much in Scotland as in England. She controlled the king not only in his childhood through Moray and successive regents but also in his adolescence and early manhood. She so managed him with the prospect of succeeding to her throne that the present union of the British crowns can be called her achievement.[1]

From the vantage-point of the 1720s, Sir John Clerk of Penicuik searched back for the roots of the parliamentary union of 1707 which he had helped to negotiate. He found them in the late sixteenth century. The Anglo-Scottish union is an important issue in itself, and there are several other issues relating to the state for which a long-term perspective is needed. This book has been centrally concerned with the period 1560–1625, and the early chapters have also discussed aspects of the previous century, between about 1469 and 1560. What this final chapter will do is to apply some of the methods and findings of this book to the *subsequent* century, up to about 1725. The result, although only an outline sketch, may illustrate some significant patterns in the development of the early modern state.

We begin by picking up some of the themes of the previous chapter: the three forms of state power—ideological, economic, and military power. This time we will look at how the resources of power developed during the period 1625–1725. This century contained at least five major landmarks: the creation of a new government by the covenanters in 1638–40; the English occupation of 1651; the Restoration of 1660; the Glorious Revolution of 1689; and the union of 1707. What new power resources did the state acquire at these dates, or in between them?

[1] Sir John Clerk of Penicuik, *History of the Union of Scotland and England*, ed. D. Duncan (SHS, 1993), 62–3.

The ideological trappings of the covenanting state were those of the opposition to James VI: a combination of radical presbyterianism and secular contract theory. Ascending principles of authority were firmly established in both church and state, with the general assembly restored to its role as a body of delegates, and the government placed securely in the hands of parliament. The royal prerogative was curtailed, and commitment to Calvinist zeal was made the test of fitness for political office—sometimes (as with the Act of Classes of 1649) with extraordinary thoroughness. The Solemn League and Covenant promoted both presbyterianism and parliamentary authority in both Scotland and England. Members of the nobility could exercise leadership in both parliament and assembly, but only if they were prepared to lead in the direction that the covenanting movement as a whole wished to go. The marquis of Hamilton and earl of Montrose were successively elbowed aside as the movement gathered momentum in the early 1640s; Hamilton was rehabilitated only much later, when its interests briefly happened to coincide with his in the Engagement. The 1640s was not a decade of deference to magnates.[2]

Formally, the Restoration regime based its claims to authority on its return to the governmental system of the 1630s. Certainly it did revive numerous aspects of this system, but it *chose* which of them to 'restore', and was as willing as any other regime to innovate when it chose. It should be regarded as essentially a new regime, though certainly a conservative one. Still, it was in the more rarefied fields of ideology that the most extravagantly reactionary claims were made. The trappings of authority were made as monarchical as possible. It was certainly a regime based very much on descending principles of authority.[3]

This was the last period of dominance for the ideology of the

---

[2] It is occasionally argued that votes were marshalled by magnates who retained real control. J. J. Scally, 'Constitutional revolution, party and faction in the Scottish parliaments of Charles I', *Parliamentary History*, 15 (1996), 54–73, puts the best possible case for this, based on the fact that two magnates (Hamilton and Argyll) headed the main parliamentary parties; but it is evident both that Argyll's party was generally more successful and that it lacked significant noble support.

[3] See in general R. Lee, 'Retreat from revolution: The Scottish parliament and the restored monarchy, 1661–1663', in J. R. Young (ed.), *Celtic Dimensions of the British Civil Wars* (Edinburgh, 1997); J. Patrick, 'A union broken? Restoration politics in Scotland', in J. Wormald (ed.), *Scotland Revisited* (London, 1991). On the role of parliament see J. Patrick, 'The origins of the opposition to Lauderdale in the Scottish parliament of 1673', *SHR* 53 (1974), 1–21.

divine right of kings. It was once more buried in 1689, this time permanently. The Claim of Right made it plain that parliament was now sovereign—that Scotland was a 'legal limited monarchy'. Both judiciary and parliament increased their independence from the crown; taxation required parliamentary consent; religion came fully under parliamentary control (thus assuring Protestant hegemony); and royalist interpretations of the prerogative were now impossible.[4]

The adoption of the language of political liberty, resistance to tyranny, and government by consent meant that the Scottish state after 1689 was using similar means of ideological legitimation to the English. It is not at present entirely clear how far these ideas were importations; there were often indigenous precedents available from the 1640s, but they were not always used. A small but clear example comes from the abolition of the estate of bishops in 1689, which used contemporary English ideas rather than precedents from the previous abolition of bishops in 1638–40. Ideological Anglicization, or perhaps convergence, continued for the next quarter-century at least. The English Habeas Corpus Act of 1679 was followed by a similar Scottish act 'anent wrongous imprisonment' in 1701. Between 1702 and 1714, recognizable Whig and Tory parties began to emerge in Scotland to complement those in England.[5]

---

[4] Surprisingly, there is no detailed study of the Claim of Right. It is printed with the related Articles of Grievances in *Source Book*, iii. 200–8, and its general political context is outlined in I. B. Cowan, 'Church and state reformed? The revolution of 1688–1689 in Scotland', in J. I. Israel (ed.), *The Anglo-Dutch Moment: Essays on the Glorious Revolution and its World Impact* (Cambridge, 1991). It is strangely absent from B. P. Lenman, 'The poverty of political theory in the Scottish Revolution of 1688–1690', in L. G. Schwoerer (ed.), *The Revolution of 1688–1689: Changing Perspectives* (Cambridge, 1992), apart from a paragraph dismissing it as 'not a radical but a conservative interpretation . . . a cautious neo-feudalism', on the alleged grounds that its forfeiture of James VII was a feudal procedure (p. 255). But parliament did not claim to be James's feudal superior.

In the circumstances, the ideological implications of the Claim of Right can best be understood through the implementation of its key demands. This was achieved through pressure from a radical parliamentary group, the 'Club', with a constitutional rather than ecclesiastical programme: J. Halliday, 'The Club and the Revolution in Scotland, 1689–1690', *SHR* 45 (1966), 143–59.

[5] J. Goodare, 'The estates in the Scottish parliament, 1286–1707', *Parliamentary History*, 15 (1996), 11–32, at pp. 29–30; P. G. B. McNeill, 'Habeas corpus in Scotland', *Scots Law Times (News)* (1960), 46–7; D. Hayton, 'Traces of party politics in early eighteenth-century Scottish elections', *Parliamentary History*, 15 (1996), 74–99.

Meanwhile, debates on the Scottish constitution paralleled those on the English one more closely than before. The basic question, as it had been since Buchanan, was whether the monarchy was absolute, or limited by parliament. Scottish Whig thinkers found less to say about the details of the medieval parliament than their English counterparts, but that did not mean they thought it was insignificant; Sir Edward Coke and his followers had been able to say even less about the Anglo-Saxon witenagemot, but it was still vital to their case for an 'ancient constitution'. Scottish Whigs were certain that parliament had exercised a check on early kings such as Robert III, Robert I, John Balliol, or the mythical Fergus I. Moreover, they asserted that the Scottish parliament had often determined the succession, as it had done in 1689.[6] This Anglicization had some paradoxical results. Even the opposition to the union of 1707 articulated by Andrew Fletcher of Saltoun was expressed in a language—classical republicanism—pioneered by James Harrington in Cromwellian England.[7]

Religious ideology declined in political importance during the second half of the century. This may seem a strange view to take when the Restoration regime had so many difficulties with covenanting dissidents. But the regime brought these difficulties on itself by committing itself to an unpopular episcopalian settlement. It was itself a firmly secular, aristocratic regime, determined not to allow churchmen to influence the government; bishops were seen (perhaps mistakenly) as the best way of keeping the lid screwed down on dissent. Bishops were given authority to implement ecclesiastical policy in their dioceses, but the *making* of ecclesiastical policy was kept firmly in the hands of the leading secular politicians.[8] As John Sommerville has pointed out for

---

[6] C. Kidd, *Subverting Scotland's Past: Scottish Whig Historians and the Creation of an Anglo-British Identity, 1689–c.1830* (Cambridge, 1993), 77–96. On Coke, see J. G. A. Pocock, *The Ancient Constitution and the Feudal Law* (2nd edn., Cambridge, 1987), 39–40; on Buchanan, see J. H. Burns, *The True Law of Kingship: Concepts of Monarchy in Early-Modern Scotland* (Oxford, 1996), 204–9.

[7] N. Phillipson, 'Politics, politeness and the anglicisation of early eighteenth-century Scottish culture', in R. A. Mason (ed.), *Scotland and England, 1286–1815* (Edinburgh, 1987), 228–9; cf. R. L. Emerson, 'Scottish cultural change, 1660–1710, and the union of 1707', in J. Robertson (ed.), *A Union for Empire: Political Thought and the British Union of 1707* (Cambridge, 1995).

[8] J. Buckroyd, 'Anti-clericalism in Scotland during the Restoration', in N. Macdougall (ed.), *Church, Politics and Society: Scotland, 1408–1929* (Edinburgh, 1983); cf. E. H. Hyman, 'A church militant: Scotland, 1661–1690', *Sixteenth Century*

contemporary England, the Clarendon Code against dissent was not 'religious' legislation; it merely punished those who refused to accept the state's authority to define religion in a certain way, and 'nobody would have related these matters to salvation'.[9]

The regime of the 1690s, basing itself more sensibly on moderate presbyterianism, ran no risk of being destabilized by religion— even though it purged two-thirds of the parish ministers. This purge had nothing to do with salvation, but occurred because of the episcopalian ministers' reluctance to endorse the Williamite regime. The regime certainly faced various forms of religious dissent—but because these dissenters were minorities, and because they *were* various and disunited (radical presbyterians, independents, episcopalians, and Catholics, none of whom had any time for the others), they did not threaten the state in the way that the single broad presbyterian movement had been able to do. Episcopalians, the largest group of dissidents, were the ideological mainstay of Jacobitism, but they were never wholly united, and they also imported an Anglican strain of non-militant latitudinarianism. Similarly, presbyterians had developed a native brand of pragmatism since the defeats of 1648–51. Disagreements rumbled on within presbyterianism, but compromises had become available. Religion was now played for party political advantage. Labels like 'presbyterian' and 'episcopalian' were regularly adopted and discarded by politicians in the 1690s who might wholly lack commitment to these causes. King William had been brought to British shores by a Protestant wind, not a presbyterian one.[10]

The positive side of religious pluralism also attracted some, like Gilbert Burnet, the Scottish bishop of Salisbury who was a leading ideologue of the Glorious Revolution. He wrote in the 1690s: 'There being such a vast difference of opinion concerning

Journal, 26 (1995), 49–74. One reason for keeping bishops under secular control was to avoid a repetition of the rivalry between nobles and bishops that had broken out in the early 17th cent.

[9] C. J. Sommerville, *The Secularization of Early Modern England: From Religious Culture to Religious Faith* (Oxford, 1992), 126.

[10] C. Kidd, 'Religious realignment between the Restoration and the union', in Robertson (ed.), *Union for Empire*; P. W. J. Riley, *King William and the Scottish Politicians* (Edinburgh, 1979), 4–7; B. P. Lenman, 'The Scottish episcopal clergy and the ideology of Jacobitism', in E. Cruikshanks (ed.), *Ideology and Conspiracy: Aspects of Jacobitism, 1689–1759* (Edinburgh, 1982); T. Clarke, 'The Williamite episcopalians and the Glorious Revolution in Scotland', *RSCHS* 24 (1990–2), 33–51.

religion, it is certainly inconsistent with the peace of mankind (the preserving which must be a great part of religion) that men should raise commotions on that account'.[11] It had been possible to argue in the early seventeenth century that differences in *church government* deserved respect, but not differences in religion itself.

Similar developments had been taking place in England since the Restoration, and Brian Levack has argued that it was here that the general outlines of religious pluralism in Britain were shaped. The Church of England became a narrow institution, hostile to Protestant dissenters (and to Catholics) and with no intention of compromising with them; persecution thus ensued. When persecution of Protestants was abandoned after 1689, the only remaining alternative was toleration. In this situation, the Church of Scotland was simply another dissenting Protestant denomination, and its existence in a united Britain was no harder for the English establishment to accept than the existence of English dissenters. The architects of the union of 1707 guaranteed the 1690 settlement within Scotland alone; no union scheme since 1670 had required Anglo-Scottish religious union. Religion was still powerful in legitimating the eighteenth-century British state, but so long as the true Briton was a Protestant, the denomination he professed mattered less than it would have done in the early seventeenth century.[12]

This left no space for one important ideological offence: witchcraft. This had been seen very much as a political crime under James VI, who had written a book about it. Witchcraft, the ultimate defection from the state religion, had required exemplary punishment by agents of the crown. New regimes in 1649 and 1661 had buttressed their authority with a burst of witch-hunting. The omission of the new regime of 1689 to follow suit is a strong indication that politics had become a more secular affair. The new ecclesiastical authorities did generate local campaigns in the early 1690s on sexual morality, but this was in effect a retreat to the church's core area of authority. There was still occasional

---

[11] Quoted in D. Reid (ed.), *The Party-Coloured Mind* (Edinburgh, 1982), 126.

[12] B. P. Levack, *The Formation of the British State: England, Scotland and the Union, 1603–1707* (Oxford, 1987), 133–7; cf. L. Colley, *Britons: Forging the Nation, 1707–1837* (London, 1992), 18–36. As a result, even England could no longer be a 'confessional state': J. Robertson, 'Union, state and empire: The Britain of 1707 in its European setting', in L. Stone (ed.), *An Imperial State at War: Britain from 1689 to 1815* (London, 1994), 248.

witch-hunting even after 1700, but the central authorities no longer took pride in it.[13]

This decline in the ideological power of religion could be seen as a loss of power for the state. If it could no longer call so readily upon divine legitimation, or threaten its opponents with damnation, this was a weakness. However, this is where we should recall that power resources, such as persuasive ideologies, can be used not only by states but by other groups, even dissidents opposed to the state authorities. The decline of religious power had been connected with the fragmentation of the Protestant movement, so that no section of that movement could any longer mount a challenge to the state. The Williamite regime could divide and rule. It could not use the power of religion so much, but neither could its opponents.

Unlike religion, the fiscal power of the state witnessed some energetic forward leaps in the century after 1625—although there were also some backward shuffles. The main forward leap was the covenanting revolution, which burst through the fiscal stagnation of Charles I's reign. The covenanters established an unprecedented and up-to-date system of state finance. The 'tenth penny' of 1639–40 was a tax of 10 per cent on all income from land and trade, on a new valuation. The antiquated assessments for parliamentary taxation were jettisoned. In 1643, the 'monthly maintenance' was introduced; it was a straightforward land tax, based on a system of quotas payable by each shire. The collectors were local lairds, the commissioners of supply, drawn from the same group as the justices of the peace (the two posts were often combined). The land tax was followed in 1644 by an excise on an English model, taxing the sale of a wide variety of commodities but particularly alcohol. Excise and land tax formed the twin fiscal pillars of the Scottish state for well over a century thereafter. Throughout the 1640s there was also a great deal of state borrowing, mostly of

[13] S. Clark, 'King James's *Daemonologie*: Witchcraft and kingship', in S. Anglo (ed.), *The Damned Art: Essays in the Literature of Witchcraft* (London, 1977); C. Larner, *Enemies of God: The Witch-Hunt in Scotland* (London, 1981), ch. 6; R. Mitchison and L. Leneman, *Sexuality and Social Control: Scotland, 1660–1780* (Oxford, 1989), 27–8. There was one incident of coercive policing of the new, broader limits to ideology, when an atheist was executed for blasphemy in 1697: M. Hunter, ' "Aikenhead the atheist": The context and consequences of articulate irreligion in the late seventeenth century', in id. and D. Wootton (eds.), *Atheism from the Reformation to the Enlightenment* (Oxford, 1992).

domestic capital—an indication that Scotland's credit infrastructure could support the financing of a modern all-out war, at least with the help of English subsidies to several Scottish armies. The wars of the covenanters were still being paid for by Scots several decades later, demonstrating (among other things) how effective their regime had been in mobilizing the nation's resources. As a fiscal machine, nothing like it had been seen in Scotland before.[14]

The covenanting fiscal system was continued and extended under the English occupation of the 1650s. Unusually, paid collectors were employed at first, though the valuation was done by local propertied folk under supervision from England. With the customs and excise (reorganized to follow the English system more closely), these exactions yielded an overall annual total, on average, of about £134,000 sterling (£1,608,000 Scots). Although this maintained the civil government, it was unable to meet more than a quarter of the cost of the occupying army—£270,000 sterling per year—and the rest had to be remitted from England.[15] A report to parliament in 1659 gave the annual income of the English state as £1,517,275, and of the Scottish state £143,653 sterling—a ratio of 10.5 to 1. The main sources of revenue in Scotland were the land tax (£72,000), the excise of beer, ale, and spirits (£47,444), and the main overseas customs (£12,500).[16]

One of the most important things the Restoration was intended to restore was a cheap civilian state. The land tax was abolished. A more modest annual revenue of £40,000 sterling (£480,000 Scots) was established from customs and excise alone. Together with some non-parliamentary customs, feudal dues, and other traditional revenues, the gross annual revenue for the mid-1660s was estimated as £678,000 Scots—a mere two-fifths of what it had been in the

---

[14] D. Stevenson, 'Financing the cause of the covenants, 1638–1651', *SHR* 51 (1972), 89–123. The 'monthly maintenance' (later known as 'assessment' or 'cess') included a provision for taxation of the royal burghs, fixed at one-sixth of the total sum raised. Since the other five-sixths fell on land, for simplicity's sake it will be referred to as a land tax in what follows.

[15] F. D. Dow, *Cromwellian Scotland, 1651–1660* (Edinburgh, 1979), 23–5, 58, 110–11, 171–3, 213, 216–17.

[16] *APS* vi, II. 785. These revenue figures may be slightly inflated, but there is no reason to doubt the broad reliability of the 10.5 to 1 ratio. There are indications that Scotland was taxed more heavily than England in the 1650s: Dow, *Cromwellian Scotland*, 216–17. However, contemporary estimates of comparative wealth were based on no more than guesswork: *The Cromwellian Union*, ed. C. S. Terry (SHS, 1902), pp. xli–xlii. More research on all this is required.

previous decade. This was a regime basing itself on the power of large landed proprietors, who were able to direct the tax burden elsewhere. As in England, customs and excise continued to be the mainstay of the state for the remainder of the Restoration period. However, in 1678 a land tax returned at the annual rate of £360,000, raising the total revenue to about a million.[17]

In 1690 the land tax rose to the swingeing annual rate of £865,600.[18] This measure, which increased the gross revenue by 50 per cent, was probably the nearest that Scotland came to the notorious English land tax of 1692. The 1690s also saw experiments with new sources of revenue, bypassing both landed property and commercial wealth. In 1690, a hearth tax of 14s. per hearth was imposed, eventually raising the disappointing sum of £151,921.[19] Then there were three poll taxes in 1693, 1695, and 1698, which raised £291,376, £276,000, and £241,000 respectively—also disappointing, since the first one had been projected to raise almost double that sum. The excise, which fell palpably on the poor, had been a success, but *direct* taxes on the poor seem not to have been so effective.[20]

Since 1640, the revenues of the state had been largely parliamentary, rather than royal. However, parliament could curtail its own power by granting revenues to the crown for long periods. The customs and excise of 1661 were granted for Charles II's life; in 1681 this was extended to his life plus a further five years, and on the accession of James VII it was made perpetual.[21] This tended to allow the royal prerogative to revive. But the fiscal settlement of 1690, which saw the land tax return as the basis of state finance, also saw it granted for only twenty-eight months—inaugurating a pattern of short grants. The parallel English settlement, in which the king was granted only a partial revenue for his lifetime and the

[17] R. A. Lee, 'Government and Politics in Scotland, 1661–1681', Ph.D. thesis (Glasgow, 1995), 105, 132, 135–7. There were periodic small land taxes before 1678.
[18] *APS* ix. 134–47, c. 8.
[19] *APS* ix. 236, c. 5; xi. 170–1.
[20] *APS* ix. 266–8, c. 17; 381–4, c. 12; x. 152–4, c. 12; xi, app., pp. 47–9. The first two poll taxes were at 6s. per head, with higher rates for those with property or status. The third was perhaps only nominally a poll tax, since it fell (heavily graduated) on property-holders only. For the way in which the tax net was broadened see H. M. Dingwall, *Late Seventeenth Century Edinburgh: A Demographic Study* (Aldershot, 1994), 28–9 and *passim.*
[21] *APS* viii. 247, c. 10; 460, c. 2.

customs were granted for four years only, has been shown to be a deliberate measure to ensure regular parliaments.[22] It is reasonable to assume that this was so for Scotland also. The crown's ministers were being kept on a short leash.

In England, there is debate over the relative significance of 1640 and 1690 as fiscal turning-points.[23] The same question could be posed for Scotland, since both dates saw substantial increases in the revenue. (The largest revenues of all were collected in the 1650s, but this was done by an occupying military regime with heavy costs in paid collectors, not to mention the army itself.) The major Scottish turning-point probably came with the covenanting revolution, since the regime of the 1690s was essentially reviving the fiscal system of the 1640s. Unlike in England, it failed to lift its exactions onto a yet higher plane of effectiveness.

This is because, from a fiscal point of view, England forged ahead of Scotland in the later seventeenth century. The ratio between the tax yields of the two states in 1659, as we have seen, was 10.5 to 1. By the eve of the union of 1707, it had become 36 to 1, and several English counties were paying more in taxes than the whole of Scotland. This was not, as is sometimes said, a disparity in 'wealth', but simply in revenue raised.[24] This was the age of the English 'financial revolution', and probably what we are seeing is not so much Scottish failure as English success in extracting resources. But since the Scottish and English economies were comparable in structure, there was probably no *economic* reason why the Scots should not have replicated that success. The reasons why the Scots failed to tax themselves as heavily as the English will be touched on below, but would repay further detailed investigation.

If Scotland had some fiscal catching up to do by the end of the seventeenth century, it was the union of 1707 that enabled it to tackle this task. The annual Scottish public revenue on the eve of union was estimated, probably optimistically, at £110,000 sterling

---

[22] C. Roberts, 'The constitutional significance of the financial settlement of 1690', *Historical Journal*, 20 (1977), 59–76.

[23] P. K. O'Brien and P. A. Hunt, 'The rise of a fiscal state in England, 1485–1815', *Historical Research*, 66 (1993), 129–76, at p. 160; M. J. Braddick, *The Nerves of State: Taxation and the Financing of the English State, 1558–1714* (Manchester, 1996), 17.

[24] G. S. Pryde, *The Treaty of Union of Scotland and England, 1707* (Edinburgh, 1950), 41; Clerk, *History of the Union*, 89. The first description of this ratio as one of 'wealth' seems to be W. Ferguson, *Scotland: 1689 to the Present* (Edinburgh, 1968), 81, where, although Pryde is cited, the ratio is given as 38 to 1. Both these errors have become common in subsequent works.

(£1,320,000 Scots), less than in the 1650s. Union was thought likely to increase this to £160,000 sterling (£1,920,000 Scots).[25] The prospect of vastly increased taxes goes far to explain the union's notorious unpopularity among the common folk. The union has been memorably described as a 'political job', but it was also very much a fiscal operation.[26]

The fiscal system after 1707 was more or less a copy of the English one. The system of indirect taxation was scrapped and replaced with the English model of customs and excise, but the latter was essentially an expanded and more efficient version of the former. This was mainly innovatory in intensity, rather than in the nature of the taxes involved. As for the land tax, still the largest single source of revenue, it continued largely unaltered after 1707. What was new was much higher rates of customs and excise, and a much larger administrative staff to collect these.[27]

A gap was filled in the fiscal system in 1725, after many years' hesitation: an excise on malt was introduced. It provoked widespread riots, legal challenges, and an attempted brewers' strike, even though the rate was only half that payable in England. The malt tax and other duties could sometimes be collected only with direct military support. By a happy coincidence, that military support was available, since the army in Scotland had just been reinforced in order to renew the military occupation of the Highlands. The army that overawed the Jacobite clans, and that built a network of Highland roads to facilitate military operations, began its sojourn in Scotland by quelling Lowland resistance to the malt tax.[28]

This brings us naturally to the exercise of military power. The covenanting regime created the first modern armies in Scotland. Not that its armies were unprecedented in size: the maximum number under arms, something over 30,000 in 1644, was

[25] A. L. Murray, 'Administration and law', in T. I. Rae (ed.), *The Union of 1707: Its Impact on Scotland* (Glasgow, 1974), 34.

[26] W. Ferguson, *Scotland's Relations with England: A Survey to 1707* (Edinburgh, 1977), 250.

[27] P. W. J. Riley, *The English Ministers and Scotland, 1707–1727* (London, 1964), chs. 2–5; W. R. Ward, 'The land tax in Scotland, 1707–1798', *Bulletin of the John Rylands Library*, 37 (1954–5), 288–308.

[28] Riley, *English Ministers and Scotland*, 283–4; C. A. Whatley, 'How tame were the Scottish Lowlanders during the eighteenth century?', in T. M. Devine (ed.), *Conflict and Stability in Scottish Society, 1700–1850* (Edinburgh, 1990), 6–9; W. Taylor, *The Military Roads in Scotland* (2nd edn., Colonsay, 1996), ch. 1.

comparable (taking population growth into account) to the army of 23,000 that had fought at Pinkie in 1547. The differences—and they were crucial—were two: the armies of the 1640s were fully equipped in the latest fashion, and they campaigned for long periods in most years of the decade. The army at Pinkie was a once-off effort, and stayed in the field for about a week; it was weak in field artillery and had hardly any handguns. The military tradition represented by the Pinkie campaign had been superseded during the reign of James VI, but James had not taken the further step of actually raising large modern armies. Not only did he rarely wish to do so, but the political classes might not have supported any war he cared to fight. From the 1640s, Scotland was once again in the mainstream of European warfare—although this newly refurbished military tradition was interrupted by the Cromwellian occupation of the 1650s.[29]

At the Restoration a Scottish standing army was established, generally numbering between about 1,000 and 3,000 men. It is a measure of how things had changed that such an army could seem small; before 1638 it would have been unsustainably large. It was the first regular peacetime army of the Scottish state. A militia, a part-time local force to maintain internal order against covenanting dissidence, was also created. After 1689 covenanting dissidence ceased, and the new threat from Jacobite dissidence was assumed to rely on foreign invasion, so the militia was allowed to fall into abeyance.[30] However, internal security still mattered. The Jacobite threat gave a new twist to the long-standing official suspicion of the political elite of the Highlands. Not only were the clans still armed, but many of them (mostly the enemies of the Campbells) had Jacobite sympathies. The idea of garrisoning the Highlands had regularly been discussed even during the Restoration period; in 1690 it was put into effect with the establishment of Fort William.[31]

The relative fiscal decline of the Scottish state after 1660 was

---

[29] See Ch. 5 above, and for the covenanting armies, E. M. Furgol, 'Scotland turned Sweden: The Scottish covenanters and the military revolution, 1638–1651', in J. Morrill (ed.), *The Scottish National Covenant in its British Context* (Edinburgh, 1990).

[30] C. Tabraham and D. Grove, *Fortress Scotland and the Jacobites* (London, 1995), 17–24; B. P. Lenman, 'Militia, fencible men and home defence, 1660–1797', in N. Macdougall (ed.), *Scotland and War, AD 79–1918* (Edinburgh, 1991), 175–85.

[31] P. Hopkins, *Glencoe and the End of the Highland War* (Edinburgh, 1986), 22, 32–3, 237–8.

accompanied by a relative military decline. The Scottish military machine in the 1640s had fought foreign wars; thereafter there was no further serious effort to enable it to do so. The contrast with England was striking, particularly after the Glorious Revolution. The English army establishment rose from 34,000 men in 1688 to 87,000 in 1695, figures which were closely paralleled in the next war between 1702 and 1707. The Scottish army meanwhile remained a home-defence force of between 2,000 and 3,000 ill-equipped men. When any of its regiments were sent to war, they were put on the English establishment. Although England's various wars did formally involve the Scottish state, Scotland's main contribution to the war effort was to act as a recruiting ground for England. The best-known 'Scottish' regiments, the Scots Greys and Royal Scots, were units of the English army.[32]

Moreover, it was increasingly questionable whether two such separate entities as the Scottish and English armies actually existed, except when the time came for the taxpayer to foot the bill. The two armies shared the same supreme commander—the crown— and gradually the two command structures were merged. The crown and its English ministers decided where army units were deployed; if they wanted a Scottish regiment sent to the Netherlands, they could achieve this without involving any institutions of the Scottish state. James VII ordered the entire Scottish army to England in 1688. Many officers of Queen Anne's Scottish army owed their commissions to her chief English minister, the earl of Godolphin. There was, in many ways, a single British army even before 1707.[33]

The Scottish state thus displayed threefold convergence with England during the seventeenth century, and particularly in the decade after 1689: in the way it deployed military power, in its ideological trappings, and in the fiscal structure which underpinned it.

---

[32] S. H. F. Johnston, 'The Scots army in the reign of Anne', *Transactions of the Royal Historical Society*, 5th ser. 3 (1953), 1–21, at pp. 10–16; J. W. Fortescue, *A History of the British Army*, 7 vols. (2nd edn., London, 1910–30), i. 307, 360, 378, 381; R. E. Scouller, *The Armies of Queen Anne* (Oxford, 1966), 80–2. Figures for army sizes are *establishment* figures, not necessarily actual troops.

[33] C. Dalton, *The Scots Army, 1661–1688* (London, 1909), p. xxvii; J. Childs, *The Army, James II and the Glorious Revolution* (Manchester, 1980), 180, 183–4; Johnston, 'Scots army', 17; K. M. Brown, 'From Scottish lords to British officers: State building, elite integration and the army in the seventeenth century', in Macdougall (ed.), *Scotland and War*, 148–51.

This is paradoxical, because the greater autonomy of the Scottish parliament often made it more difficult to superintend the country's government from Westminster than it had been before the Glorious Revolution. The political difficulties of the Williamite regime in Scotland sometimes led to *divergence* from England, notably in the Darien colonization scheme which England tried to prevent. But the Scottish and English governments, despite their periodic disagreements, were ruling over states that were increasingly similar in structure. This did not in itself cause the union of 1707, but it made such a union easier to envisage, and easier to put into effect once it had been decided on. When the structures were merged, they fitted.

This was partly because of the rise of parliament in both Scotland and England. In the Jacobean union proposals, probably the most hotly debated question was union of laws.[34] A century later, the expansion of parliamentary legislation meant that the laws as they stood had been shaped rather less by a process of adaptation through judicial precedent, and rather more by legislation. Meanwhile, the sovereignty of parliament had been established in both countries by the events of the 1640s, overturning the previous trend towards royal absolutism. Because the state regulated people's lives through statute, the creation of a unitary state required only the union of the two statute-making bodies. Existing laws could be revised later if it proved to be necessary. In fact it did not, and Scots law continued as a different system. The union of 1707 was in this sense the union of two fairly *new* institutions— sovereign parliaments in which the monarchical element had been heavily curtailed—while maintaining the separation of most of the old ones—especially laws and churches.

This brief survey of the century after 1625 has tried to do two things. First, it has highlighted developments in the power of the state. This view of state power is a linear one—the state was simply more powerful than before, or occasionally less so. Secondly, it has commented from time to time on the *type* of state that was developing in early modern Scotland. A powerful state is not necessarily a stable one. If it ignores a build-up of internal opposition, it can also be vulnerable—to revolution. And even before the Scottish state lost its independence, the state fashioned under

[34] Levack, *British State*, ch. 3.

James VI had been overthrown and transformed by the covenanting revolution of 1638. There were in fact two broad models of state structure: the absolutist state, dominant in the reigns of James VI and his Stewart successors, and the covenanting and parliamentary state of the 1640s and 1690s.[35] Seventeenth-century Scotland alternated between these two types of state, while also seeing linear developments that cut across the alternating pattern. Many of these linear developments have already been discussed; what of the alternating pattern?

The regime of James VI and Charles I relied on a powerful monarchy, a powerful landed nobility with hierarchically organized client networks, a system of regulated trade and industry in corporate towns, and a rent-paying peasantry. It believed itself to be socially conservative, respectful of ancient privilege above all else; the belief may in practice have been selective, but respect for hierarchy and tradition still formed a powerful ideological motor. Since hierarchy and tradition were central to any concept of nobility, this was important in providing new roles for the nobles after their main traditional function—recruiting and deploying their own military retinues—was removed in the early seventeenth century. The absolutist state needed above all a reconstructed, compliant nobility.[36]

Moreover, it was reluctant to use parliament. This is sometimes overlooked because its early stages in the 1580s had had a prominent role for parliament. However, the early seventeenth century saw this role decline. Parliament still met fairly regularly, but its legislation declined in quantity and was confined to a narrower sphere. More things were done by the royal prerogative instead.[37] The crown, meanwhile, began to come into conflict with parliaments and conventions of estates, notably in 1600—when the crown's programme was defeated—and 1621—when it was passed, but only with difficulty. The royal court gathered the reconstructed nobility around itself, using courtier nobles to promote central policies. Parliaments began to contain 'country' opposition groupings, hostile to taxation and religious innovation.[38]

[35] As a foreign occupation, the regime of the 1650s can be discounted for the present purposes.
[36] J. Goodare, 'The nobility and the absolutist state in Scotland, 1584–1638', *History*, 78 (1993), 161–82; cf. Ch. 3 above.
[37] Id. *The Government of Scotland, 1560–1625* (forthcoming), ch. 4.
[38] Id. 'Scottish politics in the reign of James VI', in id. and M. Lynch (eds.), *The Reign of James VI* (East Linton, 1999, forthcoming).

The covenanting state was created through reversing this system, rather than progressing from it in linear fashion. It had no court, the monarchy being eliminated in all but name; parliament governed. The essential constitutional requirement for a government was a numerical parliamentary majority. It found its readiest support among burgesses and lairds—and much less among nobles. The regime did not require the kind of peasantry that sustained traditional magnates, and made the first small official gesture towards restructuring agrarian relationships—the act of 1647 promoting division of commonties, which has been called 'the first real improving act'.[39] The elimination of the royal court weakened the influence of the nobility, who had dominated at court but could not control parliament. Many nobles increasingly found themselves at odds with the regime. The few nobles who retained a prominent role were those who had been disaffected from Charles I. The anti-hierarchical temper of covenanting government also showed in its abolition of episcopacy—a popular measure even with the nobles at the time, though by 1661 they had had enough of presbyterian dominance and wanted bishops back.

The clearest single difference between the two polities, therefore, was in the relative positions of crown and parliament. This was important in itself, and perhaps even more through the other differences which accompanied it. Parliament, when it was on top, curtailed the monopolization of power by the nobility, and abolished episcopacy altogether. It is an open question whether aristocratic disaffection under the covenanters was more of a weakness for the state than the earlier division between court and country. Certainly the covenanters mobilized the military resources of the nation with striking success; in the previous war, in the late 1620s, the crown's best efforts had achieved little such mobilization. The ability to fight wars is not the only measure of a state's power, but it is an important one.

In the positions of crown, parliament, and the nobility, the Restoration state represented another reversal. It was once more an absolutist state. The royal court regained control of policy, and readmitted the nobility to the spoils of office. So much is clear; we shall see that fiscal policy, too, tended to favour the nobility as it had not done during the 1640s. On the other hand, there were

[39] I. Whyte, *Agriculture and Society in Seventeenth-Century Scotland* (Edinburgh, 1979), 99.

areas, like economic policy, where there was little or no 'restoration' of the pre-1638 position.

The absolutist partnership between crown and nobility was one of the most important 'restorations' of 1660. But it was still a new relationship, because the development of the state since 1638 meant that the clock could not be turned back. The power of patronage possessed by the Restoration state, in lucrative civil and military offices, gained added leverage from the disastrous debts incurred by many nobles in the previous two decades. Not only was the state financially better off than before the covenanting revolution, but the nobles were worse off. They simply could not survive without office. Nobles were important to the Restoration regime, as they had been to that of the early seventeenth century; to that extent, an absolutist state was once more under construction. But they were more subservient to the state than before, and even those of ancient lineage were treated as mere functionaries.[40]

Parliament retained a more important role after 1660 than it had had before 1638, despite the remarkable revival of the royal prerogative. The lords of the articles (a much overrated body at all times) were restored to manage the agenda of parliament, but not to their full powers. The parliamentary franchise in the counties was rationalized in 1661, giving the vote to all proprietors with a current valued rent of £1,000, whether they were feudal 'freeholders' or not. A desire to enter parliament was more evident than before; elections could be keenly contested.[41]

So the nobles, too, became parliamentarians. To be sure, the royal court was again powerful in the reigns of Charles II and James VII, and formed the nobles' main sphere of influence. But even before 1689 it was advisable to have a parliamentary following too. And from that date onwards, politics was primarily the art of parliamentary management. The nobles were now simply politicians. A parvenu like the second duke of Queensberry, whose family had entered the peerage only in 1628, could engross the whole of the government's patronage and maintain his position against the combined parties of the other leading nobles. His only problem was that this patronage, in the form of pensions, offices, and army commissions, was not enough. Scottish elites battened on to the

---

[40] M. Lynch, *Scotland: A New History* (London, 1991), 291.
[41] W. Ferguson, 'The electoral system in the Scottish counties before 1832', *Stair Society Miscellany*, ii (1984), 266–8; Lee, 'Government and Politics', ch. 5.

public revenues voraciously. Less wealthy than their English counterparts, they had no choice.[42]

A fully parliamentary regime, with a firmly constitutional
monarch, was once more established in 1689. The union of 1707
continued this. Although the sovereign parliament now covered
the whole of Britain, it was still an elected assembly of the propertied classes—in Scotland, even the nobles now elected sixteen
representatives to the house of Lords. Politics thus remained a
matter of management of electors and members of parliament by
a ministry requiring a parliamentary majority.

The fiscal differences between the absolutist state and that of the
covenanters were striking, and go far to demonstrate the fundamental differences between the two regimes. After an initial
success in establishing regular parliamentary taxation of land, the
government of James VI moved steadily away from taxation of land
and towards taxation of commerce. After the revolution of 1638,
this was reversed; both the land tax of 1643, and the excise of 1644
(falling on the common folk), were the kinds of tax that commercial interests would find more attractive. The Restoration
regime, by abolishing the land tax, did its best to lighten the
burden on the nobility. The land tax had to be reintroduced in
1678, but as we saw above, it was the Williamite regime that
imposed a really heavy land tax in 1690. So there was something
of an alternating pattern here, with land taxes to the fore in the
1640s and again in the 1690s.

Many developments in early modern Scotland tended to cut
across this alternating twofold scheme, producing linear rather
than alternating patterns. A few examples can be given here. The
creation of a *sovereign* state in the sixteenth century, described in
Chapter 1, provided a framework within which all subsequent polities would operate. All governments after 1638 had substantial
military forces in being; before then they usually had not. The
English conquest in 1651 was a humbling disaster that injected
new caution into all subsequent Scottish dealings with England. All
these were once-for-all changes in which no alternating pattern was
possible.

As well as these abrupt linear transitions, there were gradual
ones. The development of absolute property rights in land was a

---

[42] Riley, *King William and the Scottish Politicians*, ch. 8.

gradual but still unidirectional process, with no single discontinu-
ity like the English abolition of feudal tenures in 1646. Instead
old freeholders and new feuars came slowly to be recognized as
'heritors' with the same rights to buy, sell, and manage their lands.
The covenanting state forged direct relationships with nobles'
tenants—taxing them, recruiting them for its armies, appealing to
their own political and religious allegiance—without asking the
nobles' permission. Tenants often refused to take their lords' line.
These trends continued in the Restoration period, when covenanting dissidents organized a resistance movement without noble
leadership and in which tenants again defied their lords.[43] These
linear patterns provide the strongest arguments against seeing the
Restoration regime as a fully absolutist state; it was trying to be one,
and had some success, but was operating in a changed world where
the nobility was no longer able to use its estates and client networks
to dominate.

All this may help to show why absolutism came to grief so early
in Scotland. In a European context, it had made a late but still
promising start in the last few decades of the sixteenth century.
Nevertheless it was overthrown in the revolution of 1638, and the
best efforts of Restoration statesmen were unable to reassemble all
its shattered fragments. The causes of the covenanting revolution
were manifold and have been much debated;[44] my purpose here
is not to review the entire issue, but to highlight a few aspects
deriving from the structure of the state. The absolutist state had
inherent weaknesses through its reliance on a nobility with
financial difficulties. Its limited popularity among the wider parliamentary classes, together with its limited ability to acquire non-
parliamentary revenues, made it unable to establish a secure fiscal
base from which to reward supporters. The nobility themselves

---

[43] D. Stevenson, 'The effects of revolution and conquest on Scotland', in R.
Mitchison and P. Roebuck (eds.), *Economy and Society in Scotland and Ireland,
1500–1939* (Edinburgh, 1988), 50–1.

[44] K. M. Brown, 'Aristocratic finances and the origins of the Scottish revolution',
EHR 104 (1989), 46–87; P. Donald, *An Uncounselled King: Charles I and the Scottish
Troubles, 1637–1641* (Cambridge, 1990); Goodare, 'The nobility and the absolutist
state'; M. Lee, *The Road to Revolution: Scotland under Charles I, 1625–1637* (Urbana,
Ill., 1985), ch. 7; A. I. Macinnes, *Charles I and the Making of the Covenanting Move-
ments, 1625–1641* (Edinburgh, 1991); Morrill (ed.), *Scottish National Covenant,* J. J.
Scally, 'The Political Career of James, Third Marquis and First Duke of Hamilton
(1606–1649), to 1643', Ph.D. thesis (Cambridge, 1992). Still unsurpassed is D.
Stevenson, *The Scottish Revolution, 1637–1644* (Newton Abbot, 1973).

could not contribute to this base—on the contrary, they required state subsidies. Here, the crucial gap in the Scottish state structure was the absence of any means of taxing the peasantry.

This gap was partly filled by the covenanters themselves, when they introduced the excise. This taxed peasants' cash purchases, although their wealth remained inaccessible. The Restoration regime thus had an opportunity. Parliament had initial responsibility for taxation, but might conceivably have been persuaded to grant the crown enough long-term revenue to render itself redundant.[45] If it had, this might in turn have led to the construction of an absolutist state on the French model, if not of the French size. There would have been other obstacles to this project. French hereditary office-holders, for instance, were on the whole a strength rather than a weakness for the central state—which could not be said of the Scottish heritable jurisdictions. Still, glancing at the route that the Scottish state did *not* take may help us to understand why it developed in the way that it did. Scotland had possibilities for absolutism, but in the end it took the unusual alternative route towards a parliamentary state with a limited monarchy and a limited role for the territorial nobility.

As a footnote to this twofold classification scheme for the development of the Scottish state, it is worth noting that Thomas Ertman has posited a *fourfold* classification for European states in the seventeenth and eighteenth centuries. The regime itself is either absolutist or constitutional, while the administrative structure is either 'bureaucratic' (that is, a 'proto-modern', centralized Weberian bureaucracy) or 'patrimonial' (that is, a patrimonial bureaucracy), and these regime types and administrative types can exist in any combination. It is common to cite France as an example, because its absolute monarchy and centralized bureaucracy are seen as typical—which of western Catholic states it was. However, eighteenth-century England had a constitutional regime but a centralized bureaucracy, while Hungary and Poland were constitutional but with patrimonial bureaucracies. This interpretation may not allow enough space for gradual, evolutionary change, but it is still thought-provoking. In these terms, as Professor Ertman notes, Scotland took the same path as England. By the

---

[45] Not that this was at all *likely*. Cf. Lee, 'Government and Politics', 196, 295–6.

end of the seventeenth century, it had a constitutional regime administered by a centralized bureaucracy.[46]

The Scottish state thus suffered many vicissitudes in the sixteenth and seventeenth centuries, but its overall story can nevertheless be seen as one of success—the successful construction of a state machine. A recognizable Scottish state was constructed, particularly in the reigns of Mary and James VI. It was a weak one, with a small and sometimes precarious fiscal and military base; still, we should judge the state of the 1590s by contemporary standards, and not by the standards of the 1690s or 1790s. However, in its long-term context, its story had several episodes of failure. The union of 1707 can be seen as upgrading the state by introducing more powerful fiscal systems into Scotland, and such a view ought to be more widely recognized. But the common view that it *extinguished* the state (seen as a *Scottish* state) is also valid. Does an understanding of the state's long-term development help to explain how Scotland suddenly ceased to be an independent state?

One significant point can be made at the outset: that Scotland was not unusual. *Most* attempts at European state-building failed, either in the short or the long run. Charles Tilly, whose works are an indispensable guide to this topic, points out that most of the autonomous or distinctive regions of late-medieval Europe never developed a free-standing system of public authority; others managed to do so, but were later absorbed into larger units.[47] Scotland falls into the latter category. It built its own state in the sixteenth and seventeenth centuries, only to see this state merged with the English one in 1707. On the other hand, to have this merger carried out through reasoned and peaceful negotiation, between two states of at least formally equal status, was most unusual. The absorption was more likely to come through conquest, suitably embellished with legitimating dynastic claims.[48]

Scotland's position in the British Isles since the establishment of the English 'amity' in 1560 (confirmed in 1603) had been that of a dependent, satellite state. This too was common enough among

[46] T. Ertman, *Birth of the Leviathan: Building States and Regimes in Medieval and Early Modern Europe* (Cambridge, 1997); cf. S. E. Finer, *The History of Government from the Earliest Times*, 3 vols. (Oxford, 1997), i. 36–67.

[47] C. Tilly, 'Reflections on the history of European state-making', in id. (ed.), *The Formation of National States in Western Europe* (Princeton, 1975), 38.

[48] M. Greengrass, 'Introduction: conquest and coalescence', in id. (ed.), *Conquest and Coalescence: The Shaping of the State in Early Modern Europe* (London, 1991), 7–10.

the composite monarchies of early modern Europe.[49] Semi-detached from the English core state, the Scottish body politic had special needs—and special privileges. Its main privilege was low taxation. Often its main need was to be left alone, and not to have policies imposed on it to meet purely English needs. This was often easy for the English to meet, since they in turn had few expectations of Scotland and were willing to ignore it so long as it did not make trouble. They probably saw it rather like the minor Spanish kingdoms that were castigated by Philip IV's great minister, Olivares: 'kingdoms and provinces that have privileges, and are naturally inclined to insurrections'.[50] The Scottish events of 1638–51 could certainly be seen in this way—as a minor kingdom using its institutions to assert itself and to resist interference from the centre.

And in the view from the centre, so could some of the Scottish events of 1689 onwards. The Highlands demonstrated that Jacobitism could mount an armed challenge to the Williamite regime; even if the bulk of the Lowland political nation was loyal, the Jacobite danger gave a sharper edge to Scottish affairs. Then the Scottish parliament established the Company of Scotland. The company's attempt to settle the Darien peninsula in 1698–1700, antagonizing the Spanish government during delicate negotiations over the Spanish succession, was a spanner in the works of English diplomacy. English obstruction of the colony was not crucial in causing it to fail, but it angered the Scots and showed that the economic interests of the two countries, as articulated by their governments, had diverged.

At this point, economic interests crossed with high political ones—the crisis of the royal succession in both realms after 1700. The English parliament solved this problem with the Act of Settlement of early 1701, adopting the Hanoverian dynasty. Because of the haste with which the measure was passed, the Scots were not consulted.[51] Still, the act did no harm to Scottish

[49] J. H. Elliott, 'A Europe of composite monarchies', *P & P* 137 (Nov. 1992), 48–71.

[50] Quoted in id., *The Count-Duke of Olivares: The Statesman in an Age of Decline* (New Haven, NJ, 1986), 524.

[51] The haste even left an important fault in the text of the act: H. Horwitz, *Parliament, Policy and Politics in the Reign of William III* (Manchester, 1977), 277–84, 293–4. However, on one point the act was not faulty. There were complaints in Scotland that the act prohibited the successor to the English crown from leaving

interests. It was open to the Scottish parliament to maintain the status quo (Protestantism and regal union) by passing a similar act. Had it done so, there would have been no crisis in Anglo-Scottish relations, and no parliamentary union in 1707. On the other hand, it was the privilege of a satellite state to use its separate status and institutions to make demands on its own behalf; and that is what the majority in the Scottish parliament chose to do.

It would be superfluous to dissect once more the events of 1703–7—how the court failed to construct a viable Scottish ministry; how the opposition was able to pass the Act of Security in 1703, threatening to end the regal union on Queen Anne's death unless free trade with England and its colonies were conceded; how the English responded with the Alien Act in 1705, threatening in turn to ban the Scottish trade altogether; how the court improved its management of the Scottish parliament, and how realignments in the English parliament made its acceptance of a union more likely; and how a union of parliaments was negotiated and passed in 1706–7. The chain of events was comprehensible in retrospect but scarcely predictable at the time. The point to note is that the chain was set off by the deliberate Scottish refusal to adopt the Hanoverian succession in 1703. It was not quite what Olivares would have called an 'insurrection', but it came close. The implicit threat to resurrect the 'auld alliance' with France, during an Anglo-French war, was one that the English could not afford to ignore.

What had the Scots wanted when they launched their campaign? William Ferguson points out that the dominant anti-court coalition in 1703 was heterogeneous, and gives the following conspectus: constitutional radicals; disappointed place-seekers; investors in the Company of Scotland, angry at the Darien disaster for which England was blamed; presbyterians threatened by the English court's Anglicanism; episcopalians hoping for a better deal; Jacobites hoping to make trouble for the regime. Of these diverse interests, the only ones to find substantive expression in the legislation of 1703 were the Company of Scotland's investors—for

England, *Scotland*, or Ireland without the English parliament's permission, thus seeming to take Scotland for granted. Some historians have treated these complaints as legitimate. But if Scotland had been omitted, and the Scottish parliament had later chosen the same successor, then a Scottish monarch would have required the English parliament's permission to go to Scotland.

whom free trade with England was now the only hope—and the constitutional radicals—who gained the Act anent Peace and War, although they failed to have 'limitations' on the crown inserted in the Act of Security.[52]

The Act of Security was probably a bluff, in the sense that its authors would not have dared, and in many cases did not even wish, to carry out its threat to break the regal union. And there is no evidence that separation from the English state system was the *preferred* option of any but a tiny minority.[53] It is reasonable to take the authors of the Act of Security at their word and to conclude that their preferred option was a better deal from England—one including, specifically, free trade. Which they duly got. But in return for conceding it, the English used the Alien Act to extract their own concession from the Scots—union of parliaments. It was an English decision to insist on union, and one may ask: how much pressure was necessary to achieve it? Which invites in turn the crucial question for present purposes: how much power did the Scottish state have *vis-à-vis* England?

From what was said in the previous chapter, it will be clear that this cannot be answered in the abstract. The question 'power to do what?' must once more be posed. The Scottish state might have several objectives *vis-à-vis* England. It might wish to foster the economy so that it could flourish despite English protectionism. It might seek to enable Scottish elites to maintain a united front against English demands, to counter the long English tradition of

---

[52] Ferguson, *Scotland's Relations with England*, 188. The Act anent Peace and War vested control of this aspect of foreign policy wholly in parliament. Ironically, the English Act of Settlement *had* included limitations on the crown.

[53] J. Robertson, 'An elusive sovereignty: The course of the union debate in Scotland, 1698–1707', in id. (ed.), *Union for Empire*, 204–5, describes the act as bluff; Ferguson, *Scotland's Relations with England*, 210, takes the opposite view; P. W. J. Riley, 'The Scottish parliament of 1703', *SHR* 47 (1968), 129–50, sees it as a cynical manoeuvre to embarrass the ministry. Similarly, the Catalans in 1640 did not *want* secession from Spain, they wanted a better deal from Madrid: J. H. Elliott, *The Revolt of the Catalans: A Study in the Decline of Spain, 1598–1640* (Cambridge, 1963).

The *ideal* option of many Scots (including some unionists) would indeed have been total separation, economic and political, from England. But the few anti-union writers advocating this carried little conviction. More typical and pragmatic was the earl of Roxburgh, who helped to draft the Act of Security. He regarded separation as 'preferable to all' in theory; but he argued in 1704 that Scotland lacked the power to achieve this in the face of English hostility, and so should accept either union or at least the Hanoverian succession. T. C. Smout, 'The road to union', in G. Holmes (ed.), *Britain after the Glorious Revolution, 1689–1714* (London, 1969), 186.

fostering a party of clients within Scotland; in practice this would mean providing material incentives to retain their allegiance. In extreme circumstances, it might wish to wage war against England.

The first of these options, although the least confrontational, was not in the least promising. The commercial sectors of the Scottish economy were helpless before the threat of the Alien Act. Not only that, but once union had been proposed, it was widely agreed to be the best way of reviving the Scottish economy. Anti-unionists could offer no credible alternative and were reduced to picking holes in unionist arguments.[54]

Scotland also lacked the resources for the most confrontational option, military resistance to England. The sole purpose of its army was to maintain internal security, and there was a question mark over its ability to fulfil even this task. It is not so much that there were two armed uprisings, in 1666 and 1679; it is that the suppression of the second one was thought to be beyond the state's means. The army that quelled it included five troops of English dragoons, and the government planned to send more if trouble continued.[55] This was an extension of English responsibility for Scotland's external defence.

The Scottish state faced a further military problem as European naval power grew: a trading nation was increasingly expected to have a navy as well as an army. A tiny Scottish navy was created in the 1690s, but it was dwarfed by the navies of the other belligerent powers, and hampered by disputes with the English. William Seton of Pitmedden made a telling point in 1706 during the union debate: 'This nation, being poor, and without force to protect its commerce, cannot reap great advantages by it, till it partake of the trade and protection of some powerful neighbour nation'.[56] So during the crisis of 1702–7, no Scots regarded their military forces as adequate against English invasion.[57]

[54] Levack, *British State*, 149–57. Despite the general persuasiveness of the unionist case, a few sectors of the economy (notably the salt industry) feared that free trade would harm them: C. A. Whatley, 'Economic causes and consequences of the union of 1707: A survey', *SHR* 68 (1989), 150–81, at pp. 158–65.

[55] Dalton, *Scots Army*, pt. 1, p. 56. For the regime's military difficulties in general, see Lee, 'Government and Politics', ch. 4.

[56] E. J. Graham, 'In defence of the Scottish maritime interest, 1681–1713', *SHR* 71 (1992), 88–109, at pp. 91–105; quotation from C. A. Whatley, *'Bought and Sold for English Gold?' Explaining the Union of 1707* (Economic and Social History Society of Scotland, 1994), 49.

[57] The Act of Security did order that the militia should be mustered. However, no anti-unionist writers, except Jacobites, even suggested that Scotland could con-

Resistance to England might have been possible with foreign support. In practice this meant French support, which would have been available only on condition of a Jacobite restoration. Given the firmness with which the bulk of the political nation had rejected the Stewarts, this was not only unattractive but would probably have led to civil war within Scotland. Which would not have furthered the aim of resisting English interference. Still, as Scots knew, this did not mean that the English could walk in and take over whenever they wished. Such an attempt might have been costly and fraught with danger. Scots did not wish to provoke civil war and French intervention, but could the English be sure that they would not do so? The Catalans in the 1640s had indeed invited in the French to protect them against Spain, and civil war had indeed resulted. Like Catalonia, Scotland had a name and identity that aroused strong feelings. Although the Scots lacked much in the way of military and economic power, they still had the power of ideas.

This, perhaps, is the crux of the ideological debates over union, which otherwise can seem irrelevant. The debates focused mainly (at least in volume of published output) on religion and nominal sovereignty. Patriotic Scots indignantly defended the autonomy of their church, and rejected attempts by English writers to re-surrect England's medieval claims to suzerainty over Scotland. This was irrelevant because the English government neither threatened the Scottish church, nor claimed suzerainty over Scotland.[58] The point is that contemplation of the idea that Scotland did indeed have an 'imperial crown' may have stiffened the resolve of anti-unionists, and may have warned unionists away from thoughts of complete union involving laws or churches. The Scottish determination to remain Scottish was what made Scotland what it was. The English could not walk in and take over because they knew that they would not be accepted as legitimate rulers. To the extent that the Scottish state was indigestible, it was the legitimacy of its institutions—seen as *Scottish* institutions—that made it so.

But by the end of the seventeenth century it was a good deal less

sider fighting: Robertson, 'An elusive sovereignty', 211. And the Jacobite position was disingenuous, since they did not want to break the regal union.

[58] W. Ferguson, 'Imperial crowns: A neglected facet of the background to the treaty of union of 1707', *SHR* 53 (1974), 22–44; P. W. J. Riley, *The Union of England and Scotland* (Manchester, 1978), 220–33.

indigestible than before. We have already looked at the convergence in state structure—ideological, economic, and military—
that England and Scotland had experienced during the
seventeenth century. Although 'Scottish' institutions furnished an
identity to the nation, they were also seen as functional entities.
Parliament was not just the embodiment of Scottish sovereignty; it
was also a representative institution connecting the propertied
classes to central authority. That function did not disappear in
1707, and its continuance was a valued part of the union project.
Meanwhile, the local patriotism that had guided electors' choice
of representatives was weakening. Numerous Scotsmen would
eventually be elected to represent English constituencies. The
functions of parliament were vital both in Scotland and in
England; on that, all the political classes agreed. In short, a union
of parliaments was possible because both Scotland and England,
unlike most countries at that time, had parliaments.[59]

So there was more to union than national identity; and even the
appeal of national identity was not a straightforward matter.
National identity is not people's *only* identity. While Scots went into
union very much as Scots rather than as Britons, they were also
mindful of their interests as Protestants, as capitalists, or as consumers. Scottish elites soon found it easy to develop a dual national
identity, as Scots and Britons. They saw positive value in both,
despite periodic affronts from English inability to differentiate
between England and Britain.[60]

This English insensitivity towards Scotland was careless and
sometimes arrogant, but not sinister. The English no longer had
expansionist ambitions north of the Border. The seventeenth-
century English state was certainly extending its territorial power—
in Ireland, in New England, and in the West Indies; but Scotland
was not on its list of regions worth exploiting. Even during the successful conquest of 1651, English commentators had tended to
regard Scotland as barbarous, poor, and probably not worth the
trouble. They had conquered it only to defeat the Scottish threat

---

[59] Colley, *Britons*, 49–52. Union with France, by contrast, would have required
abolition of the Scottish parliament and acceptance of absolute monarchy. One
anti-unionist suggested a union with the United Netherlands: Riley, *Union*, 231.

[60] T. C. Smout, 'Problems of nationalism, identity and improvement in later
eighteenth-century Scotland', in T. M. Devine (ed.), *Improvement and Enlightenment*
(Edinburgh, 1989); Colley, *Britons*, chs. 1–2.

to their own security. Thereafter they had tried to conciliate Scottish elites rather than exploiting the country's resources to the hilt—in contrast to their behaviour in Ireland. They had readily abandoned the expensive occupation when they perceived that English security no longer required it.[61]

This was probably why, even after 1707, Scotland remained a semi-detached region. The English had got what their security demanded, and were not interested in complete assimilation. Scotland's privileges (at least in fiscal terms) had been drastically reduced, and its participation in central government had been brought up to much the same level as other regions of Britain. But Scots law (including electoral law) continued, as did many Scottish institutions, so it was expedient to have a separate manager of patronage and electoral influence north of the Border.[62] Still, the Scottish political managers of the early eighteenth century fitted into a broader contemporary pattern. There was a general need in the British state for members of parliament to be connected to reliable local interest groups who could solve local problems of private legislation or patronage without choking the central machinery, preoccupied as this was with high politics, diplomacy, and warfare. When Patrick Riley outlined the activities of the earl of Islay as Scottish manager under Sir Robert Walpole, he commented that 'none of this was in essentials different from the way in which an English duke ran his interest'.[63] Eighteenth-century Scotland was semi-detached, but not divergent. Considering the convergence of the seventeenth century in state structures, this is not surprising.

---

[61] D. Hirst, 'The English republic and the meaning of Britain', in B. Bradshaw and J. Morrill (eds.), *The British Problem, c.1534–1707* (London, 1996), 196–200; D. Stevenson, 'Cromwell, Scotland and Ireland', in J. Morrill (ed.), *Oliver Cromwell and the English Revolution* (London, 1990); L. M. Smith, 'Scotland and Cromwell: A Study in Early Modern Government', D.Phil. thesis (Oxford, 1979).

[62] J. M. Simpson, 'Who steered the gravy train, 1707–1766?', in N. T. Phillipson and R. Mitchison (eds.), *Scotland in the Age of Improvement* (Edinburgh, 1970); A. Murdoch, *The People Above: Politics and Administration in Mid-Eighteenth-Century Scotland* (Edinburgh, 1980); J. S. Shaw, *The Management of Scottish Society, 1707–1764* (Edinburgh, 1983); R. M. Sunter, *Patronage and Politics in Scotland, 1707–1832* (Edinburgh, 1986).

[63] D. Hayton, 'Constitutional experiments and political expediency, 1689–1725', in S. G. Ellis and S. Barber (eds.), *Conquest and Union: Fashioning a British State, 1485–1725* (London, 1995), 283; P. W. J. Riley, 'The structure of Scottish politics and the union of 1707', in Rae (ed.), *Union of 1707*, 25. More research on this point would be desirable.

So the failure of the Scottish state was by no means complete. Union was not extinction. Partly for that reason, the eventual failure of the autonomous Scottish state in 1707 is of less consequence to this book than its medium-term success. Even in 1707, the union was at least formally an honourable, negotiated agreement, which even its opponents would surely have preferred to the military extinction that overwhelmed some smaller Continental states. Up to 1650, certainly, Scottish state-building had met with nothing but success. And this Scottish state was an indigenous creation. What the new British state took over was a going concern. Its machinery needed only a few modifications to operate as components of a larger system.

Parliamentary union, in these terms, was part of a process of upgrading those items of state machinery that were located in the region known as Scotland. That machinery had been unchanged for over a decade and may even have become a little rusty, but now received a boost from assimilation to England. England had recently seen the construction of one of the most powerful machines in Europe for extracting and reallocating its subjects' resources, and for pursuing ends relevant to rulers—principally warfare.[64] But after 1707, those who governed the region known as Scotland were in charge of a more elaborate and powerful engine of coercion than their predecessors. It had gained the ability to deliver the eighteenth-century equivalent of official brown envelopes through people's doors in larger numbers. It was now a branch of a larger unit, but that was part of the deal. To that extent, it was the consummation of the project which James VI claimed to have begun in the 1580s when he set out to rule Scotland with his pen; he knew that Anglo-Scottish union would facilitate the process, and also that union was not the *same* process as state-building. He would have been shocked at the constitutional arrangements of 1689, but that is another issue.

Should we, like James, celebrate the process of state formation in Scotland? The foregoing discussion has made free with words like 'success' and 'failure'. Historians of the early modern period often write about political 'success' or 'failure' in terms that treat success as wholly and inherently admirable, and failure as self-evidently bad. They might do well to emulate colleagues working

---

[64] J. Brewer, *The Sinews of Power: War, Money and the English State, 1688–1783* (London, 1988); Braddick, *Nerves of State*, ch. 9.

in more recent periods, who are aware that political power can be, and has been, put to reprehensible uses. Still, the question remains, and must be tackled without imposing anachronistic values on pre-industrial folk. One route towards an answer is thus through contemporary reactions to the effects wrought by the state. James assured his son that 'the most part of your people will ever naturally favour justice'.[65] We have no opinion surveys to tell us what the 'most part' thought of his regime, but the folk tradition may provide some straws in the wind.

It was the proud 'vaunt' of James and his ministers that they had made Scotland law-abiding. They did indeed uproot the tradition of bloodfeud—of self-help justice, sword in hand; and there is evidence that this was welcomed by the common people. Many of the Border ballads celebrated the derring-do of the reivers, but not all of them:

> Rookhope stands in a pleasant place,
> If the false thieves wad let it be;
> But away they steal our goods apace,
> And ever an ill death may they die.[66]

It would have been incongruous for the folk tradition, with its local rather than national perspective, to have celebrated openly the suppression of the reivers by agents of the central state. But some tacit sympathy for the government's programme may reasonably be inferred.

On the other hand, the main official authority experienced daily by the common folk was that of the kirk session. There is a sense in which one can speak of popular Protestantism, but hardly of 'popular' kirk session discipline. Hamish Henderson has pointed out that 'in the whole range of our folk song, there is hardly a reference to ministers or to religion—apart from the most formal—which is not hostile or satiric'.[67] The ideal of the godly state might have been expected to inspire at least some respect among folk

---

[65] James VI, *Basilicon Doron*, in *Political Writings*, 22.

[66] F. J. Child, *English and Scottish Popular Ballads*, ed. H. C. Sargent and G. L. Kittredge (London, 1904), no. 179. This ballad, 'Rookhope Ryde', narrates events on the English side of the Border in 1569. For elite criticism of bloodfeud, and for how it came to an end, see K. M. Brown, *Bloodfeud in Scotland, 1573–1625* (Edinburgh, 1986), pt. 3.

[67] H. Henderson, *Alias MacAlias: Writings on Songs, Folk and Literature* (Edinburgh, 1992), 28.

who aspired to be law-abiding, but if it did, it has left little trace in this quarter. The church did have its own musical genre, the metrical psalms, but they did not influence the folk tradition except perhaps by providing some tunes for it. The ballads on covenanting events—'The battle of Philiphaugh', 'Loudon Hill', and 'Bothwell Bridge'—took the covenanters' side, but were secular tales of martial heroism.[68]

And the state which began by suppressing private violence ended by sponsoring public violence on an unprecedented scale. The union of parliaments took place during the War of the Spanish Succession, and indeed was carried out to ensure that the fighting could continue. Many Scots fought under Marlborough in Flanders and Germany. They were fully capable of singing songs that celebrated martial heroism. Did they welcome Marlborough's wars, or even understand what they were about?

> Will ye go to Flanders, my Mally o?
> And see the chief commanders, my Mally o?
> You'll see the bullets fly, and the soldiers how they die,
> And the ladies loudly cry, my Mally o.[69]

Warfare was often seen as the *raison d'être* of the early modern state, yet its wars have scant claim to popular approval. With this in mind, the best that could be said of state formation in Scotland is that, because of its dependent situation before 1707, it was less militarized than some. A criticism that could be levelled against the union of parliaments—one often drowned out by the voice of nationalism—is that it changed this. Thereafter, the state in Scotland was directly responsible for all that was done in its name.

---

[68] Child, *Popular Ballads*, nos. 202, 205, 206; E. J. Cowan, 'Calvinism and the survival of folk', in id. (ed.), *The People's Past: Scottish Folk, Scottish History* (Edinburgh, 1980), 52.

[69] D. Herd (ed.), *Ancient and Modern Scottish Songs, Heroic Ballads, Etc.*, 2 vols. (3rd edn., Glasgow, 1869), ii. 213. 'Mally' = Marlborough. Cf. ibid. 122–4, for an even more detached view of the battle of Sheriffmuir (1715).

SELECT BIBLIOGRAPHY

1. MANUSCRIPTS

Aberdeen City Archives

William Kennedy's 'Alphabetical index to the first 67 volumes of the council register of the city of Aberdeen, 1398–1800', vol. i.

British Library, London

Papers of Sir Julius Caesar, Add. MS 12497.
Copies of documents relating to the revenues of Scotland, Add. MS 24275.
David Chalmers, 'Dictionary of Scots law' (1566), Add. MS 27472.
John Acheson, 'Anent cunyie, ane ample discourse' (c.1581), Add. MS 33531.
Royal MSS, 18.B.vi.

Dundee City Archive and Record Centre

Dundee council minutes, vols. i–ii.

National Archives of Scotland, Edinburgh

Edinburgh presbytery minutes, CH2/121.
Treasurer's accounts, E21.
Treasurer's accounts (Leven & Melville), E22.
Comptroller's accounts, E24.
Treasury of new augmentation, E49.
Taxation decreets, E62.
Taxation accounts, E65.
Navy papers, E90.
Mint accounts, E101.
Lothian MSS, GD40/2/9.
Cunninghame of Caprington letter book, GD149/265.
Miscellaneous parliamentary papers, PA7/1.
Minutes of council of war, 1626–9, PA7/2, no. 30a.

National Library of Scotland, Edinburgh

Balfour's Practicks, Adv. MS 24.6.3 (3).
Balcarres papers, Adv. MS 29.2.8.
Denmylne MSS, Adv. MS 33.1.1, vols. i–ix.

'Historie of the Kennedyis', Adv. MS 33.3.28.
'Concernyng the chekker and the kingis rentis', Adv. MS 34.2.17.

2. PRINTED PRIMARY SOURCES

(a) Public and Administrative Records

Aberdeen Council Letters, 6 vols., ed. L. B. Taylor (London, 1942–61).
Accounts of the Collectors of Thirds of Benefices, 1561–1572, ed. G. Donaldson (SHS, 1949).
Accounts of the (Lord High) Treasurer of Scotland, 13 vols., ed. T. Dickson *et al.* (Edinburgh, 1877–).
Acts of the Lords of Council in Public Affairs, 1501–1554, ed. R. K. Hannay (Edinburgh, 1932).
Acts of the Parliaments of Scotland, 12 vols., ed. T. Thomson and C. Innes (Edinburgh, 1814–75).
Acts of Sederunt of the Lords of Council and Session (Edinburgh, 1790).
Ayr Burgh Accounts, 1534–1624, ed. G. S. Pryde (SHS, 1937).
Booke of the Universall Kirk: Acts and Proceedings of the General Assemblies of the Kirk of Scotland, 3 vols., ed. T. Thomson (Bannatyne and Maitland Clubs, 1839–45).
Calendar of State Papers, Domestic Series, 94 vols., ed. R. Lemon *et al.* (London, 1856–).
Calendar of the State Papers Relating to Scotland and Mary Queen of Scots, 1547–1603, 13 vols., ed. J. Bain *et al.* (Edinburgh, 1898–1969).
Carnwath. *Court Book of the Barony of Carnwath, 1523–1542*, ed. W. C. Dickinson (SHS, 1937).
The Earl of Stirling's Register of Royal Letters, 1615–1635, 2 vols., ed. C. Rogers (Grampian Club, 1885).
Edinburgh. *Extracts From the Records of the Burgh of Edinburgh*, 13 vols., ed. J. D. Marwick *et al.* (SBRS and Edinburgh, 1869–1967).
Exchequer Rolls of Scotland, 23 vols., ed. J. Stuart *et al.* (Edinburgh, 1878–).
Fife. *Sheriff Court Book of Fife, 1515–1522*, ed. W. C. Dickinson (SHS, 1928).
Glasgow. *Extracts From the Records of the Burgh of Glasgow*, 11 vols., ed. J. D. Marwick *et al.* (SBRS, 1876–1916).
Glasgow. 'Extracts from the registers of the presbytery of Glasgow, 1592–1601', *Maitland Miscellany*, i (1833).
JAMES VI & I, *Letters*, ed. G. P. V. Akrigg (Berkeley and Los Angeles, 1984).
Kirkintilloch. *Court Book of the Burgh of Kirkintilloch, 1658–1694*, ed. G. S. Pryde (SHS, 1963).
Letters and State Papers during the Reign of King James VI, ed. J. Maidment (Abbotsford Club, 1838).
Letters of James V, ed. R. K. Hannay and D. Hay (Edinburgh, 1954).

Lothian. *Records of the Synod of Lothian and Tweeddale, 1589–1596, 1640–1649*, ed. J. Kirk (Stair Society, 1977).
Original Letters Relating to the Ecclesiastical Affairs of Scotland, 2 vols., ed. D. Laing (Bannatyne Club, 1851).
Records of the Convention of Royal Burghs of Scotland, 7 vols., ed. J. D. Marwick and T. Hunter (Edinburgh, 1866–1918).
Register of the Great Seal of Scotland (Registrum Magni Sigilli Regum Scotorum), 11 vols., ed. J. M. Thomson *et al.* (Edinburgh, 1912–).
Register of the Privy Council of Scotland, 37 vols., ed. J. H. Burton *et al.* (Edinburgh, 1877–).
Register of the Privy Seal of Scotland (Registrum Secreti Sigilli Regum Scotorum), 8 vols., ed. M. Livingstone *et al.* (Edinburgh, 1908–).
Selected Justiciary Cases, 1624–1650, 3 vols., ed. S. A. Gillon and J. I. Smith (Stair Society, 1953–74).
State Papers and Letters of Sir Ralph Sadler, 3 vols., ed. A. Clifford (Edinburgh, 1809).
State Papers and Miscellaneous Correspondence of Thomas, Earl of Melros, 2 vols., ed. J. Maidment (Abbotsford Club, 1837).
Statutes of the Scottish Church, 1225–1559, ed. D. Patrick (SHS, 1907).
Stirling Presbytery Records, 1581–1587, ed. J. Kirk (SHS, 1981).
Stuart Royal Proclamations, i (1603–1625), ed. J. F. Larkin and P. L. Hughes (Oxford, 1973).
The Warrender Papers, 2 vols., ed. A. I. Cameron (SHS, 1931–2).

(b) Narratives, Tracts, etc.

'Account of a Journey into Scotland', 1629, in HMC, *Report on the Manuscripts of the Earl of Lonsdale*, ed. J. J. Cartwright (London, 1893).
BALFOUR OF PITTENDREICH, Sir JAMES, *Practicks*, 2 vols., ed. P. G. B. McNeill (Stair Society, 1962–3).
BODIN, JEAN, *The Six Bookes of a Commonweale*, ed. K. D. McRae (Cambridge, Mass., 1962).
BUCHANAN, GEORGE, *The Art and Science of Government Among the Scots (Dialogus De Jure Regni Apud Scotos)*, ed. D. H. McNeill (Glasgow, 1964).
—— *The History of Scotland*, vols. i–ii, ed. J. Aikman (Edinburgh, 1830).
CALDERWOOD, DAVID, *History of the Kirk of Scotland*, 8 vols., ed. T. Thomson and D. Laing (Wodrow Society, 1843–9).
Catholic Tractates of the Sixteenth Century, 1573–1600, ed. T. G. Law (STS, 1901).
CLERK OF PENICUIK, Sir JOHN, *History of the Union of Scotland and England*, ed. D. Duncan (SHS, 1993).
COWPER, WILLIAM, *Workes* (2nd edn., London, 1629).
CRAIG, THOMAS, *De Unione Britanniae Tractatus*, ed. C. S. Terry (SHS, 1909).

CRAIG, THOMAS, *Jus Feudale*, 2 vols., ed. J. A. Clyde (Edinburgh, 1934).
—— *Scotland's Soveraignty Asserted*, trans. G. Ridpath (London, 1695).
The First Book of Discipline, ed. J. K. Cameron (Edinburgh, 1972).
GORDON, Sir ROBERT, *Genealogical History of the Earldom of Sutherland* (Edinburgh, 1813).
HAY, WILLIAM, *Lectures on Marriage*, ed. J. C. Barry (Stair Society, 1967).
HOPE, Sir THOMAS, *Major Practicks*, 2 vols., ed. J. A. Clyde (Stair Society, 1937–8).
JAMES VI & I, *Political Writings*, ed. J. P. Sommerville (Cambridge, 1994).
KNOX, JOHN, *History of the Reformation in Scotland*, 2 vols., ed. W. C. Dickinson (Edinburgh, 1949).
—— *Works*, 6 vols., ed. D. Laing (Wodrow Society, 1846–64).
LESLIE, JOHN, *Historie of Scotland*, 2 vols., ed. E. G. Cody and W. Murison (STS, 1888–95).
LINDSAY OF THE MOUNT, Sir DAVID, *Works*, 4 vols., ed. D. Hamer (STS, 1931–6).
LINDSAY OF PITSCOTTIE, ROBERT, *Historie and Cronicles of Scotland*, 3 vols., ed. Æ. J. G. Mackay (STS, 1899–1911).
MAJOR (MAIR), JOHN, *History of Greater Britain*, ed. A. Constable (SHS, 1892).
MELVILLE, JAMES, *Autobiography and Diary, 1556–1610*, ed. R. Pitcairn (Wodrow Society, 1842).
MELVILLE OF HALHILL, Sir JAMES, *Memoirs of His Own Life*, ed. T. Thomson (Bannatyne Club, 1827).
Monro's Western Isles of Scotland and Genealogies of the Clans, 1549, ed. R. W. Munro (Edinburgh, 1961).
MOYSIE, DAVID, *Memoirs of the Affairs of Scotland, 1577–1603*, ed. J. Dennistoun (Maitland Club, 1830).
'Relation of the Manner of Judicatores of Scotland', ed. J. D. Mackie and W. C. Dickinson, *SHR* 19 (1922), 254–72.
The Second Book of Discipline, ed. J. Kirk (Edinburgh, 1980).
SKENE, JOHN, *De Verborum Significatione: The Exposition of the Termes and Difficill Wordes Conteined in the Foure Buikes of Regiam Majestatem and Uthers* . . . (Edinburgh, 1599).
—— (ed.), *Regiam Majestatem* (Edinburgh, 1609).
SPOTTISWOODE, JOHN, *History of the Church of Scotland*, 3 vols., ed. M. Napier and M. Russell (Spottiswoode Society, 1847–51).

(c) Source Collections

CHILD, F. J., *English and Scottish Popular Ballads*, ed. H. C. Sargent and G. L. Kittredge (London, 1904).
Collectanea de Rebus Albanicis (Iona Club, 1847).

DICKINSON, W. C. *et al.* (eds.), *A Source Book of Scottish History*, 3 vols. (2nd edn., Edinburgh, 1958–61).

ELTON, G. R. (ed.), *The Tudor Constitution* (2nd edn., Cambridge, 1982).

GIBLIN, C. (ed.), *The Irish Franciscan Mission to Scotland, 1619–1646: Documents from Roman Archives* (Dublin, 1964).

HERD, D. (ed.), *Ancient and Modern Scottish Songs, Heroic Ballads, Etc.*, 2 vols. (3rd edn., Glasgow, 1869).

Highland Papers, 4 vols., ed. J. R. N. Macphail (SIIS, 1914–34).

HMC, *Calendar of the Manuscripts of the Marquis of Salisbury*, 24 vols., ed. S. R. Bird *et al.* (London, 1883–1976).

—— *Report on the Manuscripts of the Earl of Mar and Kellie*, 2 vols., ed. H. Paton (London, 1904–30).

—— *Report on the Laing Manuscripts Preserved in the University of Edinburgh*, 2 vols., ed. H. Paton (London, 1914–25).

The Jacobean Union: Six Tracts of 1604, ed. B. R. Galloway and B. P. Levack (SHS, 1985).

JAMES, H. (ed.), *Facsimiles of National Manuscripts of Scotland*, 3 vols. (Southampton, 1868–71).

The Maitland Folio Manuscript, 2 vols., ed. W. A. Craigie (STS, 1919–27).

Memorials of Montrose and his Times, 2 vols., ed. M. Napier (Maitland Club, 1848–50).

Scottish Population Statistics, ed. J. G. Kyd (SHS, 1952).

Taymouth. *The Black Book of Taymouth, with Other Papers from the Breadalbane Charter Room*, ed. C. Innes (Edinburgh, 1855).

3. SECONDARY WORKS

ALDIS, H. G., *A List of Books Printed in Scotland before 1700* (2nd edn., Edinburgh, 1970).

ANDERSON, P., *Lineages of the Absolutist State* (London, 1974).

ANDERSON, P. D., *Black Patie: The Life and Times of Patrick Stewart, Earl of Orkney, Lord of Shetland* (Edinburgh, 1992).

ARMITAGE, D., 'Making the empire British: Scotland in the Atlantic world, 1542–1707', *P & P* 155 (May 1997), 34–63.

AUSTIN, J., *The Province of Jurisprudence Determined*, ed. W. E. Rumble (Cambridge, 1995).

AYLMER, G. E., *The King's Servants: The Civil Service of Charles I, 1625–1637* (London, 1961).

BANNERMAN, J., 'The lordship of the Isles', in J. M. Brown (ed.), *Scottish Society in the Fifteenth Century* (London, 1977).

BARDGETT, F. D., *Scotland Reformed: The Reformation in Angus and the Mearns* (Edinburgh, 1989).

BARRELL, A. D. M., *The Papacy, Scotland and Northern England, 1342–1378* (Cambridge, 1995).

BARROW, G. W. S., *Robert Bruce and the Community of the Realm of Scotland* (3rd edn., Edinburgh, 1988).

BARTLETT, I. R., 'Scottish mercenaries in Europe, 1570–1640', *Scottish Tradition*, 13 (1984–5), 15–24.

BEIK, W., *Absolutism and Society in Seventeenth-Century France: State Power and Provincial Aristocracy in Languedoc* (Cambridge, 1985).

BJØRN, C. *et al.* (eds.), *Nations, Nationalism and Patriotism in the European Past* (Copenhagen, 1994).

BOARDMAN, S. I., 'Politics and the Feud in Late Medieval Scotland', Ph.D. thesis (St Andrews, 1990).

—— *The Early Stewart Kings: Robert II and Robert III, 1371–1406* (East Linton, 1996).

BONNEY, R., 'Absolutism: What's in a name?', *French History*, 1 (1987), 93–117.

BORTHWICK, A. R., 'The King, Council and Councillors in Scotland, *c.*1430–1460', Ph.D. thesis (Edinburgh, 1989).

BOSSY, J., *Christianity in the West, 1400–1700* (Oxford, 1985).

BOYNTON, L., *The Elizabethan Militia, 1558–1638* (London, 1967).

BRADDICK, M., 'State formation and social change in early modern England: A problem stated and approaches suggested', *Social History*, 16 (1991), 1–17.

—— 'The early modern English state and the question of differentiation, from 1550 to 1700', *Comparative Studies in Society and History*, 38 (1996), 92–111.

—— *The Nerves of State: Taxation and the Financing of the English State, 1558–1714* (Manchester, 1996).

BRADSHAW, B., and MORRILL, J. (eds.), *The British Problem, c.1534–1707* (London, 1996).

BRADY, C., 'Court, castle and country: The framework of government in Tudor Ireland', in id. and R. Gillespie (eds.), *Natives and Newcomers: The Making of Irish Colonial Society, 1534–1641* (Dublin, 1986).

BREWER, J., *The Sinews of Power: War, Money and the English State, 1688–1783* (London, 1988).

BROWN, J. J., 'The Social, Political and Economic Influences of the Edinburgh Merchant Elite, 1600–1638', Ph.D. thesis (Edinburgh, 1985).

BROWN, K. M., *Bloodfeud in Scotland, 1573–1625* (Edinburgh, 1986).

—— 'Aristocratic finances and the origins of the Scottish revolution', *EHR* 104 (1989), 46–87.

—— 'In search of the godly magistrate in Reformation Scotland', *Journal of Ecclesiastical History*, 40 (1989), 553–81.

BROWN, M., *James I* (Edinburgh, 1994).

BRUNTON, G., and HAIG, D., *An Historical Account of the Senators of the College of Justice* (Edinburgh, 1836).

BURNS, J. H., *Lordship, Kingship and Empire: The Idea of Monarchy, 1400–1525* (Oxford, 1992).

—— *The True Law of Kingship: Concepts of Monarchy in Early-Modern Scotland* (Oxford, 1996).

—— 'Institution and ideology: The Scottish estates and resistance theory', Institute of Historical Research, Electronic Seminars in History (archived 29 July 1997 at http://ihr.sas.ac.uk/ihr/esh/estate.html).

BUSH, M., *Noble Privilege* (New York, 1983).

CAIRNS, J. W., *et al.*, 'Legal humanism and the history of Scots law: John Skene and Thomas Craig', in J. MacQueen (ed.), *Humanism in Renaissance Scotland* (Edinburgh, 1990).

CALDWELL, D. H. (ed.), *Scottish Weapons and Fortifications, 1100–1800* (Edinburgh, 1981).

CHALLIS, C. E., 'Debasement: The Scottish experience in the fifteenth and sixteenth centuries', in D. M. Metcalf (ed.), *Coinage in Medieval Scotland, 1100–1600* (British Archaeological Reports, no. 45, 1977).

CHALMERS, T. M., 'The King's Council, Patronage, and the Governance of Scotland, 1460–1513', Ph.D. thesis (Aberdeen, 1982).

CLARK, S., 'King James's *Daemonologie*: Witchcraft and kingship', in S. Anglo (ed.), *The Damned Art: Essays in the Literature of Witchcraft* (London, 1977).

COLEMAN, C., and STARKEY, D. (eds.), *Revolution Reassessed: Revisions in the History of Tudor Government and Administration* (Oxford, 1986).

COLLEY, L., *Britons: Forging the Nation, 1707–1837* (London, 1992).

CONTAMINE, P., *War in the Middle Ages*, trans. M. Jones (Oxford, 1984).

COWAN, E. J., 'Calvinism and the survival of folk', in id. (ed.), *The People's Past: Scottish Folk, Scottish History* (Edinburgh, 1980).

COWAN, I. B., *The Scottish Reformation* (London, 1982).

—— and SHAW, D. (eds.), *The Renaissance and Reformation in Scotland* (Edinburgh, 1983).

CROSS, C., *The Royal Supremacy in the Elizabethan Church* (London, 1969).

—— *et al.* (eds.), *Law and Government under the Tudors* (Cambridge, 1988).

CRUICKSHANK, C. G., *Elizabeth's Army* (2nd edn., Oxford, 1966).

DAWSON, J., 'The fifth earl of Argyle, Gaelic lordship and political power in sixteenth-century Scotland', *SHR* 67 (1988), 1–27.

—— 'Calvinism in Gaelic Scotland', in A. Pettegree *et al.* (eds.), *Calvinism in Europe, 1540–1620* (Cambridge, 1994).

DICKINSON, W. C., 'An inquiry into the origin and nature of the title Prince of Scotland', *Economica*, 4 (1924), 212–20.

DIETZ, F. C., *English Public Finance, 1558–1641* (2nd edn., London, 1964).

DILWORTH, M., *Scottish Monasteries in the Late Middle Ages* (Edinburgh, 1995).

DODGSHON, R. A., *From Chiefs to Landlords: Social and Economic Change in the Western Highlands and Islands, c.1493–1820* (Edinburgh, 1998).

DONALDSON, G., *The Scottish Reformation* (Cambridge, 1960).

—— *Scotland: James V–James VII* (Edinburgh, 1965).

—— *All the Queen's Men: Power and Politics in Mary Stewart's Scotland* (London, 1983).

—— 'Problems of sovereignty and law in Orkney and Shetland', *Stair Society Miscellany*, ii (1984).

—— *The Faith of the Scots* (London, 1990).

DOW, F. D., *Cromwellian Scotland, 1651–1660* (Edinburgh, 1979).

EDINGTON, C., *Court and Culture in Renaissance Scotland: Sir David Lindsay of the Mount* (Amherst, Mass., 1994).

ELLIOTT, J. H., *The Revolt of the Catalans: A Study in the Decline of Spain, 1598–1640* (Cambridge, 1963).

—— *The Count-Duke of Olivares: The Statesman in an Age of Decline* (New Haven, 1986).

—— 'A Europe of composite monarchies', *P & P* 137 (Nov. 1992), 48–71.

ELLIS, S. G., *Tudor Frontiers and Noble Power: The Making of the British State* (Oxford, 1995).

ERTMAN, T., *Birth of the Leviathan: Building States and Regimes in Medieval and Early Modern Europe* (Cambridge, 1997).

FALLON, J. A., 'Scottish Mercenaries in the Service of Denmark and Sweden, 1626–1632', Ph.D. thesis (Glasgow, 1972).

FERGUSON, W., *Scotland's Relations with England: A Survey to 1707* (Edinburgh, 1977).

FINER, S. E., *The History of Government from the Earliest Times*, 3 vols. (Oxford, 1997).

FOSTER, W. R., *The Church before the Covenants, 1596–1638* (Edinburgh, 1975).

FULTON, T. W., *The Sovereignty of the Sea* (Edinburgh, 1911).

GALLOWAY, B., *The Union of England and Scotland, 1603–1608* (Edinburgh, 1986).

GOODARE, J., 'Parliament and Society in Scotland, 1560–1603', Ph.D. thesis (Edinburgh, 1989).

—— 'Parliamentary taxation in Scotland, 1560–1603', *SHR* 68 (1989), 23–52.

—— 'The nobility and the absolutist state in Scotland, 1584–1638', *History*, 78 (1993), 161–82.

—— 'The Scottish parliament of 1621', *Historical Journal*, 38 (1995), 29–51.

GOODARE, J., 'The estates in the Scottish parliament, 1286–1707', *Parliamentary History*, 15 (1996), 11–32.

—— 'Thomas Foulis and the Scottish fiscal crisis of the 1590s', in W. M. Ormrod *et al.* (eds.), *Crises, Revolutions and Self-Sustained Growth: Essays in Fiscal History, 1130–1830* (Stamford, 1999).

—— 'The Statutes of Iona in context', *SHR* 77 (1998), 31–57.

—— *The Government of Scotland, 1560–1625* (forthcoming).

—— and LYNCH, M. (eds.), *The Reign of James VI* (East Linton, 1999).

GRAHAM, M. F., *The Uses of Reform: 'Godly Discipline' and Popular Behavior in Scotland and Beyond, 1560–1610* (Leiden, 1996).

GRANT, A., *Independence and Nationhood: Scotland, 1306–1469* (London, 1984).

—— 'Scotland's "Celtic fringe" in the late middle ages: The MacDonald lords of the Isles and the kingdom of Scotland', in R. R. Davies (ed.), *The British Isles, 1100–1500* (Edinburgh, 1988).

GREENGRASS, M., 'Introduction: Conquest and coalescence', in id. (ed.), *Conquest and Coalescence: The Shaping of the State in Early Modern Europe* (London, 1991).

GREGORY, D., *History of the Western Highlands and Isles of Scotland, 1493–1625* (2nd edn., London, 1881).

GUENÉE, B., *States and Rulers in Later Medieval Europe*, trans. J. Vale (Oxford, 1985).

GUNN, S. J., *Early Tudor Government, 1485–1558* (London, 1995).

HALE, J. R., *War and Society in Renaissance Europe, 1450–1620* (London, 1985).

HALLIDAY, J., 'The Club and the Revolution in Scotland, 1689–1690', *SHR* 45 (1966), 143–59.

HARDY, J. R., 'The Attitude of the Church and State in Scotland to Sex and Marriage, 1560–1707', M.Phil. thesis (Edinburgh, 1978).

HARRISS, G., 'Political society and the growth of government in late medieval England', *P & P* 138 (Feb. 1993), 28–57.

HEWITT, G. R., *Scotland under Morton, 1572–1580* (Edinburgh, 1982).

HINSLEY, F. H., *Sovereignty* (2nd edn., Cambridge, 1986).

HOPKINS, P., *Glencoe and the End of the Highland War* (Edinburgh, 1986).

HURSTFIELD, J., *Freedom, Corruption and Government in Elizabethan England* (London, 1973).

INSH, G. P., *Scottish Colonial Schemes, 1620–1686* (Glasgow, 1922).

IREDELL, G. W., 'The Law, Custom and Practice of the Parliament of Scotland, with Particular Reference to the Period 1660–1707', Ph.D. thesis (London, 1966).

JOHNSTON, S. H. F., 'The Scots army in the reign of Anne', *Transactions of the Royal Historical Society*, 5th ser. 3 (1953), 1–21.

JONES, M. (ed.), *Gentry and Lesser Nobility in Late Medieval Europe* (Gloucester, 1986).

KELHAM, C. A., 'Bases of Magnatial Power in Later Fifteenth-Century Scotland', Ph.D. thesis (Edinburgh, 1986).

KELSEN, H., *General Theory of Law and State*, trans. A. Wedberg (New York, 1961).

KIDD, C., *Subverting Scotland's Past: Scottish Whig Historians and the Creation of an Anglo-British Identity, 1689–c.1830* (Cambridge, 1993).

KIERNAN, V. G., 'Foreign mercenaries and absolute monarchy', in T. Aston (ed.), *Crisis in Europe, 1560–1660* (London, 1965).

KIRK, J., *Patterns of Reform: Continuity and Change in the Reformation Kirk* (Edinburgh, 1989).

KOENIGSBERGER, H. G., 'Monarchies and parliaments in early modern Europe: *Dominium regale* or *dominium politicum et regale*', *Theory and Society*, 5 (1978), 191–217.

LAMONT, W. D., *The Early History of Islay, 500–1726* (Dundee, 1966).

LARNER, C., *Enemies of God: The Witch-Hunt in Scotland* (London, 1981).

LEE, M., *John Maitland of Thirlestane and the Foundation of the Stewart Despotism in Scotland* (Princeton, 1959).

—— *Government by Pen: Scotland under James VI and I* (Urbana, Ill., 1980).

—— *The Road to Revolution: Scotland under Charles I, 1625–1637* (Urbana, Ill., 1985).

—— *Great Britain's Solomon: James VI and I in his Three Kingdoms* (Urbana, Ill., 1990).

LEE, R. A., 'Government and Politics in Scotland, 1661–1681', Ph.D. thesis (Glasgow, 1995).

LENMAN, B., 'The limits of godly discipline in the early modern period, with particular reference to England and Scotland', in K. von Greyerz (ed.), *Religion and Society in Early Modern Europe, 1500–1800* (London, 1984).

—— and PARKER, G., 'Crime and control in Scotland, 1500–1800', *History Today*, 30/1 (Jan. 1980), 13–17.

LEVACK, B. P., *The Formation of the British State: England, Scotland and the Union, 1603–1707* (Oxford, 1987).

LYNCH, M., *Edinburgh and the Reformation* (Edinburgh, 1981).

—— (ed.), *The Early Modern Town in Scotland* (London, 1987).

—— (ed.), *Mary Stewart: Queen in Three Kingdoms* (Oxford, 1988).

—— *Scotland: A New History* (London, 1991).

McCLURE, J. D., and SPILLER, M. R. G. (eds.), *Bryght Lanternis: Essays on the Language and Literature of Medieval and Renaissance Scotland* (Aberdeen, 1989).

MacDonald, A. A., *et al.* (eds.), *The Renaissance in Scotland* (Leiden, 1994).

MacDonald, A. R., 'Ecclesiastical Politics in Scotland, 1586–1610', Ph.D. thesis (Edinburgh, 1995).

Macdougall, N., *James III* (Edinburgh, 1982).

—— (ed.), *Church, Politics and Society: Scotland, 1408–1929* (Edinburgh, 1983).

——*James IV* (Edinburgh, 1989).

—— (ed.), *Scotland and War, AD 79–1918* (Edinburgh, 1991).

Macfarlane, L. J., *William Elphinstone and the Kingdom of Scotland* (Aberdeen, 1985).

McGladdery, C., *James II* (Edinburgh, 1990).

MacGregor, M. D. W., 'A Political History of the MacGregors before 1571', Ph.D. thesis (Edinburgh, 1989).

Macinnes, A. I., *Charles I and the Making of the Covenanting Movement, 1625–1641* (Edinburgh, 1991).

—— *Clanship, Commerce and the House of Stuart, 1603–1788* (East Linton, 1996).

Mackenzie, W. M., 'The Debateable Land', *SHR* 30 (1951), 109–25.

McNeill, P. G. B., 'The Jurisdiction of the Scottish Privy Council, 1532–1708', Ph.D. thesis (Glasgow, 1960).

—— and MacQueen, H. L. (eds.), *Atlas of Scottish History to 1707* (Edinburgh, 1996).

—— and Nicholson, R. (eds.), *An Historical Atlas of Scotland, c.400–c.1600* (Conference of Scottish Medievalists, 1975).

Macquarrie, A., *Scotland and the Crusades, 1095–1560* (Edinburgh, 1985).

MacQueen, H. L., *Common Law and Feudal Society in Medieval Scotland* (Edinburgh, 1993).

McRoberts, D. (ed.), *Essays on the Scottish Reformation* (Glasgow, 1962).

Madden, C., 'The Finances of the Scottish Crown in the Later Middle Ages', Ph.D. thesis (Glasgow, 1975).

—— 'Royal treatment of feudal casualties in late medieval Scotland', *SHR* 55 (1976), 172–94.

Makey, W., *The Church of the Covenant, 1637–1651* (Edinburgh, 1979).

Mann, M., 'The autonomous power of the state: Its origins, mechanisms and results', in J. A. Hall (ed.), *States in History* (Oxford, 1986).

—— *The Sources of Social Power*, i. *A History of Power to AD 1760* (Cambridge, 1986).

Mason, R. A., 'Kingship and Commonweal: Political Thought and Ideology in Reformation Scotland', Ph.D. thesis (Edinburgh, 1983).

—— (ed.), *Scotland and England, 1286–1815* (Edinburgh, 1987).

—— (ed.), *Scots and Britons: Scottish Political Thought and the Union of 1603* (Cambridge, 1994).

MEIKLE, M. M., 'Lairds and Gentlemen: A Study of the Landed Families of the Eastern Anglo-Scottish Borders, *c.*1540–1603', Ph.D. thesis (Edinburgh, 1989).

MILLER, J. (ed.), *Absolutism in Seventeenth-Century Europe* (London, 1990).

MITCHISON, R., 'The social impact of the clergy of the reformed kirk of Scotland', *Scotia*, 6 (1982), 1–13.

—— *Lordship to Patronage: Scotland, 1603–1745* (London, 1983).

—— and LENEMAN, L., *Sexuality and Social Control: Scotland, 1660–1780* (Oxford, 1989).

MORRILL, J., 'A British patriarchy? Ecclesiastical imperialism under the early Stuarts', in A. Fletcher and P. Roberts (eds.), *Religion, Culture and Society in Early Modern Britain* (Cambridge, 1994).

—— (ed.), *The Scottish National Covenant in its British Context* (Edinburgh, 1990).

MULLAN, D. G., *Episcopacy in Scotland, 1560–1638* (Edinburgh, 1986).

MURISON, D., 'Linguistic relationships in medieval Scotland', in G. W. S. Barrow (ed.), *The Scottish Tradition* (Edinburgh, 1974).

MURRAY, A. L., 'The Exchequer and Crown Revenue of Scotland, 1437–1542', Ph.D. thesis (Edinburgh, 1961).

—— 'The procedure of the Scottish exchequer in the early sixteenth century', *SHR* 40 (1961), 89–117.

—— 'Sir John Skene and the exchequer, 1594–1612', *Stair Society Miscellany*, i (1971).

—— 'Notes on the treasury administration', *TA*, xii (1980).

—— 'Exchequer, council and session, 1513–1542', in J. H. Williams (ed.), *Stewart Style, 1513–1542* (East Linton, 1996).

MURRAY, P. J., 'The lay administrators of church lands in the fifteenth and sixteenth centuries', *SHR* 74 (1995), 26–44.

NICHOLSON, R., 'Feudal developments in late medieval Scotland', *JR* ns 18 (1973), 1–21.

—— *Scotland: The Later Middle Ages* (Edinburgh, 1974).

O'BRIEN, I. E., 'The Scottish Parliament in the 15th and 16th Centuries', Ph.D. thesis (Glasgow, 1980).

O'BRIEN, P. K., and HUNT, P. A., 'The rise of a fiscal state in England, 1485–1815', *Historical Research*, 66 (1993), 129–76.

O'CONNOR, A., and CLARKE, D. V. (eds.), *From the Stone Age to the 'Forty-Five* (Edinburgh, 1983).

OLLIVANT, S., *The Court of the Official in Pre-Reformation Scotland* (Stair Society, 1982).

PAGAN, T., *The Convention of the Royal Burghs of Scotland* (Glasgow, 1926).

PARKER, D., 'Sovereignty, absolutism and the function of the law in seventeenth-century France', *P & P* 122 (Feb. 1989), 36–74.

PAUL, J. B. (ed.), *The Scots Peerage*, 9 vols. (Edinburgh, 1904–14).

PENNINGTON, K., *The Prince and the Law, 1200–1600: Sovereignty and Rights in the Western Legal Tradition* (Berkeley and Los Angeles, 1993).

PERCEVAL-MAXWELL, M., *The Scottish Migration to Ulster in the Reign of James I* (London, 1973).

POCOCK, J. G. A., *The Ancient Constitution and the Feudal Law* (2nd edn., Cambridge, 1987).

POGGI, G., *The State: Its Nature, Development and Prospects* (Cambridge, 1990).

PRODI, P., *The Papal Prince: One Body and Two Souls: The Papal Monarchy in Early Modern Europe*, trans. S. Haskins (Cambridge, 1987).

PRYDE, G. S., 'Scottish Burgh Finances before 1707', Ph.D. thesis (St Andrews, 1928).

—— *The Burghs of Scotland: A Critical List* (Glasgow, 1965).

RAE, T. I., *The Administration of the Scottish Frontier, 1513–1603* (Edinburgh, 1966).

—— (ed.), *The Union of 1707: Its Impact on Scotland* (Glasgow, 1974).

REID, W. S., 'Clerical taxation: The Scottish alternative to dissolution of the monasteries', *Catholic Historical Review*, 35 (1948), 129–53.

REINHARD, W. (ed.), *Power Elites and State Building* (Oxford, 1996).

RILEY, P. W. J., *The English Ministers and Scotland, 1707–1727* (London, 1964).

—— *The Union of England and Scotland* (Manchester, 1978).

—— *King William and the Scottish Politicians* (Edinburgh, 1979).

ROBERTSON, J. (ed.), *A Union for Empire: Political Thought and the British Union of 1707* (Cambridge, 1995).

SANDERSON, M. H. B., *Scottish Rural Society in the Sixteenth Century* (Edinburgh, 1982).

—— *Cardinal of Scotland: David Beaton, c.1494–1546* (Edinburgh, 1986).

—— *Mary Stewart's People* (Edinburgh, 1987).

SCOTT, W. R., *The Constitution and Finance of English, Scottish and Irish Joint-Stock Companies to 1720*, 3 vols. (Cambridge, 1912).

SCOTTISH RECORD OFFICE, *Guide to the National Archives of Scotland* (Edinburgh, 1996).

SELLAR, D., 'Barony jurisdiction in the Highlands', *Notes and Queries of the Society of West Highland and Island Historical Research*, 16 (Sept. 1981), 22–6.

—— 'Celtic law and Scots law: Survival and integration', *Scottish Studies*, 29 (1989), 1–27.

SHAW, D., *The General Assemblies of the Church of Scotland, 1560–1600* (Edinburgh, 1964).

SHAW, F. J., *The Northern and Western Islands of Scotland: Their Economy and Society in the Seventeenth Century* (Edinburgh, 1980).

SIMPSON, G. G. (ed.), *Scotland and the Low Countries, 1124–1994* (East Linton, 1996).

SKENE, W. F., *Celtic Scotland*, 3 vols. (2nd edn., Edinburgh, 1886–90).

SKINNER, Q., 'The origins of the Calvinist theory of revolution', in B. Malament (ed.), *After the Reformation* (Manchester, 1980).

SMITH, A. D., *The Ethnic Origins of Nations* (Oxford, 1986).

SOMMERVILLE, C. J., *The Secularization of Early Modern England: From Religious Culture to Religious Faith* (Oxford, 1992).

SPRUYT, H., *The Sovereign State and its Competitors* (Princeton, 1994).

STAFFORD, H. G., *James VI of Scotland and the Throne of England* (New York, 1940).

STEVENSON, D., 'Financing the cause of the covenants, 1638–1651', *SHR* 51 (1972), 89–123.

—— *The Scottish Revolution, 1637–1644* (Newton Abbot, 1973).

—— 'The effects of revolution and conquest on Scotland', in R. Mitchison and P. Roebuck (eds.), *Economy and Society in Scotland and Ireland, 1500–1939* (Edinburgh, 1988).

STONE, L., *The Crisis of the Aristocracy, 1558–1641* (Oxford, 1965).

THOMPSON, I. A. A., *War and Government in Habsburg Spain, 1560–1620* (London, 1976).

THOMSON, D. S., 'Gaelic learned orders and literati in medieval Scotland', *Scottish Studies*, 12 (1968), 57–78.

TILLY, C. (ed.), *The Formation of National States in Western Europe* (Princeton, 1975).

—— *Coercion, Capital and European States, AD 990–1990* (Oxford, 1990).

ULLMANN, W., *Principles of Government and Politics in the Middle Ages* (4th edn., London, 1978).

WASSER, M. B., 'Violence and the Central Criminal Courts in Scotland, 1603–1638', Ph.D. diss. (Columbia, 1995).

WATT, D. E. R., 'The papacy and Scotland in the fifteenth century', in B. Dobson (ed.), *The Church, Politics and Patronage in the Fifteenth Century* (Gloucester, 1984).

WHATLEY, C. A., 'Economic causes and consequences of the union of 1707: A survey', *SHR* 68 (1989), 150–81.

WHYTE, I., *Agriculture and Society in Seventeenth-Century Scotland* (Edinburgh, 1979).

—— *Scotland before the Industrial Revolution: An Economic and Social History, c.1050–c.1750* (London, 1995).

WILLIAMSON, A. H., *Scottish National Consciousness in the Age of James VI* (Edinburgh, 1979).

—— 'Scots, Indians and empire: The Scottish politics of civilization, 1519–1609', *P & P* 150 (Feb. 1996), 46–83.

WILLOCK, I. D., *The Origins and Development of the Jury in Scotland* (Stair Society, 1966).

WOLFE, M., *The Fiscal System of Renaissance France* (New Haven, 1972).

WORMALD, J., *Court, Kirk and Community: Scotland, 1470–1625* (London, 1981).

—— *Lords and Men in Scotland: Bonds of Manrent, 1442–1603* (Edinburgh, 1985).

—— 'Taming the magnates?', in K. J. Stringer (ed.), *Essays on the Nobility of Medieval Scotland* (Edinburgh, 1985).

—— (ed.), *Scotland Revisited* (London, 1991).

—— 'The creation of Britain: Multiple kingdoms or core and colonies?', *Transactions of the Royal Historical Society*, 6th ser. 2 (1992), 175–94.

YOUNG, M. D. (ed.), *The Parliaments of Scotland: Burgh and Shire Commissioners*, 2 vols. (Edinburgh, 1992–3).

ZULAGER, R. R., 'A Study of the Middle-Rank Administrators in the Government of King James VI of Scotland, 1580–1603', Ph.D. thesis (Aberdeen, 1991).

INDEX